respected colleague

Alfred Publishing Co., Inc.
15335 Morrison Street
Sherman Oaks, California 91403

Printing (last digit)
10 9 8 7 6 5 4 3 2 1

Library of Congress Cataloging in Publication Data

Feinberg, Lilian O.
    Applied business communications.

    Includes bibliographies and index.
    1. Communication in management. I. Thompson, Mary C.
II. Title.
HF5718.F44   658.4′5   81-12854
ISBN 0-88284-125-4   AACR2

658.45
F299

Production Manager: Rena J. Copperman
Production Management: Robert S. Tinnon
Interior design: Robert S. Tinnon
Copyeditors: Janet Greenblatt, Marie Enders
Typesetting: Publisher's Typography
Printer: Kingsport Press

Cover photograph courtesy of
Intelligent Systems Corporation

APPLIED
BUSINESS
COMMUNICATION

Lilian O. Feinberg
Iowa State University

Assisted by

Mary C. Thompson
Purdue University

Alfred Publishing Co., Inc.
Sherman Oaks, California 91403

Contents

Preface

busi·ness com·mu·ni·ca·tion, *n.,* the imparting or interchange of thoughts, opinions, or information by speech, writing, or signs for the business of living, learning, and earning a living

Accept this definition and you accept the fact that almost everything you do involves some type of business communication. When you speak or write to an employer, business associate, teacher, family member—anyone and everyone involved in your business of living, learning, and earning a living—you are involved in this process. *Holistic* business communication signifies that good communication includes the *whole* range of communication: thinking, listening, speaking, reading, writing, reacting.

That's what this book is all about.

Purpose

The emphasis of *Applied Business Communication* is on the communication involved in earning a living. Its purpose is threefold: (1) to help improve the accuracy of information about communication in the marketplace for those who have communication skills; (2) to improve those communication skills, skills indispensable for business success; (3) to provide realistic insights into communication activities on the job and to enable men and women to use their communication skills to find and keep the jobs they want.

ix

Content

Part One: Communication—An Overview reviews with you the prerequisites: theories and models of communication and the contexts (intrapersonal, interpersonal, small-group, organizational, and intercultural) within which we communicate. Many of the selections in this section were contributed by experts in the field.

Part Two: Communication Skills begins with the skills we all learned first—listening, speaking, and reading and provides recommendations for improving these skills. Next writing is explored in depth, from several angles: (1) the target—your audience, (2) patterns—methods of organization, (3) style—choosing your words, and (4) the image—appearance. Here you will consider everything from establishing good will to analyzing your audience to organizing your writing to selecting the right word and the appropriate language for each occasion to considering the format and most suitable paper for your written message.

Part Three: Applications helps you apply the writing skills of Part Two to memos, information letters, refusal letters, selling letters, reports, and proposals. Current examples and cases from daily living, business, industry, education, and government are used throughout to illustrate the wide variety of actual situations you will encounter. The Assignments sections are designed for classroom or in-service training exercises. The "supervisor," for those that are working, is the training and development manager; for students, the supervisor is the teacher.

Part Four: Communication and Careers examines the elements of self-analysis, evaluation by others, and job opportunity resources to consider in your career research. Following are guidelines and instructions to help you with the actual job search, in the preparation of effective résumés and application letters and in the art of interviewing. On-the-job considerations, such as employee benefits and performance appraisals, as well as information on changing jobs, offer you an insider's view of the world of work. Sharpening this view and concluding this section are eight unedited, real-life diaries, or logs, written by men and women in professional, technical, and managerial occupations. These diaries should convince you of the need to learn or become better acquainted with the specific communication skills of the occupation you plan to enter or wish to advance in.

Part Five: Changing Technology introduces you to the exciting world of today—and tomorrow—to information systems, the automated office and workstation, word processing, and electronic mail. Surveyed here are developing technologies and their effects on business, industry, education, and the professions.

Appendices A through *D* contain supplementary information on effective dictation; audiovisual resources; direct mail, including a detailed explanation of mailing lists; and interpretations of selected landmark laws that affect the business community.

The *Handbook* provides a handy reference to matters of grammar, punctuation, spelling, and frequently used technical terms and abbreviations.

By now you are beginning to recognize the holistic point of view: good business communication is more than the sum of its parts. It has many dimensions: it says many things both verbally and nonverbally. Thus a clear and complete message is always carefully planned—consciously or unconsciously. With practice, your planning becomes almost automatic—much like breathing or walking.

Read, discuss, apply this material to your needs. Then plan, organize, write, evaluate, and revise. You are about to invest your time and energy in learning how to become a better communicator for the business of living, learning, and earning a living. The investment will pay you top dividends for the rest of your life.

Acknowledgments

Great teachers leave legacies—students imprinted with their philosophies, their ethical and educational standards. Five such great teachers have influenced me.

Alta Gwinn Saunders emphasized attention to detail, and the "you" viewpoint was central to her teaching just as it is to mine.

Frederick A. "Pop" Russell was responsible for my leaving school during my junior year, going out to sell and meet the "publics." "Nothing works like real experience," he said. The combination of theory and practice prepared me to be a better student and better writer on my return to the classroom.

Caroline Tupper sensitized her students to the beauty of words. "Is that *exactly* what you mean?" she would say. "Is that really the word you want?" Finding exactly the right word sometimes took hours, but she made the search seem worthwhile.

Then there was Bob Sink, editor of the *Champaign-Urbana Courier*. His red pencil taught me the art of concise writing, the need to be brief, to research my subject, and, above all, to be accurate. I hope that this search for the facts and the responsibility to report them accurately are reflected in *Applied Business Communication*.

But the one most important influence in my life as a teacher and writer is Leonard Feinberg, my husband, Distinguished Professor in Sciences and Humanities, Fulbright scholar, Wilton Park Fellow (England), and holder of almost every faculty award given at Iowa State University. Early on he helped me establish good teaching habits—returning papers to students the class period following their submission, regarding students as important individuals worthy of my very best efforts. Together, later, we wrote and published a workbook and grammar.

The friendships we have made at home and overseas have enriched this book. Professional colleagues, personal friends, and brief acquaintances have helped verify details, offered inside information, and provided published and unpublished papers. "Contributors" follow, but the list can never be complete.

Mary Thompson's devotion, expertise, and collaboration are recognized in the "Assisted by" on the title page. Quentin Johnson, Iowa State University, could be counted on to unsnarl linguistic problems; Don Pady, Iowa State University, responded immediately to every phone call for library reference assistance. Steve Manus, editor, contributed more than the usual editing advice, impressing me with his youth, maturity, and organizational ability.

The American Business Communication Association (ABCA) has been a constant source of information and inspiration. I am indebted to my mentor, Arno Knapper, associate dean of the college of business, University of Kansas, and to Francis W. Weeks, University of Illinois, Executive Director of ABCA. I have learned a great deal from sharing professional experiences at ABCA conferences and reading research in the *ABCA Bulletin* and *ABCA Journal.*

And I have learned a great deal from consulting for business and industry and writing professionally for television, popular magazines, and scholarly journals, as well as from working with community and international organizations.

Applied Business Communication reflects these many experiences and influences. It is a "hands on" book, a practical guide to good business communication. It is written for students, professionals, and nonprofessionals. May it serve you well.

Lilian O. Feinberg
Iowa State University

Contributors

ANN Z. ADAMS, Head, English Department, MacCormac Junior College, Chicago, Illinois, has been preparing court reporters for the past nine years. She is a popular speaker at court reporter conventions and author of numerous court reporting monographs.

DAVID N. BATEMAN, Director, Division of Applied Business and Organizational Communication, Southern Illinois University at Carbondale, is a consultant to business and government and the author of more than a dozen articles and papers on organizational communication. He is also the co-author, with Norman B. Sigband, of *Business Communications*.

EDMUND G. BLINN, Professor of Journalism/Mass Communication, Iowa State University, specializes in communication law.

CARLA BUTENHOFF has taught English at the University of Massachusetts at Amherst, University of Wisconsin-Oshkosh, University of Wisconsin-Milwaukee. She has been a public relations representative and company spokesperson and is presently an advertising manager.

SORRELL CAPLAN, President of Communique, a full-service Washington, D.C., public relations firm, was previously public affairs director of the National Federation of Business and Professional Women's Clubs and editor of the employees' newsletter for the U.S. Department of Labor.

JOHN CONDON began his intercultural studies 25 years ago as a college freshman in Mexico. Since then he has lived in East

Africa, Latin America, and Asia, teaching and conducting research. He is the author or co-author of a dozen books in the field. Recently, he returned to the United States, settling in San Diego where he divides his time among research, writing, and consulting.

D. DAVID DAHL is marketing industry manager for Northwestern Bell Telephone Co., Des Moines, Iowa.

HAROLD W. DAVEY, Professor Emeritus of Economics, Iowa State University, is a specialist in labor relations.

CAL W. DOWNS, Professor of Organizational Communication, University of Kansas, wears many hats: Chairperson, Organizational Communication Division, Academy of Management; Chairperson, Organizational Communication Division, International Communication Association; Director, monthly seminar, University of Michigan, Division of Management Education.

DON FABUN, iconoclast, former director of publications, Kaiser Aluminum (honored with medals and international citations), is the author of numerous books, films, and television scripts, and lectures at international, national, and regional conferences.

WILLIAM R. FEENEY, Assistant Professor, Information Systems Department, San Diego State University, has been using systems analysis techniques in data processing for the past 16 years. He is an innovative researcher, designing and conducting experiments involving human subjects, and a consultant to school districts and businesses in Europe and Asia.

KARL E. GWIASDA, Associate Professor of English, Iowa State University, has degrees in English and chemical engineering. He teaches technical writing and nineteenth-century British literature and is the co-author of *Professional Writing: A Guide for Students.*

KATHLEEN HART, lecturer in business communication, New Brunswick Community College, Moncton, New Brunswick, Canada, is an officer of International Toastmistress Clubs, Inc., and Vice President Canada, American Business Communication Association.

LARRY D. HARTMAN, Associate Professor and Director of Communication Studies, Department of Business Education, Northern Illinois University, DeKalb, is a member of the Illinois Education Association Publications Committee.

KENNETH G. JOHNSON, Professor of Mass Communication, University of Wisconsin-Milwaukee, is the author of several articles on communication, science, and general semantics in *General Semantics: An Outline Survey.* He edited *Research Designs in General Semantics* and is senior author of *Nothing* Never *Happens,* a collection of communication activities and readings.

NEIL J. KATZ is director of sales service, Alvin B. Zeller, Inc., New York, mailing list compilers and brokers.

MARJORIE M. LEESON, Chairperson of the Data Processing Discipline, Delta College, University Center, Michigan, has designed, programmed, and maintains a major financial system for Delta's 360-40. She also conducts training seminars, serves as a consultant on microcomputers and curriculum development, and recently revised *Basic Concepts in Data Processing.*

DONALD J. LEONARD, Assistant Professor of Administrative Services, Arizona State University, was selected to revise Robert L. Shurter's *Communication in Business.*

ROBERT LINDEMEYER, Director of Media Development, Media Resources Center, Iowa State University, is in charge of an extensive program of instructional media design and production. He holds offices in state and national media associations, is writer/co-producer of a 12-projector, 3-screen multimedia presentation, "The Library—A Place to Grow," which was shown at the White House Conference on Libraries and Media Services.

W. J. LORD, JR., is the recipient of numerous academic awards and grants, including the Emens Distinguished Professorship at Ball State University. Apart from his academic and administrative responsibilities at the University of Texas, Austin, he is actively involved in continuing education for adults and is a researcher, writer (four books), and consultant for business and industry.

KARYN L. MULLICA received her training in speech pathology at Iowa State University, California State University, Northridge, and the University of Colorado. Formerly on the staff of Gompers Rehabilitation Center, she is now in private practice in Phoenix, Arizona, and edits a speech pathology newsletter for professionals.

PAUL E. NELSON, Associate Professor of Speech, Iowa State University, is co-author of *Understanding and Sharing: An Introduction to Speech Communication* and *Confidence in Public Speaking.* He teaches courses in interpersonal communication, public speaking, and persuasion.

DONALD S. PADY is a reference librarian and bibliographer, Iowa State University Library.

ELIZABETH ROBERS, Assistant Professor, Department of Speech and Theater, Ohio Northern University, directs the communication skills program.

LOIS W. SEARS, Assistant Professor, Business Division, Delta College, University Center, Michigan, specializes in typewriting, office machines, filing and records management. She regularly updates her teaching with industrial work experience.

DAVID R. SEIBOLD, Assistant Professor, Department of Speech Communication, University of Illinois, teaches courses in organizational communication and small-group behavior. A consultant to business and government, he also conducts workshops on interpersonal communication, group decision-making, and public speaking.

J. MORGAN SMYTHE is branch manager, I.P. Sharp Associates, Ltd., Toronto, Ontario, Canada, a nationwide electronic mail organization.

ANN STEELE started working as a secretary before graduation from high school. Since then, she has continued secretarial work while rearing a family and accumulating two university degrees in music. A court reporter and transcriber, she is a member of the National Verbatim Stenomask Reporters Association, as well as several professional and honorary music associations.

LEE THAYER is Professor of Communication, Division of Humanities, University of Wisconsin-Parkside. His ideas on human communication are known worldwide. Trained as a psychologist, he is also active as a consultant and counselor, as well as a teacher and author.

MARY C. THOMPSON is Alumni Relations and Communication Coordinator, School of Nursing, Purdue University. She did her graduate study in business communication under the direction of Lilian O. Feinberg. She has served as administrative assistant with the division of patents and copyrights and as director of communications and alumni relations for the Krannert Graduate School of Management and Purdue School of Management. At Iowa State University, she was assistant to the engineering college placement officer, performed alumni relations work for the college of engineering and taught business communication. In addition, she has edited a variety of publications and owned and operated a public stenographer service in Champaign, Illinois.

ALMA JEAN WALKER, teaching and research assistant, Iowa State University, taught high school in Nebraska for seven years before returning to graduate school.

TIM WHALEN, senior engineer, Dravo Utility Constructors, Inc., New Orleans, Louisiana, has published articles in *Technical Communication, ABCA Bulletin, Oklahoma Professional Engineer,* and other journals.

Additional Contributors

The American Business Communication Association; Ames Greenhouses, Inc.; J. D. Armstrong (advice on bids and contracts); Ballou Farms, Inc.; Ben Berman (credit and telephone consultant); Tony Bishop (job descriptions); Buck Construction Co.; Major J. M. Chambers, Jr., USMC (military titles, memos); Lois DeBakey (writing guideline reprints); Fidelity Distribution Corporation; Vicki Fields (Beneficial Finance information); First National Bank of Ames, Iowa; Burt Gleason (forms); Eleanor Gibson (advice on reading); Haband, Inc.; Craig Hastings (legal writing); Herbert A. Harmison (employment/placement); Kenneth Hoyt (career information inspiration); IBM; International Society for General Semantics; International Paper Co., Inc.; Iowa-Des Moines National Bank; Kitakyushu Foreign Trade Association; Sanford Lebow (bits and bytes); Vickie LoPiccolo (photographer); Moore Business Forms, Inc.; Fritz Munn (credit form, information); National Research Bureau (N. J. Pasqual); Jayne Montgomery (proposals); Olive's, The Fashion Shoppe; Bill Schultz (paper information); Siegel and Gale; Donna Stine (personnel appraisal); Iris Varner (ethics); Madeline Walls (13-30 reprints); Gary Wiggins (retirement plans).

Part One

Communication—An Overview

CHAPTER ONE

Communication Theories

Communication is not a thing, it is a process. Sender, message, and receiver do not remain constant throughout an act of communication. To treat these as static entities, as they often are in our research, is questionable when applied to the most extreme form of continuous discourse, misleading when used to analyze the episodic verbal exchanges that characterize face-to-face communication, and is totally useless in probing man's communication with himself. Changes in any of these forces, and few forces remain constant very long, reverberate throughout the entire system. Students of communication are not dissecting a cadaver, but are probing the pulsing evolution of meaning in a living organism.

Dean C. Barnlund
"Toward a Meaning-Centered
Philosophy of Communication"

Because communication is so all-pervasive in our lives, it is difficult to define and understand. Surrounded as we are by communication, we cannot step outside it and see it as a whole. However, we can improve our understanding by creating models of certain types of communication. Although these models are limited and constantly challenged by thoughtful people, nevertheless they can be useful. One important model is *information theory*.

INFORMATION THEORY

Information can be defined most generally as the *selection of order out of chaos*. For example, pure noise is without information. It contains a random group of sounds at all different frequencies. However, limit those frequencies to a select few, and information is produced. The information depends on the selection; that is, if certain frequencies are selected, the information will be a bird chirp; if others are selected, a piano note.

Information involves selectivity.

To understand the communication of information, look at the dialogue between a computer and its operator. The computer stores information in the form of millions of "bits" of memory. These bits consist of magnetic pieces of material in either one state or another—in a sense, "on" or "off." What makes these bits information is that they are arranged in definite patterns; that is, the bits themselves are not information—their pattern is.

Information comes from the arrangement of patterns.

1

Encoding is the creation of patterns, or codes.

The computer does not arrange the bits by itself. Rather, the information is *inputted* into the computer by the operator. Further, the information stored by the computer (its pattern of bits) corresponds to a similar pattern outside of the computer (the information the operator wants stored). For example, perhaps today's temperature is a piece of information that corresponds to "72 degrees Fahrenheit," which in turn corresponds to the computer bits "1–0–0–1–0–0–0." We see, then, that nature provides us with information (today's temperature) we can identify, store, and transmit by creating corresponding patterns ("72 degrees" or "1001000"). In information theory, these patterns (words, numbers, computer bits, and so on) are called *codes* and the process of creating these codes is called *encoding*.

Getting back to the computer analogy, information is stored by the computer in coded form. It may then be *transmitted* or *outputted* to the operator or another computer that uses the same or a different code for storage. In transmitting to the operator, the computer encodes the information into a form the operator can understand—numbers or words. The coded information being transmitted is called a *message*. This message is transmitted through a *channel* (electric wires) to a *receiver* (a terminal or printer) and read by the operator. In reading the message, the operator *decodes* it into understandable information. Finally, the operator gives the computer *feedback* by communicating that the message was received. The operator's feedback can either continue the communication cycle or terminate it.

Transmitting is the sending of information in an understandable form.

A message is the information transmitted by a sender to a receiver, who tries to make meaning of it and provide feedback.

According to information theory, communication is most effective when messages are (1) coded clearly and unambiguously; (2) transmitted without the addition of *noise* distorting the message; (3) received without loss of any part because of channel overload, and (4) decoded accurately so that the original information is perfectly duplicated. These same rules apply to communicating information effectively in a business setting. Here are some suggestions on how to do this.

1. Use precise and understandable words.
2. Make sure your words can be heard clearly or read easily. Avoid anything interfering with your message—a noisy room, dirty typewriter keys, illegible handwriting.
3. Limit what you have to say (or write). Remember, complicated information needs explanation and time to be understood.
4. Look for feedback that shows comprehension—nodding of the head at appropriate moments, changes of expression at key points, intelligent questions, appropriate suggestions.

Just as a computer transmits millions of "bits" of stored information through a receiver which decodes it, so information is communicated in a business setting.

HUMAN COMMUNICATION

The information model implies that communication is a simple encoding–transmitting–decoding process. It also implies that if communication is done carefully enough, the message sent will be identical to the message received. However, this model omits the most important component of human communication—*meaning*.

Most people assume that the meaning of coded messages (words and numbers) can be looked up in books, and once understood, they are the same for all people in all situations. If this were true, the information model would accurately describe human communication. Human communication would merely consist of choosing the right words, saying them the right way, and then making sure the receiver understood the meaning of the words.

True, there are cases in which meaning is straightforward and communication follows this model—for example, when an operator communicates with a computer or an instructor explains the use of a piece of equipment. Yet the complexities of meaning come up even in the case of instruction. Consider a computer specialist teaching several trainees the use of a highly complicated piece of equipment.

Meaning can vary from person to person.

The instructor might start by saying, "Anyone can learn how to operate this machine." One trainee might think the statement insulting: the instructor is implying superiority. Another trainee might take the statement to mean the equipment looks more complicated than it is. Still another might interpret the statement as a challenge: if the machine can't be mastered, there is something wrong—and not with the computer.

What accounts for the different meanings in a single message? The answer to this question centers on the fact *the receiver, not the sender, creates meaning.*[1] This fact leads us to a fundamental question: *How is meaning created?* How do you use language to communicate with one another? This is the question addressed by *general semantics.*

GENERAL SEMANTICS
Kenneth G. Johnson*

General semantics considers the relationship between language and behavior.

General semantics was first developed by Alfred Korzybski in his book *Science and Sanity,* published in 1933. It is concerned with how people use language to understand the world and each other and focuses on the relationship between language and all aspects of human behavior. Understanding the principles of general semantics can help you avoid some of the confusions of meaning mentioned earlier.

Look beyond the word to the person, event, or object that it stands for.

1. *Words are not the things they represent.* A description of an event is not the event itself. You cannot use the word *pencil* to write. This seems obvious, but often we respond to words as if they were things, to descriptions as if they were events. We see this most clearly in the person who can't stand to talk about certain things, be it sex, old age, or plane crashes. In business, we see it in the boss who hires "a good résumé" without checking the person it is supposed to represent.

[1]See "Communication Theory," by Lee Thayer, pages 13–15.

*Kenneth G. Johnson is Professor of Mass Communication at the University of Wisconsin, Milwaukee.

2. *Things labeled alike are not necessarily alike.* We often talk about students, professors, businesspeople, customers, or others as if they were all alike simply because we use the same word to describe them. It is only on second thought—if we take the time for a second thought—that we recognize the uniqueness of each individual we have so neatly categorized. While we are less likely to overgeneralize about things and people we know well than about strangers, it is a trap we fall into easily. Consider the manager who refuses to purchase a sorely needed computer because of a bad experience with a primitive "monster" twenty years ago. The individual does not realize that the "computer" of twenty years ago and the "computer" of today are entirely different things.

Beware of labels and overgeneralizations.

3. *Words cannot tell "all" about a person or event.* In describing something or someone, we choose certain characteristics that seem important to us. But once we say, "He is a slow learner," or "She is a coward," we tend to act as if we've said it *all*. And that little word *is* obscures the fact that we are talking about *our* abstractions, reactions, and evaluations. We even label ourselves in ways that limit our behavior. The woman who says she *is* a data processor and the man who says he *is* a tough loner both act as if that is *all* they are and ever will be. They are blinded to other possibilities by their own labels.

We can never know or say everything about anyone or anything.

4. *Meaning is in people and situations, not in words.* For example, *when* something is said affects its meaning. As a novice, you would feel complimented if your manager told you, "You're learning nicely." After a year on the job, you would probably consider the same statement an insult.

Meaning lies in people.

These principles outline the main ideas of general semantics. Some of them seem simple, almost obvious, once they are pointed out. But internalizing them, behaving as if you know them, is much more difficult. Here are some ways to apply these principles in daily communication.

- Distinguish clearly between statements of observation and statements of inference.
- Realize that we necessarily abstract; we cannot know all or say all about anything.
- Recognize that we live in a world of process, of change, and that our "maps" are often out-of-date.
- React to unique people, things, and events, not to their categories or labels.
- Talk and write in terms of degree of probability, not either-or categories.

- Look beyond words to the objects or relationships they are intended to represent.
- Watch out for *is* and the other *to be* verbs that imply finality and certainty.
- Use *seems, appears, I think, to me, in my opinion,* and so forth.
- Ask, "What do you mean?" and "How do you know?" in a sincere effort to understand.

Language maps our world.

General semantics, then, is not the study of words or the study of meanings as these terms are ordinarily used. It is concerned with language as a way of mapping the world around us, with the potentials and limitations of humans as map makers, and of languages as map-making systems. We hear only what we understand; we communicate clearly only what we understand. The language we learn becomes our *program* and guide to the world around us.

Realizing this, many organizations, both private and public—from Ashland Oil Company and United Airlines to the United States Forest Service and the Department of Agriculture—are now incorporating general semantics into their education and training programs. They find a knowledge of semantics pays off in more creative, open-minded managers.

ASSIGNMENT: COMMUNICATION THEORY

Your employer has a strong commitment to effective communication. You have become interested in how people communicate within groups and within and between organizations. You have requested and received permission to attend a communication theory conference.

After you have submitted a memo or short report covering your experiences at the meeting, you are asked to share your material with the management-training supervisor and other interested groups. Your boss asks that you specifically show how the theories you learned about at the conference relate to your job. Select one of the following topics and prepare an oral or written report as directed.

Topics

1. "Language maps the world around us." Apply this topic to your work experience, to your geographic location, and to your colleagues. Prepare a 300- to 500-word report to be used as a handout.

2. "Stereotyping." As employees and employers, we stereotype people by title, education, and skill levels. Prepare a short presentation, oral or written, on three occupational titles in your company that are frequently stereotyped and describe how these stereotypes can cause problems for employees.
3. "Words are *not* the things they represent." Prepare a short talk or paper using at least three examples of frequently misunderstood words related to your occupation. Discuss how different perceptions affect our communication and understanding of word meanings.
4. "Words as symbols determine our attitude toward people and events." Prepare an informal report using specific work-related examples.

Words are not our only vehicle of communication. Writer Don Fabun explores the revealing medium of *nonverbal* communication. Through nonverbal communication, we often disclose more of our feelings than we realize and learn more about the feelings of others than words can ever tell.

NONVERBAL COMMUNICATION*
Don Fabun

Information theory and general semantics involve coded patterns, usually words, transmitted audibly or visibly—*verbal communication.*

Nonverbal communication is transmitted and received as *non-coded* patterns, sent and received visibly and audibly, but also possibly employing extrasensory wavelengths (ESP). While verbal communication consists of the *words* communicated, nonverbal communication can be accomplished without words or in addition to words. In fact, the *way* words are communicated carries many nonverbal messages. For example, a "hello" can be said with a smile, with indifference, or with anger, each time communicating a different message.

Nonverbal communication relays feelings.

A further way to distinguish verbal from nonverbal communications is to consider their functions. Words function to communicate thoughts. Nonverbals communicate emotions or feelings.

It is usually assumed that in the evolution of human culture nonverbal communication preceded verbal communication. And because of its greater antiquity, nonverbal communication is richer and more

*Adapted from a paper by Don Fabun, former Director of Publications for Kaiser Aluminum Corporation and a well known writer and lecturer in the field of communication.

Table 1–1: The Many Meanings of a Handshake

Type	Possible Meanings
Very firm	"I'm going to compete with you."
Firm and vigorous	"Respect me" or "Pay attention to me" or "Like me."
Firm but relaxed	"Hi. Nice to meet you. We are equals."
Weak	Either "You intimidate me" or "I'm not interested in you," depending on other nonverbal cues.

Nonverbal communication is the closest thing we have to a universal language.

varied than verbal communication. In addition, it is capable of more subtle variations than words, and as communication is more universally understood. (Most experienced travelers know they can communicate fairly well in a foreign country just by using nonverbal techniques.)

Nonverbal communication is virtually limitless, for any individual in any culture/can make use of the *three dimensions of space, time and motion, color, sound, odor, dimension/size, and posture.* General semanticists say "Words have no meanings, only people do." People convey many of those meanings through nonverbal "language."

Forms of Nonverbal Communication

One touch could be worth a thousand words.

Touch.   Shaking a hand or touching a colleague can communicate friendship, domination, competition, even anger, depending on where and how it is done (Table 1–1). No words can simulate touching experiences. Words can only describe them. Thus touching is very important in communicating your feelings to others.

Silence may be loud or soft.

Silence or failure to respond verbally.   The "sounds of silence" are a significant part of nonverbal communication. Silence may be used to indicate agreement, punishment, respect, guilt, incomprehension, censure, disapproval, malice, disbelief, disagreement, rapt attention, awe, disinterest, or dissent. Its meaning will depend on other cues as well as on context. (The language of noise is equally meaningful.)

Body language may convey more than we intend it to.

Body motions.   Standing, sitting, kneeling, bowing, trembling, turning, seeming rigid or relaxed—such gestures, posture, and especially eye contact are a few of the components of "body language." You'll want to be aware of how your body communicates to others and how you are affected by others' motions and positions (Figure 1–1). The success

Figure 1–1: Mental Attitudes Shown through Body Language

of an interview, for example, depends on how well you use body language, followed by the way you say things and the way you present yourself.

Appearance.   Through our dress, we signal our age, sex, occupation, nationality, social standing, economic level, rank in the social hierarchy, religious affiliation, and social protest. An effective communicator is aware of the impact of appearance and adjusts accordingly. For example, a company president might dress neatly and formally for an important board meeting but roll up his or her sleeves when helping a clerk in the shipping room.

Table 1–2: Using Space to Communicate Effectively*

Type of Message	Best Setting
Intimate (rarely found in a business setting)	Close, within arm's length—up to 18 inches
Personal	Relatively close, within two or three arms' lengths—18 inches to 4 feet
One-to-one discussion or instruction	Close enough to be heard with normal voice level—2 to 5 feet—preferably without intervening desk or coffee table
Group meeting (colleagues)	Around a table and/or face to face. Dominant speaker usually chooses center position at head of long table—within 3 to 12 feet of others— where easily seen and heard
Public meeting	From 12 feet onward—may require public address system, exaggerated expressions and gestures

*Space zones differ from culture to culture.

Do clothes make the man—or woman?

Certain dress habits can also reflect how an interviewer or interviewee thinks. Women wearing blouses and skirts, shoes with heels, and stockings give off a positive image. Men wearing suits, relatively short hair, and no facial hair create a favorable impression. According to studies, men in gray suits, white shirts, and burgundy ties have an advantage when being interviewed. Height, weight, and attractiveness can also play a role, with taller males having a greater advantage and usually ending up with a higher salary. (Consider, too, the impact of appearance on the written message, Chapter 7.)

Space.   The distance between speakers and listeners, the setting of their communication, and how they place themselves in that setting determine their relationships and both the tone and substance of the message (Table 1–2). In addition, around each person there is a "private space" or "bubble." Sometimes called *territoriality* or *proxemics,* this space determines the kinds of communication that can be effective. Being too close may lead to discomfort or hostility. Being too far may imply indifference, fear, or hostility.

Our private space expands and contracts depending upon the communication situation.

Top administrators divide their offices into at least two areas—a working area and a seating area. They can stay behind the desk and maintain an authority position (dominance), or they can change the

An example of an office without walls using partitions. Although it gives the working area a feeling of spaciousness, it has a definite disadvantage in the lack of privacy offered.

relationship to a more equal one by moving to the seating area. "Offices without walls" use halfway partitions and are an attempt to enlarge or stretch private bubbles to promote communication among workers and supervisors.

The allocation of work space—its size, distance from the center of authority, even the height from the ground—frequently defines the position of a person in the organization. The higher up in the building, the closer to the corner or to the choice view, and the nearer to authority, the more important the individual.

What does timing tell?

Time.   To be late for an appointment or work, to be too early, to be on time, or not to show up at all tells more than words can express about how we view the occasion and other persons. We can express contempt, eagerness, apathy, disinterest, rejection, acceptance, curiosity—a whole range of feelings—just in the way we use socially agreed upon time. Time, too, is an extremely important variable in cross-cultural communication.

In any type of message, 35 to 40 percent is communicated verbally. The remaining 60 to 65 percent of the message's overall effect comes from nonverbal influences. You must put the two together to communicate effectively—both as sender and receiver.

ASSIGNMENT: NONVERBAL COMMUNICATION

In-service training meetings this week will deal with nonverbal communication. Each participant is to select, prepare, and submit, in advance of the meeting, a short report on one type of nonverbal communication.

Your supervisor has requested that you write a memo (Chapter 8) stating your selection, including an outline (Handbook, page 554) and at least one outside reference source. The training director will coordinate the selections and cover material not chosen. Since you may be asked to make your presentation in the form of a talk or handout, plan on ten minutes or five pages. Relate the report to your work experience and use specific examples and details. Expect a spirited discussion.

Topics

1. Touch
2. Noise
3. Silence
4. Light
5. Size

6. Clothing
7. Color
8. Space
9. Body language
10. Time

Professor Lee Thayer challenges *all* communication theories, pointing out the illusions of communication. He reinforces Johnson's and Fabun's cautions about meanings being created within each of us, building barriers to effective communication.

COMMUNICATION THEORY
*Lee Thayer**

What, then, shall we say of communication? How shall we understand it? What, indeed, do we know about human communication? More than that, what do we know about human communication that has real relevance for our personal lives and for the quality of the societies in which we live?

We know, from such compelling and dramatic stories as that of Helen Keller's transformation from animal-like deaf mute to extraordinary human being, that communication is the process by which we actually create and maintain one another as human beings. We become human, and participate in the human world, only *in* communication.

Communication makes us human.

We know, too, that the world in which we humans live is a world created and maintained in words. To speak of a thing, we must name it; and in naming it, we create that thing in our minds in the form of the name we have given it. And as we have become more and more "civilized," our minds are more and more constituted of "communicational realities"—of those things and ideas and places and people and feelings and awarenesses that have the reality they have for us only because of the way we have come to talk to each other about them.

We often have the illusion—especially we Westerners—that communication is something people "do to" one another. The illusion is that if we say something to someone, and that person "understands" us, we have *caused* that understanding by what we said, or by the way we said it.[1]

Communication is not something we do to each other.

*Lee Thayer is Professor of Communication of the University of Wisconsin, Parkside.

[1] It is remarkable but true: almost all of the theories and models of communication you will come across in communication textbooks are based on that illusion.

Most are variants of this basic form: $A \blacktriangleright B = X$ (A "communicates" something to B with X result). Note that elaborations (such as David Berlo's S–M–C–R model—Sender, Message, Channel, Receiver) do not alter the underlying form or formula. Now, that approach to communication events may be adequate whenever B is interchangeable with all other Bs, or when A is interchangeable with all other possible As, as in the dinner-table request, "Please pass the salt." Here we are not concerned with the personality of the sender or the receiver, nor with their relationship or their feelings about one another. But consider saying "I love you" to someone. Will it make any difference who that someone is? Where a particular A communicates a particular message to a particular B, the result (X) will depend not so much on what is said as it will on how they feel about one another and what they intend with respect to one another.

There are other difficulties and inadequacies with our currently popular approaches to communication. Here it is only important to remember that they are based on the illusion that what we say *causes* the receiver's response. Communication does not work that way, as you will see if you examine the further readings at the end of this chapter.

From this point on in this article, an alternative approach to understanding human communication is developed.

The illusion is compelling, but the facts just don't bear it out. What we know is that communication occurs only when someone takes something into account. That something may be another person, a place, the look on the other person's face, what the other person says, something the other person said last week, or the setting sun. One is just as much an instance of communication as the other. But the setting sun does not "do" something "to" us, any more than what another person says "does" something "to" us. We do something "to" the other's utterance, and "to" the setting sun, as we attribute meaning or significance or value to our perceptions of them.

So we know that any factually based theory of communication would have to be centered in the receiver as the de facto creator of any "message" that he or she "gets." Why is this?

The answer is so simple as to be easily overlooked. It is that no human has any sensory equipment capable of receiving ideas or meaningful information or knowledge. All we can have from ourselves or the world around us has to come to us in the form of the neutral blips and bleeps—meaningless until *we* attribute meaning *to* them—of our neural networks, especially of our optic and auditory systems. And if the source is outside of us, these blips and bleeps have been transformed at our eyes and our ears from the even more neutral light waves and sound waves that can be transported in our physical surroundings. If we take something into account, we must literally create the message we "get" out of the raw data available to us.

Meaning does not lie "out there"; it is within us.

Socialization is the long process of slowly learning how to create appropriate and acceptable kinds of messages out of what we are supposed to take into account. The languages we use to "encode" and to "decode" what is going on of importance to us both enables us to "see" and "comprehend," yet disables us from "seeing" or "comprehending" in some different way.

Society affects the way in which we create meanings . . .

The implications are as profound as they are remarkable. Whether or not something makes sense to us depends solely on the sense we can attribute to it. What we see and hear and understand and believe and appreciate of the world in which we live is therefore never independent of ourselves as the creators of the messages we "get"—as the ultimate source of the sense of things, of what things "mean."

In everyday life, it is ultimately the meanings that you and I attribute to whatever we take into account that have consequences for us personally, and for the societies in which we live. We know that the kinds of communicative experiences we have will in some general way determine the kinds of people we will be, the kinds of existence we will have as humans. But here's the rub: if the kinds of communicative experiences we *can* have depend on our capacities for creating the meaning those experiences will have for us, then it is clear that the influence is reciprocal. How our societies are will determine how we will be; but how we are will determine how they will be.

. . . but how we create meanings also affects society.

Do we have a "theory" of such things? Do we have a theory of communication—of those conditions and processes and experiences out of which we create and maintain ourselves as human, and out of which we create and maintain our human societies? Do we have a theory of what kinds of communicative experiences lead to what kinds of mental health, to what kinds of perspectives on life, to what kinds of joys and griefs and pleasures and frustrations and prejudices and am- bitions and concerns, to what kinds of human societies, human rela- tionships, human beliefs, human errors?

If we *are* what we can communicate, and what others can com- municate to us, will we ever be able fully to understand the process?

Perhaps we have overlooked the obvious. Is it possible that every human who has ever lived, that every human now living, *is* a theory of human communication?

Are you a theory of communication?

Some of us are "better" theories than others, of course. But is it possible for us to understand communication—that process in which we have our very existence as humans—beyond what we have become as humans in that process?

Can we know any more about communication theoretically than we can come to understand by reflecting upon what kind of theory of communication we individually and collectively are—or might be?

FURTHER READING

Information Theory and General Semantics

Baldinger, Kurt. *Semantic Theory.* New York: St. Martins, 1980.

Bormann, Ernest. *Communication Theory.* New York: Holt, Rinehart & Winston, 1980.

Cannon, Don L. and Gerald Luecke. *Understanding Electronic Commu- nications.* Dallas, TX: Texas Instruments, 1980.

Condon, John C., Jr. *Semantics and Communication,* 2nd ed. New York: Macmillan, 1975.

Hayakawa, S.I. *Through the Communication Barrier.* New York: Harper & Row, 1979.

Johnson, Kenneth, John Senator, Mark Liebig, and Gene Minor. *Nothing* Never *Happens.* Encino, CA: Glencoe, 1974.

Johnson, Wendell. *People in Quandaries.* San Francisco: International Society of General Semantics, 1980.

Korzybski, Alfred. *Science and Sanity,* 4th ed. Lakeville, CT: Institute of General Semantics, 1958.

Lee, Irving J. *Language Habits in Human Affairs.* Westport, CT: Greenwood Press, 1979.

Littlejohn, Stephen W. *Theories of Communication.* Columbus, OH: Merrill, 1978.

Mason, Robert M. and John E. Crepps, eds. *Information Services: Economics, Management and Technology.* Boulder, CO: Westview, 1980.

McQuail, Denis. *Communication.* New York: Longman, 1975.

Percy, Walker. "The Delta Factor." *The Message in the Bottle: How Queer Man Is, How Queer Language Is, and What One Has to Do with the Other.* New York: Farrar, Straus & Giroux, 1975.

Pollock, T. C. and J. G. Spaulding. *General Semantics: A Theory of Meaning Analyzed.* Lakeville, CT: Institute of General Semantics, 1981.

Read, Charlotte S. "General Semantics." *Encyclopedia of Library and Information Science,* vol. 9, pp. 211–21. New York: Marcel Dekker, 1973.

Thayer, Lee. *Communication and Communication Systems.* Homewood, IL: Irwin, 1968.

———— . "The Idea of Communication: I. Looking for a Place to Stand." *Communication Yearbook II,* Brent D. Ruben, ed. New Brunswick, NJ: Transaction Books, 1978.

Wrangham, Elizabeth. *The Communication Revolution,* Malcolm Yapp, ed. St. Paul, MN: Greenhaven Press, 1980.

Nonverbal Communication

Birdwhistell, Ray Lee. *Kinesics and Context: Essays on Body Motion Communication.* Philadelphia: University of Pennsylvania Press, 1970.

Fabun, Don. *Three Roads to Awareness.* Encino, CA: Glencoe, 1970.

Fast, Julius. *Body Language.* New York: M. Evans & Co., 1970.

Fromm, Erich. *The Forgotten Language.* New York: Grove Press, 1951.

Hall, Edward T. *The Hidden Dimension.* Garden City, N.Y.: Doubleday, 1959.

———— . "The Silent Language in Overseas Business." *Harvard Business Review,* 38, May–June 1960, 87–96.

———— . *The Silent Language.* Westport, CT: Greenwood Press, 1980.

Knapp, Mark L. *Essentials of Nonverbal Communication*. New York: Holt, Rinehart & Winston, 1980.

Korda, Michael. *Power! How to Get It; How to Use It*. New York: Random House, 1975.

Machotka, Pavel and John P. Spiegel. *Articulate Body*. New York: Irvington, 1980.

Morris, Desmond, Peter Collett, Peter Marsh, Marie O'Shaughnessy. *Gestures*. Chicago: Intercultural Press, 1980.

Rosenthal, Robert, ed. *Skill in Nonverbal Communication: Individual Differences*. Cambridge, MA: Oelgeschlager, Gunn & Hain, 1979.

CHAPTER TWO

Communication Contexts

To be aware of the many functions of communication is to be alive and sensitive to the most basic of human needs. As our needs for bodily health and comfort are met, we become more aware of (and create new) needs for symbolic health and comfort. To be loved or respected, to help others, to feel trust—the list could be elaborated greatly—becomes extremely important. Each communication situation both reveals our frailty and offers some promise for support.

John C. Condon
Semantics and Communication

Communication begins with the self and moves into broader and broader contexts.

Communication contexts refer to particular situations and the communicators involved. This chapter examines communication in five basic contexts: intrapersonal, interpersonal, small-group, organizational, and intercultural.

Intrapersonal communication takes place within the individual. Before you can communicate with a co-worker, customer, or supervisor, you must have some idea of who you are and how you think, feel, and act.

Interpersonal communication moves beyond the individual and usually includes one other person, most often in a face-to-face situation. Most of us spend more than half of our time communicating within this context. In business you may give information to and seek information from other employees, converse with a client, answer or ask questions of your boss, and so on.

Small-group communication involves the individual and others who usually join together for a specific purpose, again, most often in a face-to-face situation. In business the purpose of the small group may be to solve problems, make decisions, or determine company policies and procedures.

Organizational communication unites the individual with an entire organization—corporation, institution, or whatever. It is concerned with how people within the organization relate to each other, and to other organizations and people with whom they must deal. The latter may include suppliers, customers, and often even competitors.

18

Intercultural communication is concerned with the entire global community, the broadest of all contexts. It requires an awareness of cultural differences as they affect values, methods of expression, and nonverbal behavior. For example, if you have business with a Japanese manufacturing company, it is important that you know that the Japanese almost never use first names.

The following selections should help you anticipate some of these important communication contexts. As you read the selections, keep in mind that none of these contexts exists in a vacuum; each is affected by some or all of the others.

INTRAPERSONAL COMMUNICATION*
Jacquelyn B. Carr

Intrapersonal communication is the process of creating meaning within the self. Before we can explore communication with others, we must have some understanding of how we create meaning patterns within the self. If we are unaware of how we process information, we will be less conscious of how we attach meaning to the external world—which includes other people as well as the environment and the situation. Knowing how I as a unique individual communicate with myself and how I can expand my consciousness of that process will enhance my ability to create meaning for myself and share that meaning with others.

We have a "memory bank" of experiences from which, at any given moment, we can select, interpret, and evaluate incoming information. Outside each of us, in the form of external stimuli, something occurs that we process through our sensory equipment (eyes, ears, skin, nose, mouth). How we deal with much of this information depends on our cultural and social environment. We select certain stimuli and block out others. We spend a great deal of energy considering, reacting to, and making *sense* out of what comes to us through our senses. In the process, we develop our own realities, our own impressions of what the world is like—we develop a "personal consciousness."

Our personal consciousness tells us who we are in relation to our world.

Intrapersonal communication, communicating with the self, occurs when we think, feel, or act, as well as when we verbalize to ourselves. By exploring intrapersonal communication, we observe ourselves and become more aware of our personal consciousness—our self-concept. We get in touch with what reality means to us and what is real to us about ourselves. We get to know ourselves better through

*Reprinted with permission from Jacquelyn B. Carr, *Communicating and Relating* (Menlo Park, CA: Benjamin/Cummings, 1979), pages 11-13.

experiencing body, emotions, and mind. As you become aware of the language you use, you will begin to hear how you talk to yourself. Moreover, observing your behavior will give you more information useful for improving communication.

Each thought we have is part of our personal consciousness. And our thoughts are always changing. We may see the same object, hear the same tone, taste the same food, but our consciousness of these experiences changes each time. This changing series of experiences is always modified by previous experiences. We often feel strange about our subsequent views of the same things. We sometimes wonder how we could have responded the way we did the first time. We all experience pluralistic thinking, duplicity, contradictions, paradoxes, and inconsistencies. We are always in flux, never the same person we were before. We continue, moment by moment, to add to what we were a minute ago.

The moment we stop changing we are dead.

ASSIGNMENT: INTRAPERSONAL COMMUNICATION

Take some time to think about how you communicate with yourself. Then, in writing, answer these questions:

1. How effective are you in "talking to yourself"? Are your thoughts often confused or disquieting? Are they clear and full of insight?
2. How do you reach conclusions and solve problems?
3. What are eight of your strengths?
4. How can you use your strengths to achieve three of your business communication goals?

Refer to your answers to these questions as you work through the rest of this chapter. Try to determine how your intrapersonal communication affects the way in which you communicate with others.

INTERPERSONAL COMMUNICATION*
Cal W. Downs and Paul E. Nelson

Communication occurs in a number of different contexts and at different levels, starting at the intrapersonal, and each of them is worth studying. But the study of interpersonal communication is particularly significant for a number of reasons.

---

*Adapted from papers by Cal W. Downs, Professor of Organizational Communication, University of Kansas, and Paul E. Nelson, Dean, College of Communication, Ohio University.

First, you have been communicating interpersonally all your life, and you probably spend more time doing so than you do with other forms of communication. In fact, a study by Samovar, Brooks, and Porter found that adults spend an average of 52 percent of their waking hours speaking, listening, and conversing in interpersonal situations.

Most of us spend half of our waking hours communicating interpersonally.

Second, an interpersonal dimension is present in communication at the group, organizational, and cultural levels. For this reason, most of the communication models have been based on the interpersonal dimension.

Third, theories of interpersonal communication can be *applied* profitably to our most important relationships. For example, they apply to friendships, marriage, superior-subordinate work interactions, negotiations, and doctor-patient relationships. These factors make the study of interpersonal communication very important.

The Components of Interpersonal Communication

Interpersonal communication can be defined as that communication which takes place when two or more people in a relationship exchange messages through oral, face-to-face interaction. While there is no particular magic in definitions, it is useful to explore some of the ramifications of this one to determine how it differentiates the interpersonal dimension from other levels of communication.

Size. Most interpersonal analyses focus on *dyads*, or two-person groups. Of course, it is possible to consider more than two people, but the more who are involved, the more complex the situation. Consequently, size is one of the considerations that differentiate interpersonal communication from intrapersonal communication on the one hand and from group and organizational communication on the other.

Relationship. Communicators interact in some kind of relationship. One of the greatest contributions of interpersonal communication theory has been to demonstrate that *the relationship may be just as important as the content of the messages in determining the success of interpersonal communication*. Whenever you send a message to someone else, it is always useful to ask yourself what kind of impact this message will have on the other individual and how it may affect your relationship with that person. Keep in mind that any relationship is constantly being built or destroyed by the communicators; it cannot remain static.

Two-way exchange. People sometimes communicate in a one-way direction, with one person the sender and the other person the receiver. However, healthy interpersonal relationships generally require that both

Interpersonal communication usually involves a one-on-one relationship in a two-way exchange of information.

people function as sources and receivers. Whether the situation is social or work related, both communicators need to be able to listen as well as to express themselves. (For more about listening, see Chapter 3.)

Feedback.   At the very center of two-way communication is the concept of feedback, a label applied to *all the messages and responses that you get back from people after you have initiated communication with them.* The responses can be verbal or nonverbal; they can be questions or comments. Since feedback is one of the most important concepts of interpersonal communication, it is sometimes useful to analyze how you use it. How do you react to different types of feedback? Are you as receptive to negative feedback as you are to positive feedback? Are you more likely to accept feedback from some individuals than from others? How do you decide when to give feedback to others? What are some of the guidelines you use?

What do you do with feedback?

Oral, face-to-face setting.   Many people consider this their richest and most pleasant channel of communication; others experience great anxiety. Therefore, it is useful to consider what advantages the oral, face-to-face channel has over other channels such as letters, memos, and telephone conversations.

Perhaps the greatest single advantage is that you get immediate feedback. Furthermore, because you are in each other's presence, your feedback can be nonverbal as well as verbal. No other channel permits this. An additional advantage is that it is easier to establish a communicative relationship with someone when you are in direct contact with that person.

Factors Affecting Interpersonal Communication

Do others see you as you see yourself? If not, why not?

Self-image.   People define themselves through their interpersonal communication. If others perceive you as ambitious, capable, and friendly, you are likely to feel that way about yourself. And the opposite is true.

How you perceive yourself affects others' perceptions of you. This communication cycle can be pleasing when you are satisfied with your self-image and the image others have of you. Changing your image requires a change in both attitude and behavior. As others see you behaving differently, they reinforce your new self-image.

Occasionally, people are unaware of the perceptions others have of them, and their self-image is in conflict with those perceptions. This can lead to communication that is ultimately unsatisfactory. For example, if you see yourself as ambitious and friendly, but your employer sees you as lazy and aloof, you will probably misinterpret your employer's hostile or cold behavior. Rather than changing those behaviors that are interpreted as laziness, you might react with your own hostility. Eventually, this pattern may lead to your searching for a new job.

Self-disclosure. Have you ever noticed that some people with whom you work reveal more about themselves than others do? Self-disclosure is the extent to which you reveal yourself to others by telling them what they otherwise would not know. Self-disclosure is reciprocal; that is, revealing yourself to others invites them to reveal themselves to you. This mutual process is the basis for good relationships.

The worker who rarely self-discloses is often regarded with suspicion and distrust, while the worker who discloses inappropriately is seen as too confessional. Between these extremes is the person who is perceived as having a "good personality" because he or she knows that self-disclosure can invite a healthy professional relationship.

The appropriateness of self-disclosure at work depends on your role, your relationship, and your time together. Ordinarily, for example, you self-disclose more to people you see as your equals, somewhat less to those you see as your superiors, and even less to those you see as your subordinates. You self-disclose more to those with whom you are friendly and cooperative, less to those with whom you are cold and competitive. And you disclose more in a business environment that encourages personal contact and a family spirit. Finally, you are likely to self-disclose more to those you have known a long time.

Ideally, the amount of information we disclose about ourselves varies from situation to situation.

Clarity. The effectiveness of interpersonal communication is bounded by how clearly messages are exchanged. Though clarity is always limited by differences in people (their background, attitudes, and interests, for example), there are two important ways clarity can be controlled.

First is the *choice of language*. As we will discuss in the section on speaking, Chapter 3, your choice of words must be precise in meaning and understandable to your listener.

Second, *feedback* indicates whether your message was understood; restate your thoughts if it was not. Repressing thoughts without clarifying them can lead to anger that leaks out in inappropriate ways: backbiting, gossip, or chronic complaining. On the other hand, a person who goes beyond clarity to verbal and nonverbal aggression can be perceived as obnoxious because he or she seems always to want the world to bend to personal likes and dislikes.

It is important to realize that clarity is somewhat *subjective*. Some people always feel they are misunderstood, no matter how clear their language is or how aggressively they express their ideas. They don't

How can we tell if our messages are being received clearly? We can look and ask for feedback.

realize that understanding is in a large part controlled by the other person and that *total* communication is neither possible nor necessary.

The degree and type of clarity needed vary from situation to situation. It is important that a service technician know exactly what problems you are having with your typewriter, for example, but not how you feel about your job. On the other hand, it is probably more important to make clear to a co-worker how much you liked his or her presentation at a company meeting than to specify the details of your praise.

Without filters we would soon grow deaf, dumb, and blind.

Personal filter.   You function as a *communication filter*, accepting some cues and messages while excluding others. You are not just a passive recipient of messages that surround you; you are actively involved in selecting, organizing, and interpreting those messages in a way that will make sense to you.

Your "filter" is made up of your own purposes, motivations, thinking patterns, biases, attitudes, and memory. Because each person becomes a unique filter, individuals interpret the same message in different ways. (This aspect of interpersonal communication will be explored further in the section on listening in Chapter 3.)

Evaluating Interpersonal Communication

There are many criteria that can be used to judge the effectiveness of communication, and perhaps all of them are appropriate at different times.

First, there is *message content*. Because (as seen in Chapter 1) meaning is created by the receiver, it is doubtful that complete understanding is ever achieved. However, unless there is some substantial degree of mutual understanding, the communication will probably be unsatisfactory.

Second, there are criteria of effectiveness that focus on the *relationship*. Interpersonal communications that are inappropriate for a certain relationship may lead to some conflict. For example, most people expect more openness and friendly banter from a co-worker than from a boss. One who is continually curt and formal should expect some hostility from colleagues. The most productive and long-lasting relationships require interpersonal communications that exhibit rapport, openness, support, and compatibility.

Communication is successful if it achieves the results we desire.

Third, there are criteria based on the *accomplishment of a desired purpose*. In other words, the communication is successful to the extent that desired results are achieved. Thus a "successful" communication could be to develop hostility in a co-worker, if that is your desired goal.

Awareness of the likely results of your communication is all-important and is a sign of a mature communicator.

You should keep in mind that people have multiple purposes. For example, you can, perhaps, fulfill one objective by getting information from another individual; but you may use methods in the process that completely ruin the relationship. Therefore, you may never get information from that individual again. (Journalists, for example, are particularly vulnerable in such a situation.) In this sense, there may be some trade-off in your effectiveness and you cannot be assessed an unqualified success.

We may achieve a result but ruin a relationship.

Remember, also, that all people in a transaction have purposes, and frequently your purposes are not compatible with those of the other person. Therefore, when you succeed, the other person may lose. Capable administrators anticipate problems of interpersonal communication and try to convert them to mutually satisfying conditions.

Mutually satisfying results are usually the best results of any communication.

Here are six excellent suggestions for effective interpersonal communication.

1. Remember that interpersonal communication takes place within relationships. Every message has a content and relational component. Be alert to the interplay between those components—your relationship and the purpose of the communication. When you get into an argument, for example, instead of expressing resentment immediately, first try to find something good to say about your opponent. This may help defuse a potentially explosive situation and gain you a hearing.
2. Recognize your "filters": your purposes, motivations, thinking patterns, biases, attitudes, and memory. Don't be afraid to admit you don't know something, don't understand a statement, don't remember. Ask questions to verify your interpretation.
3. Be sensitive to others' feedback. Encourage it from them, and give them feedback in return. Feedback is essential for clarity. Be willing to compromise, unless a principle is involved.
4. Be aware of your self-image and the image others have of you. Self-image affects your communication and all of your behavior. If you are not pleased with your image, try to communicate the image you want. Be aware that most of us tend to interact with those who agree with us, have beliefs similar to ours. You'll have a chance to grow more intellectually if you are willing to listen to and understand loners and "oddballs."
5. Use self-disclosure appropriately. Use self-disclosure to build relationships. We prefer to react/interact with individuals we feel we know as feeling human beings. Remember, however, to observe unspoken barriers of rank, age, and prestige.

6. Encourage clarity in your communication by using precise, appropriate language and by using feedback to make sure you are understood. Express your idea in several different ways, if necessary, to make another person understand you. Or use the *Rogerian Argument*,* in which you ask the other person to summarize what you have said and how you feel about it; then you do the same for the other person *before* getting into the discussion. This sets up a "psychological safety," enabling you and an adversary to feel safe and reduce misunderstandings.

ASSIGNMENT: INTERPERSONAL COMMUNICATION

People communicate all the time, but there is a great deal of misunderstanding about how and why communication is effective on one occasion and not on another.

Your supervisor has scheduled an interpersonal communication in-service workshop and asked you to select a topic from the following list. You are to prepare a presentation for the meeting relating a specific business communication experience. You may select a partner to demonstrate your activity. You may use role-play techniques, interview techniques, or another method if you wish.

Your topic may focus on a letter you have received or sent and its response; a memo you have received or sent and its response; a report you have written or received; or a description of an interview, evaluation session, telephone conversation, or group meeting. You are to direct a discussion period following your presentation. Plan to spend a total of ten minutes.

Topics

1. How messages are filtered
2. An analysis of why you choose to work with one person rather than another, one group rather than another
3. Methods of response to positive or negative feedback
4. Personal feedback mechanisms
5. Workplace constraints on interpersonal communication
6. Interpersonal communication during an employment interview
7. Interpersonal relations: how they affect you

*Named for Carl Rogers, a California-based clinical therapist.

8. Examples of verbal and nonverbal feedback encountered with an immediate supervisor, a friend at work, or a person working for you
9. How interpersonal relations shaped you
10. Factors to consider before self-disclosing at work
11. How clarity is related to assertiveness, to language choice
12. How one recognizes personal successful communication

SMALL-GROUP COMMUNICATION
Paul E. Nelson[*]

Something happens to communication when it involves more than two people: it becomes much more complex. For example, imagine two people, *A* and *B*, having a conversation. There is only *one* possible conversation, *A–B*. Add one more person, *C*, however: now there are *four* possible interactions, *A–B*, *A–C*, *B–C*, and *A–B–C*. Add another person, *D*, and there are *11* possible interactions. And so on.

This additional complexity produces dynamics not found in one-to-one communication. For example, groups of three or four persons tend to compete. In a three-person group, there is a tendency for two people to form a coalition against the third, though the members of the coalition may switch from issue to issue. In the four-person group, there is a tendency to pair in opposing teams.

Small-group communication is more complex than interpersonal communication.

The organizational pattern of a group tends to change when it has five or more members: it becomes less competitive. It changes again when it has roughly more than nine members: it loses cohesion and closeness. *The small group of five to nine members* is thus a somewhat unique communication system.

Groups of this size form for a variety of reasons—social conversation, learning, therapy—but the most important function in business is to *solve problems and make decisions*. Such groups as boards of directors, personnel committees, sales management teams, and grievance committees are charged with the responsibility of solving problems too big or complicated for one person.

Unique Characteristics of Small Groups

There are several characteristics of the small group that set it apart from other communication systems. These characteristics also help explain why the small group is used so often in business to solve problems.

*Paul E. Nelson is Dean, College of Communication, Ohio University.

Frequent interaction.   Because of its size, the small group allows each member to interact with others face to face. This produces an intense communication environment that helps produce and judge ideas quickly.

Group personality.   A small group tends to take on an identity of its own rather than remaining a conglomerate of various personalities. This *cohesion* can lead to a forceful decision-making process, but it has its risks. "Group think," the tendency for members to agree blindly to the ideas of the group, can produce disastrous decisions.

Group norms.   Groups tend to develop their own rules and value systems. For example, straitlaced managers might behave out of character in their weekly sales meetings. The group norms might encourage joke telling, swearing, and loud debate that individual managers would never engage in.

Coping behavior.   One function of a group is to protect itself from outside threats and disturbances. These threats range from simple demands on the members' time to an outright attack on the validity of the group's decisions or even its existence. In response, the group may react with briefer meetings and elaborate, technical reports.

Role assignment.   Within a group there is a variety of tasks to be performed, and individual members play certain roles to accomplish these tasks. Roles include those that are necessary for reaching a goal—such as supplying information, asking for opinions, and giving group direction—and those that are necessary to maintain a good social atmosphere—such as encouraging others, creating harmony, and controlling the flow of communication. Usually, each person adopts several roles.

Interdependent goals.   Each member of a group has a set of personal goals and a set of group goals. However, those goals shared by all the members of the group become the primary goals of the group. Personal goals contrary to those of the group must be suppressed or they may cause conflict within the group, even failure to meet the group goals.

Small groups generally interact frequently, assume an identity, develop their own values, protect themselves against outside influences, share goals, and achieve more than their members could individually.

The whole is greater than the sum of the parts.   A group is capable of greater productivity than the same number of members working individually. This is not only because of the division of labor that occurs in role assignment, but also because the ideas of one person trigger ideas and memories of others. This leads to brainstorming, which cannot be duplicated by one person.

Problem Solving

The unique characteristics of the small group make it ideal for problem solving. As a result, modern corporations rely heavily on small groups for decision making and problem solving.

The organization of the group's task inevitably boils down to two main questions: What is the problem? and What is the solution? The organizational patterns that lead to answers for these two questions are numerous. John Dewey's method of reflective thinking is one important pattern that can be adapted by most groups. Here are the steps in Dewey's method.

In business, small groups solve problems, make decisions, set policies and procedures.

1. Recognize the problem.
2. Define the problem.
3. Analyze the problem.
4. Establish standards for evaluating solutions.
5. Suggest solutions.
6. Select the best solution.
7. Test the solution.

Leading

Role assignment is an important characteristic of problem-solving groups, and one of the most important roles is that of leadership. Sometimes this is an assigned role. At other times a leader simply emerges out of the situation. In either case, the leader is the person who assumes the functions of leadership, and that person may or may not be the one who has the title of chair, director, or head. Occasionally, several members act as leaders.

One or more leaders emerge in any small group.

John Brilhart (1978) suggests five functions that a leader should serve: (1) guiding the discussion; (2) stimulating creative and critical thinking; (3) promoting clear communication; (4) promoting cooperative interpersonal relations; and (5) helping the group and its members improve their problem-solving skills.

Persuading

After a group has arrived at a decision or a solution to a problem, the solution must be "sold" to others. The office manager who assigned the committee may have to be persuaded that the committee decision is the best solution. The policy that the group decided upon may have to be accepted by the board of directors. Or the solution may have to be

*If the function of a small group is to make recommendations, it must be prepared to persuade others of the validity of those recommendations.`

voted upon by those persons affected by the decision. In any case, decisions by a group or a committee frequently must be acceptable to persons outside the committee, and that requires persuasion.

When a task-oriented small group makes a decision that must be accepted by another person or group, the group has to demonstrate, from that other person or group's point of view, why the decision or solution should be accepted. In other words, some audience analysis must take place in which the group determines why the manager or the persons who will judge the solution should accept the committee's decision.

Committees and other small groups are often surprised at the response of persons who receive the suggested solution or decision. Sometimes committee decisions are not warmly accepted because the person or persons to whom the decision has been submitted did not go through the same process of decision making. Hence a small group has to reveal the rationale for the decision or solution by "walking through" the decision with the person who must determine its acceptability.

This analysis of small-group characteristics and functions should help you to avoid conflicts and enable you to work more efficiently. Like all systems, it is easier to analyze than to put into practice.

ASSIGNMENT: SMALL-GROUP COMMUNICATION

You have been assigned by the vice-president for personnel to serve on a screening committee. The task of the screening committee is to examine the credentials of the top three candidates for district sales manager and to recommend them in rank order. The district sales manager is supposed to be a college graduate with at least two years of experience and three letters of recommendation from previous supervisors or employers. The district sales manager will supervise the activities of 16 salespersons in a large city.

One candidate is Regina Washington, a black woman who graduated with an M.B.A. from Harvard Business School. She has excellent recommendations from previous employers, but her experience is almost exclusively on the financial side; none of her experience is in sales. She is 26 years old. The second candidate is Ricardo Callatta, a white male from Boston, who has a B.A. from Boston University and some credits toward a master's degree in political science. Callatta has been a district sales manager for a competing firm for nearly ten years. He is well known in sales circles for having won top sales awards nearly every year he has been on the job. He is 35 years old. The third candidate is an inside candidate: he has worked with you and the others on the screening committee for as long as anyone can remember. He is Sam Silverberg, a man in his late forties who gets along well with everyone. His record says that he graduated from New York University, but he is more notable because all but 2 of the 16 salespersons in the district have indicated that they want Sam.

At the first meeting of the screening committee, the vice-president appoints you to chair the committee with the task of rank-ordering the three candidates. Knowing what you know about interpersonal communication and small-group decision making, what would you do with the other four members of your committee to ensure that a fair and equitable decision results from your deliberations? What are some concepts in interpersonal communication that might be most useful in this kind of decision making? How would you go about persuading the vice-president that your committee made a wise decision?

Discuss these problems in a small-group meeting. Each member should take brief notes and then compare them. (The interpretations will surprise you.) Be sure to discuss all of the following topics.

Topics

1. What are some basic questions that members of a committee task force or group must ask in organizing decision making or problem solving?
2. What are some functions that need to be fulfilled by members of a small group? Which functions are leadership functions?
3. What is the role of persuasion in small-group decision making?
4. How do the steps in Dewey's method apply to the above situation?
5. How did a leader appear in your group?
6. What divisions or pairing occurred in your group?

ORGANIZATIONAL COMMUNICATION
David N. Bateman[*]

The most frequently asked question about organizational communication is, What *is* it? Organizational communication might best be represented as a monster octopus, sprouting a new tentacle several times

*David N. Bateman is a professor of communication at Southern Illinois University.

each year. Not too long ago, organizational communication was a simple concept; today, like the monster octopus, it is growing in numerous ways.

Within the context of an organization, both interpersonal and small-group communications take place. Whatever the organization—corporation, agency, institution—it has a communication system all its own. This system affects and is affected by other communication contexts.

Organizational communication is how the employees in a group relate to one another, how the organization reports information to one of its publics, and how information flows inside and outside the organization. It is all of these things and more. And by the time this book is published, organizational communication will be many more things.

Organizational communication takes in *all* events in and around the organization. These events can involve written words (letters, bulletin boards, house organs, and memos), hardware (telecommunications, computers, and dictation equipment), speech activities (meetings, discussions, and presentations), as well as all kinds of interpersonal and nonverbal activities. Thus, *organizational communication might best be explained as the study of how an organization and its people relate to each other and to those people and organizations external to it.*

Organizational communication encompasses everyone comprising the organization and everyone with whom it deals.

Some Dimensions of Organizational Communication

Organizational communication has been approached from different perspectives. The perspectives broadly identified are *the employee perspective* (how to get needed information into the head and hands of the employee); *the flow or channel perspective* (how information is passed and routed inside and outside the organization); *the skills perspective* (how to improve the actual communication abilities of individuals' writing and speaking); and *the media perspective* (how different technologies can be employed to broadcast the message).

Some Specific Tools of Organizational Communication

Communicators have developed and used various "tools." These tools can be used to help one understand how communications work in the organization and to help the organization accomplish its goals. These tools include the following.

Communication audits. Just as an accountant can audit the finances of an organization in an attempt to discover financial problems, the communicator can also audit. Some items in the audit check list include

- listing communication policies and procedures
- classifying communication policies and procedures
- identifying communication control systems
- measuring communication program effectiveness
- evaluating communication efforts

Management by objective.   Management by objective (M.B.O.) was conceived as a technique that managers could use to make employees aware of the organization's objectives and to motivate employees to achieve those objectives. As M.B.O. has been instituted in organizations, it has become obvious that organizational communications are the catalysts making M.B.O. work. Very simply, if it is expected that employees are going to be motivated because the organization established objectives, how are the employees made aware of these objectives? Organizational communication can involve meetings, memos, supervisor-subordinate discussions, and so on, all orchestrated to make M.B.O. effective.

Communication flows.   You have probably played a game called Telephone, where one person is given a message and then the message is individually transmitted to others in turn. After being passed to about five people, the message, when repeated, is often unintelligible. To a child, the game is fun. To an organization executive, the situation is frustrating. A common tool communicators employ is the establishment of monitoring points within the organization so that they can determine where messages go haywire.

   The manner in which communication flows in an organization varies, depending on the organization's structure and the type of communication. For example, while official reporting is done through a well-organized system of memos and meetings, important news can spread quickly by rumor via the "grapevine." It's not unusual for an executive to find out about a big sale from a secretary or clerk before it is reported by the sales manager.

Organizations can improve their efficiency by monitoring communication, stating their objectives, and establishing channels for the flow of information.

   Obviously, these tools relate to more than communication. When correctly applied, they can assist the organization in becoming more efficient in its operations.

Organizational Communication for What Organizations?

Most studies have explored business operations. However, organizational communication involves all organizations—hospitals, governmental agencies, religious groups, unions, and political groups, among others. The need for improved organizational communication is obvious when we recognize that much of the work of the organization is accomplished through communication.

In its broadest sense, effective organizational communication can benefit society.

If it is possible to improve the communication in and from the organization, then the organizational communicator will have made a substantial contribution to society.

ASSIGNMENT: ORGANIZATIONAL COMMUNICATION

The public affairs director has agreed to meet with your in-service training group to talk about organizational communication. In planning for the meeting, the director asked that participants collect samples of other companies' internal and external publications for discussion and evaluation.

You are to obtain one sample and prepare an analysis of it, using a memo format. The analysis should specify the audience for the publication and identify its purpose, frequency of publication, distribution method, and other pertinent data. Attach one copy of the publication to the memo and bring it to the meeting.

Your memo should refer to as many of the following topics as appropriate.

Topics

1. From your work or personal experience, list other internal and external publications. Identify different audiences.
2. List the groups of employees in an organization involved in organizational communication and explain their relationships.
3. Describe "events" occurring in organizational communication in your organization.
4. Describe the "tools" used to audit organizational publications.
5. Chart the path of a message from the bottom to the top of an organization.

INTERCULTURAL COMMUNICATION
John C. Condon[*]

The words and gestures we make when we say we are communicating with one another are only the most apparent part of communication. Behind those outward expressions is a vast and complex set of ex-

---

[*]John C. Condon is a well known writer, educator and consultant in the field of intercultural communication.

periences and assumptions we share with others. The name we give to that collective set of assumptions, beliefs, values, expectations, and linguistic habits is *culture.* Probably many of the communication principles outlined in earlier sections are applicable only within their own cultural setting. They may not work with persons who come from other cultural backgrounds.

This is not to say that everybody from the same culture communicates well or that there are no misunderstandings among people who share a common culture. But it does mean that when we are with people who have grown up learning other values, speaking other languages, holding other assumptions, our chances of misunderstanding are greatly increased.

Communication behavior regarded as effective in one culture may be unacceptable in another.

The study of intercultural communication, what happens when persons from different cultures attempt to communicate, is important for at least two reasons. It is not only that we need to understand and get along with persons who speak different languages and who may have different goals in life, although in our interdependent world that may be reason enough. In addition, an intercultural perspective on communication allows us to understand ourselves better, including our own assumptions and goals that underlie so much of what we call "communication."

Cultural Differences

What then is "culture" as it relates to communication? Culture may be regarded as the way we have learned to perceive the world around us and to act in ways appropriate to that world. In other words, culture is not only something "out there" in the physical world, such as jazz and museums; rather, it is a way of looking and listening, a way of seeking and speaking that we have learned from our life's experiences.

A basic problem in intercultural communication is that people from different cultures in the same situation may not view that situation in the same way and may, in turn, react differently. Such differences in themselves are not necessarily cause for concern; they can be interesting, informative, even helpful *if* they are recognized as arising from cultural differences. The problem is that behavior that springs from a cultural source is easily confused with responses having to do with personalities and attitudes.

If we are to be understood in other cultures, we must first understand their manners of communicating.

Here is a simple example. A businessperson in the United States tends to value people who express themselves well, who ask good questions and give good, straight answers without a lot of hesitation. Job applicants are likely to be judged, in part, on how well they sell themselves during an interview. Direct questions are asked and quick, clear-cut answers are expected.

In Japan the situation is quite different. To begin with, background is more important than foreground: the person's family, studies, and so forth mean more than any one thing the person might say in an interview. The interviewer is expected to know this background before the interview begins. Moreover, someone who is seeking a job is supposed to be modest about his or her abilities and outwardly appreciative of being considered for the position.

Thus, when Americans interview Japanese as prospective employees for the Tokyo branch office, applicants may seem shy or lacking in self-confidence. And from the applicant's point of view, the interviewer may seem unprepared and uninformed by asking background questions (therefore the whole organization may be doubted). The straight questions may seem crude and embarrassing. The answers, viewed from the other side, may seem evasive and suspicious.

Values

How can we better understand the cultural dimensions of communication? There are several ways. One is to increase our awareness of cultural values, that part of culture we are probably least conscious of—until something goes wrong. By *values* is meant *all that we learn to do or not to do.* Values are not the same as behavior, for we don't always act as we know we should; but values are guides to action and to the evaluation of actions.

Dominant values differ from culture to culture.

Among the dominant values in the United States are *individualism* (a person is primarily responsible to self, not family or organization); the qualities associated with *youth* (imagination, energy, experimentation); *change* (many equate "newer" with "better"); *mobility; equality* (we are nervous about differences in rank, status, rules for men and women; despite a history with obvious inequalities, we continue to pursue this as a realistic goal); *separation of work and play;* a kind of *pragmatism* (which to us seems natural to distinguish from tradition or aesthetics—Does it work? is a basic question). Many other such themes might be considered.

In many respects these values are minority values in the world today. The qualities associated with age, experience, and wisdom are more likely to be valued elsewhere, where respect is paid to one who is older. "Newer" does not at all suggest "better." In many cultures, men and women are expected to act in clearly distinguishable ways, in speech, actions, and responsibilities. Mobility, as in moving onward through the ranks in different companies, may not be interpreted as a positive sign. Instead, it may suggest that the person on the move does not get along with associates and lacks maturity.

MINDING OUR INTERNATIONAL MANNERS—A SAMPLER*

Far East: Business people visiting some Far Eastern nations are expected to conform to the Pakistani custom of spending at least a few minutes on unrelated social conversation. Business can be discussed after five or ten minutes, but only if the American opens that part of the conversation.

Lima, Peru: It is impolite to show up for dinner on time. If cocktails are scheduled for 8 P.M., show up around 9 P.M. Arriving late is a socially accepted custom referred to as following Peruvian Time or *hora Peruana* in Spanish. Try to find out if business meetings are also scheduled for *hora Peruana.* They usually are.

China: Business should be settled before the meal. Do not leave business for afterward. Chinese usually get ready to leave when the last course, noodles or soup, is served. With the last bite, the company thank the host and hostess and leave for home.

Pakistan: American business people should phrase many questions, particularly concerning political issues, so that the Easterner has a graceful way of not answering. Try to avoid asking questions requiring yes or no replies.

Moslem Cultures: No liquor is served at business lunches. Do not ask for liquor; do not offer liquor (unless you know your guests *very* well).

Buddhist Cultures: Attitudes toward time are similar to those in South America. Attitudes toward liquor differ with individuals, but the Buddhist, Hindu, and Moslem religions forbid alcoholic beverages. In a Buddhist society, do not be surprised if you fail to receive a statement of appreciation for a gift or business favor. Religion and tradition sometimes assume that the act of generosity is its own reward and no acknowledgment need be made.

South America: Personal compliments are freely offered but personal questions are never asked.

Japan: Never use first names. Talk in moderation, leaving many things unsaid. It is quite all right to leave words hanging in air, sentences unfinished. Japanese need to get a "feel" for the other person, are not hesitant to let long silences develop. Japanese want complete explanations. In making a presentation, a Westerner should use every possible visual aid: samples, models, maps, blueprints, photographs, videocassettes, recordings, and other devices, including material to be given away or loaned for future showings.

Belgium: White chrysanthemums symbolize mourning. Flowers are appropriate as thank-you gifts or when visiting a colleague's home (almost everywhere), but select other varieties. The white chrysanthemum also signifies mourning in Japan.

Everywhere: "Space bubbles" or distances between people differ from culture to culture. Business people should learn approximate size of space bubbles when working overseas, as well as other cultural distinctions.

"Cultures of the world can be placed on a continuum, based on the amount of communication contained in the nonverbal context compared with the amount in the verbal message." (Hall 1979) Highly contexted societies (Arab, Chinese, Japanese, others) examine entire circumstances of an event in order to understand what is happening. Stronger emphasis is placed on personal contact and less on procedures. Less contexted societies (American, Swiss) put more emphasis on the verbal message, want to get down to business quickly. Business persons might adjust behavior to the depth of context.

*****Source:** Based on articles in *The Bridge* and personal experience.

Presentation

Styles of presentation and expression also vary. The American public speaker's advice to "stand up, speak up, shut up," with its implied value of coming right to the point and not being long-winded, is ineffectual in societies as different as Liberia, Iran, and the Philippines, where much more elaborate discourse is called for. We in the United States tend to equate silence with a person's shyness or disagreement or lack of interest. In many cultures throughout the world, however, silence speaks volumes; but to read it correctly one must have learned the meanings of silence in that culture.

Nonverbal Cues

Values, methods of expression, and nonverbal behavior vary from culture to culture and must be learned.

In all of our nonverbal behavior, how we sit, stand, and walk; the clothing, jewelry, and hair styles we wear; the ways in which we arrange our desks; and much, much more reveal as much about our culture—without our realizing it—as about our personalities or intentions. It is a common issue in intercultural communication that words expressed in a common language may seem to mean the same thing, but that the nonverbal expressions that accompany the words may yet require "translation." In the United States a smile would seem to cancel out the words of an apology; in Japan, on occasion, it may be appropriate. A listener's eyes are lowered, a reflex intended to show deference to the speaker; but if the speaker is from a society like the United States, the eye avoidance may be interpreted as indifference or impudence. The head nods and it may mean "yes" or it may just mean "I understand but do not necessarily agree." The head shakes from side to side and it may mean "no" or, in much of India, "yes."

These examples illustrate the deep concern in intercultural communication: *to know the cultural bases of communication that can aid understanding and avoid confusion when people from different background come together.*

There are few universal principles of "good" communication.

Many people believe that basic principles of communication and business management are universal. At a safe distance of abstraction such a faith may be affirmed. But in day-to-day communication, from the hiring of a receptionist to the successful merger of two large organizations into an effective joint venture, the cultural factors in communication, however subtle, cannot be denied. In the years ahead, no aspect of communication will be more important to consider seriously than intercultural communication.

ASSIGNMENT: INTERCULTURAL COMMUNICATION

Your supervisor has offered you a position in an overseas branch of the company. The position fits closely with your career objective, has good potential for future advancement, and is very challenging. You will be able to take your family and will receive a cost-of-living allowance.

The supervisor wants you to review the situation very carefully and write a memo listing the pros and cons of overseas living. You are given a selected list of references to read and consider. Choose a country and include at least four of the following topics in your memo.

Topics

1. Language
2. Religion
3. Values and attitudes
4. Social organizations
5. Education
6. Technology
7. Politics
8. Law
9. Comparative expense: housing, transportation, cost of living
10. Cultural activities
11. Culture shock
12. Advantages and disadvantages of being accompanied by family

FURTHER READING

Intrapersonal Communication

Carr, Jacquelyn B. *Communicating and Relating.* Menlo Park, CA: Benjamin/Cummings, 1979.

Massey, Morris E. *The People Puzzle: Understanding Yourself and Others.* Reston, VA: Reston, 1980.

Rogers, Everett M. and D. Lawrence Kincaid. *Communication Networks: Toward a New Paradigm for Research.* New York: Free Press, 1980.

Yadava, J. S. and Gautam Vinayshill, eds. *Communication of Ideas.* Atlantic Highlands, NJ: Humanities Press, 1980.

Interpersonal Communication

Adler, Ron et al., *Interplay: the Process of Interpersonal Communication.* New York: Holt, Rinehart & Winston, 1980.

Argyle, Michael and Peter Trower. *Person to Person: Ways of Communicating.* New York: Harper & Row, 1979.

Brooks, William D. and Phillip Emmert. *Interpersonal Communication.* 2nd ed. Dubuque, IA: Wm. C. Brown, 1980.

Byrum-Gaw, Beverly. *It Depends: Appropriate Interpersonal Communication.* Sherman Oaks, CA: Alfred, 1981.

Condon, John C. *Interpersonal Communication.* New York: Macmillan, 1977.

Gordon, William I. *Communication: Personal and Public.* Sherman Oaks, CA: Alfred, 1978.

Haney, William V. *Communication and Interpersonal Relations: Text and Cases.* Homewood, IL: Irwin, 1979.

Maddalena, Lucille A. *Communications Manual for Nonprofit Organizations.* New York: American Management Association, 1981.

Patton, Bobby R. and Kim Giffin. *Interpersonal Communication,* 3rd ed. New York: Harper & Row, 1980.

Pearson, Judy C. *Interpersonal Communication: Clarity, Confidence, and Concern.* Glenview, IL: Scott, Foresman, 1981.

Pearson, Judy C. and Paul E. Nelson. *Understanding and Sharing: An Introduction to Speech Communication.* Dubuque, IA: Wm. C. Brown, 1979.

Samovar, Larry, Robert Brooks, and Richard Porter. "A Survey of Adult Communication Activities." *Journal of Communication,* 19, 1969, 301–307.

Smith, Dennis R. and L. Keith Williamson. *Interpersonal Communication: Roles, Rules, Strategies, and Games,* 2nd ed. Dubuque, IA: Wm. C. Brown, 1980.

Sproule, J. Michael. *Communication Today.* Glenview, IL: Scott, Foresman, 1980.

Stewart, John and Gary D'Angelo. *Together—Communicating Interpersonally,* 2nd ed. Reading, MA: Addison-Wesley, 1980.

Weaver, Richard L. *Understanding Interpersonal Communication.* Glenview, IL: Scott, Foresman, 1978.

Small-Group Communication

Bormann, Ernest G. and Nancy C. Bormann. *Effective Small Group Communication.* Minneapolis: Burgess, 1980.

Brilhart, John K. *Effective Group Discussion.* 3rd ed. Dubuque, IA: Wm. C. Brown, 1978.

Cronkhite, Gary. *Communication and Awareness.* Menlo Park, CA: Benjamin/Cummings, 1976.

Drucker, Peter R. *Management: Tasks, Responsibilities, and Practices.* New York: Harper & Row, 1974.

Fisher, B. Aubrey. *Small Group Decision Making: Communication and the Group Process.* New York: McGraw-Hill, 1974.

Ritti, R. Richard and G. Ray Funkhouser. *The Ropes to Skip and the Ropes to Know.* Columbus, OH: Grid, 1977.

Organizational Communication

Bowman, Joel P. and Bernadine P. Branchaw. *Successful Communication in Business.* New York: Harper & Row, 1980.

Downs, Cal W., Wil Linkugel, and David Berg. *The Organizational Communicator.* New York: Harper & Row, 1977.

Eisenberg, A. M. *Job-Talk: Communicating Effectively on the Job.* New York: Macmillan, 1979.

Goldhaber, Gerald W. *Organizational Communication.* Dubuque, IA: Wm. C. Brown, 1974.

Haney, William V. *Communication and Organizational Behavior.* Homewood, IL: Irwin, 1973.

Huseman, Richard D., Cal M. Logue, and Dwight L. Freshley. *Readings in Interpersonal & Organizational Communication,* 3rd ed. Boston, MA: Holbrook, 1977.

Lewis, Phillip V. *Organizational Communication: the Essence of Effective Management,* 2nd ed. Columbus, OH: Grid, 1980.

Morris, John O. *Make Yourself Clear! Improving Business Communication.* New York: McGraw-Hill, 1980.

Preston, P. *Communication for Managers.* Englewood Cliffs, NJ: Prentice-Hall, 1979.

Swindle, Robert E. *The Business Communicator.* Englewood Cliffs, NJ: Prentice-Hall, 1980.

Intercultural Communication

The Bridge, Review of Cross-Cultural Affairs and International Training. Denver, CO: quarterly.

Casse, Pierre. *Training for the Cross-Cultural Mind.* Society for International Education, Training and Research, 1980.

Clutterbuck, D. "Breaking through the Culture Barrier," *International Management,* December 1980, pp. 41–42.

Condon, John C. *Communicating Across Cultures.* Tokyo: International Christian University, 1972.

Hall, Edward T. *Beyond Culture.* Garden City, NY: Anchor Press, 1976.

Harris, Philip R. and Robert T. Moran. *Managing Cultural Differences.* Houston, TX: Gulf, 1979.

Kohls, Robert L. *Survival Kit for Overseas Living.* LaGrange Park, IL: Intercultural Network, 1979.

Malick, S., ed. *The Making of the Manager: A World View.* New York: Anchor Press/Doubleday, 1974.

Prosser, Michael H. *The Cultural Dialogue: An Introduction to Intercultural Communication.* Boston, MA: Houghton Mifflin, 1978.

Smith, Elise C. and Louise Fiber Luce. *Toward Internationalism: Readings in Cross-Cultural Communication.* Chicago: Newbury House, 1979.

Terpstra, Vern. *The Cultural Environment of International Business.* Cincinnati: South-Western, 1978.

(Bibliographies on Intercultural Communication available from NAFSA, Intercultural Communications Network, 1860 19th St., N.W., Washington, D.C. 20009. In addition, Terpstra's book has excellent references for intercultural and international communications.)

Part Two

Communication Skills

CHAPTER THREE

Listening, Speaking, and Reading

The average person spends 45 percent of each day listening; 30 percent speaking, 16 percent reading, and 9 percent writing.

Ralph G. Nichols and Thomas R. Lewis
Listening and Speaking

The business world is tied together by intricate systems of communication, both human and electronic. But people—men and women—started these systems and are responsible for their continuing existence.

Basic to business success—from the first entry-level position to top administration—is the ability to communicate well with customers and colleagues. This chapter introduces you to the three communication skills used most frequently in business and daily life: listening, speaking, and reading.

LISTENING

Before you learned to read, before you learned to speak, you *listened.* You heard or felt certain vibrations that for most of us became recognizable sounds, then words. You *reacted,* first with gestures, then with speech. Later you learned to read and you enlarged your vocabulary from sounds representing objects to sounds representing ideas. Then you learned to write. But first you listened.

First you listened, next you spoke, then you read, and finally you wrote.

From the very beginning, what you heard and how you heard it helped form the individual you are, including your attitudes toward the world around you. This is still true.

In general, listening serves three essential functions: (1) it provides information; (2) it gives clues to the character of individuals and organizations; and (3) it links us to other humans and satisfies our need to interact.

45

Listen for information, character clues, interaction.

Often, all three components are active in one conversation. For example, while listening to a colleague, you might learn about a new competitor (information), find out that the person is feeling depressed (character), and show through your listening that you care (interaction). An effective listener realizes that all of these functions are equally important to communication, regardless of place, person, or purpose.

The Importance of Listening in Business

Good listening is important to earning a living and can lead to that first job and later to advancement. Colleagues, students, and friends have found jobs through their "spreading the word" and listening to others. A new business moving into town? Someone leaving or being promoted? Listening can open up opportunities for you.

Keep your ears open.

Alert and competent employees and managers constantly listen to everything—rumor, scuttlebutt, the grapevines, and reliable authorities and information sources. And they listen, too, to the "sounds of silence." (Don Fabun writes about the sounds of silence on pages 7–12.)

Salespeople are particularly aware of the importance of listening. The effective salesperson *qualifies* a potential customer before selling a product. *Qualifying* means determining the customer's needs, attitudes, and desires—both stated and hidden—before selling. A buyer may be concerned with price or flexibility. A buyer may want to be friendly or aloof. A good salesperson looks and listens for clues to what will satisfy. The sales pitch or message is then adjusted. Unsuccessful (and unpleasant) salespeople don't listen.

Open up and listen.

Employees should be encouraged to talk, participate, and feel part of the group when they are producing a service or commodity. Talking can reduce personal stress and internal tensions, solve problems, and increase productivity, but only when listeners react: *hear, understand,* and *act.*

Listening Barriers

Every teacher has stories of students who attend class regularly yet constantly miss instructions, assignments, and discussion questions. These students mishear words and phrases. What is wrong? They simply don't listen.

Being able to listen to others is an essential part of communicating. Listening provides information, gives clues to the characters of others, and links us to other humans which satisfies our need to interact.

Another classic story involves a corporate president who has a real hearing impairment but won't admit it to himself or to his employees. He refuses to wear a hearing aid and in a conversation or meeting rarely asks the speaker to talk louder or repeat a statement. He has particular trouble distinguishing between sounds and voices and in a noisy office is more likely to hear a clattering typewriter than an employee's question. As a result, his effectiveness is greatly hampered.

These stories indicate that listening is an *active* process involving both our *senses and mind, our hearing and thinking.* To

There is a difference between hearing and listening.

listen effectively, we must be able to (1) hear sounds—their tone, pitch, and intensity; (2) separate important sounds from background noise; (3) translate those sounds into comprehensible words and sentences; and (4) interpret the speaker's meaning. Each of these steps is subject to problems that are barriers to effective listening.

Hearing Barriers

There are two basic kinds of hearing barriers: physical and environmental.

Physical—deafness, age, health, tone level, fatigue, and appearance. Some physical problems can be corrected medically, some with a hearing aid. If a hearing impairment is only temporary (for example, due to fatigue), try to postpone important meetings. Never be afraid to ask a speaker to repeat a word or sentence. It shows you are listening.

Environmental—noise, outside interference, location, light, and color. Often listening is impaired because of distractions in the environment. Make sure the speaker is aware of them. Then either alter the environment or the speaker's delivery.

Thinking Barriers

There are two basic kinds of barriers to thinking: intellectual and attitudinal/emotional.

Intellectual—vocabulary, language, regional accents, word choice (colloquialisms, jargon, terminology), education. When the speaker is from a different geographic, social, economic, cultural, or professional milieu, you can expect these barriers. Don't be embarrassed. Ask for a definition of a strange-sounding word. Language snobbery is a barrier to effective communication.

Attitudinal/emotional—self-interest, preoccupation, tone, voice level, warmth/coolness (attitude toward the subject), feeling of superiority, daydreaming, confidence in speaker and self. It is easy to understand why we often pay little attention while listen-ing. After all, our brain is capable of processing 600 to 700 words per minute and the average speaking speed is 125 words per min-

The mind can outrun the ear. Listening requires concentration.

ute. We have plenty of time for other thoughts. However, many conversations demand our full attention if we are to truly understand the speaker. In addition, a sensitive speaker will know when we are daydreaming. We are sending out a silent message: "I don't care about what you say."

Here are some suggestions for overcoming some of these barriers and becoming an active listener:

1. *Stop talking.* It is difficult to listen and speak (or watch television and speak or read and speak) at the same time.
2. *Concentrate.* Focus your attention on the speaker's *message.*
3. *Listen for main ideas.* Watch for these clues:

- Speaker's mannerisms—pauses, raising or lowering voice, facial expressions, time spent on topics
- Key words or phrases—"I shall now list . . .," "It is important to know. . ."
- Transition words—"on the other hand," "however," "furthermore," "in the first place," "nevertheless"
- Foreshadowing—"There are several points of view . . ."
- Consensus—"All economists agree that . . ."
- Repetition—"Once more you will note . . ."
- Issues—"All economists do not agree that . . ."
- General-specific relationships—"The strength of China comes from its people."
- Examples, analogies, quotations, restatements, summaries

4. *Take notes.* Writing interferes with listening, but jotting down key words and main points serves as a valuable reminder. Use abbreviations, symbols, asterisks, check marks, underlining, and double horizontal lines to compose a flexible outline while the speaker repeats, summarizes, pauses, or makes transitions. *With permission,* use a tape recorder.
5. *Be patient.* Wait until the speaker finishes before making a judgment or reply.
6. *Ask questions at appropriate times.* Ask your questions at the end of a lecture, during a discussion, after instructions. Asking questions helps develop points further, clears up confusion, shows your involvement. But try to be objective and tactful. Criticism and argument can put a speaker on the defensive, annoy other listeners.
7. *Remember the speaker's viewpoint.* What is spoken is only part of the whole. The four barriers (physical, environmental, intellectual, and attitudinal/emotional) may be there—for you or for

Are you an active listener?

the speaker. Stop, look, and listen. Then review what you have heard. If possible, check the reliability of what you have heard or what you think you have heard. (The two could be quite different.)

8. *Sift and save.* Store the important information in your memory and on "hard copy." Make notes on tape or in writing. With practice you'll learn to abstract only what you need—the main ideas. Knowledge is a continuous process, fed by these bits and pieces of learning.

Almost everyone in the business world must listen every day—to a supervisor, to an employee, to a customer or client, to a colleague. Effective listening is a basic skill necessary for advancing your career and for successful everyday living.

ASSIGNMENT: LISTENING SKILLS

Your supervisor has called a meeting of your work group for a week from today. Of concern are listening skills. Recently, poor listening habits resulted in missed appointments, lost sales, and personnel conflicts.

You have been asked to prepare a 200- to 250-word paper on effective listening. The entire sales staff has been invited to attend so that they may listen to and review the subject. You may choose a situation in which you were talking or listening, on or off the job, but you must include the results of the listening activity. A suggested list of topics was attached to the supervisor's memo for your convenience. Choose one of them.

Topics

1. A recent listening experience in which you encountered physical barriers to listening.
2. A situation in which you gave or were given instructions while surrounded by environmental interference.
3. A circumstance in which there were intellectual barriers to listening.
4. The meaning of "listening from the top down, from the bottom up, across horizontal levels."
5. Employment benefits of effective listening.

SPEAKING[*]

Thirty percent or more of your day is spent speaking. Thus, there is plenty of opportunity for you to practice oral communication. You use the telephone; speak to colleagues, friends, and family; present reports, testimony, evaluations; participate in committee meetings; speak before large and small groups—both formally and informally. Your speaking extends beyond the immediate, the personal—to the larger community—for religious, social, charitable, political, environmental, and other concerns. You may speak in person or via the media—on radio or television.

Now it's someone else's turn to listen.

Your purpose may be

- to interest or amuse
- to inform or teach
- to stimulate or impress
- to convince or persuade

In business communication, these purposes frequently overlap.

Presentation

It is not enough just to speak your thoughts when you are communicating orally. Your listener must clearly hear your message and understand its meaning. Therefore, the listener's attention should focus on what you say rather than how you say it. If the listener is distracted by the way you deliver your message, he or she may become bored, confused, or irritated, and the message you are trying to convey will be lost.

Speaking involves message, meaning, and method.

Barriers to effective speaking include

- poorly organized and incomplete ideas
- excessive detail and rephrasing
- ambiguous terms
- incorrect grammar and long, awkward sentences
- inappropriate and monotonous decibel level, pitch, and speaking rate

*This section is an edited version of two papers: one written by Karyn L. Mullica, speech pathologist, Phoenix, Arizona; the other by Kathleen Hart, teacher of business communication and an officer of International Toastmistress Clubs, Inc., Moncton, New Brunswick, Canada.

- omitted and distorted sounds
- excessive nasality, breathiness, and hoarseness
- meaningless words and phrases, such as "um," "and-uh," "Okay?" and "you know"

Transform your speaking skills into an art.

Thus, effective speaking involves not only the content of the speech but also your manner of speaking. Like all skills, effective speaking requires constant practice followed by evaluation to hone it to a fine art. You can acquire this practice in many ways. (1) Courses in public speaking are available at many levels in most schools, in adult education classes and seminars. (2) Professional consultants offer to revamp not only your speech but also your appearance: clothing, walk, hair—the entire image. (3) Toastmasters International and International Toastmistress Clubs, Inc., have thousands of units throughout the world.

The clubs hold weekly lunch or dinner meetings and provide a forum for practicing one's speaking skills. Members give prepared and impromptu (table-topic) speeches, report on committee meetings, participate in oral evaluations of talks, and serve as club officers. These clubs have training programs offering members continued practice and local, state, regional, national, and international competition.

The courses and clubs help you organize your material and present it effectively in various situations. In addition, they may teach you how to use visual aids and help you to understand body language.

But you can also learn to be a better speaker by (4) working on your own. You can build your vocabulary (see pages 59–60), and you can improve your diction and enunciation by using a tape recorder. Tape speeches you prepare, stories you read, meetings you attend. Then play back your efforts and evaluate your performance, or, better yet, get a friend to evaluate it, paying particular attention to pronunciation, articulation, voice quality, tonal color. Retape sections and try to improve on quality. You will find that constant practice followed by intelligent evaluation and then further practice will soon improve your speaking ability. And you'll develop a sense of confidence in yourself.

Prepare, practice, polish; then practice some more.

But even the most experienced speakers sometimes "freeze," forgetting words, phrases, sometimes the entire talk. Robert Orben, former director of the White House speechwriting department and special assistant to the president, advises a distressed speaker to admit the anxiety to the audience—but to try to deliver this admission with the urbanity of a Bob Hope. Orben, a comedy writer, suggests that a speaker say, "Some people suffer from stage fright.

I don't. The stage doesn't frighten me. It's the audience that scares the heck out of me."

Other experts suggest variations on that theme plus physical exercises to relax: (1) breathe rhythmically, slowly, deeply; (2) yawn several times; (3) move your body—loosen your arms, swallow, shrug your shoulders.

Still others advise you to think of the audience as a group of friends who are eager to take part in a conversation. Look around as you speak, to find your special favorites. Most of all, *be yourself.*

Here are some suggestions for organizing a business speech.

1. *Keep it concise.* Unless you are a very entertaining speaker, use as few words as possible to make and explain your points. Rarely is it necessary to speak longer than 20 minutes (ten double-spaced typewritten pages), and often a few minutes will do.
2. *Use short words, phrases, and sentences.* At times, eloquence calls for complicated passages, but most audiences are not impressed with long words and lengthy sentences. Modern American life and business are fast and direct. Speak simply, clearly, directly.
3. *State your main ideas clearly.* Begin with the conclusion, not a question. Lead quickly to your main point. Present one idea, support it with a series of short points, and then present the next idea in logical order. Ask questions to stimulate thinking.
4. *Analyze your audience.* Translate what you have to say into potential benefits to your listeners. Use relevant examples.
5. *Use quotations, cite authorities, give specific and concrete details.* These provide support for your ideas and enable the audience to "see" what you mean. Try to appeal to all of their five senses.
6. *Use key words, repetition, and the "you" viewpoint.* Winston Churchill's speeches provide many good examples of this. ". . . we shall fight on the beaches, we shall fight on the landing grounds, we shall fight in the fields and in the streets, we shall fight in the hills; we shall never surrender. . . ."
7. *Use 3-by-5 cue cards or a typed outline (all capitals) filled in with examples.* These will help you remember, help you relax.
8. *Prepare warm opening remarks and a strong conclusion.*
9. *Use visual aids whenever appropriate.* These reinforce your words.
10. *Check out the details of your presentation.* Time, place, position on the program, introducer, lectern, and audiovisual aids are important factors affecting the success of your speech.

If your mind goes blank, don't be afraid to admit it.

Effective speaking rewards both listener and speaker.

Knowing your topic, being well prepared for your particular audience, and checking the physical arrangements should put you at ease. You'll be ready to enjoy people liking you, understanding your point of view. You will have become an effective speaker.

ASSIGNMENT: SPEAKING SKILLS

Your supervisor was pleased with the feedback from the listening-learning meeting and has decided to hold regular in-service training sessions. The next one will focus on speaking skills.

Your assignment for the next meeting is to prepare a three-minute talk on one of the topics listed below. Using organizing suggestions from page 53, discuss a work-related situation. Try to include current reference material.

Because speaking is so important (frequently making your first impression), the work group has been asked to complete an evaluation for each speaker. A copy of the evaluation sheet (Figure 3–1) follows. Review this sheet as you prepare the assignment.

Topics

1. Explain the difference between the content of speech and the manner of speaking.
2. Name and describe three specific situations in which the ability to speak effectively is an advantage to anyone in business.
3. Discuss a business example for one of the four purposes of giving a speech.
4. Describe the importance of the physical arrangements involved in giving an informal talk or formal speech.

READING

Reading—your life may depend on it.

Many educated men and women have difficulty reading effectively. They have problems filling out employment applications, learning new techniques from printed material, understanding texts and contracts.

Some of these people may suffer from dyslexia, "a condition of failure to master reading at a level normal for age when this failure is not the result of a generally debilitating disorder such as

SPEAKER _____

TOPIC _____

INTENDED AUDIENCE _____

LENGTH (TIME) _____

	Excellent	Acceptable	Unacceptable
Organization			
Introduction			
Gains audience attention	☐	☐	☐
Orients listener	☐	☐	☐
Body			
Makes main points clear	☐	☐	☐
Limits points in scope and number	☐	☐	☐
States advantages and disadvantages	☐	☐	☐
Organizes material logically	☐	☐	☐
Conclusion			
Summarizes problem	☐	☐	☐
Makes clear-cut recommendations	☐	☐	☐
Content			
Has clear sense of purpose	☐	☐	☐
Has knowledge of subject	☐	☐	☐
Has substantial ideas	☐	☐	☐
Fields questions well	☐	☐	☐
Delivery			
Shows positive attitude	☐	☐	☐
Articulates well	☐	☐	☐
Emphasizes important points	☐	☐	☐
Uses visual aids	☐	☐	☐
Makes good use of gestures	☐	☐	☐
Varies voice (not a monotone)	☐	☐	☐
Paces talk, makes good use of time	☐	☐	☐

Please give any additional comments that will be helpful to the speaker:

_____

_____

_____

_____

_____

_____

_____

_____

Figure 3–1: Speech Evaluation Form

mental retardation, major brain injury, or severe emotional instability" (Gibson, pp. 5, 485–86). However, we also know that, across cultures, economic status, parents' education, and reading resources in the home consistently show up as the major factors influencing motivation and stimulation for reading.

Many experts claim that television has changed the learning and reading abilities of American students. Some believe that this is because television teaches children to think visually rather than linearly (in words). Others believe that the quick pacing of programs and the ease of channel changing lower attention spans. And there are still other theories.

The decline in reading ability in the United States has become a national crisis.

Whatever the reason—dyslexia, home environment, or electronic influence—a growing number of men and women are graduating from high schools and colleges with poor reading ability. And most of them go on to jobs that require this basic skill—reading.

The Importance of Reading

The rise of electronic communication—television, radio, telephone, and computer—has persuaded many people that reading and writing are old fashioned, slow, and inefficient. Yet in 1979, 161,476 new books, pamphlets, and other written materials were published in the United States. Hundreds of thousands of other publications were produced throughout the world. These written materials contain the rapidly increasing knowledge of humankind. Much of this knowledge is technical, more and more important to understand as technology increasingly molds our lives at home and at work.

More written materials are being published today than ever before.

The written word is still the most effective tool we have for storing and transmitting information. Letters, reports, and books are portable, compact, relatively permanent; they can be read and reread at any speed, any time, and any place. In the office of the future, messages will be transmitted electronically by computers, but they will still have to be written and read. Illiteracy is extremely expensive—to the individual and to the economy.

Who will read the printouts?

Improving Reading Skills

In business, read first for information.

The fundamental purpose of reading and writing in business is to transmit information. Modern society requires that this be done as quickly and as efficiently as possible. Fortunately, one can develop reading skills: skills to help a slow reader improve compre-

Table 3–1: Fitting Reading Strategies to Types of Reading Materials

Type of Material	*Methods of Reading*
Long journal articles, business reports, proposals, nonfiction	*Preview* for speed. 1. Read first two paragraphs. 2. Read first sentence of each of next two paragraphs. 3. Read last two paragraphs. *Survey* for comprehension. 1. Read table of contents. 2. Read chapter overviews, summaries, abstracts. 3. Skim publication rapidly. 4. Read first sentence of every paragraph (usually main idea). 5. Look at pictures, graphs, charts. 6. Read headings, bold or italicized type.
Popular magazines, sports, entertainment, fiction, some business material	*Skim* for speed. 1. Think of eyes as magnets. 2. Force them to move fast. 3. Sweep them across every line of type. 4. Pick up only a few key words in each line.
All material	*Cluster* for speed and comprehension. Train your eyes to see all words in clusters of three or four words. This takes practice: 1. Choose something light to read. 2. Read as fast as you can. 3. Concentrate on seeing three to four words at once. 4. Reread at normal speed and see what you missed. 5. Practice on different material until you miss very little on first reading. 6. Practice 15 minutes daily for at least one week.

hension and speed, skills to help an average reader to become a better reader—and writer.

For both comprehension and speed, adapt your reading strategies to the type of material you are reading and your purpose in reading it. You might read an important legal document very carefully, looking for "fine print," unclear terms, or loopholes. On the other hand, you might skim something you've read before or something new that is not of vital interest, picking out only the main points. Table 3–1 suggests several strategies to adapt to different types of reading materials.

Adjust your reading to type of material and your purpose.

Table 3–2: Fitting Reading Strategies to Purpose

Purpose	Reading Speed
To "get the gist"	Very rapid
To understand general ideas	Fairly rapid
To retain detailed facts	Moderate to slow
To locate specific information	Skimming
To determine value of material	Skimming very rapidly
To enjoy	Rapid or slow, depending on writing style and your needs
To build general background	Rapid

Although skimming has its uses, speed kills comprehension.

Your reading speed can be increased through training of eye movement, the basis for most courses of speed reading. But reading quickly is most useful for judging what to ignore and what to reread. (Most people who "read" more than 800 words per minute are actually skimming.) The survey method is a compromise between skimming and preview and helps you to focus on key points and remember them. Still, you will need to adapt your reading speed to different purposes, as shown by Table 3–2.

Are you an active reader?

The average adult reads at a speed of 200 to 400 words per minute, usually closer to 200. To extract information efficiently and remember it, you should (1) look for key words; (2) find topic sentences; (3) find summary sentences; (4) underline, star, or check the above; (5) outline; and (6) write key terms and definitions in the margin.

For example, a manager of a trucking firm concerned with rising fuel costs might *skim* parts of a news article like this.

A sudden leapfrogging of foreign oil charges is shaping up as just the first round in a prolonged series of *new price hikes* for Americans.

Mid-May price boosts by several major oil-exporting countries probably will *add 4 cents a gallon to U.S. gasoline* costs. *More increases* are expected from a meeting of the Organization of Petroleum Exporting Countries that starts on *June 6* in Algiers.

Before the end of this year, *decontrol* of domestic oil prices will *boost* gasoline costs *4 more cents* a *gallon. Another dime* will be added if the president's *oil-import fee* survives challenges in the courts and Congress.

If all these costs are passed on to *consumers*, the *average price* of gasoline—*$1.23 a gallon* in late *May*—could hit *$1.50* by the *end of 1980.*

With cluster reading, the manager would see:

Before the end   of this year,   decontrol of domestic

oil prices   will boost gasoline costs   4 more cents a

gallon.   Another dime   will be added   if the president's

oil-import fee survives   challenges in the courts

and Congress.

In general, *decrease speed* when you find unfamiliar words not made clear by the sentence (underline, try to understand in context, read on); long and involved sentence and paragraph structure (slow down, untangle until clear, use question mark in margin); unfamiliar or abstract ideas (look for examples, ask for help); detailed, technical material, complicated directions, abstract principles (again, question, ask others for help); material you wish to remember (make notes in margin, rephrase).

Increase speed when you find simple material with familiar ideas; unnecessary examples and illustrations used to clarify familiar ideas; detailed explanations and elaboration of familiar material; and broad, generalized ideas easily understood.

Efficiency in reading is affected by knowing what to read, when to speed up or slow down, and by the *size of one's vocabulary.* You can increase your vocabulary as you read. Here are some suggestions for increasing your word power.

Reading can expand your vocabulary.

1. Write out all new words and their definitions on 3-by-5 cards and try to learn and use several of the words daily.
2. Try to get the meaning of an unfamiliar word from its context in the sentence or paragraph; then check its definition in the dictionary.
3. Pronounce the word, checking the phonetic symbols in the dictionary.
4. Use the word in a sentence of your making.
5. Learn the common *prefixes* (a word, syllable or letter) placed before the *root*, or base, of a word to form a new word (*dis*appoint, *im*possible, *un*likely, *ultra*sonic).
6. Learn the common *suffixes* (a sound or letter or sequence of sounds or letters) placed after the *root*, or base, of a word to form a new word (fam*ous*, bring*ing*, opposi*tion*, instru*ment*).

7. Associate the root word with its synonyms (words with similar meanings) and antonyms (words with opposite meanings).
8. Associate the word with a mental image or picture, something familiar to you.
9. Write the word over and over until your hand *feels* the word and your eyes recognize it immediately.

There's no better way to learn a word than by reading it, speaking it, hearing it, writing it.

The suggestions in this chapter should give you a good plan of action, helping you to read better and faster than before.

ASSIGNMENT: READING SKILLS

In your company, employees have missed staff meetings because of failure to read memos carefully. Equipment has been damaged because of careless reading of instructions. Expense vouchers have been filled out incorrectly, delaying payment. These and other experiences have prompted your supervisor to call for an in-service training session to improve reading skills.

You have been asked to give a five-minute presentation on one of the following topics.

Topics

1. Explain to the group why good reading skills are mandatory in business despite advances in electronic communication.
2. For approximately one minute read aloud a passage from a legal business document. Then discuss the reasons why such documents must be read very carefully.
3. Discuss the advantages of using different reading speeds for different types of materials. As you do so, read aloud a one-paragraph example of each type of material that you discuss.
4. Keep a list of *all* the material you read for one week. Next to each item note the method you used to read it (preview/survey, skimming, clustering). Share the list and methods with the group. See if they agree with the methods you used.

Table 3–3: Summary of Listening, Speaking, Reading, and Writing Skills

Skill (applied to . . .)	Listening	Speaking	Reading	Writing
Concentration	Stop talking; focus on speaker's message	Keep it concise; use relevant examples	Slow speed for difficult passages	Help the reader's concentration by writing concisely, using relevant examples.
Clarity	Listen for main ideas	State main ideas clearly	Find and outline topic and summary sentences	Use topic and summary sentences; use headings and italics to set off main ideas
Retention	Take notes; ask questions; "sift and save"	Use key words, repetition, and the "you" viewpoint	Write key terms and definitions in the margins	Use key words, repetition, and the "you" viewpoint; outline and summarize important ideas

APPLYING LISTENING, SPEAKING, AND READING SKILLS TO WRITING

Starting with Chapter 4 and continuing through Chapter 14, this book will focus on writing in the business setting. However, as you work, keep in mind the *holistic* nature of communication. That is, listening, speaking, reading, and writing are *not* separate and independent skills. They are parts of the whole process of communication.

Note that the skills used by good listeners, informative and interesting speakers, and effective readers can be applied to writing. For example, maintaining concentration is a problem common to many listeners. It also applies to many readers. How many times have you been distracted from a book, article, or report because it moved too slowly or simply "looked" boring?

A good writer overcomes these barriers and tries to find ways to *help the reader concentrate on the writing.* Table 3–3 summarizes the main skills covered in this chapter and suggests how they apply to writing.

Now apply your listening, speaking, and reading skills to your own writing.

FURTHER READING

Listening

Astmann, Herbert K. *Four Big Steps to Success: Reading, Writing, Speaking, Listening.* Dubuque, IA: Kendall-Hunt, 1978.

Banville, Thomas G. *How to Listen—How to be Heard.* Chicago: Nelson-Hall, 1978.

Colburn, D. William and Sanford B. Weinberg. *An Orientation to Listening and Audience Analysis.* Chicago: Science Research Associates, 1976.

Coriell, Ron and Rebekah Coriell. *Listen, Look and Live.* Old Tappan, NJ: Fleming H. Revell, 1980.

Geeting, Baxter and Corinne Geeting. *How to Listen Assertively.* New York: Monarch Press, 1978.

Keefe, William F. *Listen Management!* New York: McGraw-Hill, 1971.

Kerman, Joseph. *Listen,* 3rd ed. NY: Worth, 1980.

Nichols, Ralph G. and Leonard A. Stevens. *Are You Listening?* New York: McGraw-Hill, 1957.

Nichols, Ralph G. and Thomas R. Lewis. *Listening and Speaking.* Dubuque, IA: Wm. C. Brown, 1963.

Rogers, Carl E. and Richard E. Farson. "Active Listening." *Readings in Interpersonal and Organizational Communication.* Boston: Holbrook Press, 1969.

Weaver, Carl H. *Human Listening: Processes and Behavior.* New York: Bobbs-Merrill, 1972.

Speaking

Adler, R. *Talking Straight: Assertion Without Aggression.* New York: Holt, Rinehart & Winston, 1978.

Baird, John E., Jr. *Speaking for Results: Communication by Objectives.* New York: Harper & Row, 1980.

Booth, J. L. and others. *Public Speaking: Theory and Practice.* Winston-Salem, NC: Hunter, 1978.

Cronkhite, Gary. *Public Speaking and Critical Listening.* Menlo Park, CA: Benjamin/Cummings, 1978.

Ehninger, Douglas, Alan H. Monroe, and Bruce E. Gronbeck. *Principles and Types of Speech Communication,* 8th ed. Glenview, IL: Scott, Foresman, 1978.

McCabe & Bender. *Speaking Is A Practical Matter*, 4th ed. Boston: Allyn & Bacon, 1981.

Makay, John J. *Speaking with an Audience: Communicating Ideas and Attitudes*, 2nd ed. Dubuque, IA: Kendall-Hunt, 1980.

Nelson, Paul E. and Judy C. Pearson. *Confidence in Public Speaking*. Dubuque, IA: Wm. C. Brown, 1981.

Verderber, Rudolph F. *The Challenge of Effective Speaking*, 4th ed. Belmont, CA: Wadsworth, 1979.

Reading

Durkin, D. *Children Who Read Early*. New York: Teachers College Press, 1966.

Gibson, Eleanor J. and Harry Levin. *The Psychology of Reading*. Cambridge, MA: The MIT Press, 1978.

Mangieri, John and R. Scott Baldwin. *Effective Reading Techniques: Business and Personal Applications*. New York: Harper & Row, 1978.

Mayfield, Craig K. and Wayne R. Herlin. *Improving Reading, Speech and Comprehension*. Dubuque, IA: Kendall-Hunt, 1978.

Reading Skills in Business Education. Monograph 128. Cleveland, OH: South-Western, 1975.

Santeusanio, Richard P. *Reading Skills for Business and Industry*. Boston, MA: CBI, 1980.

Smith, Frank. *Reading Without Nonsense*. New York: Columbia University, Teachers College Press, 1979.

Sticht, Thomas G. *Reading for Working*. Alexandria, VA: Human Resources, 1975.

Taylor, Halsey P. and Sheila F. Taylor. *Read to Write*. Glenview, IL: Scott, Foresman, 1980.

CHAPTER FOUR

Writing:
The Target—
Your Audience

Perhaps you have never been told to think about the *purpose of your audience* in reading what you write—what do they hope to learn from you, and what do they intend to do with that knowledge?

You must understand not only the purpose but also the background of your audience. You must know who your readers are, what they already know, and what they don't know.

Kenneth W. Houp and Thomas E. Pearsall
Reporting Technical Information

In Chapter 3, you learned more about three basic business communication skills: listening, speaking, and reading. Beginning with this chapter and continuing through the rest of Part 2, you will be dealing with the skills and principles of business writing: how to reach your target—your audience (Chapter 4); how to plan and organize your messages (Chapter 5); how to improve the style and content of your messages (Chapter 6); and how to create a favorable appearance for your messages (Chapter 7).

Determine the background and purpose of your audience.

In every kind of business writing, you must keep your intended audience uppermost in your mind. If you focus on yourself, the impact you are making—how smart you are, how much you know—you might as well write in shifting sand.

If, on the other hand, you focus on your audience—the person or group who needs or wants to know what you have to say—by showing your interest and concern, you will establish good will and your message will receive a positive reception.

GOOD WILL

Good will is an intangible that has dollars and cents value. In commercial transactions it may be included as a line item in the purchase price of property. In daily business communication it is equally important.

In whatever you write first establish good will.

Good will may be defined as the desire to help someone who has helped you or the feeling of friendship toward an individual or organization, based on previous pleasant experiences.

64

Good will implies service—a satisfying two-way transaction involving, for instance, vendor and consumer or sender and receiver. In business communication, you establish good will by

- analyzing your audience
- using the "you" viewpoint
- relying on specific content
- personalizing your message
- establishing a common ground of experience
- being positive
- offering service beyond the initial contact

You sell more goods and services, and keep goods sold, through good will. You earn trust and loyalty, both personally and for your organization. With good will, you can cut through red tape and circumvent a chain of command. It takes time to accumulate this intangible, to credit good will to your account. But it's worth it.

Good will reaps many rewards.

ANALYZING YOUR AUDIENCE

The first step in establishing good will is to analyze your audience and consider the reader's needs (Table 4–1). Ask yourself these questions: Who is the reader? What do we have in common? What is the reader's likely attitude toward my message? What does the reader want? How can I help? When you analyze your audience, you determine why that person or those people would like to hear from you.

Logical Considerations

Perhaps the reader needs to receive concrete information such as what, where, when, how, and how much. You should communicate this kind of information concisely and in detail (see Chapter 6). This avoids confusion and misunderstanding.

Ask yourself how much your audience knows about the subject. We often assume too much knowledge and confuse our readers by using unfamiliar terms or by leaving out important details. However, don't insult a knowledgeable person by giving too much explanation. An engineer writing about plant design should send one report to a technician and another to a layperson.

What does your audience already know?

Table 4–1: Analyzing Your Audience: Some Sample Situations

Who Is the Reader?

Characteristic	*Possible Analysis*
Present customer	Knows your company; probably on good terms.
Former customer	Knows your company; what happened to break relationship?
Vendor	Wants to sell you something and keep you happy.
Potential customer who has contacted your company	Knows something about your company and wants to know more; what is this person looking for?
Your superior	Wants respect, but is probably looking for knowledge and enthusiasm.
Your subordinate	Wants your acknowledgment or praise.

What Do We Have in Common?

Characteristic	*Possible Analysis*
Professional authority	Use technical terminology and assume similar knowledge and problems.
Colleague	Look for areas of commonality with a colleague; do you have similar responsibilities, motivations, and goals?
Consumer	Keep in mind your own needs and frustrations as a consumer.

What Is the Reader's Likely Attitude?

Characteristic	*Possible Analysis*
Friendly	Acknowledge good relationship and show interest in maintaining it; avoid undue familiarity.
Neutral	Try to make a good first impression.
Hostile	Try to find an area of agreement or a neutral "buffer."

What Does the Reader Want? How Can I Help?

Characteristic	*Possible Analysis*
Status or respect	Show your respect for the reader.
Convenience (time)	Get right to the point; show what you can do to help.
Savings (money)	Make a special offer.

Emotional Considerations

Always consider your audience's emotional needs and expectations. The reader may want to be recognized, to avoid conflict, to be kept informed, to feel important. Often simple *courtesy,* showing that you are considerate of his or her needs and concerns, is sufficient to emotionally satisfy your reader.

Courtesy involves putting yourself in the reader's place—having *empathy*. Imagine yourself the recipient of your own correspondence. For example, consider this notice regarding an overdue bill.

```
    It has been six weeks since Invoice 1407
was mailed to you.  We have not yet received
payment.  Acme Lawnmower requires all bills to
be paid within 30 days. Failure to remit pay-
ment immediately will precipitate legal action.
```

The information in this notice may be completely accurate, but the tone is insulting, cold, and overly demanding. Such a notice would probably make the reader feel hostile toward Acme, thus destroying good will and complicating a simple problem of late payment. Courtesy dictates a different approach.

```
    Several weeks ago you purchased an Acme
Easi-Cut Lawnmower.  Undoubtedly it has made
your lawn easy to maintain and minimized your
labor.

    More than 250,000 Easi-Cut mowers have
been sold during the past three years--more
than any other mower on the market.  It has
truly earned its reputation for dependability
and ease of use.

    However, as we have not yet received pay-
ment from you, we are wondering if there is a
problem or if you have simply mislaid Invoice
1407 for $128.59.  Your purchase agreement
required complete payment within 30 days, and
the bill is now two weeks overdue.

    Please write or phone our Customer Rela-
tions Office to clear your account.  We would
appreciate your cooperation.
```

Knowledge of Your Audience

Your analysis of your audience will depend on how well you know (or if you know) who the readers are and what their expectations are.

You know your audience personally. If you have had prior contact with your audience, in person or through correspondence, then it is important to acknowledge this in every communication. If you don't do this, in even the most routine memo, you risk insulting your audience. However, avoid an intimate tone unless you are close friends. (Knowing the reader makes it easier to analyze his or her needs. But you should still be *objective* and complete in your replies.)

```
Dear Mr. Reynolds:

     It was a pleasure seeing you again at the
Chicago Dealers' meeting.  I particularly en-
joyed your talk on marketing in the '80s.

     Enclosed is the price schedule you wanted.
Please feel free to write or phone me when I
can be of further service.
```

You are responding to a specific request or complaint but don't know the audience. Many business situations require responding to specific correspondence from an unknown person. This correspondence should tell you a great deal about your reader. Friendly, hostile, or neutral? Dealt with your company before? Knowledgeable about your products? In a rush? Looking for a bargain? Answers to these kinds of questions give you a clue to (1) the positive aspects of your company's relationship to the reader; (2) the reader's specific needs; (3) the reader's probable attitude toward your message.

In this situation it is particularly important that you make specific reference to the reader's initial correspondence to you and that you answer each of the specific points. This lets the reader know that someone has indeed read and understood the letter.

```
     Enclosed is information you requested re-
garding the translation services offered by the
Michel Thomas Language Centers.

     There is, however, no information regarding
costs since we quote according to the degree of
technicality and the size of the particular job.
All work is by experienced and thorough
professionals.
```

```
     For quotations regarding a specific job,
please call our office.  We look forward to
hearing from you and appreciate your interest
in our services.
```

You have had no contact with your audience.   Often sales messages are sent to a general audience with which you have not had prior contact. However, these messages are usually sent to a *targeted* audience—people who have something in common. They may be former customers of your company. They may be professional women or news magazine subscribers or dentists. Mailing lists can be obtained for almost any group imaginable. (See Appendix C.)

Why is a targeted sales message more effective than an untargeted one? Because it enables you to know something about your audience. Most important, they are people likely to be interested in your product. For example, new magazines send their subscription offers to subscribers of other magazines, since such persons have already demonstrated a willingness to buy.

Also, you can use your knowledge of the targeted audience to direct the tone and content of your sales message. What do these people have in common? How can you appeal to that common characteristic?

A targeted sales message is more effective than an untargeted one.

THE "YOU" VIEWPOINT

To establish good will treat the reader as an individual. Use the "you" viewpoint.

Think of that special individual—first, last, and always. Make the reader the center of attention in your message. Imagine the reader sitting beside you. "Talk" with the reader. Ask yourself what information the reader needs. How much detail? What level of language? Emphasize the second person "you" instead of the first person "I." Begin and end your writing with the reader constantly in mind and you'll achieve the "you" viewpoint.

Write always for a special individual

```
     I think you'll be interested in our
investment plan.
```

Self-centered

```
     As a successful farmer, you'll be interested
in the XYZ Farmer's Investment Plan.
```

Reader-centered

For most of us, this is a new way of thinking when we write. Yet the "you" viewpoint is centuries old, the main idea behind the Golden Rule.

Personalizing

You *personalize* within the body of a letter or memo by addressing the individual by name:

Personalized

```
    As a successful farmer, Mr. Reynolds,
you'll...
```

Overuse has cheapened this device. Automatic, computerized typewriters and word processors insert individual names in mass mailings. Recipients no longer take these inserts seriously. But genuine personalizing in individually written correspondence can still be effective.

Specific Content

What does your audience need or want to know?

For your writing and personal contacts to be as helpful as possible, address your audience's specific needs and concerns. Ask yourself these questions: Are there several ways to deliver this product or service? Which method would be best for this person? Will it save money? Save time? Guarantee damage-free delivery? After you consider these types of questions, address them in your communication. This shows your concern, your good will. (Figure 4–1 illustrates an extremely effective use of specific content.)

Personalized

```
    As a successful farmer, Mr. Reynolds, you'll
be interested in the XYZ Farmer's Investment Plan
For farmers in higher tax brackets, FIP offers
regular, insured dividends and diversification
in farm-related companies, companies you know:
```

Specific content

```
    John Deerfield        International Harvest
    Masser Furgeson       Cargille
    General Foodstuff     Purena Ralling
```

SHARED EXPERIENCE

The world's greatest direct-mail campaign started out with an idea and a common problem: the high cost of made-to-order menswear. Offering mail-order pants—a limited choice, individually sized—for less than half the store price brought in thousands of orders—and launched a multimillion-dollar company.

2609 Frederick Drive
East Grand Rapids, Michigan
May 11, 1942

Mr. Humphrey Billingsley
412 Queen Street
Sault Ste. Marie
Ontario, Canada

Dear Mr. Billingsley:

　　For many years I have been intensely interested in the
Algoma district of Ontario. Each year for the past eleven
years I have managed to explore a little more of Algoma on
short canoe and fishing trips, and have come to be very much
at home in the bush. I will be graduated from the school of
Forestry of Michigan State College in June and want very
much to become a member of one of your crack timber-cruising
parties.

　　I want you to know, Mr. Billingsley, that I realize there
is a vast difference between theoretical and practical experience. In view of this fact, will you please consider my
qualifications?

　　From the time I was old enough to become a Boy Scout, I
have taken every opportunity to get out in the bush. By so
doing I have acquired an understanding of self-preservation
and the self-confidence of an experienced woodsman.

　　I have become thoroughly acquainted with the Ranger Lake
district, the Sand River District, the Montreal River district, the Michipocoten River district, and the area from
Mill 155 on the Algoma Central Railroad north to James Bay
along the Missinabie River.

　　I am as much at home in a canoe as I am on land, having
traveled in canoes more than 7,000 miles. My canoeing experience includes the shooting of Hell's Gate on the Missinabie
River, a feat no other white man can claim. In the spring of
1941 I traveled the full length of the Sand River without
making a portage, and once, on the Montreal River, successfully shot all eleven steps of the Golden Stairway alone.

　　I am a good bush cook, can string a tarp in a minimum of
time in the rain, and have never been unable to kindle a
fire, even in the heaviest of thunderstorms. I am a good
swimmer, can carry a heavy pack or a canoe, and am handy with
an ax.

Figure 4–1: A Classic Job Application Letter Using Specific Content Persuasively

Mr. Humphrey Billingsley   2   May 11, 1942

My theoretical experience includes a knowledge of the instruments, methods, and techniques used by timber cruisers. As a special project, my surveying crew made a closed traverse of 40 acres of hilly, wooded country. The traverse was made with reference to the true meridian, and precision of one in 5,000 was required. We achieved that precision. Also taken into account on the project were elevation, direction, area, monument placing, random lines, and the corrections for temperature, wind, slope, and misadjustment of instruments.

As a member of an advanced mensuration class, I estimated, by the strip method, the volume and number of board feet of lumber by species of a 360-acre tract. From the data compiled on this cruise, I then constructed a complete set of local tree volume tables by species from four inches D.B.H. to 46 inches D.B.H.

In a special course in mapping I became adept at both reading and constructing topographic and geologic maps. My term project was the construction of a topographic map of a square mile with a contour interval of five feet.

Mr. Billingsley, I fully realize that a timber cruiser's life isn't all tea and crumpets. All too often the tea is black and the crumpets are soggy. Also, among my intimate acquaintances are the blackflies and muskeg--but the bush is in my blood.

I shall be glad to attend an interview any time after the 16th of June.

Yours sincerely,

Daniel Decker

Figure 4-1: *continued*

Your audience identifies with you when you identify with your audience. Showing that you understand the audience's problems because you've had similar ones establishes common ground.

Show your audience that you understand

> As you may know, Mr. Reynolds, the XYZ <u>Farmer</u> Investment Plan was started by <u>farmers</u> such as yourself: successful <u>farmers</u> looking for safe investments in industries they understood. Today, the XYZ Plan continues to help the high-tax-bracket <u>farmer</u>.

Shared experience

POSITIVE ATTITUDE

Attitude affects the content and tone of your message. It affects how the reader will respond to your communication. Ask yourself how you would like to be treated, and guard against

anger	flattery	sarcasm
bragging	insolence	servility
curtness	pomposity	sexism
exaggeration	preaching	stereotyping
undue pessimism	whining	undue familiarity

Angry? Write what needs writing but wait before sending the message. Cool off. Then read what you've written. You'll probably decide to rewrite it. Then, too, there may be legal reasons for not immediately sending in writing what you may be sorry for later.

A *positive attitude* means showing sincere and genuine concern for your audience. It means dwelling on the positive aspects of your relationship and choosing positive words (see Chapter 6).

Think twice before allowing curtness, insolence, or condescension to creep into your communication with those you consider less important than yourself. And be sufficiently secure within yourself to be honest—to eliminate servility, fawning, flattery, or whining when writing (or speaking) to superiors.

Use positive language

Undue familiarity can cause you to lose friends and alienate people. You are showing maturity and tact when you use a courtesy title (Mr., Mrs., Ms., and so on) to address someone older or in a "higher" position until that person gives you permission to shorten the distance.

Use appropriate language

Stereotyping, too, shows up in language and attitude, affecting your tone. Stereotyping in language results from using clichés and platitudes—overused, tired expressions (Chapter 6). Writing

Avoid triteness in your writing.

to the hypothetical masses instead of to the individual is another type of stereotyping: applying to a unique individual uncritical, unfounded, general characteristics.

SERVICE ATTITUDE

Show that you have something positive to offer.

A *service attitude* (Figure 4–2) indicates that your interests are in harmony with those of your audience; your ultimate concern is their satisfaction. There are a number of phrases that show this attitude: "The customer is always right"; "we will not be undersold"; "refunds with a smile"; "one week's free trial without obligation"; "up-to-date service at last year's prices"; "free fill-up if our attendants fail to check under the hood."

Public service also develops good will for you, the writer, and your organization and attracts future customers.

- A bank offers additional service without charge.
- A savings and loan institution offers free meeting rooms to community clubs.
- Hairdressers volunteer to visit nursing homes bimonthly.
- An automobile agency sponsors a children's athletic contest.
- A furniture store lends its stock to theatrical groups.
- Men and women serve long hours without pay on city boards, committees, campus organizations, and service clubs.

A service attitude, when conveyed correctly, will enable you to maintain and improve your relationship with your audience. To accomplish this, *you must point out how your existing product or service has helped the audience and suggest or ask for new ways in which you can be of service.* These two important parts of service are known as *resale* and *sales promotion.*

Resale

Resale keeps a customer sold on a company and its products or services. In letters, brochures, and memos you reinforce the customer's satisfaction with a *previous* purchase or relationship.

Resale basically consists of reminding the audience of why they dealt with your company in the first place. This involves

- pointing out desirable qualities in the product
- indicating the satisfaction of other buyers

Full-service banking right where you need it... in North Ames!

Our North Grand office at Randall's Food Store is more than simply a mini-bank or courtesy counter. We offer all of the banking services you'll find at our Downtown and Campustown locations. Checking and savings accounts, safe deposit boxes, loans, money orders, traveler's checks and many more. You'll like our convenient customer hours, too.

After hours . . . or whenever you wish . . . you're invited to use our FIRST BANK 24 automated teller at Randall's. It's located just outside the front door of the store, and available 24 hours daily.

Our North Grand office offers just what you need . . . full-service banking. And it's right where you may need it most . . . in the north part of town.

1st
FIRST NATIONAL BANK

North Grand office:
    Randall's Food Store,
    24th and Grand

North Grand hours:
    Mon.-Fri. — 10:00 a.m. to 6:00 p.m.
    Saturday — 9:00 a.m. to 12:00 noon

Other offices:
    Downtown, Fifth and Burnett
    Campustown, 2320 Lincoln Way

Member: FDIC, Federal Reserve System

Figure 4–2: Conveying a Service Attitude

- listing the services you provide
- offering aids for better utilization of your product
- making reordering convenient and simple
- offering willingness to accept customer suggestions

The situations in which resale can be used are virtually limitless. Here are a few examples.

Delayed deliveries

Pointing out qualities makes your product worth waiting for. Also notice how specific information important to the reader—scheduled delivery date—is included.

Your Hickory Park chest of drawers is completely handcrafted, stained, and sealed for lifetime beauty and service. Such custom finishing requires more than the usual time, resulting in a temporary backlog of orders.

You'll be happy to know that your order is scheduled for March 1 delivery.

Reorders

Pointing out the product's success and profitability and listing the accompanying services and aids reminds the customer of your product.

Remember how quickly you sold our the Bend West Humidifiers last winter? You were not alone. In fact, the Bend West is the most popular humidifier available.

You'll find them even more profitable this year. With each purchase, your customers will receive

- an extended factory warranty--two years instead of one
- a free sample of Bend West Purifier Water Softener
- discount samples worth $10 on humidifier accessories

Anticipating complaints

Pointing out the company's service and indicating willingness to accept suggestions promote good will.

We sincerely appreciate having had the opportunity to serve you. We have done our best to give value with quality. If there are any questions regarding the bill, or our work,

```
please feel free to call, and we will be happy
to discuss them with you.

    Thank you.

            Buck Construction Company
```

Sales Promotion

The other component of the service attitude, sales promotion, is
the desire to find new ways to satisfy customers and thereby increase sales. In this regard, selling goes beyond promoting existing
products. Market researchers investigate and analyze the consumer's needs and wants through telephone, mail, and personal
interviews. Research laboratories develop new products. Existing
services are extended and new ones offered.

In business communication, this extension of service natu-
rally follows resale, since by offering *new, related* products or services you are offering greater satisfaction. The following example
clearly illustrates the effectiveness of sales promotion.

```
    Your new HiHoSnomobile left the factory
this morning.  Expect prepaid delivery by R&Y
Truckers Saturday morning.

    We welcome you as a new client, knowing
you'll be delighted with the HiHoSnomobile.
You'll appreciate its instant start in below-
zero weather, its quick steering response, its
Down-Foam Comfort seat.

    For additional comfort and safety, check
the HiHoSnomobile accessories, pages 5-10 in
the enclosed catalog.  Lightweight, designer-
styled Snomobile suits for men, women, and
children are now 30% off regular prices.
```

Resale

*Promoting from resale and
providing a final emphasis on
further service.*

Ideally, resale and sales promotion complement each other:
sales promotion offers new products and services; resale keeps it
sold and leads to new business.

ASSIGNMENT: THE TARGET—YOUR AUDIENCE

After studying this chapter, you and your work group gather for a coffee break and quiz each other about what you have learned.

Topics

1. How do you find the "individual," your audience?
2. What is empathy?
3. Define good will, using examples from personal experience.
4. How do you "personalize" a message?
5. Explain sales promotion and resale using examples from your experience.
6. How can you show your desire to be of service—the service attitude?
7. What motivates people to continue to read a letter?
8. How can you use the "you" viewpoint in your writing?
9. Why should you depend on specific content to reach your reader?
10. Analyze the Billingsley letter (pages 71–72). What do you know about the writer? The receiver?

FURTHER READING

Bernstein, T. *The Careful Writer*. New York: Atheneum, 1965.

The Communication of Ideas. Montreal: The Royal Bank of Canada, 1972.

Ferguson, Jeanne and Maria B. Miller. *You're Speaking—Who's Listening?* Palo Alto, CA: Science Research Associates, 1980.

Hayakawa, S. I. *Language in Thought and Action,* 2nd ed. New York: Harcourt Brace Jovanovitch, 1964.

Houp, Kenneth W. and Thomas E. Pearsall. *Reporting Technical Information,* 4th ed. Encino, CA: Glencoe, 1980.

Lipman, Michel and Russell Joyner. *How to Write Clearly*. San Francisco: International Society for General Semantics, 1979.

Oliu, Walter E., Charles T. Brusaw, and Gerald J. Alred. *Writing That Works*. New York: St. Martin's Press, 1980.

Pearsall, Thomas E. *Audience Analysis for Technical Writing*. Encino, CA: Glencoe, 1969.

Tichy, H. J. *Effective Writing for Engineers, Managers, Scientists*. New York: Wiley, 1966.

CHAPTER FIVE

Writing: Patterns—Methods of Organization

The principal error in most writing . . . is *lack of adequate organization.* It does the contractor no good to know all about building a house unless he [or she] is able to arrange for the subcontractors and workmen to come and to do their jobs in a specified, logical order. Without this logical order the house will not get built. In the same way, no matter how much a person knows, he has not accomplished anything in writing unless he has communicated what he knows to someone else. And he cannot communicate effectively without logical order.

Robert C. Wylder and Joan G. Johnson
Writing Practical English

A method of creating good communications is POWER. POWER (*P*lan, *O*rganize, *W*rite, *E*valuate, *R*evise) is a tool to help you cover all the important steps of writing, and it is applicable to all types of writing.

Planning is deciding *what* to write. You do this by evaluating the needs of your audience, the situation, and your purposes.

Organizing consists of arranging what you want to say to make a coherent and effective presentation. To do this, you must vary the organization of your message according to the situation.

Writing is the actual process of putting words together to make a message. Here you bring everything together: your ideas, organization, and choice of words.

Evaluating is an important step often omitted by impatient writers. It involves reading your writing objectively and critically and noting places for improvement. It means checking to see if you have followed the ABCs of accuracy, brevity, and clarity.

Revising means polishing your work. You correct errors and try to create an attractive image.

Effective writing involves preparation, composition, and follow-up.

PLAN

There are no shortcuts. You must plan on paper or in your mind before you write. As you learned in Chapter 4, you must

- exhibit good will
- analyze your audience

79

- use the "you" viewpoint
- rely on specific content
- include shared experience

One planning technique is to consider the five Ws and one H. Ask yourself these and other questions, depending on your purpose. Then jot down the answers—facts and figures—in the appropriate columns in Figure 5–1.

Who. Who will be affected by the message? Who said what to whom? Who is the reader? Who is a mutual friend? Who is involved? Who did what? Who told me about the situation, the job opening, the product?

What. What is the purpose of my message? What is the status of the reader? What does the reader want? What steps have I taken to solve the reader's problem? What is the problem? What action is desired? What should the reader know, do? What details should I include? What do I want? What evidence do I have? What am I proposing? What resources are required? What means will be used to solve the problem?

Why. Why did it happen? Why is it important to the reader? Why should I be involved? Why should the reader take action? Why this time, place, action? Why am I taking this approach? Why will this benefit the reader? Why am I writing (justification)? Why is this solution better than another? Why is the problem important?

When. When will I write (timing)? When will I deliver? When will I send? When is it wanted? When is it available? When is it expected? When will I take action?

Where. Where did it happen? Where will I deliver? Where will I go? Where can I be reached?

How. How do I plan to solve the problem? How many copies of the message are there? How many items? How was it sent? How was it paid for? How will it be used? How can the reader benefit? How will I raise the money? How will I use the money? How will I work out procedure (steps to take)? How will I assess or evaluate the situation before and after action?

Another technique is to use a planning sheet such as the ones in Figures 5–2, 5–3, and 5–4.

Who	What	Why	When	Where	How

Figure 5–1: Planning Sheet for the Five Ws and One H

(Fill in blanks; circle one or more approaches.)

1. What is my primary purpose? _____

2. Is there a second purpose? _____

3. What do I want the reader to know—or do? _____

   _____

4. Why? _____

5. How can the reader benefit? _____

6. Points to cover in my message. _____

   _____

7. What approach should I take?

   Admission of Guilt   Apologetic   Appreciative

   Arouse Curiosity   Ask for Help—Cooperation

   Ask Question   Awareness of Reader's Problem

   Complimentary or Congratulatory   Good News

   Humorous   Personal   Positive vs. Negative

   Regretful   Sense of Urgency   Sympathetic

Source: Adapted from *The Modern Business Letter Writer's Manual*, Marjane Cloke and Robert Wallace, Doubleday & Co., Inc., Garden City, New York, 1969. Originated for Mutual of New York (MONY), life and health insurance company, for its Letterwriting Training Program.

Figure 5–2: Plan Sheet for Originated Message

Complicated writing, like that involved in reports and proposals, requires more sophisticated planning strategies. *Idea grids, outlines,* and *time tables* are three useful tools (see Chapter 13). Discussions with friends and colleagues, group conferences, or planning sessions may help you in dealing with complicated problems.

After you have planned what you want to say, decide on the format of your message (see Chapter 7). Is a traditional approach called for? A more contemporary one?

ORGANIZE

Communication, in general, falls into three main patterns, whether spoken, written, or nonverbal:

(Fill in blanks; circle one or more approaches.)

1. What is the purpose of my message? _____

2. What does the writer want to know—or have us do? _____

3. Can we give the reader the information—do as asked? _____

   _____

4. What points should I cover in my message? _____

   _____

5. Is there any way the reader benefits? _____

   _____

6. What approach should I take?

   Admission of Guilt   Apologetic   Appreciative

   Arouse Curiosity   Ask for Help—Cooperation

   Ask Question   Awareness of Reader's Problem

   Complimentary or Congratulatory   Good News

   Humorous   Personal   Positive vs. Negative

   Regretful   Sense of Urgency   Sympathetic

Source: Adapted from *The Modern Business Letter Writer's Manual,* Marjane Cloke and Robert Wallace, Doubleday & Co., Inc., Garden City, New York, 1969. Originated for Mutual of New York (MONY), life and health insurance company, for its Letterwriting Training Program.

Figure 5–3: Plan Sheet for Reply

- those that *i*nform (disclose)
- those that *r*efuse (reject)   = **IRS**
- those that *s*ell (persuade)

IRS is easy to remember but greatly oversimplified. There are numerous overlaps and combinations between and among these patterns. All communication is supposed to inform someone of something. Furthermore, research has shown that all messages can actually be separated into two categories:

- messages expecting acceptance
- messages expecting resistance

No one formula guarantees successful writing. Patterns are merely general outlines or guides suggesting the progression of

(Fill in blanks; circle one or more approaches.)

1. What do I want the reader to do? _____

_____

2. What likely reasons would the reader have for not having done this?

_____

_____

3. What appeal can I make to get action? _____

_____

4. How can I phrase my approach to make it more attention getting?

_____

What technique can I use? _____

5. Points to cover. _____

6. What approach should I take? _____

Admission of Guilt   Apologetic   Appreciative

Arouse Curiosity   Ask for Help—Cooperation

Ask Question   Awareness of Reader's Problem

Complimentary or Congratulatory   Good News

Humorous   Personal   Positive vs. Negative

Regretful   Sense of Urgency   Sympathetic

Source: Adapted from *The Modern Business Letter Writer's Manual,* Marjane Cloke and Robert Wallace, Doubleday & Co., Inc., Garden City, New York, 1969. Originated for Mutual of New York (MONY), life and health insurance company, for its Letterwriting Training Program.

Figure 5–4: Plan Sheet for Follow-up

There are no magic formulas but there are some general guidelines to good writing.

your material. Although certain technical and professional writing (law, medicine, engineering, for example) require you to fill out preprinted forms or to follow traditional formats, you should always *rely on specific content, concern for the reader, and POWER to eliminate both indifference and resistance and to ensure acceptance.*

There is, however, one rule you can safely apply to almost all communication patterns. *The beginning and ending of a message, sentence, or paragraph should contain your most important ideas, words, and phrases. Material in these positions is easily read and catches the reader's attention quickly.*

Information Messages

Information messages offer good will and good news in a neutral tone. Usually you can expect acceptance of these messages. Here is the pattern to follow with most information messages.

a. Begin with most important information.
b. Add details in order of decreasing importance.
c. Conclude with (1) reference to opening or (2) good-will sentence or phrase.

The reader wants to know (and should be told immediately) why you are writing and whether he or she should spend time reading what you have written. In the pattern above, (a) answers those questions and contains the most important material; (b) offers further necessary information; (c) reinforces by repetition of (a), adds a final important detail, or establishes additional good will.

Can you provide information that someone else needs?

An information message may be as short as one sentence.

```
Yes, I'll be in your office, Saturday, June 16,
at 9:30 A.M.
```

or as long as a report.

For multiple mailings, word-processing typewriters can be programmed to reproduce routine confirmations, instructions, or other messages. (See Chapter 7.) Easily organized paragraphs may be placed on tape, cassettes, diskettes, or magnetic bubbles (Figure 5–5). In addition, some printed forms may be helpful (Figure 5–6).

Refusal Messages

Refusal messages present bad or disappointing news. They may include an outright rejection of a request, an offer of a substitute product or service, or a combination of rejection and acceptance. Here is the pattern to follow with most refusal messages.

a. Begin with buffer.
b. Add logical reasons leading to
c. Stated or implied disappointing news.
d. Offer (1) possible compromise, (2) substitute, or (3) omit
e. Conclude with call for action or another buffer.

ISU Alumni Association

Alumni Suite | Memorial Union
Iowa State University | Ames, Iowa 50011
Phone 515-294-4607

Date

Name
Street Address
City, State, Zip Code

Dear (Name):

We've received your most recent $xxxxx payment in response to
our membership reminder and appreciate your prompt reply. Our
records indicate that you have now paid a total of $xxxxx toward
life membership in the Alumni Association leaving a $xxxx balance.

On behalf of the Alumni Association's Board of Directors, please
accept our sincere thanks for your interest in and support of Iowa
State University through life membership in the Alumni Association.

Sincerely,

Karen S. Tow
Coordinator of Alumni Activities

KST/cw

P. S. Please consider this letter your official receipt.

Figure 5–5: Programmed Thank-you Letter

ROUTING AND TRANSMITTAL SLIP Date

TO: (Name, office symbol, room number, building, Agency/Post)	Initials	Date
1.		
2.		
3.		
4.		
5.		

Action	File	Note and Return
Approval	For Clearance	Per Conversation
As Requested	For Correction	Prepare Reply
Circulate	For Your Information	See Me
Comment	Investigate	Signature
Coordination	Justify	

REMARKS

DO NOT use this form as a RECORD of approvals, concurrences, disposals, clearances, and similar actions

FROM: (Name, org. symbol, Agency/Post)	Room No.—Bldg.
	Phone No.

5041–102

☆ U.S. Government Printing Office: 1977—241-530/3363

OPTIONAL FORM 41 (Rev. 7–76)
Prescribed by GSA
FPMR (41 CFR) 101–11.206

Figure 5–6: Routing and Transmittal Slip

Present disappointing news with tact and sensitivity.

You've probably heard the saying, "You can catch more flies with honey than with salt." The *buffer* attempts to sweeten the unpleasant message, to establish rapport, harmony. Thus the buffer is a neutral *area of agreement between the writer and reader.* The buffer that opens the message should be friendly, concerned, usually agreeing with something the reader wrote. It should be non-committal, avoiding implications of "yes" or "no" and related to the content, thus serving as a transition.

Note that a message in the refusal pattern does not follow the general rule to place important ideas first. But such a message is less likely to offend, annoy, irritate, or anger the receiver. It implies that both sender and receiver are intelligent and reasonable. Sometimes unpleasant situations arise, but objective, calm discussion can help solve the problem.

Some writers resist the buffer opening, protesting that the reader knows what is coming and should be told the bad news first. Therefore, ask yourself how you would react if you received a refusal message in the information pattern, with the unpleasant information first, rather than in the refusal pattern, with its softening buffer. Then remember the "you" viewpoint and plan accordingly.

Bad-news messages include "flush letters," rejections of employment applications. Any rejection hurts one's ego, but the buffer opening (a) helps soften the blow.

Paragraph 1: Buffer

Thank you for your letter expressing an interest in our firm. Your desire to obtain experience this summer in professional accounting is commendable.

Following the opening with logical reasons (b), shows you care enough to explain. You want the reader's understanding, good will, future consideration.

Paragraph 2: Logical reasons

As you may know, ours is not the type of business that is conducive to temporary summer employment. We are less busy during the summer months than at any other time of the year because of the high concentration of companies on a calendar-year basis. Further, early summer is the time when most of our newly engaged permanent personnel begin their careers.

Following the explanation with the stated or implied disappointing news (c), gets to the heart of the message. The disappointing news may be buried within the last part of the explanation (logical reasons) paragraph, or it may follow in its own paragraph. It may be expressed in the passive voice or the active voice. It may be expressed positively (see Chapter 6), or it may be expressed bluntly and directly.

For these reasons we are not in a position to offer temporary summer positions.	*Paragraph 3: Stated refusal*

Following logical reasons as it does, the disappointing news loses its sting. The final paragraph in this illustration is a combination of a possible compromise (d) and a call for action (e).

I wish you success in obtaining a suitable summer position and would appreciate hearing from you when you become available for a permanent professional appointment.	*Paragraph 4: Compromise and call for action*

The student receiving this letter believed the sender. He thanked the writer for his response and kept in touch with the company. Before graduation, the student had an interview and accepted a permanent position with the company.

The following illustrates another variation of the refusal message, a response to a customer's letter of complaint.

You are right in expecting your Gourmet Broiler to function properly for more than two years. Our products are designed to give you such service under normal use and care. Therefore we always appreciate receiving information from customers like you, because it helps us to provide better products for your money.	*Paragraph 1: Buffer; note agreement; use of "normal"; "you" viewpoint*

The Gourmet Broiler was tested in homes under varying conditions for two years before it was put on the market. Any major defect usually showed up within thirty days, and five years was established as a minimum life expectancy. Frequent moves plus lack of use, allowing moisture to collect, decreased this life expectancy.	*Paragraph 2: Logical reasons; note use of passive voice, eliminating personal blame*

Our repair lab has given your broiler a thorough analysis for defects in workmanship as specified in the one-year guarantee. They report finding everything in order except a rusted heating element with coils snapped in several places. Coils are weakened by rust and	*Paragraph 3: Implied refusal—expired guarantee; note positive explanation using passive voice, eliminating personal blame*

```
are more likely to break when the broiler is
moved.
```

*Paragraph 4: Buffer/
adjustment offer*

```
    Your satisfaction is as important to us
as the thorough testing we give our products.
Therefore, we would like to rewire the entire
heating unit for only the actual cost of $18.50.
```

*Paragraph 5: Call for action;
note "you" viewpoint*

```
    Your broiler can be back in your home and
operating like new within three weeks of your
reply.  Just check the appropriate box on the
enclosed postcard and sign it to indicate your
decision.
```

Selling Messages

The beginning and ending of a selling message should contain your most important ideas, words, and phrases. Material in these positions is easily read and catches the reader's attention quickly. Here is the pattern to follow with selling messages.

a. Capture the reader's attention immediately.
b. Continue with details of specific interest.
c. Convince the reader to become involved.
d. Call for specific action.

The information in Chapter 7 (Writing: The Image—Appearance) can help your message escape the wastebasket. But color, printing, and layout merely assist. *Rely on content and concern for the reader to eliminate both indifference and resistance and to ensure acceptance.* Remember, you are writing to a specific individual, not to the faceless masses. You must plan first, then you must organize.

An attention-getting opening (a) should quickly involve the reader and motivate him or her to read on. Personalizing, using the reader's name, is one way to do this. But the excessive use of computerized personalizing has diminished the effect.

Interest (b) consists of continuing attention from the opening, stimulating the reader's curiosity, answering the unspoken questions, What comes next? and Why should I be interested?

*Selling a product, an idea,
yourself? Show how you can
help your reader.*

Conviction (c) helps to make the reader decide that the message applies to him or her personally and that he or she should probably take action.

Action (d) consists of specific instructions for the reader to follow: mail, phone, fill out, reply, and so on.

```
Some time ago, Mr. Tilley . . .
```

```
you or another service-oriented person at Moore
sent me a batch of M-4092 booklets--forms for
the "9 key operations" of business.  I've passed
these out each quarter to my students in Business
Communication to illustrate the diversity of
needed and available forms.  Now I'd appreciate
another service.
```
Attention-getting opening (a) personalized, contemporary format

Details of specific interest (b) to reader

```
    I am writing a book on business communica-
tion--Applied Business Communication, to be pub-
lished by Alfred Publishing Co., Inc., Sherman
Oaks, California.  I would like to use your book-
let or parts of it in my "Forms" section.  Of
course, I will credit Moore with the material.
Your services will be acknowledged.  And the
readers--mainly college students, some profess-
ionals--will be directed toward Moore for future
needs.  I can't think of a better illustration
for the purpose than your booklet.
```
Benefits to reader, leading to conviction (c)

```
    May I have your written permission, please?
```
Call for action (d)

```
    With great appreciation,
```

```
    (signature)
```

Asking a question of the reader is another attention-getting device.

```
    WOULD YOU BE WILLING TO PAY 50 DOLLARS TO
    HAVE A TOP-NAME DESIGNER PINCH YOUR BOTTOM?*
```
Attention (a)

Think about the reader; think about how the reader can benefit from your message; think of what will interest the reader. Select the *one* most important idea of your message and create an opening around it.

---

*Duke Habernickel, Haband for Men, 265 N. 9th St., Paterson, N.J., spring 1979 promotion.

In the Haband direct-mail letter, Duke Habernickel uses humor to gain customer attention, and then he continues to interest customers in good-looking American jeans with correct fit. Correct fit is the controlling idea, the most important idea.

Interest (b)

```
     Now, while that sounds crazy, millions of
American men are now paying $20.....$30.....and
even $50 for a pair of what they call "tight
designer jeans." In order to get into them,
you have to take off your boots and 20 pounds!
But today some are calling those sprayed-on
jeans the most important fashion development of
the decade.

     I say THEY'RE CRAZY! If tight jeans, al-
most impossible to get into and priced higher
than a box of raisins and a bus ride to Boston
...if those denim dandies are the development
of the decade, I say thank goodness the decade
is nearly over.
```

Shared experience

```
     Now don't get me wrong...I like that jean
look just as much as you do...Jeans are the most
welcome change of pace a man can have in his
wardrobe. But I think they ought to fit! I
think a man should be able to get them on with-
out a fight...and that's exactly why I'm here
today with the new HABAND ALL-AMERICAN JEANS...
I think you'll love 'em because
```

Note "you" viewpoint throughout this form letter

```
     GOOD LOOKING AMERICAN JEANS CAN BE THE
     FAVORITE PAIR OF PANTS OF YOUR LIFE!
     CORRECT FIT FROM HABAND IS THE MOST
     IMPORTANT INGREDIENT!
```

Interest (b) leading into conviction (c)

```
     Okay. So you say, "What does he mean by
correct fit?" And I say the answer depends on
the cut of your jib! Even if your jib is gen-
erous, our new HABAND American jeans will sat-
isfy because we've made them to fit the mature,
seasoned man about Main Street. The Marlboro
Man can shell out fifty bucks for his pants if
he wants to, but even he would have to admit our
HABAND ALL-AMERICAN JEANS are easy-wear, easy-
care, and easy to get on and off.
```

The letter continues with details of correct fit; contrasts no-pocket designer jeans with five-pocket HABAND jeans; highlights the easy-care 100 percent no-iron, wash-and-wear fabric; then discusses price.

```
...less than the most widely touted chain store       Conviction (c)
discount price!  Two pairs for $19.95 only at
HABAND, and only while they last!
```

Action follows—both before and after the signature.

```
...Look at these jeans in the big full-color ad      Action (d)
enclosed.  Make your choice of the great casual
colors.  And then let me hear from you today
with your order.  I predict that of all the
weekend slacks you have ever owned, you'll like
these All-American HABAND jeans the best of all!
And you sure don't have to pay any $50 to join
the fun!

Looking forward to your reply

HABAND OF PATERSON

(signature)

Duke Habernickel
```

```
P.S.  It's easier to shop by mail from HABAND      Action (d) again, plus
too.  Saves gas.  No traffic.  No tumult.  Just    conviction (c)
tell us what you want and have them delivered
right to your door, quick as a wink!
```

This folksy appeal built a multimillion-dollar mail-order business for its founder. (A story is told that it all began with a test letter, sent out without merchandise on the shelves. The overwhelming response created momentary panic and involved the whole community. Men and women rushed in to cut, stitch, measure, package, and mail. They've since been replaced by their children—possibly their grandchildren—but the letterwriting goes on.)

Subject and attention lines (Chapter 7) are additional devices to focus the reader's attention:

```
Attention: Personnel Director

Subject:  Request for Job Description
```

Tabulating, itemizing, using "bullets" (Chapter 7), and underlining call attention to material, but nothing substitutes for specific content and concern for the reader. Beginnings and endings cause more problems than middles. However, once the writer thinks up an opening that will interest the reader, the body of the message usually seems to flow.

To sum up: devices are helpful, but material gains emphasis and reader attention primarily through

- position—beginning and ending of sentence, paragraph, message
- space—short sentences, short paragraphs, surrounding white space
- style—active verbs rather than passive, specific nouns rather than general, exact details
- structure—simple sentences rather than complex

All messages, whatever the type, contain elements of selling or persuasion. You may be convincing the reader of your integrity or dependability in a good-will, information message. You may be trying to overcome resistance to disappointing news in a refusal message. You may be selling a product, a service, a point of view, or you may be applying for a job. Organizing can help you order your material for a particular situation.

But planning comes first. Only after you have researched your subject and developed a respectable quantity of material should you write. (See Chapter 13.)

WRITE

Writing—putting words down on paper—is easy. Writing well, writing effectively is difficult. But there's only one way to learn to write well. Practice. Write, write, write. In the following chapter, we will examine matters of writing style.

To write well you must write often. Practice, practice, practice.

Just as you must practice to become proficient in a sport or craft, you must practice writing. Just as you develop a "feel" for golf or skydiving or swimming, you develop a "feel" for writing. You can develop this "feel" for your own writing. You can develop this "feel" for other people's writing. You can even develop this sensitivity for prewritten, computerized paragraphs.

But it takes time.

As you practice, you'll develop your own method, possibly one of these.

1. Plan mentally. Then jot down the message sentence by sentence, revising constantly. Polish each word and phrase. Then proceed to the next.
2. Plan mentally. Then outline according to IRS. Fill in your outline. Then write a complete rough draft.
3. Plan mentally. Listen (see Chapter 3). Then collect clippings on the subject from magazines, newspapers, brochures, letters. Write notes to yourself about the subject. File or store the material until you are ready to write by reshuffling the data physically and mentally until a logical pattern forms.
4. Work out a combination of 1, 2, 3.

The actual *process* of writing may involve one of the following.

1. Composing directly on a typewriter.
2. Writing longhand, perhaps using every other line of regular or legal-size paper.
3. Dictating into a recorder or to a secretary and later correcting the hard copy.
4. Using variations of 1, 2, 3.

Some writers do their best work before breakfast or during the morning hours. Others prefer different times, including after midnight. Some demand absolute quiet. Others can write anywhere. But all agree that the only way to get the job done is to apply the seat of one's pants to the seat of a chair.

And write, write, write.

EVALUATE

With practice, you develop a feel for the correct word or phrase, the rhythm of a sentence. You develop a reasonable sense of doubt about the spelling of a word. You will refer to your dictionary and thesaurus more often than before. You will substitute one word for another, shorten a sentence or paragraph, rearrange the order of material.

You will remember, again and again, until it becomes automatic, *the beginning and ending of a message, sentence, or paragraph should contain your most important ideas, words, phrases. Material in these positions is easy to read and catches the reader's attention quickly.* Check each sentence, each paragraph, each message to make sure you've followed this general directive. You'll be surprised how helpful it can be.

Did you begin and end with your most important ideas?

Colleagues and classmates can also be helpful. In some classes, students read each other's papers and write their comments. If the writer of the paper disagrees with the evaluation, the reader must explain the judgment, specifically. Then it's up to the writer to decide whether to make the change. In an office, you can ask a friendly colleague or supervisor for advice (but don't ask too often). In Canada, military officers evaluate each other's writing. A clipboard or "Float File" of correspondence at all levels is circulated daily. Content, expression, mechanics, form, and need for the communication are criteria.

Evaluate, revise, refine. There is always room for improvement.

Evaluation of your writing by others is necessary until you gain experience and the "feel." With experience will come self-confidence and competent self-evaluation.

HOW DO I CREATE?
Sorrell Caplan, Washington, D.C., Public Relations Account Executive

As a public relations counselor, I develop communications programs for a variety of clients. That requires the ability to analyze a client's problems and potential in order to determine with whom the client needs to communicate and to select the appropriate media to disseminate the message.

In addition, in the course of my work I develop or create stories for the print and broadcast media, plan photographic slide shows for which I determine what photographs must be taken, often taking the pictures myself, to tell the story visually, and produce television shows by working out the story line and suggesting the visual situation.

So, to answer, How do I create? Sometimes, I sit at my typewriter and pound out a story from scratch. If the story is long and complicated, I may outline it at my desk, writing by hand on a yellow pad. But ideas are not confined to the office! When my problem is particularly complicated, I do my best creating walking home from work, waiting in

a doctor's office or for some other appointment, riding on a train or plane, taking a bath, or lying in bed at night.

I usually carry a small notebook in my purse for quick notes. If I know ahead of time that I'll be sitting awhile, as on a plane, I usually take along a larger notebook or yellow pad. If I find myself without paper and pen, I try to locate some as soon as possible after an idea surfaces. I've not yet had to get up in the middle of the night to make notes. So far, I've been able to remember my ideas in the morning. But if the time comes when I either forget or begin to lose sleep in order to remember, I'll keep a pad and pen by my bed.

I used to feel guilty if I'd spend a restless day in the office when ideas didn't flow. I realize now that the best thing to do when that happens is to shift to some more mechanical job such as cleaning out files or developing lists. More often than not, the ideas come when I least expect them.

REVISE

Different people rely on different means of revising material. Here are some common methods.

1. Write down the *whole* message. Then revise the *whole*.

   - Renumber paragraphs.
   - Correct expression.
   - Insert additional material.
   - Clip and paste—cut pages apart and paste relevant pieces on clean paper in a new order. (Try rubber cement; it's inexpensive and easy to use.)
   - Verify accuracy—proofread spelling, grammar, punctuation, word/number usage, names, addresses, titles, data, dates, all details including syllabication, abbreviations, capitalization (refer to dictionaries, a thesaurus, handbooks, sources of information).

2. Write down small sections of the message, revising sentence by sentence, word by word.

   - Retype each piece, each page as you make revisions or rethink your message.
   - Use commercial correcting fluids or tapes to facilitate minor corrections.

3. Revise backward, from the end to the beginning, especially to catch spelling and punctuation errors.
4. Read aloud to ensure clarity of meaning.
5. Solicit others' opinions. (Publishers hire professional readers to judge manuscripts and suggest possible revisions.)
6. Set the writing aside, if possible, for several hours or several days to develop perspective, objectivity.
7. Revise, one or more times, using the steps in method 1, and, finally, give special attention to

   - headings
   - beginnings and endings of lines
   - vertical and horizontal columns
   - bottom of one page and top of next

Errors are more likely to occur in these positions.

Word-processing equipment speeds revision by enabling writers to correct a message as it appears on a video screen or playback. The corrected communication is then automatically reproduced with readjusted margins and spacing. Mechanized revision is efficient but must be preceded by thorough planning, careful organization, sensitive writing, honest evaluation. Whatever the revision method, always remember the most important goal of the message—communicating with the reader.

ASSIGNMENT: PATTERNS—METHODS OF ORGANIZATION

Your training and development director has asked your group to prepare a booklet of tips on how to plan and organize written business messages. You are to address the following topics in the booklet—which will be distributed to all employees.

Topics

1. The planning technique of the five Ws and one H
2. Various kinds of planning sheets
3. IRS patterns
4. When to use the I pattern. The R pattern. The S pattern.
5. The buffer
6. The importance of beginnings and endings in your messages
7. Methods of gaining emphasis or attention in your messages
8. Some methods of writing
9. The process of writing
10. Evaluating your messages
11. Revising your messages
12. The main concern of all communicators

FURTHER READING

Barker, Larry L. *Communication*, 2nd ed. Englewood Cliffs, NJ: Prentice-Hall, 1981.

DeVito, Joseph A. *Communication: Concepts and Processes*, 3rd ed. Englewood Cliffs, NJ: Prentice-Hall, 1981.

Fisher, Dalmar. *Communication in Organizations.* St. Paul, MN: West, 1981.

Gilmore, Susan K. and Patrick W. Fraleigh. *Communication at Work.* Eugene, OR: Friendly Press, 1980.

Holcombe, Marya W. and Judith K. Stein. *Writing for Decision Makers.* Belmont, CA: Lifetime Learning Publications, 1981.

Vervalin, Charlie, ed. *Communication Guidelines for Technical Professionals.* Houston, TX: Gulf, 1981.

Weeks, Francis W. and Kitty O. Locker. *Business Writing Cases and Problems.* Champaign, IL: Stipes, 1980.

Wilkinson, C. W., Peter B. Clarke, and Dorothy Colby Menning Wilkinson. *Communicating Through Letters and Reports.* Homewood, IL: Irwin, 1981.

Wylder, Robert C. and Joan G. Johnson. *Writing Practical English.* New York: Macmillan, 1966.

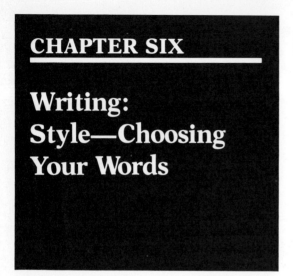

CHAPTER SIX

Writing: Style—Choosing Your Words

The best style is plain, simple, sincere. To write this way, you must honestly care about your reader. You must be able to think from the other person's point of view.

Ellis Gladwin
There Are No Strangers

Adjust your style to fit your message.

Knowing your reader, approaching your reader with good will, and planning the organization of your message will help you select the correct tone for your message. But unless you also select your words with care to attract and maintain the reader's interest, all your good intentions will be lost. Style is the writer's voice; it not only reflects the writer's attitude, but it also affects the reader's reaction to the message.

It is nearly impossible to offer hard and fast rules for choosing words. Style is personal and varies according to culture, profession, and situation. Legal jargon is acceptable on contracts, but hardly anywhere else (even legal language is being simplified). And the styles of most evangelists or politicians are hardly appropriate in the typical business setting.

Nevertheless, there are some general principles of style that apply to modern business writing. They reflect the need in business for efficiency and precision. To quote the hackneyed motto of the manager, "Time is money." Translated into business writing, "Say what needs saying—quickly, simply, and directly. Then stop."

"Have something to say, and say it as clearly as you can." That, according to Matthew Arnold, is the only secret of style. Know what your writing is supposed to accomplish, and make sure it adheres to the ABCs of business communication: *accuracy, brevity, and clarity.*

In an initial message, anticipate questions the reader might ask. Be sure your facts are accurate—names, addresses, numbers, quantities, dates, titles, instructions, area and zip codes—everything to make a reply simple and easy. In a written reply, answer every question that has been raised.

USE APPROPRIATE LANGUAGE

Use everyday English whenever possible. When technical or specialized terms are necessary, use them. But be sure that your reader knows their meaning; if he or she does not, then explain the meaning. Thomas E. Pearsall recommends dividing readers into "laymen, executives, experts, technicians, and equipment operators" (Pearsall, p. v). Each group requires a different vocabulary.

Select the right word for the right audience.

Many beginning writers think that elaborate, pompous wording makes writing more formal and precise. It doesn't. Write as though you want your reader to understand you. You do.

USE SPECIFIC, CONCRETE WORDS

Specific Words

Use specific words instead of generalizations. *Specific words* are accurate and clear, while generalizations may be misleading or confusing. Consider the following interoffice memo.

```
It has been stated that we must have information
available on warranties carried on some products
before selling them.  A written warranty on any
item of a certain price must have the appropriate
explanation.  Failure to comply could subject us
to penalties.
```

The underlined words are so vague in this context that the message hardly tells us anything. More specific language clarifies the memo.

```
Last Wednesday the FTC warned our legal depart-
ment and 16 other major chain stores that all
retail stores must make sure that shoppers can
study complete terms of warranties carried on
consumer products before the sale.  A written
warranty on any item priced higher than $10 must
clearly state whether it is "full," thus includ-
ing a right to refund, or "limited."  More-
detailed disclosures must be made when the
item is priced above $15.  Failure to comply
```

```
could subject us to civil penalties of up to
$10,000 for each violation.
```

Be particularly careful of your use of pronouns. They take the place of nouns and provide needed variety in a sentence, but if you use them improperly they can cause confusion.

```
Tom thinks that Mr. Jenkins knows that he is
unhappy with his job and Fred is incompetent.
He thinks this problem can be solved by firing
Fred and giving Tom the job, but I'm not sure
he can handle it.
```

The preceding statement is unclear because it can be interpreted in several different ways, depending on the meanings of the underlined pronouns. Here is a clearer statement.

```
Tom thinks that Mr. Jenkins knows that Tom is
unhappy with his job and that Fred is incompe-
tent.  Tom thinks his own problem can be solved
by firing Fred and giving Tom the job, but I'm
not sure Mr. Jenkins can handle firing Fred.
```

The words *this* and *which* frequently occur in dangling modifiers—parts of sentences relating back to earlier nouns. The reader finds it difficult to decide which noun *this* is replacing. *Which* clauses slow down sentences and require added punctuation and concentration. Go on a "which hunt." Revise *most* sentences with such construction. Change *which* to a verbal, or rewrite the sentence for clarity. Rewrite, revise, remove. Instead of

```
Somebody has to take over all the tasks which
are currently making people nonproductive.
```

write

```
Somebody has to take over all the currently
non-productive tasks.
```

The word *this* should be followed by the answer to the question "what?" until you are certain that the noun reference is clearly understood: "This year," "This action," instead of "This is it," "This will help you."

Adjectives and adverbs should also be specific. When used correctly they help to clarify and add detail, but they can also

Table 6–1: Abstract and Concrete Words

Abstract	Less Abstract	Concrete
Equipment	Typewriter	IBM Selectric II
Transportation	Vehicle	Boeing 747
Communication	Message	Letter
Hostility	Physical violence	Fistfight
Automation	Computer	Burroughs 500

exaggerate and overgeneralize. What is a "once-in-a-lifetime offer"? What does it mean when something "remarkably out-performs" something else? What is "appropriate action" and how much is "substantially reduced"? What constitutes an "amazing proposal"? Unless you can back these generalizations with specifics, don't use them.

Concrete Words

Concrete words are not only specific; they also refer directly to one or more of our five senses (sight, sound, taste, touch, and smell) or to tangible objects and individuals. They contrast with abstract words, which convey ideas of groups of things.

Use concrete words that appeal to the senses.

Use concrete words to help the reader visualize your message. Good storytellers and newspaper reporters use the concrete to attract and maintain the reader's attention. Table 6–1 shows the relationship between abstract and concrete words.

You have limited space and time for your messages. Each word must count. Rely heavily on specific and concrete words. Be selective and accurate in word choice.

Eliminate Deceptive Euphemisms

Euphemisms substitute for specific, concrete words to create a more favorable image. They have their uses.

> If you employ a *security guard* . . . he is likely to conduct himself differently on the job from a *watchman*. . . . A *director of a hospital* will probably act the part better than if . . . called a *superintendent*.

This effect of labels on behavior undoubtedly contributes to the prevalence of euphemistic titles in our status-conscious society. A *bartender* prefers to be called a *mixologist*, a *hairdresser* a *cosmetologist*, a *garbage collector* a *sanitation engineer*, and a *bookie* a *commission agent*. (Italics added.) (DeBakey, Sec. 9-2, p. 3.)

Choose words with generally agreed upon meanings.

Nevertheless, euphemisms can obscure meaning and when used incorrectly or inappropriately can create serious problems. Millions of dollars of government aid to the "disadvantaged" were delayed because legislators and recipients could not agree on the people included.

It is usually best to say what you mean simply, clearly, directly. Your purpose in writing, tact, and the image you wish to project should govern your use of euphemisms.

> *"termination" (when required)*
>
> *means your working time's expired*
>
> *means you are no longer hired*
>
> *translated truly means "you're fired"*
>
> (Burdick, p. 2.)

Use Figures of Speech

Another way to make your thoughts more specific and concrete and vivid is to use *similes*, *metaphors*, and *analogies*. Familiar examples explaining the unfamiliar can help you share experiences and develop a common ground with your reader. Imaginative comparisons, either stated or implied, help to transfer your mental image.

Figures of speech can show connections and make your writing fresh and lively.

Use a simile. Use *like* or *as* to imply similarity between two things.

```
    The stationery was as impressive as a $1000
bill.

    The stationery felt like paper money.
```

Use a metaphor. Omit the *like* or *as* and state that one thing *is* another.

```
    "A writer is a gunner...."
```

Use an analogy. Extend the metaphor or simile to state or imply more than one similarity between the original and the imaginative comparison.

```
    "A writer is a gunner, sometimes waiting in
his blind for something to come in, sometimes
roaming the countryside hoping to scare something
up.  Like other gunners, he must cultivate pa-
tience; he may have to work many covers to bring
down one partridge,..." (Strunk, p. 69)
```

Figurative language in business is especially helpful in explaining complex ideas and equipment. But the *figures of speech* must be fresh, and they must fit the situation and the reader.

Good writing is imaginative, appealing to both emotion and logic. In business writing as in literature, the imaginative involves the writer and the reader, compelling both to pause and think.

USE POSITIVE LANGUAGE

Your choice of words and your attitude develop the *tone* of your communications. Words have both informative dictionary meanings *(denotations)* and "halo," or emotional, associated meanings *(connotations).*

Positive words create a bright halo around your message. They say what you can do rather than what you can't. They make people feel good about you and your message.

Discouraged before you write? Your writing will sound discouraged and be discouraging. Confident you're really trying to help the reader (listener)? You will sound confident. You will eliminate *if, anxious, maybe,* and other downbeat words. Instead of

Develop a positive tone to gain a positive response.

```
    If you are interested, phone...
```

write

```
    Just phone for further information.
```

Instead of

```
    We hope you enjoy your new toaster.
```

write

```
    You'll have years of enjoyment with your
new toaster.
```

USE THE ACTIVE VOICE

Use vivid verbs to make your writing come alive.

Verbs signal movement. Verbs tell you what you must do, can do, should do. *Active verbs,* the more exact the better, make your sentences move, come alive. Use them.

Verbs have what grammarians call *voice,* active or passive. In the *active voice,* the subject of the sentence acts. In the *passive voice,* the subject of the sentence is acted upon.

Active ("you" understood)

```
Write a 2,500-word essay.
```

Passive ("by you" understood)

```
A 2,500-word essay should be written.
```

Passive voice verbs obscure, blur, dilute. They are useful in delivering bad news (see Chapter 10) and for shunting responsibility to an unknown entity, away from the sender or receiver. Some hints on how to use the active and passive voice most effectively are shown in Figure 6–1.

KISS—KEEP IT SIMPLE, STUPID

KISS first surfaced in military circles. Now it is appearing as a humorous/serious directive in respected educational institutions.

Use Short, Simple Words

Never use a long word when a short word will do.

Short words tend to have more impact and are easier to read and remember than long words. However, short words can become monotonous. A good rule is to avoid trying to impress your reader by intentionally adding long words. Instead, let your writing, in this respect, resemble good, clear speech.

Not all long words are unclear (try to find a short word for *dictionary*), but many can be stuffy and pompous. In some professions these words are so common that their users are not even aware of the confusion such words cause. These people end up speaking and writing "gobbledygook"—like the following.

```
It will work if we adopt a balanced contingency
policy based on integrated management options
with optional organization projections utiliz-
ing responsive transitional programming and
parallel reciprocal mobility implemented by
functional third-generation hardware and a
synchronized monitored time-phase that has a
```

For a strong presentation...	We just purchased a computer.	☑	...use the active voice
	A computer was purchased recently.	☐	
For brevity...	Increase productivity.	☑	...use the active voice
	Productivity should be increased.	☐	
When the subject is unknown...	Someone is robbing the office.	☑	...use either voice depending on emphasis ("office" or "someone")
	The office is being robbed.	☑	
When you don't wish to call attention to the subject...	I will be conducting tests tomorrow.	☐	
	Tests will be conducted tomorrow.	☑	...use the passive voice
When down-playing bad news...	We lost your shipment.	☐	
	Your shipment has been lost.	☑	...use the passive voice

Figure 6–1: Using Active or Passive Voice

```
compatible incremental capability and is sys-
tematized with digital options and integrated
into a logistical concept.
```

Philip Broughton, a United States Public Health Service official, guarantees that this passage can be used in any situation to impress or confuse your reader or listener. You'll sound great and nobody will disagree with you. Nobody will be exactly sure of what you said! Table 6–2 suggests some ways to simplify and shorten your writing.

Avoid Wordy Sentences

Long, twisted sentences are hard to read. Short, simple sentences— one after another—indicate a lack of verbal maturity. The short sentence of one to ten words carries more emphasis. Sometimes, however, one must include a number of related details within one sentence, and it grows and grows. Try to limit sentences to less

Short sentences give impact to your message.

Table 6–2: Use Short Words

While the words in the first column have their uses, try to use simple words. Write the way you talk.

Don't Say	Say
advise	write
affirmative	yes
complete	fill out
cooperate	help
disclose	show
execute	sign
forward	send
furnish	send
inasmuch as	since
indicate	show, say
in lieu of	instead of
insufficient	not enough
negative	no
pertaining to	of, about
presently	now
residence	home
state	say
substantial	big, large

Source: *Furst and Furst Newsletter*, Vol. 6, No. 1, 1980.

than 20 words. And vary those sentences for both appearance and attention.

It's up to the writer to select, reject, and compress. Concise writing results from your including only necessary material and using only necessary words. A well-written message may be both brief and concise. *Brevity* refers to length. *Conciseness* refers to content.

There's no substitute for rewriting. Each time you take a fresh look at your writing, you can think of better ways to say something. Count words. Are there more than 16 to 20 in an average sentence? Cut. Can one word do the job of two or three? Substitute. Can rephrasing help? Try.

```
It is quite possible          Have you seen this
that this report has          report?  (5 words)
come to your attention.
(12 words)
```

```
I should like to express      Thanks for the
my thanks for the helpful     suggestions.
suggestions you have made.    (4 words)
(14 words)
```

Table 6–3: Simplify Long-Winded Phrases

One-word substitutes convey your ideas quickly and clearly with no loss in meaning.

Windy	*Write*
along the lines of	about, like
at this point in time	now, currently
be in a position to	can
despite the fact that	though
due to the fact that	since, because
few and far between	seldom
for the purpose of	for
in a position to	able
in the amount of	for
in connection with	about, of
in spite of the fact that	although
in view of	since
make inquiry of	ask
on behalf of	for
on or before	by
sometime in the near future	soon
under the circumstances	because
with reference to	about

Source: *Furst and Furst Newsletter,* Vol. 6, No. 1, 1980.

```
This is an alternative        Please consider
to which I hope you will      this alternative.
give careful consideration.   (4 words)
(12 words)
```

In each of these examples, the shorter sentence is more effective, crisper, easier to read.

Eliminating unnecessary phrases will help shorten your sentences. Table 6–3 lists a few common phrases and their one-word substitutes.

Using conjunctions accurately will strengthen the impact and clarity of your sentences. Using too many "ands" or other joiners creates long, weak sentences. Conjunctive adverbs (*accordingly, also, besides, consequently, furthermore, however, indeed, likewise, moreover, nevertheless)* are extremely useful as bridges from one paragraph or idea to another. Subordinating conjunctions (*after, although, because, if, since, until, unless, when, where, while*) connect important ideas to less important ideas. (Professional writers call connecting links the "bucket brigade.")

The longer the sentence, the more time it takes to read, the less attention it receives. So use these conjunctions, but use them accurately, when they alone will serve your purpose.

Ernest Hemingway was a foreign correspondent in his youth. To save money telegraphing his Canadian publisher, he simplified, cutting messages to a minimum. Later, his short stories and novels reflected this crisp, brisk, almost sparse style, and won him great acclaim. *Telegraphese* is useful to know. It is stripped-down language, rich in specific verbs and nouns. It is almost bare of prepositions, pronouns, conjunctions, and other "understood" words (not present but "filled in" by the reader's mind). *This style is too informal for most business letters.* But memos, brief reports, and instructions can benefit from this style.

```
Need more envelopes.  Please send.
```

Formulas have been developed to measure reading levels. To test your writing, use one of the standardized readability tests. Lipman and Joyner (p. 8) recommend this variation as shown in Table 6–4.

USE SENTENCE VARIATION

Vary sentence length to hold your reader's interest.

Using short, simple words and sentences will make your writing clearer and stronger. But variation will make it more interesting. Variation enables you to emphasize some points and deemphasize others.

To understand word order and variation, one must first know what a sentence is. Grammarians can't agree on a single definition. Two may be helpful.

- A sentence is a group of words expressing a complete thought.
- A sentence is the smallest independent unit of complete thought.

The first is the traditional definition. The second enables you to use one or more words—the fewer the better—for emphasis. Additional words are understood, automatically filled in by the reader's mind. Try it and see. (In the sentence you just read, the "you" is understood.)

Vary Sentence Types

Declarative

```
Federal government bonds are safe investments.
```

The sentence above is a *declarative sentence* because it declares, or tells, something. It is a strong, positive sentence, emphasizing a belief. But sentence after sentence written in that word order

Table 6–4: Reading Level Measurement Test

Take a 100-word sample. Count the total number of syllables in the sample. Then count the number of sentences and find the average number of words per sentence. If you get 6 words per sentence and 125 syllables per sample, you're in the "very easy" category. But 35 words per sentence and 185 syllables would show your writing is "very difficult."

Words Per Sentence	Syllables Per 100 Words	Readability	Approximate Percent of Adults in U.S. Who Can Read This	School Grade Level
6 plus or minus 5	123 plus or minus 10	Very easy	93%	5th
10 plus or minus 3	135 plus or minus 10	Easy	90%	6th
13 plus or minus 2	141 plus or minus 8	Fairly easy	88%	7th
16 plus or minus 2	150 plus or minus 8	Standard	76%	8–9th
18 plus or minus 2	160 plus or minus 10	Fairly difficult	52%	9th
22 plus or minus 8	170 plus or minus 10	Difficult	24%	College
35 plus or minus 10	185 plus or minus 15	Very difficult	6%	College graduates

(Like all charts, this is an approximation. It is intended as a guide to readability rather than a formula yielding scientific accuracy.)

Michel Lipman and Russell Joyner, *How to Write Clearly.* San Francisco: International Society for General Semantics, 1979. Reprinted with permission.

would be dull and monotonous. No one wants to listen to someone telling, telling, telling.

You have a choice of three other types of sentences: the *interrogative*, which asks a question; the *exclamatory*, which expresses strong emotion; and the *imperative*, which gives a command.

COMMUNICATION SKILLS

Interrogative	Are federal government bonds safe investments?
Exclamatory	Federal government bonds are the really safe investments!
Imperative	Buy federal government bonds.

The declarative and interrogative forms are the ones used most frequently. Questions involve the reader by requiring an answer. Don't they? Questions break the monotony of the declarative.

Limit your use of the emotion-laden exclamatory sentence. At times business communicators appeal to the emotions, but most often they should rely on objective facts and reason.

Vary Sentence Structure

The number of main ideas and limiting or conditional ideas in a sentence labels it simple, compound, complex, or compound-complex.

A *simple sentence* contains only *one* main idea. The period forces you to a full stop, to pause and think. A simple sentence is easy to read. It is more emphatic than sentences containing two or more ideas.

Simple

Federal government bonds are safe investments.

one main idea

A *compound sentence* contains two or more main ideas. Closely related ideas are frequently written in this sentence form. But joined, given equal time, each idea loses some emphasis. (Joiners are conjunctions such as *and, but, or, for, nor,* or adverbs used as conjunctions.)

Compound

Federal government bonds are safe investments,

main idea

and they are state tax exempt.

main idea

A *complex sentence* consists of one main idea and one or more limiting or conditional ideas. These limiting ideas are *dependent* or *subordinate* to the main idea. Subordinate conjunctions (page 109) signal such limiting ideas. This construction is useful for emphasizing necessary qualifications that limit the main idea.

<u>If you want a safe, short-term investment,</u>   *Complex*
      limiting or qualifying idea

<u>you might consider U.S. Treasury Notes.</u>
            main idea

A *compound-complex sentence* consists of at least two main ideas and one or more limiting ideas. Therefore, it usually contains more words than simple or complex sentences. Obviously, it takes longer to read, longer to understand.

<u>If you want a safe, short-term investment,</u>   *Compound-complex*
      limiting or qualifying idea

<u>you might consider U.S. Treasury Notes;</u>
            main idea

in addition, <u>they are state income tax exempt,</u>
            main idea

<u>useful if your state has high tax rates.</u>
      limiting or qualifying idea

Count the words—33, 13 over the maximum suggested for ease of reading. Look at the punctuation—four commas and one semicolon. Not too bad, but it's a good idea to rewrite when punctuation becomes complicated. However, where is the important information? Remember: *The beginning and ending of a message, sentence, or paragraph should contain your most important ideas, words, and phrases. Material in these positions catches the reader's attention quickly and is easily read.*

It should be noted that the "fine print" currently being eliminated from business contracts and papers is usually filled with compound-complex sentences—tiresome, unclear writing (see Figure 6–2).

Figure 6–2: Simple Is Smart. This is the installment loan form used by Citibank a few years ago. It's typical of the traditional consumer contract. Written by lawyers, for lawyers it's obviously not written to be read. The form suffered from:

- long sentences
- elaborate constructions
- anachronistic and confusing words
- traditional legal language
- elaborate listing of remedies

PBR 668 REV. 9-74

FIRST NATIONAL CITY BANK
PERSONAL FINANCE DEPARTMENT - NEW YORK
APPLICATION NUMBER ____________
ANNUAL PERCENTAGE RATE ________ %

$ ____________
TOTAL OF PAYMENTS (4) + (7)

PROCEEDS TO BORROWER	(1)	$ ______
PROPERTY INS. PREMIUM	(2)	$ ______
FILING FEE	(3)	$ ______
AMOUNT FINANCED (1) + (2) + (3)	(4)	$ ______
PREPAID FINANCE CHARGE	(5)	$ ______
GROUP CREDIT LIFE INS. PREMIUM	(6)	$ ______
FINANCE CHARGE (5) + (6)	(7)	$ ______

FOR VALUE RECEIVED, the undersigned (jointly and severally) hereby promise(s) to pay to FIRST NATIONAL CITY BANK (the "Bank") at its office at 399 Park Avenue, New York, New York 10022 (i) THE SUM OF

P.L. NO. — AND DATE LOAN MADE

____________ ($ ______) (TOTAL OF PAYMENTS) ( ) IN ______ EQUAL CONSECUTIVE MONTHLY INSTALMENTS OF $ ______ EACH ON THE SAME DAY OF EACH MONTH, COMMENCING ______ DAYS FROM THE DATE THE LOAN IS MADE; OR ( ) IN ______ EQUAL CONSECUTIVE WEEKLY INSTALMENTS OF $ ______ EACH ON THE SAME DAY OF EACH WEEK, COMMENCING NOT EARLIER THAN 5 DAYS NOR LATER THAN 45 DAYS FROM THE DATE THE LOAN IS MADE; OR ( ) IN ______ EQUAL CONSECUTIVE BI-WEEKLY INSTALMENTS OF $ ______ EACH, COMMENCING NOT EARLIER THAN 10 DAYS NOR LATER THAN 45 DAYS FROM THE DATE THE LOAN IS MADE, AND ON THE SAME DAY OF EACH SECOND WEEK THEREAFTER; OR ( ) IN ______ EQUAL CONSECUTIVE SEMI-MONTHLY INSTALMENTS OF $ ______ EACH, COMMENCING NOT EARLIER THAN 10 DAYS NOR LATER THAN 45 DAYS FROM THE DATE THE LOAN IS MADE, AND ON THE SAME DAY OF EACH SEMI-MONTHLY PERIOD THEREAFTER, (ii) A FINE COMPUTED AT THE RATE OF 5¢ PER $1 ON ANY INSTALMENT WHICH HAS BECOME DUE AND REMAINED UNPAID FOR A PERIOD IN EXCESS OF 10 DAYS, PROVIDED (A) IF THE PROCEEDS TO THE BORROWER ARE $10,000 OR LESS, NO SUCH FINE SHALL EXCEED $5 AND THE AGGREGATE OF ALL SUCH FINES SHALL NOT EXCEED THE LESSER OF 2% OF THE AMOUNT OF THIS NOTE OR $25, OR (B) IF THE ANNUAL PERCENTAGE RATE STATED ABOVE IS 7.50% OR LESS, THE LIMITATIONS PROVIDED IN (A) SHALL NOT APPLY AND NO SUCH FINE SHALL EXCEED $25 AND THE AGGREGATE OF ALL SUCH FINES SHALL NOT EXCEED 2% OF THE AMOUNT OF THIS NOTE, AND SUCH FINE(S) SHALL BE DEEMED LIQUIDATED DAMAGES OCCASIONED BY THE LATE PAYMENT(S); (iii) IN THE EVENT OF THIS NOTE MATURING, SUBJECT TO AN ALLOWANCE FOR UNEARNED INTEREST ATTRIBUTABLE TO THE MATURED AMOUNT, INTEREST AT A RATE EQUAL TO 1% PER MONTH AND (iv) IF THIS NOTE IS REFERRED TO AN ATTORNEY FOR COLLECTION, A SUM EQUAL TO ALL COSTS AND EXPENSES THEREOF, INCLUDING AN ATTORNEY'S FEE EQUAL TO 15% OF THE AMOUNT OWING ON THIS NOTE AT THE TIME OF SUCH REFERENCE, FOR NECESSARY COURT COSTS. THE ACCEPTANCE BY THE BANK OF ANY PAYMENT(S) EVEN IF MARKED PAYMENT IN FULL OR SIMILAR WORDING, OR IF MADE AFTER ANY DEFAULT HEREUNDER, SHALL NOT OPERATE TO EXTEND THE TIME OF PAYMENT OF OR TO WAIVE ANY AMOUNT(S) THEN REMAINING UNPAID OR CONSTITUTE A WAIVER OF ANY RIGHTS OF THE BANK HEREUNDER.

IN THE EVENT THIS NOTE IS PREPAID IN FULL OR REFINANCED, THE BORROWER SHALL RECEIVE A REFUND OF THE UNEARNED PORTION OF THE PREPAID FINANCE CHARGE COMPUTED IN ACCORDANCE WITH THE RULE OF 78 (THE "SUM OF THE DIGITS" METHOD), PROVIDED THAT THE BANK MAY RETAIN A MINIMUM FINANCE CHARGE OF $10, WHETHER OR NOT EARNED, AND, EXCEPT IN THE CASE OF A REFINANCING, NO REFUND SHALL BE MADE IF IT AMOUNTS TO LESS THAN $1. IN ADDITION, UPON ANY SUCH PREPAYMENT OR REFINANCING, THE BORROWER SHALL RECEIVE A REFUND OF THE CHARGE, IF ANY, FOR GROUP CREDIT LIFE INSURANCE INCLUDED IN THE LOAN EQUAL TO THE UNEARNED PORTION OF THE PREMIUM PAID OR PAYABLE BY THE HOLDER OF THE OBLIGATION (COMPUTED IN ACCORDANCE WITH THE RULE OF 78), PROVIDED THAT NO REFUND SHALL BE MADE OF AMOUNTS LESS THAN $1.

AS COLLATERAL SECURITY FOR THE PAYMENT OF THE INDEBTEDNESS OF THE UNDERSIGNED HEREUNDER AND ALL OTHER INDEBTEDNESS OR LIABILITIES OF THE UNDERSIGNED TO THE BANK, WHETHER JOINT, SEVERAL, ABSOLUTE, CONTINGENT, SECURED, UNSECURED, MATURED OR UNMATURED, UNDER ANY PRESENT OR FUTURE NOTE OR CONTRACT OR AGREEMENT WITH THE BANK (ALL SUCH INDEBTEDNESS AND LIABILITIES BEING HEREINAFTER COLLECTIVELY CALLED THE "OBLIGATIONS"), THE BANK SHALL HAVE, AND IS HEREBY GRANTED, A SECURITY INTEREST AND/OR RIGHT OF SET-OFF IN AND TO (a) ALL MONIES, SECURITIES AND OTHER PROPERTY OF THE UNDERSIGNED NOW OR HEREAFTER ON DEPOSIT WITH OR OTHERWISE HELD BY OR COMING TO THE POSSESSION OR UNDER THE CONTROL OF THE BANK, WHETHER HELD FOR SAFEKEEPING, COLLECTION, TRANSMISSION OR OTHERWISE OR AS CUSTODIAN, INCLUDING THE PROCEEDS THEREOF, AND ANY AND ALL CLAIMS OF THE UNDERSIGNED AGAINST THE BANK, WHETHER NOW OR HEREAFTER EXISTING, AND (b) THE FOLLOWING DESCRIBED PERSONAL PROPERTY (ALL SUCH MONIES, SECURITIES, PROPERTY, PROCEEDS, CLAIMS AND PERSONAL PROPERTY BEING HEREINAFTER COLLECTIVELY CALLED THE "COLLATERAL"): ( ) Motor Vehicle ( ) Boat ( ) Stocks, ( ) Bonds, ( ) Savings, and/or ____________

SEE CUSTOMER'S COPY OF SECURITY AGREEMENT(S) OR COLLATERAL RECEIPT(S) RELATIVE TO THIS LOAN FOR FULL DESCRIPTION.

IF THIS NOTE IS SECURED BY A MOTOR VEHICLE, BOAT OR AIRCRAFT, PROPERTY INSURANCE ON THE COLLATERAL IS REQUIRED, AND THE BORROWER MAY OBTAIN THE SAME THROUGH A PERSON OF HIS OWN CHOICE.

IF THIS NOTE IS NOT FULLY SECURED BY THE COLLATERAL SPECIFIED ABOVE, AS FURTHER SECURITY FOR THE PAYMENT OF THIS NOTE, THE BANK HAS TAKEN AN ASSIGNMENT OF 10% OF THE UNDERSIGNED BORROWER'S WAGES IN ACCORDANCE WITH THE WAGE ASSIGNMENT ATTACHED TO THIS NOTE.

In the event of default in the payment of this or any other Obligation or the performance or observance of any term or covenant contained herein or in any note or other contract or agreement evidencing or relating to any Obligation or any Collateral on the Borrower's part to be performed or observed; or the undersigned Borrower shall die; or any of the undersigned become insolvent or make an assignment for the benefit of creditors; or a petition shall be filed by or against any of the undersigned under any provision of the Bankruptcy Act; or any money, securities or property of the undersigned now or hereafter on deposit with or in the possession or under the control of the Bank shall be attached or become subject to distraint proceedings or any order or process of any court; or the Bank shall deem itself to be insecure, then and in any such event, the Bank shall have the right (at its option), without demand or notice of any kind, to declare all or any part of the Obligations to be immediately due and payable, whereupon such Obligations shall become and be immediately due and payable, and the Bank shall have the right to exercise all the rights and remedies available to a secured party upon default under the Uniform Commercial Code (the "Code") in effect in New York at the time, and such other rights and remedies as may otherwise be provided by law. Each of the undersigned agrees (for purposes of the "Code") that written notice of any proposed sale of, or of the Bank's election to retain, Collateral mailed to the undersigned Borrower (who is hereby appointed agent of each of the undersigned for such purpose) by first class mail, postage prepaid, at the address of the undersigned Borrower indicated below three business days prior to such sale or election shall be deemed reasonable notification thereof. The remedies of the Bank hereunder are cumulative and may be exercised concurrently or separately. If any provision of this paragraph shall conflict with any remedial provision contained in any security agreement or collateral receipt covering any Collateral, the provisions of such security agreement or collateral receipt shall control.

Acceptance by the Bank of payments in arrears shall not constitute a waiver of or otherwise affect any acceleration of payment hereunder or other right or remedy exercisable hereunder. No failure or delay on the part of the Bank in exercising, and no failure to file or otherwise perfect or enforce the Bank's security interest in or with respect to any Collateral, shall operate as a waiver of any right or remedy hereunder or release any of the undersigned, and the Obligations of the undersigned may be extended or waived by the Bank, any contract or other agreement evidencing or relating to any Obligation or any Collateral may be amended and any Collateral exchanged, surrendered or otherwise dealt with in accordance with any agreement relative thereto, all without affecting the liability of any of the undersigned. In any litigation (whether or not arising out of or relating to any Obligation or Collateral or other matter connected herewith) in which the Bank and any of the undersigned may be adverse parties, the Bank and each such undersigned hereby waives their respective right to demand trial by jury and, additionally, each such undersigned waives his right to interpose in any such litigation any counterclaim of any nature or description which he may have against the Bank. In addition, the Bank shall not be deemed to have obtained knowledge of any fact or notice with respect to any matter relating to this note or any Collateral unless contained in a written notice mailed, postage prepaid, or personally delivered to the Personal Finance Department of the Bank at its address set forth above. Each of the undersigned, by his signature hereto, hereby waives presentation for payment, demand, notice of non-payment, protest and notice of protest with respect to the indebtedness evidenced by this note, and each such undersigned hereby agrees that this note shall be deemed to have been made under and shall be construed in accordance with the laws of the State of New York.

Each of the undersigned hereby authorizes the Bank to date this note as of the day the loan evidenced hereby is made, to correct patent errors herein and, at its option, to cause the signatures of one or more co-makers to be added without notice to any prior obligor.

RECEIPT OF A COPY OF THIS NOTE, APPROPRIATELY FILLED IN, IS HEREBY ACKNOWLEDGED BY THE BORROWER

	FULL SIGNATURE	COMPLETE ADDRESSES
BORROWER	______	______
WIFE OR HUSBAND OF BORROWER AS CO-MAKER	______	______
CO-MAKER	______	______
CO-MAKER	______	______

ASSIGNMENT OF WAGES, SALARY, COMMISSIONS OR OTHER COMPENSATION FOR SERVICES

This Assignment is executed as security for, or as a manner or method of repayment of, money advanced by a bank, trust company or credit union doing business in New York.

To: FIRST NATIONAL CITY BANK – AS ASSIGNEE
PERSONAL FINANCE DEPARTMENT
810 SEVENTH AVENUE
NEW YORK, NEW YORK 10019

Date ____________, 19 ____

I, the undersigned, being the "Borrower" indicated on the promissory note which appears above, in consideration of your making the loan evidenced by said note, do hereby assign to you, as collateral security for the payment of the indebtedness evidenced thereby, any and all monies which may hereafter become due or owing to me as salary, wages, commissions or other compensation for services from any present or future employer of mine (herein referred to as my "Employer"), to the extent of an amount equal to 10%, thereof, computed at the time when such salary, wage(s), commission(s), or other compensation is (are) payable, and you are hereby authorized to apply the same, as and when received by you, to the satisfaction of all such indebtedness as shall then be due and owing by the undersigned on account of said note until all such indebtedness shall be fully paid.

I hereby authorize my Employer to give full force and effect hereto, he being hereby released and discharged from any and all liability to me for or on account of any and all monies which may be paid you hereunder.

I hereby acknowledge receipt of a copy hereof.

THIS IS AN ASSIGNMENT OF WAGES, SALARY, COMMISSIONS OR OTHER COMPENSATION FOR SERVICES.

SIGNATURE OF ASSIGNOR — SIGN FULL NAME ____________
(SIGNATURE OF COMPLETE NAME OF ASSIGNOR)

First National City Bank

Consumer Loan Note   Date_____, 19_____

(In this note, the words **I, me, mine** and **my** mean each and all of those who signed it. The words **you, your** and **yours** mean First National City Bank.)

Terms of Repayment To repay my loan, I promise to pay you _____ Dollars ($_____). I'll pay this sum at one of your branches in _____ uninterrupted _____ installments of $_____ each. Payments will be due_____, starting from the date the loan is made.

Here's the breakdown of my payments:

1. Amount of the Loan $_____
2. Property Insurance Premium $_____
3. Filing Fee for
   Security Interest $_____
4. Amount Financed (1 + 2 + 3) $_____
5. **Finance Charge** $_____
6. Total of Payments (4 + 5) $_____

Annual Percentage Rate_____%

Prepayment of Whole Note Even though I needn't pay more than the fixed installments, I have the right to prepay the whole outstanding amount of this note at any time. If I do, or if this loan is refinanced—that is, replaced by a new note— you will refund the unearned **finance charge,** figured by the rule of 78—a commonly used formula for figuring rebates on installment loans. However, you can charge a minimum **finance charge** of $10.

Late Charge If I fall more than 10 days behind in paying an installment, I promise to pay a late charge of 5% of the overdue installment, but no more than $5. However, the sum total of late charges on all installments can't be more than 2% of the total of payments or $25, whichever is less.

Security To protect you if I default on this or any other debt to you, I give you what is known as a security interest in my ○ Motor Vehicle and/or _____ (see the Security Agreement I have given you for a full description of this property), ○ Stocks, ○ Bonds, ○ Savings Account (more fully described in the receipt you gave me today) **and** any account or other property of mine coming into your possession.

Insurance I understand I must maintain property insurance on the property covered by the Security Agreement for its full insurable value, but I can buy this insurance through a person of my own choosing.

Default I'll be in default:
1. If I don't pay an installment on time; or
2. If any other creditor tries by legal process to take any money of mine in your possession.

You can then demand immediate payment of the balance of this note, minus the part of the **finance charge** which hasn't been earned figured by the rule of 78. You will also have other legal rights, for instance, the right to repossess, sell and apply security to the payments under this note and any other debts I may then owe you.

Irregular Payments You can accept late payments or partial payments, even though marked "payment in full", without losing any of your rights under this note.

Delay in Enforcement You can delay enforcing any of your rights under this note without losing them.

Collection Costs If I'm in default under this note and you demand full payment, I agree to pay you interest on the unpaid balance at the rate of 1% per month, after an allowance for the unearned **finance charge.** If you have to sue me, I also agree to pay your attorney's fees equal to 15% of the amount due, and court costs. But if I defend and the court decides I am right, I understand that you will pay my reasonable attorney's fees and the court costs.

Comakers If I'm signing this note as a comaker, I agree to be equally responsible with the borrower. You don't have to notify me that this note hasn't been paid. You can change the terms of payment and release any security without notifying or releasing me from responsibility on this note.

Copy Received The borrower acknowledges receipt of a completely filled-in copy of this note.

Signatures   Addresses

Borrower:_____   _____

Comaker:_____   _____

Comaker:_____   _____

Comaker:_____   _____

Hot Line If something should happen and you can't pay on time, please call us immediately at (212) 559-3061.

Personal Finance Department
First National City Bank

Source: Siegel & Gale, 445 Park Avenue, New York, NY 10022.

Figure 6–2, *continued.* This is a reorganization of the form on the left. It's been totally redone from the consumer's point of view using headings, sentences, active verbs, a personal tone, contractions, and defined terms.

Vary Sentence Word Order

Word order in an English sentence is usually *subject, verb, object*.

<u>Your investment program</u>/<u>should be determined</u>/
      subject   verb

<u>by your particular needs.</u>
        object

Varying this word order is another way to avoid monotony.

Begin with a verb.

<u>Investigate</u> before you invest. <u>Take</u> time to study
your circumstances: age, family needs, capital,
liquidity, plans for retirement.

Begin with a verbal (form of verb not used as verb).

<u>Planning</u> comes first. (verbal noun, or gerund)
<u>To be</u> safe rather than sorry, plan before you
invest. (infinitive used as an adjective)

<u>Having studied</u> your needs, you are ready to
study investments. (verbal adjective, or
participle)

Begin with a conjunction.

<u>But</u> remember, each type of investment has
limitations.

Begin with a phrase.

<u>For the conservative</u>, for safety and a fixed
interest rate, government bonds seem to be a
good investment.

Begin with a limiting clause.

<u>If you want capital growth</u>, some common stocks
offer potential.

Begin with an adjective.

<u>Tax-exempt mutual</u> funds offer good long-term
investments for people who want someone else
to manage their portfolios.

Begin with an adverb.

<u>Yearly</u>, mutual-fund ratings appear in the
August 15 issue of <u>Forbes</u>. <u>Very</u> specialized
funds offer you a wide investment choice,
including tax-exempts, bonds, "money market,"
speculative, chemical, and energy.

You can write short sentences and long sentences. You can
use short words and long words. You can use different types of
sentences. You can put together an infinite number of word arrangements and variations. Your writing can be fresh and stimulating. Experiment! Write, write, write.

USE REPETITION

Repetition is an easy device for gaining emphasis. You can gain
emphasis through repetition—repeating words *immediately*.

The <u>more</u> you <u>write</u>, the <u>more</u> you experiment,
the <u>more</u> you'll <u>feel</u> comfortable with <u>writing</u>
variations. And you'll <u>feel right</u> about your
<u>writing</u>.

Careful repetition hammers home your meaning, clarifies it beyond
doubt.

Too much repetition, however, can bore or insult your reader.
Use it wisely. And never use repetition merely to fill up space. If
you have no legitimate reason for using it, avoid repetition.

AVOID SEXIST LANGUAGE

Using sexist language is another example of lazy thinking, writing, and speaking. Use of the pronouns *he, his,* and *him,* for the third person singular in reference to men *and* women is traditional. But many women resent this verbal "second-class citizenship."

Because of society's biases and stereotypes, women have been considered unsuitable for many occupations; many have been denied administrative posts. Sexist language has restricted job opportunities by reinforcing such stereotypes. Since Title VII of the 1964 Civil Rights Act created the Equal Employment Opportunity Commission, more people have become aware of the need to abolish discriminatory language. Men, too, resent stereotyped roles and opportunities resulting from language usage. As one of your writing goals, be aware of sexist language and eliminate its offensive tone from all letters, memos, reports, and speeches. Here are some guidelines.

1. Use a *unisex* plural instead of the generic (universal) *man* or *he.*

Biased

Man has certain needs and wants. His needs are many.

Unisex

Men and women have certain needs and wants. Their needs are many.

2. Use *he* or *she* only to refer to a specific man or woman.

Biased

If a teacher knows what he is doing, he'll be sensitive to his students.

Specific

If Mr. Jones, a teacher, knows what he is doing, he'll be sensitive to his students.

3. Use genderless *one, individual, person, audience, listener,* or their plurals.

Biased

The office manager is responsible for harmony. She must know her job and those of the workers.

Unisex

The office manager is responsible for harmony. That individual must know the workers' jobs.

4. Substitute *the* for *his, her, hers.*

```
The office manager has to solve many problems          Biased
with his staff.
```

```
The office manager has to solve many problems          Unisex
with the staff.
```

5. Eliminate pronouns by rephrasing (a great many variations are possible).

```
Interviews are given when he schedules them.           Biased
```

```
Interviews are given when scheduled.                   Unisex
```

6. Use job titles and functions instead of sexist titles.

```
The firemen took turns preparing meals.                Biased
```

```
The firefighters took turns preparing meals.           Unisex
```

Biased	*Unisex*
policeman, policewoman	police officer
businessman, businesswoman	businessperson, executive
salesman, saleslady	salesperson, sales clerk
chairman, chairwoman	chairperson
insurance man/woman	insurance agent
mailman	mail, or letter, carrier

7. Use the full name without a courtesy title in the inside address if you don't know the courtesy title (Mrs., Miss, Ms.):

```
Ellen F. Reynolds
3221-F Rodolpi St.
Seward, GA 30561
```

8. Omit the salutation. Not sure of the courtesy title? Use a contemporary format and omit the traditional salutation:

```
Dear T. J. Beers:                                      Doubtful
```

```
Dear T. J.:                                            Poor
                                                       (too familiar)
```

```
Winds are howling....Snow is piled high....            Better
What better time to think of
          SPRING PLANTING
```

9. Substitute current pronoun usage.

Unisex

```
he/she   she/he   he or she   himself or herself
```

No truly neutral acceptable substitute exists. Suggestions—*un-acceptable*—include

Do not use these.

```
thon    hir    s/he    e   E    S'he
```

Rephrase to eliminate possible sexist references or substitute the acceptable.

Removing stereotypes is difficult and takes a long time. A good place to begin is with language—with word choice and attitude.

ASSIGNMENT: STYLE—CHOOSING YOUR WORDS

For this week's in-service training session, your work group is to analyze writing style. You will experiment with words, sharing and discussing samples you have read and received. You are developing criteria for effective word choice. Select any two of the following topics for presentation to the group.

Topics

1. Collect four examples of concrete and specific language from mail you have received and advertisements you have read. Discuss why the examples are effective.
2. Listen to yourself. Then discuss the different vocabularies you use during a typical day. When do you use each one? Why?
3. Think of four euphemisms used in your profession, business, or hobby. Which are useful? Why? Which are deceptive? What word or phrase might you substitute for these?
4. Find examples of similes, metaphors, and analogies in your reading or correspondence. Why are they effective?
5. Write two versions of the same statement, one using negative language, the other positive language. Explain why the positive version is more effective.
6. Write two versions of the same statement, one in the active voice and one in the passive voice. When is each appropriate?
7. Write four versions of the same statement, varying sentence *type*. Explain what purpose each variation serves.

8. Write four versions of the same statement, varying sentence word order. What are the advantages of varied word order?
9. Find an example of effective repetition in a brochure or sales letter. Why is the repetition effective? When is repetition ineffective or even detrimental to good writing?
10. Select a passage in a current newspaper, magazine, or legal document that uses sexist language. Rephrase it in unisex language. Why is stereotyping offensive? How can you most sensibly eliminate it?

FURTHER READING

America The Datsun Student Travel Guide. Knoxville, TN: 13–30 Corporation, 1978.

Barzun, Jacques. *Simple and Direct, A Rhetoric for Writers.* San Francisco: Harper & Row, 1975.

Bernstein, T. *The Careful Writer.* New York: Atheneum, 1965.

Brusaw, Charles T. and Gerald J. Alred. *Practical Writing.* Boston: Allyn and Bacon, 1973.

Burdick, Carole. "Marginalia." *The Chronicle of Higher Education,* January 29, 1979, p. 2.

The Communication of Ideas. Montreal: The Royal Bank of Canada, 1972.

DeBakey, Lois. "The Intolerable Wrestle with Words and Meanings."

Proceedings, 18th International Technical Communications Conference, San Francisco, June 1971.

Flesch, Rudolf. *The Art of Readable Writing.* New York: Harper, 1949.

Howard, Godfrey. *Getting Through: How to Make Words Work for You.* North Pomfret, VT: David & Charles, 1980.

Lipman, Michel and Russell Joyner. *How to Write Clearly.* San Francisco: International Society for General Semantics, 1979.

Oliu, Walter E., Charles T. Brusaw, and Gerald J. Alred. *Writing That Works.* New York: St. Martin's Press, 1980.

Pearsall, Thomas E. *Audience Analysis for Technical Writing.* Encino, CA: Glencoe, 1969.

Strunk, William, Jr., and E. B. White. *The Elements of Style,* 3rd ed. New York: Macmillan, 1979.

Tichy, H. J. *Effective Writing for Engineers, Managers, Scientists.* New York: Wiley, 1966.

Zinsser, William. *On Writing Well,* 2nd ed. New York: Harper & Row, 1980.

CHAPTER SEVEN

Writing: The Image— Appearance

While accuracy and clarity are always of paramount importance, remember that a written message makes an impression on its reader even before he or she has an opportunity to determine whether its contents are accurate and clear. A well-known engineer once told a story of visiting an industrialist's office and seeing the industrialist pick up a handsomely bound report just as it was delivered to his desk, leaf through it, and remark that it was a fine job of engineering report writing. He hadn't read the report; he made this judgment solely on the basis of its appearance.

Gordon H. Mills and John A. Walter
Technical Writing

At a subconscious level, appearance triggers our behavior. A Rolls Royce or Mercedes Benz projects an aura of quality by means of its very appearance. It symbolizes distinction and seems to be an extension of its owner, creating a unique image.

Communications, too, are extensions of the individual or group (government, business, education, industry)—and by their appearance create images of the person, product, organization.

Appearance in written communication is determined by

- Correctness and neatness
- Design
- Format
- Paper
- Reproduction quality

CORRECTNESS AND NEATNESS

More than anything else, the image you present to the reader will be best achieved by correct grammar and spelling and a neat appearance. It is important that you familiarize yourself with the basic rules of grammar and spelling outlined in the Handbook section of this text; that you use reference works such as the dictionary whenever you are in doubt; and that you carefully proofread your work.

Grammar

The musical *My Fair Lady* describes the transformation of a lower-class English flower girl into an upper-class "lady." Language change—in word choice and pronunciation—is responsible for Eliza Doolittle's new image.

The grammar you use helps create your image.

Depending on the formality of the situation, you must adjust and control your vocabulary. (We have many vocabularies—for family and friends, teachers, business colleagues, people of various ages and so on.) Written or spoken, your grammar tells other something about your background, the organization you represent, your role in that organization.

Your grammar tells a great deal about you.

Like Eliza, you can change your verbal image—if you want to or need to. If you are in doubt about a word, refer to a dictionary or grammar handbook, like the one at the end of this text. Don't hesitate to question former or present teachers or attend continuing education classes. (Caution: Some television performers frequently use poor grammar—they are play actors, cast in certain roles, devised to appeal to particular audiences. *Do not use television performers as role models for correctness.*)

Spelling

You are responsible for everything that appears over your signature. Spelling errors indicate (1) you are sloppy, (2) you are careless, (3) you are inattentive to details, or (4) you don't know any better. Occasional errors are understandable, but regular slip-ups can prevent your being hired or can hinder your advancement. Like Eliza, you'll find that correctness may be superficial as a criterion of personality, but it does establish a favorable image. Remember that no one is a perfect speller. Even professionals use guides and memory tricks to spell correctly.

Spelling errors spoil an otherwise effective message.

Punctuation

Open punctuation eliminates most marks of punctuation except in the body of your message. The major marks of punctuation (period, question mark, exclamation mark, semicolon, comma) indicate the pauses within and terminations of sentences. But there are many jobs these marks cannot perform.

If you find yourself using more than two or three such marks in

Proper punctuation tells the reader when to slow down, when to speed ahead.

one sentence, *revise.* Try to simplify, using punctuation only to speed reading and understanding.

Syllabication

A good dictionary indicates where words may be broken.

A good dictionary or an inexpensive wordbook indicates where words should be broken or hyphenated when you reach the end of a typed line. As a general rule, double consonants split; but play it safe by consulting a guide. Syllables are indicated by dots or short dashes (depending on the style of the publication). You can break a word at these points. Improper syllabication damages your image and sometimes makes it difficult for the reader to recognize a word.

Lack of Erasures

There is no excuse for a messy message.

There is no excuse today for obvious erasures on any message you send. Erasable bond paper, correction fluid, self-correcting typewriter ribbons—a host of aids are available to help you put your best page forward. Word-processing equipment simplifies the process but, even so, mistakes happen. Proofread your work carefully and then make corrections carefully. Obvious erasures indicate the informality of the message, your lack of respect for the receiver, or your lack of attention to detail.

Overall Neatness

The *total image* of your written message, like the total image of a person, is composed of far more than appearance. But appearance, including overall neatness, does trigger behavior—it captures (or repels) the reader. Once captured, the reader wants to · know more and will read on.

DESIGN

A good appearance may be deceiving, but it can never hurt you or your message.

A company's name is often imprinted on its stationery and other writing materials. Stationery usually includes a *letterhead,* with the name, address, and often the phone numer of the company. This letterhead conveys an image of the company, and its design greatly affects the appearance of corporate messages.

Figure 7–1: A Corporate Logo Easily Recognized Around the World

Often a company recognition symbol, or *logo* (a letter, symbol, or sign—usually a seal or a name), is incorporated into the letterhead. Typically, the logo is also used for all company-written materials such as

An organization's letterhead and logo help present its image to the world.

- note pads
- memos
- receipt books
- sales tickets
- note-o-grams (with or without carbons)
- folders
- phone-o-grams
- labels
- internal operation forms for buying, stockkeeping, receiving, producing, selling, delivering, billing, collecting, and disbursing.
- invoices
- action requests
- cards (post, booster, business)
- envelopes (self-sealing, window, return payment)
- routing orders
- bulletins
- purchase orders

Many large corporations have paper made to order with a private "watermark" consisting of the logo. (You can see this design by holding the paper up to a light.) The logo helps the customer remember the company and its unique image. If you doubt its importance, consider the internationally recognized logo in Figure 7–1.

Design options are limited only by imagination and cost. Most companies seek professional designers to create a logo and letterhead. Stationery letterheads are enhanced by line drawings, screen printing, embossing, engraving, hot stamping, or die cutting.

- Line drawings are reproductions of designs and lettering. Crisp and clear, they permit a wide range of color applications.
- Screen printing gives halftones (photos) a wide variety of shading and textures.
- Embossing names, symbols, and art elements is growing in popularity. A special press produces an image in relief by squeezing paper fibers.
- Engraving, although expensive, results in a raised ink surface that can be very appealing. (Run your finger over engraving and you can feel the raised letters.)
- Hot stamping, or thermography, is dramatic but also expensive if done with metal, silver, gold, or metallic colors. This process is frequently used for wedding announcements and business cards.
- Die cutting uses cutouts of signs or symbols to create open space, usually at the top of the sheet of paper.

Two examples of letterhead design are illustrated in Figure 7–2.

When not professionally designed and printed, the letterhead can be typed or hand lettered on bond paper. Inexpensive hand-lettering kits are available in office supply stores. A do-it-yourself letterhead with three or four lines of type can also be designed for an embossing stamp, which can be purchased for less than $20.

FORMAT

Format refers to the elements or parts of various types of written business communication and their arrangement on the page or within the piece of writing.

For example, most of the business letters you write will contain the following elements: (1) letterhead or typed heading, (2) date, (3) inside address, (4) salutation, (5) body, (6) complimentary close, (7) signature block, and possibly (8) various other special letter parts. See Figure 8–3, page 141. Many of the memos you write will contain these elements: (1) heading, (2) date, (3) "To" line, (4) "From" line, (5) "Subject" line, (6) body, with possible subheadings, (7) signature. See Figure 12–3, page 244. Similarly, other kinds of business writing, such as reports and proposals, will contain fairly standard elements of their own.

Figure 7–2: Sample Letterheads

Arrange the elements of your message logically and attractively.

Your positioning and arrangement of these elements will include the order in which they appear, vertical spacing within and around them, and horizontal spacing (indentions, margins).

Format also involves your use of capitalized and lowercased letters, underlining or italics, and type of punctuation (open or closed).

Although none of these matters has been standardized for all occasions and for all times, certain conventions do govern good format. A good format is one that is logical, makes reading easier, and is attractive. A good format invites the reader into your written communication.

Specific formats will be discussed in Part 3 along with the major types of written business communication: letters, memos, reports, and proposals.

Specialized Formats

Not all written business communication consists of letters, memos, reports, or proposals. Many important business procedures rely on efficient specialized forms.

Supervisors at all levels of government and the armed forces are required to follow rigid formats. Style manuals, which differ for each military service (and even within services and departments), contain forms, illustrations, and exact directions for completing a wide variety of communications.

PAPER

Select the right paper for each occasion.

Another element of image is the paper you use. It would be foolish to print an expensive art book on newsprint. Likewise, a conservative accounting firm will not be impressed by a resume on colored paper. Thus it is important to be aware of the choices you have in selecting paper to fit a message.

Basically, there are two kinds of paper: one made of a percentage of cotton fibers, the other of only wood fibers. *Cotton fiber paper* lasts longer and stays whiter. The quality (and cost) of this kind of paper is determined by the percentage (10 to 100) of rag content, referred to as *bond*. The 25-percent bond is most commonly used for stationery.

Bond paper also varies according to weight (from 9 to 24 pounds) with the heavier paper usually stiffer and more opaque. A 20-pound stock is most often used in printing and for stationery.

Wood fiber paper, also known as *sulfate* or *sulfite paper,* is made exclusively from wood pulp. It tends to yellow quickly, it deteriorates in less time than bond, and it is susceptible to insect damage. However, it is a good deal less expensive than bond paper and is often used for typing paper, as well as ditto, copier, newsprint, and certain offset printing paper.

Both bond and sulfate paper can have many different *finishes.* Either can be coated with chemicals to allow for easy erasing, absorb ink readily, resist ink or other liquids, be more opaque, or be more durable. Finishes range from the familiar kraft or uncoated paper for bags, to text paper, specialized form paper, and even imitation animal and snake skin for book and program covers.

Paper is also available in a variety of colors. White is traditional and provides the best contrast for reading black type. But color can call attention, convey an image, or create a mood for the reader. Advertising pieces are often done on colored paper because of its attention-getting effect. Your choice should depend predominantly on the purpose of your message.

REPRODUCTION

Typing

Most written business messages are typed—at least initially. Technological developments have revolutionized the slow, manual typewriter. Electric typewriters are available with computer tapes and magnetic ("mag") cards to reproduce and personalize numerous copies of the same message when multiple copies are required.

Several companies now offer computer-typewriters capable of typing 500 and more words per minute and of storing hundreds of thousands of characters. Word-processing equipment with video screens, video display terminals tied in with computers, and even a voice-activated typewriter offer exciting possibilities for large-scale message duplication (see Part 5).

Other Methods of Reproduction

There are many other reproduction methods that range widely in cost, number of copies that can be made, and quality.

There are many ways to reproduce your message. Consider quality, quantity, and cost.

Ditto or Spirit Duplicator.   An inexpensive copier, the *ditto* uses an alcohol-type base dispensed by a wick to reproduce copies. Quality of reproduction is relatively low, corrections are difficult to

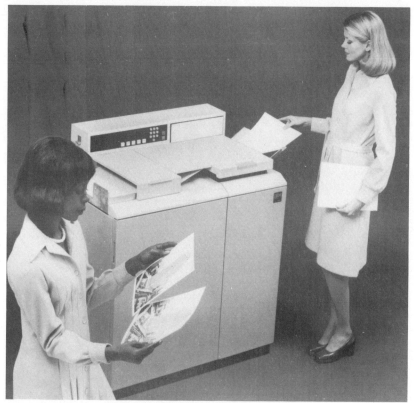

Figure 7–3: An electrostatic copier capable of making 4,500 copies per hour and automatically copying on both sides of the paper.

make, and this method is rarely used to make more than a hundred copies.

Mimeograph or Stencil Duplicator. The *mimeograph* provides a low-cost, good-quality reproduction. It can be used to make several hundred copies of better quality than the ditto. However, a stencil must be used, and this makes corrections difficult. Also, the mimeograph is not designed to print books, color, or elaborate art work.

Copiers (Reprographics)

Copiers use heat, light, electricity, and chemical reactions. *Electrostatic copiers* (Figure 7–3) are the most common today and are frequently referred to as "Xerox," regardless of the brand or pro-

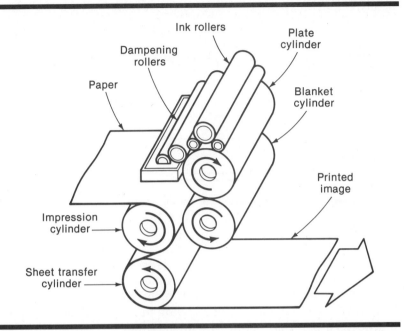

Figure 7–4: In offset printing the ink is first transferred to a rubber blanket from the plate cylinder.

cess. Not all copiers can reproduce nonwhite paper, and at times typed messages cannot be copied cleanly. Generally, copiers provide good-quality reproduction, but the machines are delicate and tend to break down easily. Some equipment requires special paper.

"Intelligent copiers" are already on the market. Operating with lasers or fiber optic tubes, tied in with optical character readers (OCR), they automatically read figures and other data and convert them into charts, graphs, and documents—at incredibly high speeds and in a variety of typefaces. Expect to see more of these during the 1980s.

Offset Lithography

Offset printing produces high-speed, high-quality, low-cost printing on a wide variety of paper and materials. As can be seen in Figure 7–4, the inked image is first transferred to a rubber blanketed cylinder and then is "offset" to the paper, hence the term *offset*.

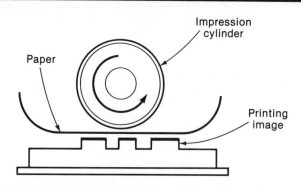

Figure 7–5: The letterpress method of printing is the only method from which you can use type directly.

The versatility of offset printing is so great it can be used for almost any printing need: from 100 copies of a flyer seeking a lost family pet done at your local instant printer, to a one-million copy plus, 200-page, 4-color run of *Playboy* magazine done at a huge midwestern printing plant. Of course, while the cost and the sophistication of the printing equipment in these two examples is vastly different, the basic offset principle is exactly the same.

Letterpress

Letterpress, the oldest method of printing, will work on any type of paper and the results are usually excellent. Letterpress is most often used for books, catalogs, advertisements, and packaging products that must be produced in large numbers. See Figure 7–5.

Because of the wide variety of paper and duplicating methods currently available, it is a good idea, when buying paper or planning to reproduce your work, to determine exactly what you need. Then follow the recommendations of experts. Suggestions for designing letterheads, booklets of sample papers, and examples of typefaces are available free of charge from most printshops and paper distributors.

ASSIGNMENT: THE IMAGE—APPEARANCE

Your in-service training session this week will be a round-table discussion on the importance and ingredients of the image—appearance—in written business communication. Select one of the following topics and lead a discussion of it with the rest of the group.

Topics

1. Bring to the session any aids to correct grammar, spelling, and punctuation that you use regularly. Explain the key features of each one. What other aids are available?
2. Select a product (real or imaginary). Design a letterhead for a company that sells that product or service. Clip and paste; hand letter, draw, type, etc. Ask for the group's reactions to your letterhead.
3. Explain the considerations with which format is concerned. Discuss the features of a good format, illustrating them with examples.
4. Collect ten samples of paper. These should include business stationery, your own personal stationery, typing paper, and business forms. Briefly analyze them in terms of image, product, status of sender, and intended audience.
5. Discuss the duplicating methods with which you are familiar. How did you learn about them? What are the advantages and disadvantages of each?
6. Locate sources of printing and duplicating. Watch the processes and report your observations to your colleagues.

FURTHER READING

Boulding, Kenneth E. *The Image.* Ann Arbor, MI: The University of Michigan Press, 1956.

Competitive Paper Grade Finder, 1979, 13th ed. King of Prussia, PA: Grade Finders, 1978.

Glaister, Geoffry. *Glaister's Glossary of the Book: Terms Used in Paper-Making, Printing, Bookbinding and Publishing.* Berkeley, CA: University of California Press, 1979.

A Manual of Style, 12th ed, rev. Chicago: The University of Chicago Press, 1975.

Mosher, R. H. and D. S. Davis, eds. *Industrial and Specialty Papers: Their Technology, Manufacture and Use.* New York: Chemical Publishing, 1979.

Pocket Pal, 11th ed. New York: International Paper Co., 1974.

Turner, Mary C. *The Bookman's Glossary.* New York: R. R. Bowker, 1961.

Van Derveer, Paul D. and Leonard E. Haas, eds. *International Glossary of Technical Terms for the Pulp and Paper Industry.* San Francisco: Miller Freeman, 1976.

Words into Type, 3rd ed. Englewood Cliffs, NJ: Prentice-Hall, 1974.

Part Three

Applications

CHAPTER EIGHT

Letter Format

. . . communication depends as much on the nonverbal message as it does on the verbal. Your ideas may be brilliant, your statements clear, tactful, concise, accurate, and in correct English—but if those beautiful statements are thrown together haphazardly on paper, with no form or balance, the recipient will probably not even read them; if he does, it will be with prejudice.

Norman B. Sigband
Communication for Management and Business

Most business letters fit one of these three patterns: information, refusal, selling (IRS). Regardless of the pattern, however, in nearly all cases, business letters follow the same general format.

As you learned in Chapter 7, certain conventions have traditionally determined what elements the business letter should contain and how these elements should be arranged on the page. These conventions affect both the content and appearance of the message.

Today you no longer address a business person as "Dear Most Honorable Sir or Madam." Nor do you close a letter with "Your most obedient servant." You may use more creative, more personal phrases, or you may even omit the *salutation* or *complimentary close*. But you still cling to the tradition of identifying the sender and receiver of the message.

You may change the position of certain letter elements to create a desired image or to increase readability. Almost any position is acceptable, as long as there is a logical reason for the shift from traditional to contemporary.

Use logic in your letter format.

You may also adjust spacing—on the page and between different elements of the letter. Again, however, there should be a logical reason for the shift from the traditional, which usually calls for single-spacing between lines; double-spacing between paragraphs and letter parts; and four spaces for the signature in the signature block.

LAYOUT

Plan the placement of your letter on the page.

Placement of the message on the page is traditionally determined by two methods: *the picture-frame plan* and *the standard-line plan.* For the first, estimate the length of the message (minus the letter-head or heading) and plan equal-width margins around the top and right and left sides. The bottom margin should be approximately one and a half times as deep as the others (just as a cardboard mat around a picture is deeper at the bottom). See Figure 8–1.

You can set keyboard stops on the typewriter for equal-width side margins. However, you must watch the bottom margin until you have become experienced enough to automatically judge the distance or learn to use the keyboard gauge. At first you may find it necessary to retype a message, adjusting the margins for longer or shorter lines to secure eye-pleasing surrounding white space.

Some people find the standard-line plan easier to use. With this plan, all letters are given the same side and top margins, no matter what the length of the message. Again, the bottom margin is approximately one and a half times as deep as the others. Adjustment is made by varying the spacing between letter parts and paragraphs for messages of varying lengths. Some large corporations use the standard-line plan (Figure 8–2). And most large organizations have their own style books with directives for most communication situations. (If you are not given such information, ask for it.)

Indention and punctuation decisions depend on several factors: individual preference, an organization's directives, who the receiver of the communication will be. Typically, the first line of a paragraph is *indented,* as many spaces as you like, usually two to six (Figure 8–3); *blocked*—typed flush left with other lines (Figures 8–4, 8–5, and 8–6); or *hanging*—typed flush left with the following lines indented (Figure 8–7).

Some business letters include punctuation (commas or other marks) at the end of lines in the heading, inside address, salutation, and complimentary close. This is called *closed punctuation.* But efficiency and simplicity save time and money. You can type faster when you do not punctuate these elements. This is called *open punctuation.* Combinations of open and closed punctuation are acceptable and popular.

ballou farms, inc.

January 1, 19___

Mr. Gerald Dorstal, President
Dostal Manufacturing Company, Inc.
Ankeny, Iowa 50161

Dear Mr. Dorstal:

XXXXXXXXXXXXXXXXXXXXXXXXXXXXXXXXXXXXXXXXXXXXXXXXX
XXXXXXXXXXXXXXXXXXXXXXXXXXXXXXXXXXXXX

XXXXXXXXXXXXXXXXXXXXXXXXXXXXXXXXXXXXXXXXXXXXXXXX
XXXXXXXXXXXXXXXXXXXXXXXXXXXXXXXXXXXXXXXXXXXXXX
XXXXXXXXXXXXXXXXXXXXXXXXXXXXXXXXXXXXXXXXXXXX
XXXXXXXXXXXXXXXXXXXXXXXXXXXXXXXXXXXXXXXXXXXXXXXX
XXXXXXXXXXXXXXXX

XXXXXXXXXXXXXXXXXXXXXXXXXXXXXXXXXXXXXXXXXXXX
XXXXXXXXXXXXXXXXXXXXXXXXXXXXXXXXXXXXXXXXXXXXXX
XXXXXXXXXXXXXXXXXXXXXXXXXXXXXXXXXXXXXXXXXXXXXXXX
XXXXXXXXXXXXXXXXXXXXXXXXXXXXXXXXXXXXXXXXXXXXXX
XXXXXXXXXXXXXXXXXXXXXXXXXXXXXXXXXXXXXXXXXXXXXX
XXXXXXXXXXXXXXXXXXXXXXXXXXXXXXXXXXXXXXXXXXXXXX
XXXXXXXXXXXXXXXXXXXXXXXXXXXXXXXXXX

XXXXXXXXXXXXXXXXXXXXXXXXXXXXXXXXXXXXXXXXXXXXXX
XXXXXXXXXXXXXXXXXXXXXXXXXXXXXXXXXXXXXXXXXXXXXX
XXXXXXXXXXXXXXXXXXXX

Sincerely yours,

BALLOU FARMS, INC.

John J. Ballou, President

R.R. 2   MONTICELLO, IOWA   52310   319-465-4390

Figure 8–1: Picture-frame Plan

Space is adjusted between the date and inside address and between the body and complimentary close. Other adjustments may be made between paragraphs and other parts. Text (body) may be double-spaced instead of single-spaced, with triple-spacing between paragraphs.

Letterhead

MICHEL THOMAS
LANGUAGE CENTERS

Date

January 1, 1981

Inside
address

Kathleen Donovan
Geist and Geist Advertising
2345 Sohio Avenue
Los Angeles, CA 90025

Salutation

Dear Ms. Donovan:

Body

XXXXXXXXXXXXXXXXXXXXXXXXXXXXXXXXXXXXXXXXXXXXXXXXXX
XXXXXXXXXXXXXXXXXXXXXXXXXXXXXXXXXXXXXXXXXXXXXXXXX
XXXXXXXXXXXXXXXXXXXXXXXXXXXXXXXXXXXX

XXXXXXXXXXXXXXXXXXXXXXXXXXXXXXXXXXXXXXXXXXXXXXXXX
XXXXXXXXXXXXXXXXXXXXXXXXXXXXXXXXXXXXXXXXXXXXXXXXX
XXXXXXXXXXXXXXXXXXXXXXXXXXXXXXXXXXXXXXXXXXXXXXXXX
XXXXXXXXXXXXXXXXXXXXXXXXXXXXXXXXXXXX

XXXXXXXXXXXXXXXXXXXXXXXXXXXXXXXXXXXXXXXXXXXXXXXXX
XXXXXXXXXXXXXXXXXXXXXXXXXXXXXXXXXXXXXXXXXXXXXXXXXX
XXXXXXXXXXXXXXXXXXXX

Complimentary
close

Sincerely,

Signature block

Ann Schumaker

Special
parts

Enclosures

2700 West Coast Highway, Newport Beach, CA 92663, (714) 631-0880

Figure 8–2: Standard-line Plan

March 22, 1981

Mr. Tom Farmer
Rural Route 1
Casper, WY 72135

Dear Mr. Farmer:

    Now you can rent instead of buy high priced farm
equipment on a short-term basis, or lease it for a period
of up to one year.

    This plan could greatly reduce your capital needs. It
would also eliminate repair costs and high fixed costs such
as taxes, interest, and depreciation. As you already know,
these large, modern machines are necessary because of the
labor savings and increased field capacity they provide.

    You can rent a tractor for as little as $10 per hour.
Available are units up to 175 horsepower. You can also rent
power-matched equipment for any size tractor that fits your
needs. Cabs and duals are also available for a slight additional charge.

    All rented equipment is delivered to your farm. The
farmer is expected to treat the equipment as if it were his
own. The farmer must furnish fuel and lubricants for the
equipment. If a breakdown does occur, and we cannot repair
it within 24 hours, we will bring you a comparable machine
to keep you operating on schedule.

    Enclosed is a rate schedule for all our rental equipment.
To discuss the benefits you can gain from leasing our equipment, please call us collect. The machinery is available on
a first-come, first-served basis, so call soon to make your
arrangements.

              Cordially yours,

              M V EQUIPMENT RENTAL

              Lester James
              Sales Manager

Enclosure: Rate Schedule

Date

Inside address

Salutation

Body

Complimentary close

Signature block

Special parts

Figure 8–3: A Traditional, Indented Style

APPLICATIONS

Date

Inside
address

Salutation

Body

Complimentary
close

Signature block

Special
parts

April 15, 1981

Paul D. Crone, President
Crone Furniture Company
2318 Willow Avenue
Minneapolis, MN 65409

Whale beds, giraffe chairs, elephant toy chests. . .

join the safari leading to exciting discoveries in the land
of two-through ten-year-olds. As a furniture dealer, you
are constantly looking for vibrant new concepts in children's
furniture. At MENAGERIE, we have gone exploring and are now
introducing a hardboard revolution.

Children in various test situations have been delighted to
jump on our whale's stomach and to store their toys in the
bright red elephant. Our collection of animal furniture is
made from industrial tri-wall hardboard and is painted in
bright, appealing colors. The materials are inexpensive,
yet very durable. The designs provide a learning experience
while also matching the imaginativeness of a child.

As a parent, you realize the child's need for a stimulating
environment during the formative years. Our "menagerie"
fulfills this need as demonstrated by our sales records for
test sales. Enclosed is our brochure containing more detailed information. We are sure our designs will add a new
creative dimension to your present inventory.

You can make an appointment to meet with our representative,
John Michaels, by calling our Des Moines number. He can
arrange to demonstrate our furniture in your showroom.

Yours for better business,

Daniel D. Wayne
President

DDW:gp

Enclosure

Figure 8–4: A Contemporary, Block Style

October 3, 1981   *Date*

Mr. Michael Thompson   *Inside*
The Head Shop   *address*
2200 Sunset Drive
Carson City, NV 82946

Dear Mr. Thompson: *Salutation*

Fashionable sideburns and moustaches are now available at   *Body*
profit-making prices. Research has proved that men desire
to grow better sideburns and moustaches than nature has
granted. Help your customers satisfy this desire with
reasonably priced hair products by Hair Incorporated.

Hair Incorporated products retail from $3 to $20. You can
purchase them for $1.50 to $10. You make a 100 percent
profit on each sale.

Our products are made of 100 percent human hair and come in
a wide variety of popular styles. Custom-made and matched
to your customers' own hair color, all products are shipped
within 21 days of receipt of order.

You can return any of the products within 30 days of purchase
for a full refund. We will also buy back products up to one
year after purchase for half their retail value.

Our products are available only at better hairstylers in
Nevada. A limited supply is also available through nationally recognized Barbers, Incorporated distributors.

Enclosed you will find a catalog and price list. Harold
Handlebar, our specialist in your area, will be calling on
you within the next week to answer any questions you may
have and to present you with a point-of-purchase display.

Serve your customers more completely and make a profit at
the same time.

Sincerely yours,   *Complimentary close*

Thomas L. Morehair   *Signature block*
Vice-President and
   Sales Manager

ENC.   *Special*
                                                         parts
TLM:mwc

Figure 8–5: A Traditional, Block Style

APPLICATIONS

Date

Inside address

Salutation

Body

Signature block

Special parts

```
                                                July 10, 1981


        Mr. John Apple
        Security Department Manager
        Grapple Line, Pier 72
        New York, NY  07111


        Your burglary, Mr. Apple,

        could have been prevented.  An attack-trained lion roaming
        your premises would have kept your valuable property safe
        from intruders.

        For a cost of only $8.50 per night each three months, our
        experienced trainers deliver your hungry lion at closing
        time and pick him up in the morning just before you open
        for business.  The cost compares favorably with our com-
        petitors' prices who only offer dogs.

        The King of Beasts Security Service offers a sure solution
        to your problem.  We can train one of your employees to
        patrol with the lion or he can be released to prowl stealth-
        ily on his own.  One lion can replace three armed guards.

        Phone for an appointment to learn more about these and
        other benefits offered you by our service.  Our roar is
        better than a bark.

                                    KING OF BEASTS
                                    SECURITY SERVICE



                                    Douglas Allan
                                    Marketing Manager

        DA/pn
```

Figure 8–6: A Contemporary, Modified Block Style

November 15, 1981

Ms. Deidre Winters
Physical Education Department
University of Tennessee
Knoxville, TN 37901

                    SUBJECT: Your order #127493

Dear Ms. Winters

The Strokeze Swimwear you ordered was shipped freight prepaid
    this morning by United Parcel; it should arrive in Knox-
    ville by Wednesday, November 21.

Your order for

    7   1525 S 0178 @ $15.95 ....$111.65
   10   1525 M 0179 @ $15.95 .... 159.50
    8   1525 L 0180 @ $15.95 .... 127.60
                                            $398.75
                Sales Tax 11.96
                   Total $410.71

    has been debited to your account under our regular terms
    of 2/10, n/60. A 1½% monthly finance charge will be
    added to the unpaid balance after 60 days.

Included as a bonus with the order, you will receive an
    attractive Strokeze warm-up suit color-coordinated with
    the team suits. The warm-up outfits are available for
    only $45.00 each and can be imprinted with your school
    or team name.

Thank you for your order and best wishes for a successful
    swimming season.

                    STROKEZE SWIMWEAR

                    (Ms.) Joanne Brown
                    Sales Representative

JB:gp

Date

Inside address

Salutation

Body

Signature block

Special parts

Figure 8–7: An Example of Hanging Paragraphs and Open Punctuation

STANDARD LETTER PARTS

Letterhead

Whether you choose a traditional or contemporary format, ease of reading should be your aim.

As discussed earlier, the letterhead is usually imprinted on stationery and consists of the name, address (with zip code), and possibly telephone number (with area code), telex or cable address, filing reference (Ref:), slogan, and logo. Traditionally, all this information appears at the top of the page. However, contemporary design offers a wide variety of positions, although the name is still usually placed at the top for ease of reading. (Refer to Figure 7–2, page 127, for examples.)

The *heading* is the equivalent of a letterhead on unprinted stationery. This may be typed or handwritten. It does not include the writer's name, only his or her address.

For a contemporary, more practical position, place your address *beneath* your signature. In this position, it can be more easily transposed into an inside address for the reply to you.

Date

The date may mark the left or right margin, appear centered, or even appear beneath your signature. It is best located two to six spaces above the inside address. It should be written out: February 21, 1981, *not* Feb. 21, 1981. (Military and some international forms place the day first, month next, abbreviated: 21/2/1981.)

Inside Address

The inside address consists of the name and address of the individual or organization to whom you are writing and duplicates the mailing address. Traditionally, it is placed two to six spaces below the date, at the top of the page. You may, however, acceptably place it three to eight spaces below your typed signature, marking either left or right margin, instead.

Wherever possible, use an individual's name and title.

```
Professional:  Dr., Professor, President,
               Secretary, Treasurer, Judge,
               C.P.A., and so on.

Honorary:  Colonel, Sir, Dr., Dame, and so on.
```

```
Position:  Chairperson, Dean, Manager, Director,
           and so on.

Courtesy:  Mr., Mrs., Ms. (or Ms without a
           period), Miss
```

Traditionally, when one title precedes the name, a position title follows it.

```
Dr. Wallace Russell, Dean
```

Today it is acceptable to use only the name and position title.

```
Wallace Russell, Dean
```

```
Dean Wallace Russell
```

Of course, if you know both titles, use them. When in doubt, address letters to individuals using the title you know.

If you do not have a specific name, substitute a descriptive title for the individual or department you wish to reach.

```
Buyer, Children's Wear
```

```
Personnel Director
```

Your message will be routed through channels more quickly, by-passing mail room delays.

Many widows and divorcees continue to use their husband's name and prefer to be addressed as "Mrs." (The form is acceptable for widows, confusing when used by a divorcee.) They indicate their preferred title in the signature block.

```
Mrs. Judson H. Ballou
```

```
Marian Ballou, Ph.D.
```

```
(Mrs.) M. Ballou
```

```
(Ms.) M. Ballou
```

Increasing numbers of career women use a professional name at work and a married name socially. Some married women choose to retain their maiden name or to hyphenate their own and their husband's names.

```
Marian Goodman (professionally)

Marian Ballou (socially)

Marian Goodman-Ballou (both professionally and
    socially)
```

In some cultures, the husband adopts the wife's family name. As names become less clearly defined sexually and living arrangements become more casual, you should be guided by the signature block.

When initiating correspondence to two individuals at the same address, either send separate letters or use both names, alphabetically listed, for the inside address and salutation.

Salutation

The traditional salutation is placed two spaces below the inside address and ends with a colon (:) or nothing (closed or open punctuation, respectively). A comma is used only in informal social correspondence.

Old habits die hard, among them traditional salutations. In general use are

```
Dear Sir:    Dear Madam:    Gentlemen:

Dear (Mr., Mrs., Miss, Ms.) Jones:

Dear (appropriate title) Jones:

(Mr., Mrs., Miss, Ms.) Jones:
```

Acceptable but strained or phony are

```
Dear Sir/Madam:    Dear Gentleperson:
Dear Chairman:     Chair Jones:
```

Informally, we address friends as

```
Dear Ellen:    Dear Len:    Dear Aunt Emily:
```

and these informal salutations may begin a formal business letter *if* the person is a friend or relative. Undue familiarity can alienate people.

Contemporary, creative salutations appear a minimum of three spaces below the inside address if an address is used at the top of the page. These salutations may or may not include the name of the addressee in the first sentence or phrase. They are attention-getters—personal, unique, and, usually, sincere. But they call for ingenuity and creative writing on your part (see Figures 8–4 and 8–6).

Creative salutations can be indented and punctuated as you wish. Dots or dashes are acceptable. Indenting the salutation line only is acceptable. Acceptable, too, is "hanging" the line—blocking it to the left margin and indenting all the other lines of copy.

Simplified letters eliminate the salutation and complimentary close. Or attention lines or subject lines replace the salutation and are placed two spaces below the inside address followed by two spaces to the body. Although these are rather cold and lack the personality and charm of the creative salutation, you may prefer them, depending on the purpose of the correspondence and the addressee.

Body

The letter body begins two spaces below the salutation (or attention or subject line). Unless you are adjusting spacing for the standard-line plan, single-space between lines and double-space between paragraphs. Of course, to adjust for short messages, you can double-space between lines, triple-space between paragraphs, or use half-spaces regardless of the selected format.

To ensure readability, use one to four lines for opening and closing paragraphs and no more than eight to ten lines for intermediate paragraphs.

There are other ways to make material easy to read. You may set up a series of items in columns (tables) under headings. Or you may use numbers either horizontally or vertically on separate lines to list (itemize) information. And you may use display bullets or dots (·), of various sizes, as well as dashes (—) and asterisks (*) to call attention to various points.

Arrange the body of your letter, the heart of your message, to hold your reader's attention.

These devices help reduce boredom in a long piece of writing. They create white space between and around parts, and they emphasize important items. (At any one time, though, try to limit the number of items in a list to about seven. Recent learning theory indicates that a reader loses interest when the list is much longer than that.)

Complimentary Close

The complimentary close is usually placed two spaces below the last line of the body of a letter. Typical traditional examples are

```
Yours truly,    Very truly yours,      Sincerely,

Sincerely yours,    Cordially,

Very cordially yours,
```

and in rare, very formal cases,

```
Respectfully yours,
```

Creative, contemporary closings begin a minimum of three spaces below the body. In short messages, adjust the spacing as you wish. The creative closing follows from the message. Each is unique. Each is created for the receiver of the correspondence, created to fit the situation. A dairy industry letter might close with the phrase, "With milk in mind." Figure 8–4 illustrates another creative close.

Signature Block

The first typed line of the signature block is usually placed four or more spaces below the complimentary close or, if there is no close, four spaces below the last line of the body. The space is for your written signature, followed by your typed name, including position and professional title, if any. Women may want to add courtesy titles or a married name, but this is a matter of choice. The signature will establish the first line of the inside address in a reply.

As the writer of a business letter, you represent an organization.

If you are writing about company business, *for the company,* you should protect yourself against legal action by typing the company name in capital letters two spaces below the complimentary close (or two spaces below the body if the close is omitted). This indicates you are a legally authorized correspondent.

Many authorized writers omit this protection, preferring the more personal individual name only. Make sure your company or organization will back you up before you commit to paper any statements that can create legal problems.

To ensure legibility in handwritten correspondence (try to get it typed), print your name or paste on a name-address label under your written signature.

SPECIAL LETTER PARTS

Subject Line

The subject line is located two spaces below the inside address, flush with the left margin or centered, in capital letters or underlined for visibility. Unless you are using a printed form that contains the abbreviation "Re:" or some other such marker, simply type the word "Subject:" followed by the briefly stated topic. It is unnecessary to use a complete sentence; in fact, it is better if you include only key words.

```
Subject:  REQUEST FOR APPLICATION BLANKS

Subject:  Itinerary for Voyager IX

Subject:  COLLECTIVE BARGAINING
```

The subject should be of interest to the receiver of the communication. It's a time-saver and a "flag," catching the reader's immediate attention.

Attention Line

The attention line is placed two spaces below the inside address, flush with the left margin or centered, if the communication is sent to an organization and you have been unable to find an individual's name. (Did you try telephoning?) Use the position title or a reasonable guess at such a title.

```
Attention:  Purchasing Agent

Attention:  Director of Freshman English
```

Better yet, use the attention line as the first line of the inside address to speed delivery of your message.

Multipage Headings

Do not use stationery imprinted with a letterhead for additional pages of a letter unless it is specially printed to be used this way. Otherwise, the second and any other additional pages should be of the same type of paper as the first sheet and you should add a heading. Position the heading at least as far from the top of the page as the width of the side margins. Include the *first line* of the *inside address,* the *page number,* and the *date.* Usually the name appears first, but you may switch elements. This information is an aid for filing.

```
Mary C. Thompson, Director - 2 - July 4, 1981

Mary C. Thompson, Director
July 4, 1981
Page 2

Mary C. Thompson, Director, July 4, 1981, Page 2
```

Continue the message two to four spaces below the heading.

Initials

Initials (dictator's and typist's) are placed two spaces below the signature block, flush with the left margin, to indicate the message was dictated to and typed by someone other than the writer. The dictator's initials always appear first, followed by the typist's. They may appear in lower or upper case or a combination of both. Use a colon, slash (/), or dash between the two.

```
LOF:MCT     LOF:mct     lof/mct     LOF--mct
```

If you type your own message, omit the initials. If the typist or secretary composes the letter and types it in someone else's name, only the typist or secretary's initials appear.

```
mct     MCT
```

Enclosure

The enclosure line is placed two spaces below the initials or in their place. The notation may appear by itself or it may be followed by a dash or colon and a listing of the enclosed material. It serves as a reminder to you and a cue to the receiver to look for additional material in the envelope.

```
Enc.: 3     Enclosure: Plane Tickets
```

```
Encl.--receipt for donation
```

Carbon Copy

Information regarding carbon copies is placed one or two spaces below either the initials or the enclosure. It indicates that others have received copies of the correspondence. Such an indication may have political overtones in an organization. Who does or does not receive a copy is important. Even the listing of names indicates the "pecking" or rank order. You can eliminate implications of rank order by listing the names alphabetically.

```
CC: Jane Espry    Cc: John Smith, Mary Thompson
    Marcus Smith
```

BCC—blind carbon notation—appears on the carbon copy *only,* not on the original. Without informing the addressee, this reminds the writer of other people receiving the message.

Postscripts

Postscripts are the last thing on the page, at least two spaces below the previous material. A "P.S." may be typed or handwritten. It may be a genuine afterthought—an important addition, but one that you do not want to retype the letter for. Or it may be a pre-planned ploy, a punch line in an emphatic position, an integral part of a (usually) persuasive message.

```
P.S. For even greater savings, mail your orders
     before December 1, midnight.  All orders
     postmarked before that date earn an addi-
     tional 10% discount!
```

ENVELOPE FORMAT

Size and Variety

Most premium correspondence papers are letter size, 8½ by 11 inches, with matching number 10 business envelopes. Legal-size sheets, 8½ by 13 or 14 inches, can also fit in number 10 envelopes with additional folding. Some executives also use the monarch

Table 8–1: Envelope Types and Their Uses

Type	Use
Window	Eliminates need for addressing, since inside address shows through if letter is folded correctly.
Prestamped or business reply	Usually enclosed with a letter to encourage a reply—used when soliciting contributions or orders.
Self-sealing	Also enclosed with a letter to encourage a reply.
Bulk rate	Bulk-rate permit number imprinted on envelope to facilitate large mailings—bulk rate is slower and cheaper than first class.
Air mail	Often used for international correspondence, since U.S. first class is automatically sent by air.
Padded	For mailing damageable items.

size, 7¼ by 10½ inches, with matching envelopes. Postal regulations govern the acceptable sizes of mailing pieces. Information can be obtained from any post office.

A variety of envelopes are available, each with special features. Table 8–1 lists some of these along with their uses, and Figure 8–8 shows a sample envelope design and format.

Addressing Envelopes

Help ensure the safe arrival of your message.

The *return address* should be located in the upper-left corner. If imprinted, it may appear anywhere on the left. The name and address of the receiver are usually located slightly off-center right, between the stamp and the return address (on the number 10 business envelope approximately five inches from the left, approximately two inches from the top). Addresses of more than three lines should always be single-spaced.

Air mail, registered mail, or special delivery should be indicated *under the stamp.* Air mail stickers, stamps, and envelopes are available and ensure special attention for messages that go outside of the United States. Registered letters and special delivery mail must be arranged for at a post office.

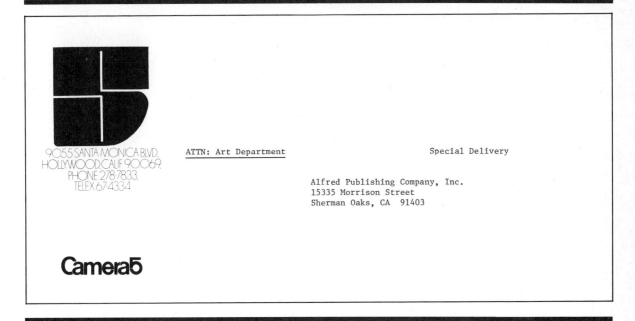

Figure 8–8: Sample Envelope Design and Format

If the mailing piece is confidential, personal, or directed to a specific location or individual, that information should be typed or printed in capital letters and underscored (<u>CONFIDENTIAL,</u> <u>PERSONAL,</u> <u>ATTN: ACCOUNTING DEPARTMENT</u>) on the left side of the envelope three lines above or even with the mailing address.

The post office reads addresses from the bottom up, beginning with the zip code, state, and city. In its "Memo to Mailers," the United Parcel Service recommends the following format:

- Name of individual
- Title
- Company name
- Street address (or P.O. box and suite)
- City, state, and zip code

The memo further cautions against putting an "attention" line immediately below the address block. Whether or not you follow this format, remember that the zip code should be the last item in any address.

Folding Stationery

Before inserting a letter into an envelope, proofread and sign the letter and attach any accompanying enclosures. Then carefully fold the material in either of two acceptable ways.

Standard fold:
1. Fold bottom first, a little less than one-third of page.
2. Fold top *down* over first fold (top will extend beyond the first fold).
3. Place message in envelope with extended flap against the front (on opening envelope, receiver easily grasps this extension).

French fold:
1. Fold bottom first, a little less than one-third of page.
2. Fold top *back* over first fold.
3. Place message in envelope with extended flap against the back (on opening envelope, receiver sees typed copy immediately).
Note: When using a window envelope, extended flap should face forward so that the inside address appears.

Folding machines can fold single pages at high speed, using either the standard or French fold.

Legal documents—deeds, warrants, mortgages, contracts, and others—are protected by a traditional *blue binder*. Many law firms imprint their firm name on the section folding over the top of the pages. This fold is stapled to hold the documents in place.

1. Fold oversized 9½-by-16-inch sheets in fourths, for delivery.
2. Store flat in legal files.

Blue folders are available at most office supply stores.

Now that you have mastered matters of letter format, you are ready to proceed to the actual writing of various types of business letters.

ASSIGNMENT: LETTER FORMAT

In preparation for this week's in-service training meeting, write a letter to a prospective customer using a contemporary format. Then rewrite the letter using a traditional format. Bring both versions to the training session and exchange letters with the other members of your group. After everyone has examined all of the letters, the group should discuss the following topics.

Topics

1. The importance of the format of the business letter.
2. Specific differences between the traditional format and the contemporary format.
3. When you would use the traditional format and why. When you would use the contemporary format and why.
4. The role of creativity in the contemporary format.

FURTHER READING

Cloke, Marjane and Robert Wallace. *The Modern Business Letter Writer's Manual.* Garden City, NY: Doubleday, 1969.

Hemphill, Phyllis D. *Business Communication with Writing Improvement Exercises.* Englewood Cliffs, NJ: Prentice-Hall, 1981.

Whalen, Doris J. *Handbook for Business Writers.* San Diego, CA: Harcourt Brace Jovanovich, 1978.

CHAPTER NINE

Information Letters

Carrier of news and knowledge, instrument of trade and commerce, promoter of mutual acquaintance among men and nations and hence of peace and goodwill.

Inscription
Post Office, Washington, D.C.

I n order to write effective business letters you must apply the skills outlined in chapters 4 through 7 and follow an appropriate format according to the steps explained in Chapter 8. Before you begin, however, it is also important that you know the various *types* of business letters and the basic content *patterns* into which they fall. Study Figure 9–1. As you will note, there are many types of business letters but most take one (or a combination) of three patterns: information, refusal, or selling (IRS). Each pattern requires its own special writing technique, so when you talk about patterns you are speaking of content and writing patterns.

In this chapter you will deal with the information pattern; in Chapter 10 you will examine the refusal pattern; and in Chapter 11 you will study the selling pattern.

For any letter you write, follow this procedure:

- Visualize your reader(s)
- Think through your purpose
- Assemble your content
- Select your format
- Determine your pattern
- Proceed with POWER

Types of letters in the information pattern and the purposes of each type are listed in Table 9–1. Easiest of all to write, these letters consist of content the reader wants to read or at least has no objection to reading.

158

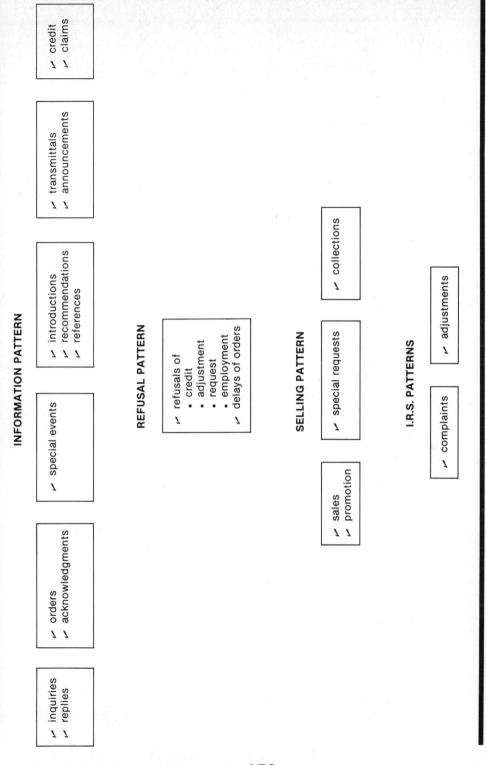

INFORMATION PATTERN

✓ inquiries ✓ replies	
✓ orders ✓ acknowledgments	
✓ special events	
✓ introductions ✓ recommendations ✓ references	
✓ transmittals ✓ announcements	
✓ credit ✓ claims	

REFUSAL PATTERN

✓ refusals of
  • credit
  • adjustment
  • request
  • employment
✓ delays of orders

SELLING PATTERN

✓ sales
✓ promotion

✓ special requests

✓ collections

I.R.S. PATTERNS

✓ complaints

✓ adjustments

Figure 9–1: Types of Business Letters and Writing Patterns

159

Table 9–1: Types of Letters in the Information Pattern

Type	Purpose
Solicited Inquiry	Response to an advertisement, selling letter, or inquiry
Unsolicited Inquiry	Usually a request for a favor
Favorable Reply	Statement of good news
Order	A request to purchase goods or services
Acknowledgment	Confirmation of receipt of an order, important letter, package
Special Events Congratulatory Letter	Praise for a job well done, a promotion, election, outstanding achievement
Appreciation Letter	A thank-you for another's time, effort, or money
Sympathy Letter	Expression of concern in a time of misfortune
Letter of Last Instruction	Collection of information for family to follow after death
Introduction, Recommendation, and Reference Letters	Introduction: a letter written on behalf of another to ask for help for that person; recommendation: a letter that evaluates or endorses a job candidate; reference: an objective report on a candidate
Transmittal	A letter introducing, justifying, evaluating, or summarizing a report, proposal, or questionnaire
Announcement	A statement of information concerning company policy, meetings, actions, or job openings
Claim or Complaint	An explanation of a problem and a statement of desired action
Adjustment	A response to a claim or complaint
Credit Application	A request for credit providing necessary financial information
Request for Further Information	A response to an application for credit
Explanation of Terms	An acknowledgment of credit approval and detailed information
Letter of Credit	A substitute for money, usually used in international trade

LETTERS OF INQUIRY

Solicited Inquiries

Solicited inquiries are written in response to an advertisement, a sales letter, or a program for confidential upward communication between employees and management. These letters require a simple, straightforward style.

1. In the first sentence ask immediately for the specific information desired. Do not refer to your source unless absolutely necessary—the reader usually knows.

   Determine what you want to know, and ask for it directly.

2. Add personal details to explain your interest, to establish yourself as an individual instead of a faceless cipher, to encourage thoughtful response.
3. Close pleasantly, perhaps indicating your appreciation for action. Be sure to include the complete heading and signature. The message can be as short as one or two sentences or paragraphs. For longer, more detailed inquiries, itemize your questions (Figure 9–2).

Unsolicited Inquiries

Frequently a request for a favor, the *unsolicited inquiry* is often a combination of the information and selling patterns. However, inquiries requiring "yes" or "no" responses or minimal effort for a reply may follow the information pattern of the solicited inquiry. When writing to request something for nothing, always enclose a self-addressed stamped envelope (SASE). Your chances of receiving a response are much better.

FAVORABLE REPLIES

Favorable replies, like most inquiries, need no introduction. The reader should be told the good news immediately. "Congratulations! You've won the Irish Sweepstakes." See Figure 9–3.

Everyone appreciates good news; give it immediately.

1. Begin with good news.
2. Answer all questions in the order they were asked or follow up with further details.
3. Close with repetition of the opening or another warm, friendly statement. Show your good will, your desire to be of service. You may want to incorporate resale and/or sales promotion.

*To-the-point
opening*

*Easy-to-follow
questions*

Special problem for Grapple

Further response indicated

```
                        GRAPPLE LINE
                          Pier 72
                 New York, New York  07111

John Apple, Security Manager        Phone: 212-667-1196

                                    March 21, 1981


     Mr. Kenneth N. Drake
     Marketing Manager
     King of Beasts Security Service
     100 Park Avenue
     New York, NY  07110

     Dear Mr. Drake:

     Before further considering your security service, I would
     like the following information:

        1.  Who is responsible for any damage done by the lion?

        2.  Will your handlers clean up after the lion?

        3.  Will food for the lion be provided or is that an
            extra charge?

        4.  How quickly can the lion be retrieved?  Cargo hand-
            ling occurs at sporadic times during the night.

        5.  What are the charges--monthly, yearly?

     Upon receipt of your answer, I will phone you about possible
     rental.

                              Yours truly,



                              John Apple
                              Security Manager

     lrc/
```

Figure 9–2: Solicited Inquiry

Price T. Rowe
1250 West Avenue
Chicago, IL 51293

April 15, 1981

Mr. James T. Litt
6428 Wilson Hall
Idaho State University
Boise, ID 00000

Dear Mr. Litt:

    Your proposal regarding an analysis of Passey-Terguson, Ltd. has been accepted.

    The limited amount of information about management and foreign operations will, of course, decrease the degree of detail in those sections of the report. However, the annual report does provide some information concerning foreign operations.

    Obviously, your main source of information will be the annual report. Other sources that may prove helpful are Value Line Investment Survey, Standard and Poor's Industrial Survey, and Survey of Current Business.

    Several stock valuation models may be used to supplement the intrinsic value method: the Walters Model, the Kurtz Model, the Gordon Model, and the Graham-Dodd Model.

    I look forward to receiving your analysis.

Sincerely yours,

R. T. Hall
Growth Fund Manager

Begin with good news

Answer questions

Supportive close

Figure 9–3: A Favorable Reply—Letter of Authorization

ORDERS

Whenever possible, use a printed order form. Order forms include all the necessary details to ensure your satisfaction. Or use the telephone if a toll-free 800 area code is available for your convenience. It's a good idea to request hard copy—a confirmation of a hotel reservation or acknowledgment of an order. Ask for a name or number for reference until you receive an official response.

When placing an order, be specific and ask for confirmation.

A third choice is to write your order in a letter. Begin directly: "Please send . . ." Continue with details, aligning the data in easy-to-read columns. Use separate, single-spaced paragraphs for each item (Figure 9–4).

ACKNOWLEDGMENTS

Acknowledgments confirm receipt and establish good will.

Always acknowledge receipt of an order, an important letter, or a package. By doing so, you confirm that it has not been lost, misplaced, or stolen, that the proper steps are being taken to satisfy the sender.

A brief form letter, a card, or a check-list memo will often do the job. Include, if applicable:

TIPS FOR TRAVELERS

Requesting hotel space? Address your letter to "Reservations" or "Reservation Clerk." If you are attending a convention, say so, and ask for the convention rate or one of the many special rates available to traveling salespersons, educators, senior citizens, clergy.

When writing overseas for reservations (instead of having a travel agent do it for you), enclose a self-addressed envelope with international postage coupons to cover the cost of the reply. (Buy coupons at your post office.) Be sure to stipulate bath or shower if writing to local rather than international hotels. And ask about meals.

Some overnight lodgings include bed and complete breakfast. Others offer American and European plans. The American plan includes two or three meals: breakfast, lunch, and dinner or a choice of the last two. The European plan includes only a breakfast of coffee or tea and some kind of bread.

When planning a stopover on an international or domestic flight, ask the airline agent about tie-in reservations. Many airlines own hotels and have available package deals. But you may have to ask for the information and speak to several people. The prices are attractive enough to warrant the effort.

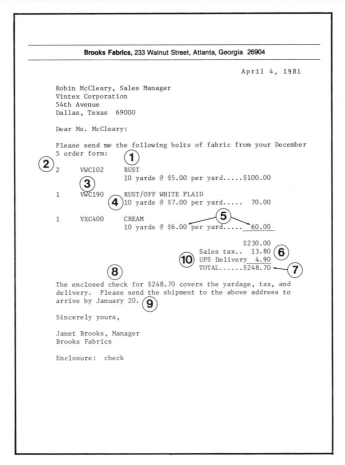

1. Exact name of product or a thorough description
2. Quantity desired
3. Catalog number, model number, parts number
4. Size, color, grade, pattern, monogram, first and second choice, other specifications
5. Unit price, quantity price
6. Sales tax and shipping charges, if applicable—no tax for nonprofit organizations, no tax if merchandise ordered from states without reciprocal tax agreement; some delivery charges are included in price
7. Total charges minus credits, if any
8. Method of payment—personal check, certified check, money order, other; charge to credit card, number enclosed; charge to account; c.o.d.—expensive—additional collecting charge on delivery
9. When and where of delivery—special instructions
10. How delivered—UPS, prepaid freight, cheapest way, air freight, fourth- or first-class mail—save by designating carrier of choice, is possible. No preference? Include approximate charges, offer to pay difference on notification. Most large organizations will accommodate.

Include all the necesary details to identify what you want whether it is a product or service.

Figure 9–4: Key Ordering Components

- referral number, order number, file number
- statement of procedure, policy
- expression of appreciation

See Figure 9–5.

Acknowledgments may be used as selling messages by emphasizing resale and sales promotion. Actually, all acknowledgments show your concern for the receiver and build good will.

SPECIAL EVENTS

When you receive birthday greetings from your insurance agent or a congratulatory note from a banker, you are pleased and amused. You know that all their clients receive the same "personal" treatment, that it is a device or tactic to gain your good will.

You may be amused, but you like being singled out for attention. And you'll probably return to that bank or to that agent the next time you need such services.

Sharing a special event shows that you care and promotes further business.

Everyone likes to receive special-event letters. Business device or heartfelt, these letters make acquaintances out of strangers, friends out of acquaintances. They are the single most effective way to develop good will.

Congratulatory Letters

A *congratulatory letter* praises someone for a job well done—a promotion, election, graduation, outstanding achievement of any kind. Such letters also acknowledge a happy event, such as an engagement, marriage, or birth of a child. React honestly to the event. Express yourself with the degree of warmth warranted by your relationship.

If there is a printed announcement, a news story, clip it to your stationery and send it along. It makes a great opening for your message. But with or without a clipping, begin directly with the praise. Usually one or two sentences, one or two paragraphs, typed or handwritten will do. (If necessary, follow up with additional information data.)

Congratulatory letters have an important place within organizations. Effective administrators recognize their value in establishing good employee relations.

Corporate expressions of good will may be sent as printed form letters, personalized with the reader's name. Such letters are

```
THE UNIVERSITY OF CHICAGO - THE LAW SCHOOL
1111 East 60th Street - Chicago, IL  60619

Since we received a letter of recommenda-
tion from you in support of Jay Thompson's
application to the Law School, I thought
you would be interested to know that he
has been admitted for our 19__ entering
class.  Our Admissions Committee gives
special attention to letters of recommen-
dation in trying to select the best can-
didates from a group of highly qualified
applicants.  On behalf of the Committee,
I want to thank you for the letter you
prepared for this candidate.

                Richard Badger, Assistant Dean
```

Figure 9–5: Acknowledgment

usually signed by an important official. But original or form, hand-written or typed, signed by a friend, official, or stranger, receiving them is a special event.

```
Dear Professor Jones:

Congratulations on being selected Professor of
the Year.

You certainly deserve the honor.

Sincerely
```

Appreciation Letters

Appreciation letters say "thank you." They show individual or organizational appreciation for another's time, efforts, behavior. They cover a wide range of situations: formal, informal, official, and personal. Traditionally handwritten, today they may be printed or typed. Or a stamped "thank you" superimposed on a bill may be used instead.

Appreciation letters from business firms are a good example of resale—keeping the customer sold on the company, product, or service. Often they

- welcome a new customer, explain services
- thank an old customer for prompt payments
- set aside "preferred" time for sales
- acknowledge gifts, bequests
- offer mementos, souvenirs, or refunds
- assure a client of continuing interest in a completed project
- extend season's greetings

Individuals usually acknowledge congratulatory letters and other personal favors with a simply written, brief message. In addition, it is thoughtful to inform employers when an employee has been especially helpful.

Warm and friendly, these letters both create and extend good will and demonstrate good manners as well as good business relations.

Sympathy Letters

Sympathy, or *condolence, letters* show you care. Whatever the misfortune, temporary or permanent, sharing and caring make the experience more bearable.

Acquaintances sometimes send printed cards with single or multiple signatures. But an individually written letter, however difficult it may be to write, means far more to the reader.

Illness, death, accident—fires, tornadoes, labor problems—your response and offer to help reveal your humanity.

Again, begin directly. Follow the information pattern, including specific detail whenever possible.

```
Dear Mrs. Snider:

Alfie was a good workman and an honest one.  We
could always depend on him to see the problem
and solve it--quickly and competently.

And he was more than that.

For the past thirty years he's been a friend.
Everyone who knew him enjoyed hearing about
```

the family, about his "wild" ideas like mulch-
ing crops with old newspapers, his numerous
inventions.

He'll be missed.

Within any organization, large or small, opportunities to write sympathy letters occur. Both intimate and official remembrances are greatly appreciated.

Letters of Last Instruction

A *letter of last instruction* may include the following information:

- Names and addresses of those to be notified when you die
- Location of your will
- Name and address of your estate executor and, perhaps, the name of family religious leader
- Brief explanation of actions taken in the will, such as disinheritance
- Father's name and mother's maiden name for a death certificate
- Location of safe deposit boxes and keys
- List and location of stocks and bonds, if not in safe deposit box
- List of insurance policies, especially life insurance, and location of policies
- Location of birth certificate or other evidence of birth, marriage license and other personal papers, Social Security card, certificates of automobile and other ownership
- List of all checking and saving accounts
- Names and addresses of people familiar with your personal and business affairs—physician, attorney, insurance agent, accountant, employer
- List and location of all personal property and instructions regarding distribution of this property
- List of any prepayments that have been made, especially for funeral arrangements
- A brief obituary
- Funeral and burial instructions, including any special burial benefits to which you are entitled (veteran's burial benefits, lodge or fraternal benefits)
- Location of burial plot
- Indication of a memorial fund or charity desired

You may want to update this letter every three to five years or when your family situation changes. Be sure to tell family members or close friends where the letter is.

INTRODUCTION, RECOMMENDATION, AND REFERENCE LETTERS

Introduction, recommendation, and reference letters differ in purpose, but sometimes the distinctions blur.

Introduction letters are written on behalf of employees, friends, business acquaintances. Such letters (1) indicate your relationship, (2) explain why you selected the reader, (3) ask for general assistance, and (4) state or imply appreciation.

Dear Mr. Pruit:

Relationship

  Paulie Chu is a former graduate student of mine, one of the very best I've ever had.

Reader's connection: request for assistance

  She's looking for a job and it is possible you can help. In your position with the Chamber of Commerce, you may have some leads or suggestions.

Evidence

  With her knowledge of Cantonese and Mandarin, an English M.A., and work in business, she could prove valuable to the right company.

Action

  Please do what you can.

Obviously, the letter is also a recommendation. It states the writer's belief in the candidate's ability. The purpose of the letter, however, is to receive help, not employment.

Introduction, recommendation, and reference letters provide information about an individual's character, qualifications, background.

Letters of introduction vouch for a person's character or status and are backed by the writer's character or status. For local or national introductions and immediate feedback, use the telephone—even if a letter is necessary for hard-copy follow-up.

Internationally, letters of introduction can cut red tape, speed business and social activities.

A *recommendation* evaluates or endorses someone looking for a job. A *reference*, on the other hand, gives an objective report of a candidate's employment or other history referred to on a resume or job application (Figure 9–6). Include relevant positions, satisfying experiences.

Reference Form

Please Return to: Career Planning and Placement, College of Home Economics, Iowa State
University, Ames, Iowa 50011 515/ 294-7246

To the Registrant:
1) Please type your name, major, degree, and graduation date on the reference form below.
2) Check A or B to inform the reference writer whether or not his/ her statement will be available for your review.
3) Sign your name and the date.
4) Please provide off-campus reference writers with a stamped envelope addressed for return to Career Planning and Placement.

To the Reference Writer:
1) Please type your statement because this reference will be duplicated exactly as you submit it.
2) This statement may include comments on the following qualities of the registrant: knowledge of subject matter, oral and written communication, creativity, initiative, leadership, quantity and quality of work, dependability, judgment, and relationships with others.
3) Please indicate the extent and type of opportunity you have had to observe the individual.

Reference for:

last name	first name	middle/ maiden	major	degree	graduation date

_____ A. I wish to have personal access to this reference.

_____ B. I waive the right of personal access to this reference.

Signature: _____   _____ Date _____

REFERENCE STATEMENT

Name of writer	Title
Organization	Address
Telephone	Signature
	Date

Figure 9–6: Standard Reference Form

Always ask permission before listing someone as a character reference and state whether your record will be *open* or *confidential*. You now have the legal right to decide. (Open records enable you to see and read everything in your personnel or placement file. Confidential records are closed to you, open to placement or other employment officials.)

Because open records can occasionally lead to lawsuits over unfavorable evaluations, telephone inquiries are becoming increasingly popular. Indeed, written recommendations and references have lost their impact on most would-be employers. They are often discounted as honest appraisals of performance.

Traditionally the recommendation consists of (1) the reason for the letter, (2) duties or knowledge of the applicant, (3) applicant's qualifications, and (4) the author's recommendations. Tone is important; it always conveys more than the actual words would indicate.

Some organizations supply forms; others request individually written letters. Writer or requester, let your conscience be your guide.

Here is an example of a recommendation.

Reason for the letter

Rick Smith, a former employee of mine, has asked me to write you.

Duties of applicant

Rick worked for me for three years, during the summers of 1977 to 1980. He washed floors and windows, took care of the garden, made deliveries and pickups, typed manuscripts. In short, he did whatever we needed during his summer vacations from the University of Southern California.

Knowledge of applicant

We depended on him and he never let us down. He was prompt, cheerful, and courteous, always keeping his word. He became one of the family.

Qualifications

With graduation, he's looking for a full-time position in accounting. As a straight A student in accounting, obviously he is qualified. As a person, he has our unconditional endorsement.

Recommendation

Our loss will be your gain. We congratulate you on this opportunity to hire Rick Smith.

Here is an example of a reference.

    Rick Smith worked for us as a houseboy
during his summer vacations from the University of Southern California from June 1977
to September 1980.

    He performed his duties satisfactorily.   *Objective report*

TRANSMITTALS

Officially, a *letter of transmittal* accompanies a formal or semi-formal document (Figure 9–7). This letter is sent to (1) the person(s) who authorized research or (2) the person(s) expected to act upon the findings. Although associated with reports (Chapter 13) as the "primary formal document," a transmittal is far more versatile. It may be used as

A letter of transmittal explains or justifies accompanying documents.

- an introductory letter, explaining how or why a report originated
- a cover letter serving as official proof of report completion—date requested, date submitted
- a first page justifying a questionnaire
- an insider's letter evaluating accompanied material
- a summary or abstract of a study

    Within a company, use (if available) a special transmittal stamp or printed form with spaces for the required information, or clip a personal memo to the document. Better yet, write a short report in memo form (see Chapter 13).

    Sometimes, however, substantial bid or proposal specifications or government documents require formal letters of transmittal.

ANNOUNCEMENTS

Letters and memos frequently contain information concerning company policy, meetings, actions, or job openings. A memo tacked to a bulletin board or a memo sent to a client may be overlooked; on the other hand, it may do the job. A letter, however, receives more attention because it indicates a personal concern or connection. For important announcements that need broad distribution, use a form letter (Figure 9–8).

Important announcements require an information letter.

2423 Dodge Street
Omaha 2, Nebraska
Telephone 402-346-7600

Northern
Natural
Gas Company

November 6, 19

<u>David K. Johnson's Report</u>
DHM – 605 – 64

W. Paul Jones
Professor of English
Iowa State University
Ames, Iowa

Dear Professor Jones:

I am enclosing the report by Mr. David K. Johnson. This report has
been reviewed by our Electrical Engineers and minor notations have
been made in case you desire to include these slight modifications.

This material is hereby released for publication and the use for
which you have requested it. I am quite pleased that we were able
to contribute to your efforts in this minor way. However, I wish to
again apologize for the delay which we encountered in reviewing
this material. Our work load has been very severe for the past few
months.

In the event that you, or any of the other faculty members at Iowa
State, can find a means by which Northern can aid in your excellent
efforts in any field of your endeavors, we will be most happy to
contribute. I hope that our delay in returning this material has not
caused you any scheduling difficulties.

Yours very truly,

D. H. McGee, Director
Design Department

bjk

Enclosure

Figure 9–7: Letter of Transmittal

Arizona State University/Tempe, Arizona 85281

An Equal Opportunity/Affirmative Action Employer

Announcement of Vacancy

COLLEGE:	College of Business Administration
DEPARTMENT:	Department of Administrative Services
POSITION AVAILABLE: ☒ FACULTY ☐ STAFF ☐ GRAD STUDENT	Assistant Professor of Administrative Services (Position Available August, 1981)
QUALIFICATIONS:	Ph.D. or appropriate doctor's degree with specific qualifications to teach and to conduct research in all areas of <u>Business Communication</u>.
SALARY:	Open
APPLICATION DEADLINE:	January 31, 1981

APPLICATION PROCEDURE:	Write to: Professor Lohnie J. Boggs, Chairman
	         Department of Administrative Services
	         College of Business Administration
	         Arizona State University
	         Tempe, AZ 85281

GENERAL INFORMATION:	The Department of Administrative Services includes the areas of Elements of the Business Enterprise, Small Business Management, Business Communication, Report Writing and Research, Business Law, Office Administration and Business Education. In cooperation with several areas, the Department is involved in the awarding of the MA, MBA, PhD, DBA and EdD degrees with concentrations in Business Education. We are particularly interested in strengthening the business writing area in our graduate programs.

Form PER 20 (REV 7/77) (Previous editions are not to be used)

Figure 9–8: Letter of Announcement

CLAIMS AND COMPLAINTS

Suppliers—from airlines to manufacturers—want to know when something is wrong with a product, order, or service. You are usually protected by printed warranties, guarantees, and the agents' desire for repeat business through good will.

When your claim seems reasonable and justified, write a letter in the information pattern (Figure 9–9). Address it to the president of the company or to the designated office for claims. You can phone the company's consumer affairs or customer relations department, using a toll-free number if available, but they will still need hard copy.

Before you begin to write, collect *all* the specific details and cool down. Your thinking will be better organized if you are calm and objective. Begin with an explanation of the problem, possibly using a subject line. Tell what happened—refer to the five Ws (who, what, when, where, why) and one H (how). Include as needed:

- dates—purchase, problem, flight, contact
- numbers—serial, model, flight, credit-card, phone
- names—personnel involved (or description)
- copies—tickets, receipts, bills, itemized expenses
- photographs—before and after
- product sample—visual proof
- personal details to stimulate interest.

Close with an explanation of the action you desire (repair, replacement, refund) and your name, address, and phone number to ensure a reply. Always remember tone and the "you" viewpoint. Be considerate; write as you would receive.

To show the importance you attach to the claim, you may want to send your letter registered mail, return-receipt-requested. You will receive an immediate, official record and later a signed postal card—proof that your message was received. This approach should bring results. However, sometimes it is necessary to be more persuasive. If there is no response within two or three weeks, you may want to write again or phone the company president. Or you can omit that step and write or phone a government or trade agency (see box). Be sure to include copies of everything you sent in the original claim *plus* a cover letter (transmittal) updating the complaint.

When you take the time to write, you are helping yourself and others. But watch your timing—make the claim immediately after

April 10, 1981

Customer Service
Unique Stationery Co.
75 W. Cienega Blvd.
San Jacinto, CA 00000

Subject: Transposed Numbers

I use your service frequently, for you do such an excellent
job and your prices are competitive. However, I'm enclosing
a recent card order, received April 8.

Please check the original copy for the apartment number. I
moved recently, after ten years--making old cards and previously ordered stationery obsolete. The new address on
cards and your courtesy gift of stickers should be

                    3650 Lynn, #701

The apartment numbers were transposed in printing. (I enclose
a copy of the original order, January 8.)

Should I return the order and await reprinting? Or should I
keep the present order and expect a new one? The stickers,
too, should be corrected.

I'd appreciate your adjustment.

Cordially,

Jean Lafitte
3650 Lynn, #701
Philadelphia, PA 00000

Enclosures

Problem identified
Sample enclosed
Date

Personal details
stimulate interest

Specific detail
Problem

Problem; action expected

Legible, complete address

Figure 9–9: Letter of Claim or Complaint

GOT A GRIPE? HERE'S WHERE TO WRITE*

WASHINGTON (UPI)—Dear readers:

Go now to the place where you keep your scissors. Then cut this out.

The following list of names, addresses, and phone numbers is by no means complete, nor does it constitute an endorsement of any of those mentioned. But we hope it will help you deal with some of the most common consumer problems.

Some sources have toll-free hotlines to call. For others, a letter might be the best bet.

—You've just opened a can of tuna and suspect you got catfood. The Food and Drug Administration has offices in more than 100 cities that will accept consumer complaints about food safety. Check your telephone directory or write the FDA, 5600 Fishers Lane, Rockville, Md., 20852.

—Your new deodorant gave you a rash or the shampoo you've been using burned your scalp. The FDA again, but this time write Heinz J. Eiermann, director, division of cosmetics technology, FDA, 200 C St. SW, Washington D.C., 20204.

—Your electric skillet shocked you and that new toy looks as if it might cut your two-year-old. Call the Consumer Product Safety Commission free at (800) 638-2666 (Maryland residents, 800-492-3927).

—You've just moved and the moving company lost Aunt Sarah's breakfront. Or you took the train to Denver and got there a day late. The Interstate Commerce Commission has a free hotline, (800) 424-9312. Or write the Office of Communications and Consumer Affairs, ICC, Room 1211, Washington, D.C. 20423.

Amtrak also has a complaint address: The Adequacy of Service Bureau, Amtrak, 955 L'Enfant Plaza North, SW, Washington, D.C. 20024. Amtrak advises sending a copy of your complaint to the ICC address preceding.

—You showed up at the airport for the flight to Toledo but the plane was overbooked. You weren't certain what your rights were or how much money they owed you. Jack Yohe is the Civil Aeronautics Board consumer representative for service complaints about air travel. Write him at the CAB, 1875 Connecticut Ave. NW, Washington, D.C. 20428. Or call (202) 673-5158).

—That double widget, wingbacked screwdriver you ordered six months ago still hasn't come and the company won't answer your letters. Write Thomas Chadwick, consumer advocate, U.S. Postal Service, Washington, D.C. 20260.

—The landlord was willing to rent you the apartment but turned you down. You think he's guilty of discrimination on the basis of race, sex, or marital status. Try the Department of Housing and Urban Development, assistant secretary for fair housing and equal opportunity, 451 7th St. SW, Washington, D.C. 20410. The free hotline, (800) 424-8590.

—You suspect you've been defrauded as a public-housing tenant or in a deal involving an FHA backed mortgage. Try HUD again, this time Gwendolyn King, division of consumer complaints, HUD, 451 7th St. SW Washington, D.C. 20410. Or call (202) 755-5353.

—You've just bought some vacation property in another state and find out it's underwater. HUD again, this time Allen Kappeler, director of the Office of Interstate Land Sales and Registration, HUD, 451 7th St. SW, Washington, D.C., 20410. Or call (202) 755-5860.

—The family car lost its steering and you think there's a safety defect. Make a toll-free call to the

---

*Individual names may change but often offices and addresses are valid. For a more complete listing of government agencies and trade organizations, consult your local library.

National Highway Traffic Safety Administration, (800) 424-9393, or write the Office of Public Affairs and Consumer Services, NHTSA, 400 7th St. SW, Washington, D.C. 20590.

　—Your Social Security check didn't arrive or you don't think you're getting what you deserve. Check with your district Social Security office.

　—The Grade A large eggs look smaller than they should or the chicken at the poultry counter looks suspect. Try Carol Foreman, assistant secretary for food and consumer services, Agriculture Department, 14th St. and Independence Ave. SW, Washington, D.C. 20250.

　—And, of course, you can always write Buyer's Billboard, UPI, 315 National Press Bldg., Washington, D.C. 20045. We'll try to get your consumer complaint or suggestion into the right hands.

the occurrence, while the details are fresh and clear. Whether personal or organizational, prompt claims usually result in prompt adjustments. (The Federal Truth in Lending Act requires prompt correction of billing mistakes. See Appendix D.)

Here are some additional suggestions.

1. Always check the *invoice* mailed earlier or accompanying merchandise.
2. Always check the *original order;* the mistake may be yours.
3. Always read the fine print, the agreement on order forms.
4. Always write or phone—honest errors occur.
5. Always advise local or regional Better Business Bureaus of serious problems.
6. Always be persistent—consult authorities, keep the claim active until settled satisfactorily.

ADJUSTMENTS

Prompt *adjustments* increase good will and company loyalty. Of course, each claim must be investigated thoroughly before an adjustment is offered; the claimant is not always right.

　But satisfied customers increase profits; satisfied employees increase productivity. Enlightened administrators try to keep everyone happy (a difficult task) and encourage open lines of communication.

　Internally, adjustments take place through face-to-face encounters with managers and supervisors and through confidential open lines (see page 46). When these fail, official grievance procedures take over, differing from company to company, organization to organization.

In the following example, a confidential complaint receives a courteous, complete, prompt response, probably adjusting an employee's attitude.

Confidential complaint

Problem (specific details withheld from publication)

Recently, my pay statement was handed to me by my supervisor, who stood in front of me and examined it. After he checked it out, he commented on how well I was doing and how everyone was making more than he was.

Personal details stimulate interest

Action desired

I resent this invasion of my privacy. My pay is my business. I think our pay shold be distributed in individual envelopes to protect our privacy. In addition, it would help avoid any resentment that may develop because of the differences.

Published response, signed by executive vice president

Personnel Information Center, Employee Services and Systems, and Equipment Research are at present reprogramming our pay system. A feature of the new system will be a Statement of Earnings in a self-enclosed envelope.

Immediate solution

Courteous, empathetic response

This will ensure you the privacy mentioned. As yet, we do not have a definite conversion date for the new system.

Compromise

Until our new system is implemented, I would encourage you to discuss your supervisor's remarks with your manager, department head, or an employee relations officer.

Externally, adjustments may take place through face-to-face meetings, phone calls, or letters. When these fail, official grievance procedures take over.

To forestall the expense and unpleasantness of legal actions and to increase good will, administrators favor adjustments. Adjustment letters follow the information pattern and should be signed by a high-ranking official. (The signature signifies that the claim or complaint is taken seriously.) Usually these letters admit the problem, explain the situation, and take action. Or the action/solution may appear in the first paragraph, followed by an explanation and courteous close.

Rubber stamps with fill-in blanks and responses written at the bottom of claim letters save time but annoy and irritate the claimant. The *personal touch* is important. Even the personalized form letter can sound like one caring human being responding to another.

> Enclosed with this letter is a replacement Land Over Fire Truck, No. 57, together with one of our new model toy cars, a gift to you.

Adjustment

> We appreciate your writing us about your experience with plastic in our products. When zinc increased in price last year, a few models were constructed of plastic.

Problem

> Fortunately this period is past, and you will note from our new releases that all models are now in zinc.

Explanation

>   With kind regards,

CREDIT

From birth to death, each of us is involved in some way with *credit*. Less than 15 percent of American business consists of cash transactions—with the percentage steadily shrinking.

Whether requesting, granting, or refusing credit, know the law and provide complete information.

As an individual or as a representative of an organization, you may find it necessary to write a letter

- requesting credit or an application form (loan companies prefer in-person requests)
- acknowledging a credit application
- requesting further information
- requesting recommendations, confirming references
- giving recommendations
- acknowledging recommendations and references
- granting credit, welcoming a client, explaining conditions, expressing appreciation for an order
- refusing credit, explaining conditions, maintaining good will
- soliciting further credit business

To an individual seeking credit, the term means "buy now, pay later." To a business person, granting credit involves deciding on an individual's ability and willingness to pay at a future specified time.

In a community where you are known, you may take credit for granted. You may have an "open account" without application, on a person-to-person basis.

Application

Under ordinary circumstances, you will have to apply for credit. Application for credit usually consists of filling out a company-supplied form (Figure 9–10). Such forms are readily available— just ask. The information requested differs from company to company but usually includes

- name, address, telephone number
- annual earnings
- employment history (job stability)
- personal references
- business references
- credit record
- housing (residential stability)

Some companies and banks may require even more personal, in-depth disclosures, but they are now being limited by law.

A credit manager checks the application for credit against computer printout, information acquired by phone from a national network of credit bureaus, and personal references or responses to mail inquiries.

The Associated Credit Bureaus of America have millions of individual files. Payment histories are a matter of record and will determine one's ability to get future credit. Credit records, for example, show a bankruptcy for up to 14 years.

For credit information on businesses, Dun and Bradstreet continues as the main source. Other reliable sources are credit, trade, and industry associations. In addition, The Credit Research Foundation traces debt trends for corporations.

Without a regular job, income, or credit history, individuals find it difficult to obtain credit. Thus it is a good idea to formally *establish* credit early, perhaps while still living at home, before you actually need the money.

Women, particularly married women, may want to open at least one account under their own name in order to establish a *personal* credit record. And remember that consumer transactions are open to your inspection under the Fair Credit Reporting Act. If rejected for credit, you can now request an explanation and

BUYER'S STATEMENT (For Dealer Use)	SOURCE	SELLER'S NAME					BUYER'S DR. LIC. NO.		STATE	DATE

TO BE COMPLETED BY DEALER	TOTAL PURCHASE $	DN. PMT. CASH $	TRADE-IN $	NET BALANCE $	TERMS @	MERCHANDISE

IF MARRIED, YOU HAVE THE RIGHT TO APPLY FOR CREDIT SEPARATELY FROM OR JOINTLY WITH YOUR SPOUSE ☐ MARRIED ☐ UNMARRIED

I APPLY FOR ☐ JOINT CREDIT WITH MY SPOUSE ☐ INDIVIDUAL CREDIT IN MY NAME ONLY ☐ SEPARATED

NAME — LAST	FIRST	M.I.	TITLE (OPTIONAL)	AGE	BIRTHDATE	CO-BUYER (SPOUSE) LAST NAME IF DIFFERENT FIRST M.I.	COBUYER'S BIRTHDATE	NO. DEP.

DO YOU HAVE CREDIT ESTABLISHED IN ANY OTHER NAME? _____ IF YES, IN WHAT NAME? _____

ADDRESS — NUMBER	STREET	APT. #	CITY	STATE	ZIP	HOW LONG YR. MO.	☐ HOME PHONE ☐ N/B	1.

RENT BUY/OWN ☐ FURN ☐ HOME ☐ UNFURN ☐ MOBILE HOME ☐ OTHER	LANDLORD OR MORTGAGE HOLDER AND ADDRESS	RENT OR 1ST. MTG. PMT (INCL. TAXES & INS.) $	BAL. OWED 1ST. MTG. $	2.
	2ND. MORTGAGE HOLDER AND ADDRESS	2ND. MTG. PMT. $	BAL. OWED 2ND. MTG. $	3.

PREVIOUS ADDRESS (IF LESS THAN 5 YEARS AT PRESENT ADDRESS)	HOW LONG YR MO.	NO. YRS. CONT. RES. IN AREA YRS.	BUYER'S EST. VALUE OF PROPERTY $	4.

BUYER EMPLOYED BY	ADDRESS OR LOCATION	HOW LONG YR. MO.	SOCIAL SECURITY NO. — —	5.

SUPERIOR	DEPT. #	BADGE #	PHONE NO.	EXT.	OCCUPATION	PAYDAY	MONTHLY TAKE HOME PAY $	6.

CO-BUYER EMPLOYED BY	PHONE NO.	EXT.	OCCUPATION	HOW LONG YR. MO.	MONTHLY TAKE HOME PAY $	7.

OTHER INCOME — EXPLAIN (IF INCOME IS FROM ALIMONY OR CHILD SUPPORT, SEE IMPORTANT INFORMATION BELOW)*	ALL OTHER MONTHLY NET INC. $	8.

BUYER'S PREVIOUS EMPLOYER	OCCUPATION	HOW LONG YR. MO.	TOTAL NET INCOME $	9.

CO-BUYER'S PREVIOUS EMPLOYER	OCCUPATION	HOW LONG YR. MO.	CO-BUYER'S SOC. SEC. NO.	10.

YR. AUTO	MAKE	MODEL	☐ PAID FOR ☐ FINANCED	YR AUTO	MAKE	MODEL	☐ PAID FOR ☐ FINANCED

BANK OR SAV. & LOAN CO. AND ADDRESS	☐ CHECKING ☐ SAVINGS ☐ LOAN

LIST CREDIT REFERENCES OF BANKS, FINANCE COMPANIES, DEPT. STORES & MAJOR CREDIT CARDS (OPEN OR CLSD WITHIN LAST 2 YRS.)

	NAME OF CREDITOR OR COMPANY	ADDRESS OR LOCATION	ITEM OR SECURITY	OPEN	CLSD.	PAYMENT	BALANCE
1.							
2.							
3.							
4.							
MAJOR CREDIT CARD OR OTHER REFERENCE 5.							
DEPT. STORE OR OTHER REFERENCE 6.							
FINANCE CO. OR OTHER REFERENCE 7.							

LIST TWO RELATIVES AND ONE FRIEND NOT LIVING WITH BUYER

NAME	ADDRESS	RELATIONSHIP

FOR OFFICE USE ONLY	ACCOUNT NO.	R-N	DATE PURCH.	TERMS (# MOS.)	1ST. PMT. DUE	DLR. CODE	DLR. RATE	MAX. LN.	DATE BOOK SENT

* IMPORTANT INFORMATION — INCOME FROM ALIMONY, CHILD SUPPORT OR MAINTENANCE PAYMENTS NEED NOT BE REVEALED IF YOU DO NOT CHOOSE TO RELY UPON SUCH INOME IN APPLYING FOR CREDIT.

00-1372 (REV. 12-78)

Figure 9–10: Typical Application for Retail Consumer Credit

review company findings. Business corporation transactions remain confidential.

Credit is extended on the basis of point systems closely supervised by federal regulation. Taken into account are the four Cs:

- character—personal honesty, reliability, activity
- capacity—income, ability to work, payment of debts, length of time with same employer
- capital—ownership of "real" property—home, car, land, cash, securities, jewelry
- conditions—length of time at a specific address, regularity in payments of utilities, whether or not you have a phone, the general or specific business climate

Letters and phone calls verify the information on the application form. ("Your application is being processed.")

With an established credit rating, your first contact could be a brief letter *requesting credit or an application form.*

Direct beginning

Please send me a credit application form and open an account for us with the enclosed order.

Billing name, address

John L. Lacey
Lacey Furniture Interiors
3600 N. Granite Reef
Houston, Texas 77052

We are listed in Dun and Bradstreet and have been at this location for fifteen years. We have accounts with, among others, the following furniture manufacturers:

Reference sources

A. J. Dunbear, Inc.
Worthington, Indiana 47471

C. W. Thomanson, Inc.
High Point, North Carolina 27261

Whittier, Inc.
621 Le Fourneau
New Orleans, LA 70140

Summary

We would appreciate your filling this order promptly on a credit basis, your usual terms.

Acknowledgments, recommendations, and references have already been discussed. Details vary, but all follow the information pattern.

Request for Further Information

If you expect acceptance from the reader, requests for further in-formation may be equally direct. But be cautious. Recent federal and state laws concerning credit matters prohibit some questions, apply restrictions regarding the release of information, confuse the inexperienced. Protect yourself and your company by using a le-gally approved request form (Figure 9–11).

`    Thank you for requesting a charge account at Donnelsons.`	*Direct beginning*
`    Just fill out and mail the enclosed form, a convenience for both of us.  Processing takes a very short time when you send the needed information.`	*Request for information* *Explanation*
`    In the meantime, you'll want to see the Fall Collection, arriving daily from world fashion centers.  Your charge account can be your pass-port to the many services we offer preferred customers.`	*Sales promotion, good will*

Always enclose a stamped, self-addressed envelope to speed the response, or use multipage stationery, enabling the receiver and you to have copies of both messages.

Explanation of Terms and Conditions

Terms and conditions are important to you. As a consumer, you want to know all the terms or conditions involved in receiving credit. As a business person, you are by law required to disclose such details when *granting credit.*

Explaining finance charges and billing procedures can be an opportunity for creating good will. For a new customer, enclose detailed information in a letter of acknowledgment. A small bro-chure can be a handy reference and reminder. It is equally useful for established customers when rates change. And rates do change.

Finance charges must include the *monthly* and *annual* per-centage rate and computation method. (These differ from state to state.) By referring to terms positively, you can encourage pur-chases and prompt payments.

`    Thank you for opening a Pytton Flexible Charge Account.  You will find your charge plate`	*Direct beginning*

Established 1976

LUMBERMENS CREDIT ASSOCIATION INC.

The nation-wide specialized credit reporting agency serving the
lumber, woodworking and related industries.

**55 EAST JACKSON BLVD.
CHICAGO, ILLINOIS 60604**

This inquiry pertains to *business* transactions—*not* consumer transactions. It
does not come within the scope of the
Fair Credit Reporting Act.

Gentlemen: _____ has given us your company as a credit reference, and we would appreciate having your answer to each question below so we may form a correct idea of their financial standing.

Yours very truly,

LUMBERMENS CREDIT ASSOCIATION INC.

Account #_____

It is important that you answer each question fully.

Date account was opened with you? _____	Amount of average balance $ _____
How much do you loan on own paper? $ _____	How much owing you now $ _____
What line of credit do you grant on discounted notes? $ _____	Are loans always met promptly? _____
Have you had to renew or extend maturing notes; if so, when? _____	
Are sales invoices assigned to you? _____	Value of real estate above exemptions $ _____
Do you require judgment notes? _____	Do you require endorser or security on loans? _____
Brief description of the real estate. _____	
What is the reputed net worth? $ _____	Character, habits and business ability? _____
Is the business risk regarded good? _____	

Remarks: (Please supplement above information by giving your opinion regarding financial standing. We shall
be pleased to have the benefit of your analysis of the current position as indicated in the latest
balance sheet.)

_____
_____
_____
_____
_____
_____

Figure 9–11: Typical Inquiry Form for Business Credit Record

enclosed. This plate will instantly identify you as a customer entitled to full charge account privileges.

This account gives you ALL the conveniences and privileges of a regular 30-Day Charge Account, PLUS important added advantages. When your shopping needs are at a peak, for instance during the Christmas season, you can, if you wish, budget your payments in accordance with your individual needs.

Explanation in general

Please read thoroughly the enclosed brochure. It will answer any questions you may have.

Explanation in particular in brochure

We look forward to your making frequent use of this account, using any one of our eight locations. Your patronage is sincerely appreciated.

Good-will closing

Consumer credit relations are frequently more personal and involve less money than do business-to-business accounts. Credit card companies offering services to a restricted (by income) clientele are slower to demand payment, more tactful than, for example, record and book clubs that attract men and women of all ages and incomes.

When business is slow or competition particularly strong, some merchants will extend consumer credit without carrying charges, sometimes for as long as 90 days. Technically called an *open account,* this arrangement enables customers to take goods with them on the understanding that they will pay when billed, usually within 30 days.

A more common agreement is the *revolving charge,* an account having a maximum limit and a minimum monthly payment, set by the credit manager. Usually credit plans that allow customers to carry a balance-due for more than a month impose a finance charge. Both the open account and revolving charge are limited to relatively inexpensive items.

Larger and more expensive purchases like refrigerators and automobiles are also sold on *installment contracts.* These contracts require regular payments and use the item itself as security for the debt. If the customer fails to make the payments, the seller (or holder of the contract—for contracts can be turned over to a third party) can repossess the item, sell it at auction, and use the proceeds to pay off the remainder of the debt. Rates on installment contracts vary widely; sometimes they are as much as 42 percent. Figure 9–12 is a form letter indicating terms of credit.

BUILDING MATERIALS ... LUMBER & COAL

OPERATING RETAIL YARDS
IN IOWA & SOUTH DAKOTA

GENERAL OFFICE
HAWARDEN, IOWA

DEAR CUSTOMER:

Effective November 1, 19   , the **FINANCE CHARGE** on a balance more than 30 days old will be raised to   % per month (which is an **ANNUAL PERCENTAGE RATE OF**   %) on $500.00 or less, and   % per month (which is an **ANNUAL PERCENTAGE RATE OF**   ) on the amount in excess of $500.00.

THANK YOU for the opportunity to serve you as a valued **CHARGE CUSTOMER.**

Sincerely

SCHOENEMAN BROS. COMPANY

Figure 9-12: Terms of Credit

Not all credit cards are alike, and it is important to know the difference to get the most for one's money. There are single-purpose cards issued by oil companies, motel chains, car-rental agencies, others. You pay nothing for them and they allow you to charge merchandise or services, paying when billed. Again, overdue payments are charged interest. Specialty cards like Diners Club, Carte Blanche, and American Express require a yearly fee. Card holders are billed within 30 to 60 days and are expected to pay on receipt of the bill.

Banks issue MasterCard, Visa, and other credit cards. These cards are used in place of cash at participating businesses. The merchants turn in the charge slips, usually to a central collection bureau, and the customer receives a statement. If the bill is paid within the time specified—usually 25 days—the use of the credit card may be free. After that a service charge is levied. Today, most banks charge an annual fee plus interest on the unpaid balance and, sometimes, a late payment penalty.

Banks, credit unions, savings and loan associations, small loan or finance companies, and insurance companies are prime lenders of lump-sum cash. Interest rates vary from the low 5 percent per year on a life insurance policy with cash value, to the high of up to 36 percent a year for a small loan company. One can borrow up to 95 percent of the cash value of an insurance policy, reducing the coverage by that amount until the debt is repaid. Insurance companies will not call in a loan as long as the interest payments are maintained.

Credit relations between companies are extremely sensitive to economic conditions. Some of the very largest companies are frequently the slowest to pay, thus forcing their smaller and more vulnerable suppliers to finance them. As a result, the suppliers may be forced to pressure their accounts for payment, or may even be pushed into bankruptcy. Conditions change so quickly—including interest rates for borrowing money—that in spite of in-depth investigation, there is never an absolute indicator of whether a firm will always be solvent.

Additional terms must be explained when granting business credit. For example, merchandise is discounted to dealers at varying percentages—depending on the product, condition of delivery, initial cost. This discount is permissible only if the bill is paid within a prearranged time from the date on the invoice.

Invoices are mailed when merchandise leaves a factory. Whether or not the product has arrived, the purchaser must pay as of the prearranged date to qualify for the discount. Beyond that date, the total amount (with no discount) is also due within a specified time before finance charges apply. These terms appear on the invoice as follows:

$$5/10, \text{N}/30$$

This means "There is a discount of 5 percent if the bill is paid within 10 days of the invoice date. The total amount (N = Net) is due within 30 days."

Reputable dealers reevaluate and update their financial position regularly. The statement is usually the basis for credit evaluation.

Dear Mr. Lacey:

Direct beginning, credit granted

Your order of July 25 was shipped by ABC Fast Freight today. You should receive the six recliners by the first of next week.

Basis for credit

You are to be congratulated on your excellent financial record. Your references were unanimous in praising your business practices.

Terms

Our usual terms are 2/10, N/30. We will bill you the tenth of each month for goods purchased the previous month. Payments within ten days of the date of an invoice entitle you to a two percent discount. (Detailed finance charges enclosed.)

Resale

You'll find the recliners popular with your customers. The attractive and sturdy fabrics, the heavy-duty construction, and the reasonable suggested selling price have attracted wide attention. National advertising has helped establish our trade name--a fact you'll appreciate.

Resale

Let us know as soon as you wish to reorder. Just use the phone and our toll-free number.

Good will—credit firmly established

We look forward to a mutually beneficial association.

Credit limits for customers or dealers are rarely indicated. When a limit is necessary, the writer states it in *positive terms*.

...For the first six months you may use your newly opened account for charge purchases up to a total of $750.

```
    For additional credit, just talk over your
needs with C.W. Parker, Customer Consultant,
fourth-floor Annex.  We are sure you will find
just the program you want.
```

You should be aware that credit terms and limits are flexible—restricted only by federal and state usury laws. For example, banks, savings and loans, finance companies, and credit unions offer many programs, a surprising variety based on the four Cs: character, capacity, capital, conditions.

In some agricultural areas, bills may not be due until after harvest. In some locations, real estate may be purchased on contract with moderate down payments and "balloons." (A "balloon" enables the buyer and seller to renegotiate terms up or down or require refinancing after a certain number of years.) Some securities can be purchased on "margin"—a down payment plus interest on the balance.

Fascinating and sometimes frightening, the credit picture changes almost daily, responding to local, national, and international events and conditions.

Letters of Credit

Letters of credit have long been used instead of money in international trade. Traditionally, exporters have found that this means of obtaining payment usually eliminates certain risks.

The traditional letters of credit involve both the importer's and exporter's banks and require a great number of documents before payment: bills of lading, commercial and consular invoices, insurance forms, trucker's receipts, and so on (Figure 9–13).

To simplify the procedure, an *instant letter of credit* or *international commercial credit card* is now available. Qualified holders may now ship with a single document, a payment voucher, similar to papers used in an individual's MasterCard transaction. The commercial credit card takes care of one or more payments of the following:

- merchandise
- transportation—point to point
- insurance—warehouse to warehouse
- brokers' fees
- bank charges
- bureau of customs
- supplier invoices

Figure 9–13:
Letter of Credit

IB 013

IOWA-DES MOINES NATIONAL BANK
Seventh and Walnut Street
Des Moines, Iowa 50304

Dirección cablegráfica Adresse télégraphique Cable address **IADESMBANK**	Nos. de télex Nos. de telex Telex number 478-474	Lugar y fecha de expedición Lieu d'émission et date Place and date of issue Des Moines, Iowa May 10, 19--

Crédito Documentario/Crédit Documentaire/Documentary Credit Irrévocable	Número de crédito / Numéro du crédit/Credit number del banco emisor / Numéro de la banque émettrice of issuing bank **1208** del banco avisador de la banque notificatrice of advising bank

Banco avisador / Banque notificatrice / Advising bank Banco Nacional, S.A. Av. Revolucion 12 Buenos Aires, Argentina	Ordenante / Donneur d'ordre / Applicant American Imports, Ltd. 1417 So. 126th Des Moines, Iowa 50000

Beneficiario / Bénéficiaire / Beneficiary Industria Agricola, S.A. P.O. Box 49-A Buenos Aires, Argentina	Importe / Montant / Amount US$4,176.80 (United States Dollars Four Thousand one hundred seventy-six and 80/100)
	Vencimiento / Validité / Expiry Fecha / Date / Date October 30, 19--
Estimado(s) Señor(es): / M / Dear Sir(s),	para negociación en pour négociation a' for negotiation in Argentina

Por la presente expedimos este crédito documentario a su favor el cual es disponible mediante negociación de su giro
Nous émetions en votre faveur ce crédit documentaire qui est utilisable par négociation de votre traite ó
We hereby issue in your favour this documentary credit which is available by negotiation of your draft at   sight

a cargo de
tirée sur
drawn on Iowa-Des Moines National Bank, Des Moines, Iowa

mostrando la cláusula: "Girado al amparo del crédito documentario No.   de (nombre del banco emisor)"
et portant la mention: "Tirée en vertu du crédit documentaire No.   de (nom de la banque émettrice)"
bearing the clause: "Drawn under documentary credit No.   **1208**   of (name of issuing bank)"

acompañando los siguientes documentos:
accompagnés des documents suivants:
accompanied by the following documents:

1. Full set of clean on board ocean bills of lading XXXXXXXXXXX consigned to American Imports, Ltd., 1417 So. 126th, Des Moines, Iowa 50000, marked "freight collect" and

   "Notify SS Brown Co., Box F, San Francisco, California."

2. Signed commercial invoice in   triplicate   covering: 14 spare parts kits for XG7 Tractor, F.O.B. Vessel any Argentine port.

3. Certificate of Origin in triplicate, if required.
4. Certificate of Origin Form A in duplicate, if required.

5. Special customs invoice in duplicate.
6. Packing list in duplicate.
   Insurance covered by XXXXXXXXX applicant.

OTHER CONDITIONS:
A. Shipments must be effected on or prior to September 15, 19--.

Expedición /Embarque de Expédition /Embarquement de Despatch /Shipment from Argentina a 6 to San Francisco, California	Embarques parciales Expéditions partielles Partial shipments Permitted.	Transbordos Transbordements Transhipments

Condiciones especiales:
Conditions spéciales:
Special conditions: All bank fees outside the United States are for the account of the beneficiary.

Por la presente nos comprometemos con los girados y/o tenedores de buena fe que los giros emitidos y negociados de conformidad con los términos de este crédito serán debidamente honrados a su presentación y que los giros aceptados dentro de los términos de este crédito serán debidamente honrados a su vencimiento. El importe de cada giro debe ser endosado al reverso de este crédito por el banco negociador.
Nous garantissons aux tireurs et/ou porteurs de bonne foi que les traites émises et négociées en conformité avec les termes de ce crédit seront dûment honorées à présentation et que les traites acceptées conformément aux termes de ce crédit seront dûment honorées à leur échéance. Le montant de chaque traite doit être inscrit au verso de ce crédit par la banque négociatrice.
We hereby engage with drawers and/or bona fide holders that drafts drawn and negotiated in conformity with the terms of this credit will be duly honoured on presentation and that drafts accepted within the terms of this credit will be duly honoured at maturity. The amounts of each draft must be endorsed on the reverse of this credit by the negotiating bank.

Suyos atentamente / Vos dévoués / Yours faithfully,
Iowa - Des Moines National Bank

Nombre y firma del banco emisor:
Nom et signature de la banque émettrice:
Name and signature of the issuing bank.

Unless otherwise stated, the negotiating bank is to forward all original and duplicate documents to us by one registered airmail.

Notificación del banco avisador
Indications de la banque notificatrice
Advising bank's notification

Lugar, fecha, nombre y firma del banco avisador.
Lieu, date, nom et signature de la banque notificatrice.
Place, date, name and signature of the advising bank.

ESTE CRÉDITO ESTA SUJETO A LAS REGLAS Y USOS UNIFORMES RELATIVOS A LOS CREDITOS DOCUMENTARIOS (REVISION 1974) DE LA CAMARA INTERNACIONAL DE COMERCIO (PUBLICACION #290) SAUF STIPULATIONS PARTICULIERES EXPRESSEMENT DEFINES, CE CREDIT DOCUMENTAIRE EST SOUMIS AUX "REGLES ET USANCES UNIFORMES RELATIVES AUX CREDITS DOCUMENTAIRES" (REVISION 1974) CHAMBRE DE COMMERCE INTERNATIONALE (PUBLICACION #290). EXCEPT SO FAR AS OTHERWISE EXPRESSLY STATED, THIS DOCUMENTARY CREDIT IS SUBJECT TO THE "UNIFORM CUSTOMS AND PRACTICE FOR DOCUMENTARY CREDITS" (1974 REVISION) INTERNATIONAL CHAMBER OF COMMERCE (PUBLICATION #290).

Personal letters of credit may be issued by an individual's bank as a safeguard against one's running out of money while traveling. Today, however, credit cards have worldwide acceptance.

ASSIGNMENT: INFORMATION LETTERS

Write and bring to your in-service training session letters in the information pattern for at least two of the following topics. Make each letter complete by supplying all letter parts. Attach a blank sheet of paper to each letter for others' comments. Then swap them with your colleagues. Each of you write down your comments and suggestions, basing your judgments on the following criteria: analysis of audience, content, organization, style, correctness, and neatness.

Topics

1. Inquiry letter about a product advertised in a magazine.
2. Letter of reply from the provider of the service inquired about in the letter in Figure 9–2.
3. Complimentary letter on a newsworthy accomplishment.
4. Formal letter of transmittal accompanying a report.
5. Order letter ordering at least five separate items, including all details for efficient delivery.
6. Adjustment letter asking for adjustment of your earlier order— the shipper was at fault.
7. A cordial response to the letter in Figure 9–9.
8. Application for credit in order to buy winter clothing (or sports equipment, farm supplies).
9. Acknowledgment of a request for credit and explanation of your credit terms.
10. Information letter informing clients of a change in your organization's procedures (collections, repair services, and so on).

FURTHER READING

Cass, Angelica. *Letters for Everyday Use.* NY: Monarch, 1981.

Christopher, Martin et al., *Customer Service and Distribution Strategy.* New York: Halsted, 1979.

Director's and Officer's Complete Letter Book, 23rd ed. Englewood Cliffs, NJ: Prentice-Hall, 1981.

Feldman, Laurence P. *Consumer Protection: Problems and Prospects,* 2nd ed. Ann Arbor, MI: West, 1980.

Foxall, Gordon R. *Consumer Behavior: A Practical Guide.* New York: Halsted, 1980.

Pearsall, Thomas E. and D. H. Cunningham. *How to Write for the World of Work.* New York: Holt, Rinehart and Winston, 1978.

CHAPTER TEN

Refusal Letters

Yet the first bringer of unwelcome news
Hath but a losing office, and his tongue
Sounds ever after as a sullen bell,
Remembered knolling a departing friend.

William Shakespeare
King Henry the Fourth

Most disappointing to receive, most difficult to write are letters of refusal. As the writer of such letters, use the refusal pattern to try to overcome the reader's resistance to the message and, at the same time, to maintain good will. Search for something pleasant or tactful to write to soften bad news. This takes time but shows your sensitivity to the reader and often promotes future business.

Refusal letters require tact and logic.

In general, apply the refusal pattern to any written or oral communication of unpleasant, disappointing, or bad news. Remember the following steps:

1. Soften the refusal with a buffer opening.
2. Follow the buffer with logical reasons.
3. Imply or state the refusal in positive language (see p. 105), avoiding unpleasant words.
4. Offer an alternative if possible.
5. Close pleasantly.

And remember that although refusal situations have much in common, each is also unique in many ways. Respond according to the individual situation.

Types of letters in the refusal pattern include

- refusals of credit
- refusals of adjustment
- delays of orders
- refusals of requests
- refusals of employment

195

CREDIT REFUSALS

The Equal Credit Opportunity Act (ECOA) of 1975 stipulates that a lender can no longer

- refuse credit because of age, sex, marital status
- refuse to grant credit to widows or divorcees
- demand financial information about a spouse when the applicant is individually creditworthy
- refuse a married person credit because of the credit rating of the spouse, unless the application is for a joint account
- refuse to consider alimony and child support as income
- refuse to consider a wife's income when a couple applies for joint credit
- ask about an applicant's birth control practices or childbearing plans
- refuse to consider income from regular part-time employment or retirement benefits
- terminate, revise the terms of, or require reapplication for a credit transaction because of retirement or a change in the borrower's name or marital status
- require a spouse or anyone else to cosign for an unsecured loan if the individual applicant is creditworthy
- refuse to extend or continue credit because age makes one ineligible for credit insurance

When refusing credit, try to offer an alternative and retain good will.

One or more of the four C's (character, capacity, capital, conditions) may dictate refusal of an applicant's credit request. But since many things change with time, credit managers (1) show appreciation for an order, for the application, or for interest in a product; (2) analyze the situation within the law; (3) imply or state the refusal; (4) offer alternatives, if possible, *benefiting the applicant;* (5) close pleasantly, suggesting immediate or future action to promote good will and sales.

Keep in mind several cautions. First of all, watch your language. Remember, some words have unpleasant connotations (see Chapter 6). Make your opening short, warm, but objective. Too hearty an opening may suggest acceptance. Keep your explanation logical, reasonable, and geared to the specific applicant (omit "company policy"). Deemphasize the refusal aspect of your message, using transition words and phrases. Suggest some alternatives in a positive, helpful manner. Alternatives may include buying with cash, earning a discount; decreasing the original order; using C.O.D.; making a sizable down payment; delaying the order temporarily; buying with cash for a stated period to establish credit; using a layaway service, paying as convenient until paid up. (Note the combination here of refusal and selling patterns.) Then close your letter with a hopeful, pleasant tone, building good will.

A Red Carpet Credit Card is certainly worth having on a trip or at home. We appreciate your wanting one as you move to a new job in a new state.	*Buffer—area of agreement, appreciation for application*
Following our usual procedure, we checked the financial references on your application.	*Logical explanation*
Printed on line 3 is the requirement of a minimum income of $7500 from all sources, established to safeguard our members.	*Implied refusal for applicant's benefit*
You should soon qualify for Red Carpet. When you do, please apply again. In the meantime	*Hopeful, pleasant ending*
we invite you to enjoy the enclosed booklet listing regional member restaurants and their specialties.	*Sales promotion/good will*

Bon Appétit!

Here you try to convince the customer of the benefits of buying for cash.

Thank you for applying for a Bonker's credit account. Your request indicates your experience with our merchandise and reputation.	*Buffer—area of agreement*
Each year students from Farwell College, your school, form a good percentage of our local business. They work for Bonker's and with Bonker's. As consumer advisors, they recommend a past credit record as an important basis for new accounts.	*Logical explanation*
Such information as you have given us so far does not meet current credit requirements. But you can easily establish a credit record. Here's how:	*Stated refusal softened by suggestion*
Just use our Personalized Layaway Plan (PLP) for your next purchase. A small deposit plus moderate installments at your convenience will	*Alternative*

```
                         hold your selections.  And as in a
                         regular charge account, there is no
                         finance charge if paid within 30 days!
```

Resale
```
                         With your final payment, we will gladly
                         review your application.  In the meantime, how-
                         ever, you will receive regular announcements of
                         special promotions and services reserved for pre-
                         ferred customers.
```

Sales promotion
```
                         For example, you are invited to take advan-
                         tage of Bonker's annual preschool sale now in
                         progress.  All fall and winter clothing is
                         offered for a full 20% off--until September 1.
```

Pleasant ending
```
                         Come in, see the fresh new merchandise at
                         reasonable prices, and use your PLP.  It's yours
                         alone.
```

Note the use of positive expressions—the reader is told what can be done. The credit refusal is softened by "so far," "current," "gladly review," phrases implying a temporary situation. When you've put together satisfactory sentences and paragraphs, adapt them to particular cases. Professional writers learn from each other; you can do the same.

ADJUSTMENT REFUSALS

Keeping customers and clients satisfied, happy with products and services, develops good will. Thus requests for adjustments usually receive considerable attention, frequently at many levels.

In addition to checking the adjustment request itself, check the writer's credit, paying habits, "return" record, and other buying history with your firm. Whenever possible, whenever justified, make adjustments quickly, cheerfully. It is the infrequent fraudulent or unreasonable request that should be refused. The letter follows the refusal pattern.

Here a request for adjustment concerning an electric range is refused—firmly and reasonably.

Buffer—appreciation for comments (complaint)
```
                         Thank you for your letter about your All-
                         American Range.  I am forwarding your comments
                         to the proper departments involved.
```

Concerning the sensi-temp unit: the more automatic something is, the more chance for something to get out of adjustment. This is the reason we have a one-year warranty on all of our appliances.

Logical explanation

Anything that could possibly be our fault shows up in a short period of time and you are protected.

Resale (range still under warranty)

The service described in your letter comes from persons who do not understand or have never been trained on the operation of our appliances. Mr. Sam Jones has not attended any of our training sessions. Furthermore, parts <u>are</u> always available from our Kansas City office. Functional parts are stocked for most appliances and there should have been no delay in getting them if properly ordered.

Specific response to statements in request for adjustment

I understand that S & P Appliance, Topeka, Kansas, is going to check and finish the repair of your range. I am sure they will have it back in operation shortly. If the range had been purchased from a franchised G.D. Dealer, there would be no labor charge for this work. But since this is not the case, any labor charges are your responsibility.

Further logical explanation

Firm statement of what can be done

Thank you again for your letter. I am sure your All-American will give you many years of satisfactory service.

Hopeful, pleasant ending

The customer is not always right. Thus it is good business to establish adjustment policies governing specific situations in order to protect yourself and your clients. But resist rigidity. Even with an established policy, review each request and judge it holistically.

DELAY OF ORDER

It is disappointing to learn that something ordered has been delayed. But tactful words can turn away wrath, keep the goods sold. The principles illustrated in the following letter apply to most situations of this kind. Your concern is for the customer. The delay is unavoidable. The wait will be worth it.

APPLICATIONS

Buffer—neutral area of agreement	On October 1 you placed an order for a green velvet Lawson couch. At that time we advised you that we expected delivery by November 14.
Explanation—word kept but unexpected occurred	The promised delivery date would normally have provided us with ample time to fill your order. However, we received the couch with slight damage incurred in delivery.
Logical decision	Since we maintain high standards of quality, we reordered your couch on an urgent delivery basis. We have been assured by the manufacturer that it will receive priority attention.
Resale	Incidentally, it may be of some comfort for you to know that your particualr couch has had a 15 percent price increase by the manufacturer. This, of course, will not be applied to you.
Pleasant, hopeful ending	Thank you again for your order and patience. Please know we are doing everthing we can to expedite delivery.

REQUEST REFUSALS

Requests for donations of money can be ignored. After all, it is up to you how you spend your money. Requests for donations of time or effort, however, often require a response. When you are unable to fulfill a request, explain. Simply saying no frustrates and annoys people. A reasonable explanation shows your interest and consideration.

Buffer—appreciation for invitation	I appreciate very much the invitation to speak under your auspices.
Logical explanation	Over the next several months, however, I have several conferences to attend overseas and an overly full schedule of speaking engagements already planned. I find that I must, therefore,
Implied refusal	limit more sharply than I would like the additional engagements that I accept during the remainder of this academic year.
Further explanation	As you will understand, I feel I must concentrate additional activities in the field in

which I have direct responsibilities--international education and cultural affairs.

I am glad you and Mrs. Thomas thought of inviting me even though, regretfully, I cannot accept.

Buffer—thanks for invitation

The same refusal pattern shows up in this letter rejecting a request for free booklets.

Thank you for your nice letter concerning the possibility of mailing various New York Life booklets to a group of educators overseas.

Buffer

As you may know, we receive a great many requests for our materials and we are pleased to make them available when we can. For the present, because of a number of reasons, not the least of which are budgetary considerations, we find we have all we can do to fill the requests that come in from normal channels.

Logical explanation

Implied refusal, possibility of future help

I am sure you understand our position and realize how sorry I am we cannot fulfill your request. Thank you again for thinking of New York Life.

Stated refusal melded with buffer

"FLUSH," OR EMPLOYMENT, REFUSALS

Being turned down for employment hurts—but the hurt is less ego-wounding when the refusal is delivered tactfully:

Thank you again for taking the time to visit with us in Portland. I hope that it was as enjoyable and informative for you as it was for us.

Buffer

Your qualifications have been thoroughly studied and evaluated, and we believe you are well qualified for many responsible management-training positions. However, we feel that the qualifications of other applicants more closely meet our established requirements.

Explanation—positively stated

Implied turndown

Your folder will be retained in our active

APPLICATIONS

Resale—keeping the applicant interested in the company, showing continued interest

Buffer

file, and should a suitable vacancy occur, you may be sure we will contact you again.

Thank you for your continued interest in our company. Good luck in your search for a rewarding position.

The recipient of the preceding letter received eleven refusals before getting a position with a large bank. At present, he is stationed in London as the bank's international representative.

ASSIGNMENT: REFUSAL LETTERS

Write and bring to your in-service training session letters in the refusal pattern for at least two of the following topics. Make each letter complete by supplying all letter parts. Attach a blank sheet of paper to each letter for others' comments. Then exchange them with your colleagues. Each of you write down your comments and suggestions, basing your judgments on the following criteria: analysis of audience, content, organization, style, and appearance. After reading and commenting on at least three letters, each member of the group is to revise his or her letters and pass them around again for other comments.

Topics

1. Letter refusing credit to a college senior who has a "slow pay" record on past transactions. Be specific.
2. Letter refusing to repair a product no longer under warranty. Offer the customer a compromise; try to keep the customer sold on the product.
3. Letter informing a customer of a delay in delivery of a product.
4. Letter refusing an invitation to join a service club.
5. Letter refusing a request for a donation of food or clothing to a bazaar raffle.
6. Letter refusing a job to a recent applicant.
7. Think of a disappointing situation you were involved in recently. Write a letter *to* yourself, *from* the other person, breaking the news but trying to keep your good will.

FURTHER READING

Hughes, H. *Letter Writing in Business.* Brooklyn Heights, NY: Beekman, 1979.

Persing, Bobbye Sorrels, *Business Communication Dynamics.* Columbus, OH: Merrill, 1981.

Wells, Walter. *Communications in Business,* 2nd ed. Belmont, CA: Wadsworth, 1977.

Wiener, Solomon. *Mastering Business Letter Writing,* rev. ed. Rochester, WA: Sovereign, 1978.

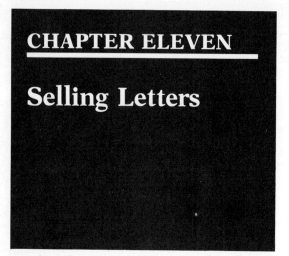

CHAPTER ELEVEN

Selling Letters

Persuasion . . . is verbal communication that attempts to bring about a voluntary change in judgment so that readers or listeners will accept a belief they did not hold before. The purpose of persuasion is to cause a change in thinking. That change may be simply the substitution of one belief for another, or it may result in action, such as voting for A instead of B, giving up smoking, or buying a product.

James M. McCrimmon
Writing with a Purpose

In a sense, every letter provides you with an opportunity to "sell" or persuade someone of something: yourself, your company, your product or service. Every letter, including those in the selling pattern, involves three essentials:

- the character of the speaker or writer
- the feelings and emotions of the listener or reader
- the reasons for the proposed action, suggested policy, or message

Effective selling letters appeal to character, emotions, logic.

The famous Greek philosopher Aristotle described these essentials twenty-three hundred years ago, calling them *ethos, pathos,* and *logos.* Character, emotions, and logic are still basic to selling products and ideas, still basic to persuasive writing.

You apply these essentials when you use thorough planning to analyze the situation and the reader. During this analysis, you try to anticipate objections, penetrate the other's mind, feelings, and emotions. You collect, reject, and accept appeals to the reader, material to include in your message—material most likely to result in action or reaction. You sift and sort mentally, frequently intuitively.

You organize the material logically to find mental paths of least resistance to your message. You use one or a combination of the following methods (described in detail in most rhetoric texts):

- from simple to complex
- from familiar to unfamiliar
- from specific examples to a general conclusion

- from a series of causes to a conclusion based on the effect of these causes
- comparison, contrast, or analogy (comparing two things different in most respects, similar in some)
- from a general truth or law to a specific application

The first five methods in the list are considered *inductive* reasoning. The sixth, and last, method is *deductive* reasoning. Logical thinking begins with early experiences. These experiences form the basis of our knowledge. We build on that knowledge, making "inductive leaps" to form general truths or laws. Then we apply these general laws to new specific applications, anticipating logical outcomes. Reasoning from a general truth to the new application is one of the most common of the reasoning processes employed in everyday life.

But that general truth, decision, or conclusion—call it what you will—is based on inductive thinking. (Daydreams, some night dreams, and intuitive knowledge are frequently examples of the subconscious using personal experience to reach new insights.)

Types of letters in the selling pattern include

- sales
- promotion
- special requests
- collections

In addition, many letters in the information pattern (unsolicited inquiries, favorable replies, acknowledgments, adjustments, credit) may also contain elements of the selling pattern.

FUNCTIONS OF SELLING LETTERS

There are many functions of the selling letter, an instrument of persuasion. In an organization, the selling letter serves to

Effective selling letters persuade someone to do something.

- build employee morale
- secure data from employees
- stimulate salespeople to greater effort
- pave the way for salespeople
- sell stockholders and others interested in your company
- keep a contact with customers
- further sell prospective customers after a demonstration
- collect accounts

In building a new business, the selling letter serves to

- secure new dealers
- initiate direct orders
- strengthen weak territories
- win back inactive customers
- create sales in territories not covered by salespeople
- develop sales among specified groups
- follow up inquiries
- drive home sales arguments
- sell other items in a line
- get product recognition
- classify and sell new types of buyers
- bring buyers into showroom

In assisting present dealers, the selling letter serves to

- help present dealers sell more
- educate dealers about your product
- train retail clerks in selling your product
- secure information from dealers or clerks

In interesting the consumer, the selling letter serves to

- create a demand or need for a product
- increase consumption of a product among present users
- bring customers into a store to buy
- open a new charge account
- capitalize on special events

Finally, the selling letter serves to

- capitalize on other advertising
- act as a "leader" for other forms of advertising. (*Leaders,* usually special bargains, lead customers into a store where, in addition, they purchase other items. But leaders may also alert the public to forthcoming programs—radio, television, film, question-naires—and other types of advertising.)
- break down resistance to a product
- stimulate interest in forthcoming events
- distribute samples
- announce a new product, new service, new policy
- keep a concern or product in mind
- research for new ideas and suggestions

- secure names for permanent lists
- protect patents or special processes
- raise funds, solicit volunteers
- secure a position

Each selling letter requires the same careful planning. Of course, each will differ from the others in appeal(s) used to motivate the reader to action. But apply the techniques suggested in this section to all persuasive writing. They work.

DIRECT-MAIL SALES

Invited sales letters are responses to inquiries about a product. The reader wants to receive your reply. For these, use the information pattern explained in Chapter 9 and close with a suggested action. Resistance to the message is minimal.

Invited sales letters require the information pattern.

The unsolicited *direct-mail* sales letter, on the other hand, must overcome massive resistance. Composing such a letter calls for experience in writing and human relations. Professional writers command top salaries for their ability to use words to sell something. Amateur or professional, you must begin with in-depth planning—research about the product and its possible market. (The term *product* refers to both goods and services.)

Unsolicited direct-mail sales letters must overcome reader resistance.

Market Research

Marketing information/research agencies use these three steps: exploration, screening, and analysis. They train investigators to sample opinions and attitudes in person, by telephone, or through mailed questionnaires. By means of this research, they hope to discover the prime prospects (people), the prime prospects' problem (need/want), the prime product to solve the problem, and how to break the boredom barrier (packaging).

Determine your prime prospects, their problem, and your solution (product or service) to their problem.

The analysis includes psychological, physical, educational, and environmental statistics. One company includes seventeen demographic categories for definition. Thus organizations hope to determine what appeal or appeals to use in promoting the product in general, as well as in conducting the direct-mail campaign.

Adapt your appeal(s) to local conditions and events where these affect the reader. For example, hail insurance appeals logically to farmers living in hail-prone areas. In a letter, you might motivate someone to buy such coverage by recalling a previous crop season with severe crop damage due to hail and pointing out how insured farmers, your clients, saved money and averted disaster. (Obviously, emotions are also included in this appeal.)

Banks appeal to customers by offering them numerous plans to choose from, describing varying interest rates designed to fight inflation. In the same letter, they may offer free gifts or premiums. The value of the gift appeals logically; the beauty of a matched set of cookware, however, appeals to the emotions.

Knowing the *prime prospects* and their *problem* assists you in selecting appeals. Knowing the *prime product* to solve the *problem* enables you to offer a solution, a service—enables you to sell.

When you can provide the kinds of information requested in the following analysis, then you can begin to think about writing a direct-mail sales letter. In-depth research and analyses probe much more deeply than the analysis presented here, but this analysis will help get you started. (It is how one student team analyzed their imaginary product.)

WHY PEOPLE SPEND MONEY

The Direct-Mail Advertising Association lists 25 reasons people spend money:

- To make money
- To save money
- To save time
- To avoid effort
- To achieve comfort
- For cleanliness
- To have health
- To escape physical pain
- To gain praise
- To be popular
- To attract the opposite sex
- For enjoyment
- To conserve possessions
- To gratify curiosity
- To protect family
- To be in style

- For beautiful possessions
- To satisfy appetite
- To emulate others
- For safety in buying
- To avoid criticism
- To be individual
- To protect reputation
- To take advantage of opportunities
- To avoid trouble

To these add four current appeals:

- To conserve energy
- To protect against inflation
- To protect the environment
- To promote equal rights

MARKET ANALYSIS

1. **Name:**
   MENAGERIE
2. **Product:**
   Children's furniture
3. **Physical description:**
   Durable tri-wall cardboard
   Nontoxic paints—primary colors
   Various animal shapes
   > Whale beds
   > Rhino bureaus
   > Kitten chairs
   > Cat tables
   > Giraffe chairs
4. **Psychological description:**
   Identifies with child's imagination
   Attractive appearance
   Inexpensive
   Provides stimulating environment for child
5. **Method of operation:**
   Same as traditional furniture
6. **Uses:**
   For sleeping, relaxation, play surfaces, storage
7. **Distinctive characteristics:**
   Arrives flat—easy to transport
   Easily assembled
   Easily stored
   Heavier-quality cardboard than used by competitors
   Only animal-designed cardboard furniture (others in traditional shapes)
   Low price—fits most low budgets
   Guaranteed for two years against tearing
   Tri-wall construction instead of duo-wall
8. **Servicing facilities:**
   Assembled furniture available for additional $7.00 each
   Replacement within two years upon receipt of damaged piece (no servicing required)
9. **How sold:**
   Through distributors
10. **Price:**
    From $7.50 to $40.00 each piece, unassembled, plus freight
    Assembled, add $7.00 each piece
    Single pieces, prepaid only—retail price

11. **Terms of payment:**

   Quantity purchases—credit terms of 2/10, n/30, finance charges
   1½ percent per month, 18 percent per year

   Discount to dealers, 15 percent from list—minimum purchase
   12 pieces

12. **Method of distribution:**

   Shipping by truck or air freight, f.o.b. (freight on board) destination

   Customers receive order at nearest airport or direct to door

13. **Buyers:**

   Furniture distributors

   Buyers of moderate-priced children's furniture, possibly Target, K-Mart, Sears, Montgomery Ward, other chains—large volume

14. **Users:**

   Children ages one to eight years

   Live in contemporary-minded homes

   Lower- and middle-class families

   Educated at least high school level

   Transient families—frequently moving

   Military families

   Young families stretching budgets

15. **Location:**

   Anywhere in the United States or overseas (Could enter into multinational agreement for manufacture)

16. **Buying power:**

   Limited—usually young families

17. **Desires of buyers/users:**

   Convenient, attractive, long-lasting furniture—innovative, priced low

18. **Promotional efforts:**

   Interior design magazines
   Interiors
   House and Garden
   House Beautiful
   Better Homes and Gardens
   Architectural Digest
   Television
   Children's shows using our furniture
   "Sesame Street"
   "The Banana Splits"
   "The Magic Window"
   "Captain Kangaroo"
   "The Muppets"

"Mr. Rogers"
Commercials
Saturday mornings during cartoons
Early evenings weekdays
Displays
Furniture dealers carrying our line
Furniture dealer conventions
Furniture shows
Interior design conventions
Written communication
Sales promotion letters—direct mail to distributors/dealers
Brochures for dealers
Magazine inserts
Miniflyers at displays for public to take home

19. **Possible market:**
Enormous—new baby boom in making
20. **Major appeal:**
Animal shapes unique—child's enjoyment
Minor appeal:
Cost, convenience, durability
21. **Sources of mailing lists of furniture dealers and distributors:**
Dun and Bradstreet *Middle Market Directory*
The Thomas Register
Moody's publications
Zeller, Inc.

Obviously, the mailing list is of major importance. With a well-organized, well-maintained mailing list, you can reach most of your probable prime prospects. The list supplies the base for your promotional efforts and is an important budget item. Appendix C contains a detailed discussion of mailing lists.

Offers

After you have completed your market research, you must choose an offer that will attract attention to your product. *Propositions*, or *offers*, will differ depending on your objective and prime prospects. Decide on *one* offer and emphasize it in your letter. Various types of offers are outlined in Table 11–1.

These basic propositions may be used singly or in various combinations depending on your objectives (see pages 205–206). Special offer letters are shown in Figure 11–1.

Make your prime prospects an offer they can't refuse.

Table 11–1: Types of Sales Letter Offers

Offer	Description
Free Information	Develops leads for salespeople or screens out nonprospects.
Sample	Enclosed with mailing or offered for nominal price. Usually results in increased sales.
Free trial	Frequently 15 days but length of trial varies with product.
Conditional sale	Prearranges the possibility of long-term acceptance, based on a sample. (Magazines urge trial subscriptions at introductory rates. If client is not delighted with first issue, may write "Cancel" on bill and return it without paying, keeping the first issue as a gift.)
Till forbid	Prearranges for continuing shipments on a specified basis. Customer has the option to forbid future shipments at any specified time. Works well for some business services and continuity book programs.
Yes-no	Involves the reader. Prospect is asked to respond through a token or stamp, indicating acceptance or rejection. More favorable than unfavorable responses usually received.
Time limit	Forces action by a specific date.
Get-a-friend	Offers reward—gift, discount, certificate—for assistance. Based on the theory that the best source for new customers is present satisfied customers.
Contest	Creates excitement, sells. Publishers Clearing House, Readers Digest, charitable foundations use these currently. Subject to stringent FTC rules.
Discount	Attracts consumers and business people, particularly where value of product has been established. Three types: for cash, for an introductory order, for volume purchase.
Negative option	Prearranges for shipment if customer does not mail rejection form prior to deadline date. Popular with book clubs, record/cassette clubs. FTC guidelines necessary.
Positive option	Based on direct action by a club member who must request book or record, food shipment, and so on. Immediate response usually less than for negative option but better for long-run sales.
Lifetime membership	Guarantees substantial savings from established retail prices for payment of one lifetime fee. Popular with consumer product organizations. Customer likely to purchase because of initial investment.

Table 11–1: Types of Sales Letter Offers, *continued*

Offer	*Description*
Load-up	Favored by publishers of continuity series. After purchaser buys and pays for first three of ten books in series, for example, publisher offers to send remaining seven in one shipment, extending payment as originally contracted. Results in more complete sets of books being sold.
Free gift	Increases response to mailing. Best to test several gifts to select most appealing. Tricky—customers may expect free gifts in order to buy again or cost may outweigh long-range profits.
Deluxe alternative	Gives prospects a choice, for example, between two dictionaries: regular edition or thumb-indexed for $2 more. Increases responses and profit.
Charter	Plays on human desires to be first, be innovative. Indicates special situation. Includes special reward for early support, for example, collector's edition of new magazine.
Guaranteed buy-back	Pledges to buy back goods at original cost if the customer so requests a number of years after original purchase. Used for mattresses, automotive supplies, others.
Multiproduct	Takes the form of a series of post cards, bound or unbound, or a collection of individual sheets, each with separate order form. Popular with mail order clothing presentations—Haband, NPC, others.
Piggyback	Rides along with major offer or at no additional postage. Many statement envelopes have piggyback flap advertising, offering fill-in coupon ordering. Useful for continuous series.
Bounce back	Included in shipments or with invoices or statements. May offer more of the same purchased product, related items, or totally different items.
Good-better-best	Gives the prospect a choice among three qualities: for example, Franklin Mint offers medallions and collectors' items in 24K gold on sterling, solid sterling silver, and solid bronze. Prices vary, attract a wide range of buyers.

Source: Adapted from Stone, pp. 160–162.

Bon Appétit

P.O. Box 2426, Boulder, CO 80322

Cut the cost of good living by saving on the _magazine_ of good living.

Use the Early Renewal Certificate enclosed. You'll save (and _protect_ your savings!) on Bon Appétit!

Dear Subscriber:

There's a perfect implement for trimming Italian parsley...slicing Beef Wellington...<u>and</u> cutting the cost of your Bon Appétit subscription. By returning the attached Certificate and extending your <u>current</u> subscription now, you can save over 30% off the newsstand price!

You may not have noticed, but the cover price of Bon Appétit has gone up to $1.75 per issue...and $2.25 for our two beautiful holiday issues. Which means that if you purchase our magazine at the newsstand, you'd be paying $22.00 a year. But by extending your subscription now, you can keep your cost at just $1.25 per copy. That comes to $15.00 a year instead of $22.00. A saving of $7.00! Use the savings to splurge on huile de noix -- walnut oil that turns an ordinary salad into an exotic treat...porcini -- dried wild mushrooms from Italy...a special quiche pan or a classic mouli cheese grater. Any $7.00 reward your heart desires!

I know that your subscription isn't expiring at this time, but I urge you to take advantage of this extension offer for three sensible reasons:

1. You'll save money.
2. You won't receive any more renewal notices for a good long time.
3. Your rate will be <u>guaranteed</u> for the full additional year of your subscription.

Just fill in your Certificate <u>now</u> and return it to us in the postage-- paid envelope we've provided. Send your payment or have us bill you. What's important is that either way, you'll <u>save</u>!

Cordially,

Rosalie E. Bruno

Rosalie E. Bruno
Senior Vice President, Circulation

2Y–18–AR81

Figure 11–1: Special-offer Letters

Attention-Getting Devices

With your selection of a proposition, or offer, for your prime prospect(s), you have begun to break down the boredom barrier. Here are some further suggestions from Stone and other marketing/advertising specialists. Consider them *before* you write.

Letters. Indent paragraphs in form letters; indented paragraphs usually outpull letters without indention. Underline important words, phrases, and sentences; emphasis slightly increases results. Use *both* a letter and a separate circular or filler; the two will generally do better than a combination letter-circular. Use either a running headline or a computerized, filled-in inside address; both are effective. Include authentic testimonials to increase the pull. Write a two-page letter with specific details to outpull a one-page letter. Select a computer-printed personalized letter over a printed letter, but keep the tone low-key.

Envelopes. Increase response by using illustrated envelopes tied in with the offer. Consider a variety of types and sizes of envelopes for a series of mailings.

Reply forms. Increase response by using reply cards with receipt stubs rather than cards without stubs. Produce more response with "busy"—important-looking, heavily printed—order and/or request forms rather than clean, sparsely printed forms. Include postage-free business-reply cards for added response; the receiver hesitates to affix postage.

Reply envelope (SASE: Self-addressed, stamped envelope). Increase the cash-with-order response by including envelopes. Increase the response to collection letters by including envelopes.

Color. Use two-color letters to outpull one-color letters. Use colored ink or colored stock for order and/or reply forms rather than black ink on white stock. Use two-color circulars to outpull one-color circulars. Promote food items, apparel, and other merchandise in authentic full color.

Postage. Use third-class instead of first-class mail; save money; results are equal for outgoing mail. Use postage-metered mail to outpull postage-stamped mail. Use ordinary postage-meter stamping or a specially designed printed meter permit; they are equally effective.

Consider physical characteristics (length, indentions, special headings, color, and so on) before you write a selling letter.

Other devices.   Get ideas from others; adapt and adjust them to your needs.

Use connecting links, professionally called "the bucket brigade." They help carry the reader along from one thought to another, help the copy flow smoothly, and give it continuity (see page 109). Examples: "but that is not all," "in addition," "so that is why," "but please remember," "as I mentioned."

Use short words and sentences.

Recognize the importance of *timing*. Holidays and special events may interfere. The receiver may ignore your mailing or the mailing piece may be misplaced or lost because of heavy volume. Many business people prefer to receive important mail on Monday. Others do not. Try to gauge time logically; try test runs for series.

Remember supersalesman Elmer Wheeler's advice: "Don't sell the steak; sell the sizzle." Sell the benefits to your audience, not just the features. Use logical reasons, facts *(logos)*, but include an appeal to the feelings and emotions *(pathos)*.

Improve your writing by continually writing and by testing your writing in the prime market.

Organization

Follow this organization in selling, or persuasive, letters:

- attention
- interest
- conviction
- action

Promise a benefit in your headline or first paragraph—your most important benefit in the most important position—to attract *attention.*

Enlarge immediately upon the benefit to build up *interest.* Give the reader specific details: size, color, weight, sales terms *(logos),* plus intangibles *(pathos).* Do not assume the reader knows the details of the offer. For example: "24K gold on sterling medallion increasing in value with time, commemorating historic visit of Pope John Paul II to Illinois in 1979—collectors' item in limited edition—to wear with pride." Build *interest.*

Back up your statements with proof and endorsements if possible. List satisfied users or previous record of dependability. Readers are skeptical; they need convincing.

Rephrase the benefits in order to intensify the reader's conviction or desire. Show the reader the need to take action to reap the benefits.

Incite *action*. Close your letter with a call for action and a logical reason for acting immediately.

Attention-getting openings.   A short opening paragraph—one to four lines, no more—invites further reading. Indeed, the *first 50 words* are the most crucial. Capture your reader's attention and you can go on to write two, three, or more pages.

Capture the reader's attention in the first paragraph.

In general, keep your messages concise rather than brief. Research indicates that the long, concise letter outpulls the short. With the long letter, you can create a mood for buying concocted from a mixture of reasons and emotions—facts and feelings.

Here are some time- and market-tested themes or topics to adapt to your product and prospects. Each helps break down the boredom barrier. Each relies on carefully selected lists.

We are pleased to announce a most exciting new service, FIRST BANK 24, a totally automated teller machine available day or night, 365 days a year.

News: Promises a new product, offers new opportunities, experiences; extremely effective.

What is it, would you say, that makes your career more challenging and demanding than that of executives or managers in most other fields?

Question: Arouses curiosity.

I don't know you and yet I have been sitting at my desk for the last two hours trying to figure out how to word this letter so it won't end up in your wastebasket.

Narrative: Appeals to the emotions, creates empathy.

Why you should insulate your attic this winter.

How successful men really get ahead.

What to do about unexpected guests.

How, who, what, when, where, why: Answer the main questions going through a reader's mind.

Warning: This offer expires in 21 days. It will never be repeated. Among the rarest stamps in all the world...the official-seal stamps of the thirteen original colonies in commemoration of the American Bicentennial...minted of 23 KARAT Gold...Examine Stamp No. 1 for 15 days FREE.

Startling offer: Appeals to logic and emotions.

Command: Suggests possibilities within reach of reader.	`Earn a college diploma in your spare time.`
	
	`Own your own home--you can with our plan.`
	
	`Plan for retirement NOW and extend your vital years.`

Numbered ways: Emphasize choice, simplify interest.	`Six ways to save money and make money at Blank Savings and Loan.`
	
	`17 little-known ways to improve your on-the-job performance--and one big way to make it pay off.`

Catchword, phrase, or sentence: Creates a mental image of the product each time it is repeated.	`It's the real thing.`
	
	`Arcticwear stops the cold cold.`
	
	`The life you save may be your own.`

Free gift: Bribes the reader to read on.	`We'll give you $5 for your gas tank, a pizza dinner at your neighborhood Pizza Hut, an instamatic camera with film, and two tickets to a hockey game!  Why?  Because we've a fun place to tell you about!`
"You are special": Singles out present customers or special categories of readers and says so.	`As a preferred Mobil customer . . . you may have, FREE for 15 days, the beautiful American Bicentennial Collection of six Commemorative Pewter-inspired Plates.`

Negative thought: Frightens sometimes, annoys other times. Use sparingly.	`Everyday, Mr. Shultz, you face the chance of injuring yourself in an accident--maybe even fatally.`
	
	`Don't be embarrassed by . . . (dandruff, bad breath)`

The preceding examples include the most popular openings, but there are others. Whichever you use, keep tone in mind. Understatement is more effective than exaggeration. Simplicity is better than too much detail or too technical an explanation. Zero in on one main point, one proposition. Make each word count—especially the first 50.

Show interest in your reader and conviction in your product or service.

Interest and conviction.   Interest and conviction form the body of your letter. You achieve both by your constant awareness of the reader—your awareness of how what you offer can be of service.

But you must believe in it yourself—know it thoroughly, its good qualities and its faults.

Select key words or ideas from the *attention-getting* opener and elaborate on them, using the "bucket brigade" or connecting links to move smoothly from one point to another point. In general, you can

- appeal to fundamental emotions and sentiments
- refer to conditions and happenings of general interest
- play up certain types and classes of people
- appeal to local and human interest
- stimulate a receptive attitude in the prospect
- feature some unique or novel detail of the product

You establish belief, or credibility by offering

- guarantees
- free trials
- free samples
- testimonials
- statistics
- references
- illustrations of all kinds
- enclosures such as charts, catalogs, coupons

Once you have connected the product with the needs and desires of the prospect, the prospect is ready to become a customer. But readiness and action are frequently different.

Action ending.　Your ending must motivate action, overcome inertia and boredom. Variations on the following are most common.

Close with a call to action.

```
One word of caution please. Only reservations
received within 21 days can be considered for
participation. Of course, the earlier you mail
your reservation, the lower your number in the
limited edition, and the greater value it has,
and the better your chance of your subscription
being accepted.
```

Limited-time or limited-quantity offer

```
With prices rising so rapidly, it's hard to tell
how long I can guarantee my current low prices
. . . . As always, all your selections come to
your home for a no-obligation-to-buy week's Free
```

Time urgency

APPLICATIONS

Trial. But you must act now--tomorrow may be too late! Rush your selections to me TODAY in the attached postage-paid envelope.

Gifts for ordering

A handsome binder to house the reports you receive will be sent to you on receipt of payment for your subscription.

Salesperson's call

Call today for a free demonstration. We will send a representative at your convenience.

Making response easier: Cards, coupons, stamped reply envelopes, requiring no payment with order, suggesting toll-free telephone call

Right now, all you need do is remove the Visa/ MasterCard charge-card on the front page of this letter, place it in the reply envelope, seal the envelope, and mail it. No need for any stamps-- postage is paid. Why not take this simple and sensible step to credit-card protection now, while it's fresh in your mind.

"There is one infallible test of the effectiveness of a sales letter—the number of sales it brings in. As one professional letterwriter said: 'Make your letter so convincing that the prospect would rather have the product you are selling than the money he must part with to buy it'" (Mager, 1976).

SPECIAL REQUESTS

Special requests also require the selling pattern. Again you must overcome the reader's resistance to taking action. But instead of selling goods or services, you are trying to

- sell an idea
- solicit contributions—time, money, goods
- register a complaint
- request an adjustment

Special requests demand your powers of persuasion.

You may urge voters to support your favorite candidate. You may solicit funds for a political, religious, social, philanthropic, or professional organization. You may try to persuade someone to speak to your group, to contribute something for a raffle or other fund raiser. You may feel it necessary to justify a complaint or adjustment—to win someone over to your point of view. Or you may have other objectives.

Whenever you must persuade someone, use the sales pattern. Follow the POWER procedure. Whether writing to one person or many, you'll need to decide on the best blend of emotion and logic to motivate favorable action.

Selling an Idea, Soliciting a Contribution

For "mass" mailings, make sure you have the best mailing list you can buy or compile. Prime prospects are more likely to listen to your special request—to read past the first 50 words. Openings and closings are more likely to appeal to the emotions than to logic. But every situation is different and must be carefully analyzed. Adapt the suggestions for writing direct-mail sales letters.

Will you help us demonstrate that metropolitan Atlanta is a gracious hostess as well as a wide-awake business community?

Pride—pride in self, in company, in country—is a strong motivation to action. When the effort is minimal, the rewards great, the individual is likely to grant the special request.

The American Business Communication Association will send about 150-200 delegates to attend its annual national convention to be held this year at the Sheraton-Biltmore in Atlanta from December 27 to December 30.

Not to be outdone by Chicago, which last year provided these teachers of modern business communication with small mementos representative of business institutions in the area (the Toni Company was among them), we propose to put Atlanta's best foot forward by reminding these delegates of the world-famous businesses that headquarter here--firms such as the Coca-Cola Company, Scripto, Lockheed-Georgia, Rich's Inc., and Avon Cosmetics, to name a few.

Can you provide some small promotional item as a souvenir from Avon Cosmetics Company? We anticipate that about 125 men and about 100 women (delegates and spouses of delegates) will attend the business luncheon where these assembled souvenirs will be presented.

Addressed to different companies, this letter raised $5,000 in gifts. Note: It also appeals to self-interest—a chance to promote the company's name and show good will.

We plan to list the names of Atlanta's cooperating institutions in the official program, thanking them for their help.

I hope you will write and tell me what you can do to help impress Avon's name on these visitors.

APPLICATIONS

Breaking down the contribution to an insignificant amount or showing a favorable tax break can incite action.

> A dime a day. For just ten days. Please care that much.

> Anything you can do to help is greatly needed. We have received clearance from the Internal Revenue Service so every gift is tax deductible.

Showing where the money goes appeals to many contributors.

> This letter to you costs 22¢, including postage. With the first dollar you contribute, my campaign benefits by 78¢. But for every dollar you contribute after that, the entire 100¢ goes directly to finance my reelection effort.

Emotional appeals, however, loosen more purse strings than do logical appeals.

> Please don't say no, because when you do, I have to unwrap his little arms from my waist and walk away. Help me, say yes.

Determine the kind of appeal that will work best with your prime prospects.

> If you decide to help, try to envision a face. A child you know, a neighbor, a fellow worker, a relative. Then say to that face, "Yes, I care. Today I made a life or death decision." Will you please take the card and decide now?

> No one can do more and the Lord will know and He will reward you.

Complaints and Adjustments

Requesting an adjustment or registering a complaint sometimes requires special persuasion, and thus the selling pattern as well as the information pattern is needed. Although the consumer is protected today as never before, some organizations need to be prodded into action. The selling pattern is useful; persistence is useful; facts, tact, and humor help.

Attention and buffer

> I'm getting nervous--needlessly, I'm sure. But my watch has been with you since September. You've cashed two checks: one dated September 26 for $1.50, another dated October 2 for $20.50. And now it's November 4.

Details

> You still have the watch, model USA 212, sent in for repair to the band and overhaul for accuracy.

Part of my nervousness stems from the length of time you've had the watch. In addition, I realized before I sent the additional $20.50 that it was a good chunk to pay for repair. And, on top of that, I've been aware for several years of the article in Consumer Reports concerning your company.

I went ahead with your request because the purchase of the watch and now its repair are being used as an exercise in my business communication courses at Iowa State University. I've admired the initial promotion--everything from the stationery to the U.N. stamps--and several of my students have purchased watches and written to you over the past few years.

But I'd like the watch back, please. Perhaps you've been swamped by work. Perhaps the mails are slow. Whatever the reason, I'd like to hear from you and I'd like the watch. I hope it won't be necessary to write again or to contact friends and authorities in New York.

Call for action

The letter received a reply by return mail. But it was necessary to write again.

You'll be interested in knowing that I have NOT received my watch (USA 212) in spite of your reassuring card of early November stating it would be shipped insured parcel post, December 10. (As you can see, it's now exactly thirty days later.)

Buffer

I've been patient, understanding, cooperative. You've had the watch since September. You've cashed checks totaling $22.00.

You owe me the watch, of course, but I'd like an explanation for the delay if I do not receive that watch by January 15.

The next step is the New York Police Department, New York Better Business Bureau, and/or United States Post Office action. I assure you that I'll take steps on January 16, much as I dislike doing so.

Threat

Surely, you, too, would prefer conciliation rather than harsh accusation.

The company sent the watch immediately, closing the claim.

Complaints and adjustment letters combine facts—requiring the information pattern—bad news—requiring the refusal pattern—and persuasion—requiring the selling pattern. Note the combination of attention and buffer openings. Note the action and buffer closings. In addition, the letters illustrate two stages in the *collection* series.

Not all complaint letters need to be dour and sober in tone to get the desired results. For example, consider the humorous interchange between claimant and insurer in Exhibit 11–1.

COLLECTIONS

Use the selling pattern for collection letters.

When credit is extended, it is given on the basis of the four Cs (character, capacity, capital, conditions). The credit manager hopes to have made a good decision, expects the customer to pay as promised. But conditions change. Sometimes it is beyond the capacity of the client to pay, for the capital has disappeared or diminished. Inflation, job loss, illness, failure of others to pay their debts, cancellation of contracts, political complications—all can contribute to financial problems.

However, it is usually safe to make certain assumptions:

- Most people are honest.
- Most people pay their bills.
- Most people dislike being in debt.
- Most people welcome professional financial advice.*
- Keeping the customer's good will is important.

A minority of men and women deliberately set out to defraud; thus one must be constantly alert. Nevertheless, customers with overdue accounts are still customers, and customers are the life-blood of a company. Investigate thoroughly before giving credit; then treat each collection as carefully as possible.

You may need to write a progressively sterner series of letters to collect a debt.

Traditionally, creditors use a *collection series* of progressively sterner letters, but series differ from company to company, from customer to customer. One's past history of purchases and payments makes a difference. Whether the customer is a consumer or a business makes an even bigger difference. And collection procedures vary within these categories.

---

*For the credit-counseling service closest to you, write: The National Foundation for Consumer Credit, 1819 H Street, N.W., Washington, D.C. 20006.

Date ___9/29/69___

Policyholder _____

> The Seattle Times
> Fairview Ave. and N. John
> Seattle, Washington

Please refer to the item(s) checked below and furnish us with the missing information for

| ___James C. Heckman___ | ___6695___ |
| Claimant | Certificate Number |

**Employer's
Certification
Notice of Claim**

☐ Date of Employment _____

☐ Certificate Number _____

☐ Social Security Number _____

☐ Occupation _____

☐ Date (Dependent, Employee) Insured _____

☐ Date Disability Caused Lost Time _____

☐ Date Last Worked _____

☐ Date Returned to Work _____

☐ Daily Hospital Benefits _____

☐ Effective Date of Major
  Medical Coverage _____

☐ Cash Deductible _____

☐ Other ___Please advise
  when and where hornet
  stings were gotten.___

☐ Employee's Annual
  Earning Code No. _____

☐ Employee's Statement of Claim _____

☐ Date of Accident _____

☐ Certificate of Attending Physician _____

☐ Itemized Medical Bill _____

☐ Itemized Hospital Bill _____

☐ Itemized Medical and/or
  Surgical Bill _____

☐ Portion of Hospital Bill Paid by Your Basic
  Benefits Carrier or Medicare _____

☐ Receipts from Drug Store Prescription Listing
  Numbers, Charges, and Doctor's Name

Exhibit 11–1: A Humorous Claims Adjustment Dialogue

October 1, 1969

Sirs:

I thought you'd never ask when and where my
hornet stings were gotten. The experience was
so harrowing, I am just yet able to talk about
how they were gotten.

The time: About 9 a.m. on a cool day in
mid-August, 1969.

The place: Southeast 40th Street, a mere
lane adjacent to the Newport Yacht Club, north of
Newport Shores but south of the Mercer Slough.

I, J. Canfield Heckman, had departed my aging
station wagon, accompanied by my daughters, Lael,
8, and Hollie, 12, and my Great Dane, Katrina,
about 3.

The party paused on the edge of a seemingly
trackless sea of grass, punctuated here and there
only by dark green masses, formidable in appearance, that we knew to harbor the delectable black-
berry. A zephyr caressed the grass, and shivers
played up and down our spines. The Great Dane
bayed mournfully.

"Fear not, J. Canfield," I told myself, "You
and your loved ones are protected against accident
and injury by one of the citadels of Free Enterprise, the Aetna Casualty & Surety Co., and any
claim will be processed rapidly and efficiently
by the firm's Group Claim Department."

Having reassured myself, I buckled tighter my
only weapon, a Webley-Vickers revolver carried by
my father, the late Brevet Maj. Steinly-Armstead
Heckman, during the Manitou Insurrection, and led
my party into the waste.

Exhibit 11–1, *continued*

We soon encountered a patch rich in berries, and were well on our way to gathering in several bucketsful. I had edged closer and closer to the center of a patch, while my daughters picked some distance away.

I reached for an especially lucious-looking garland of berries and then is when it happened: I was gotten.

At least 40,000 members of the genus Hornetis Mostmeanest rose from the patch in buzzing waves. I stepped back, assumed the kneeling position used by the troops of Gordon in Africa, and emptied my Webley-Vickers. Still they came.

Some gotten me on the left hand. Some gotten me on the right.

"Flee, my beloved offspring, they are gotten me," I shouted.

"Father, oh father, what is it that is gotten you?" they called.

"Hornetis Mostmeanests are gotten me," I replied.

We regrouped and beat a disciplined, orderly retreat.

And that, my friends in the Group Claim Department, is when and where my hornet stings were gotten.

Thank you for your interest.

J. Canfield Heckman

Attachments:
  Document A--Map.
  Document B--Drawing of Hornetis
    Mostmeanest, in triplicate

Exhibit 11-1, *continued*

October 7, 1969

Mr. James C. Heckman
3842 East Mercer Way
Mercer Island, Washington

Dear Mr. Heckman:

    I would first like to apologize for our request for further information regarding your hornet stings. Our request at that time was not really necessary, and we obviously did a poor job of requesting it. We pay between 15,000 and 20,000 claims a month from this office. Sometimes the quality of work processed by our people is not up to that quality which we would like.

    Most of the errors that we make are pointed out to us immediately. However, very few of our errors are pointed out to us with such humor and charm. We all enjoyed reading your letter, and can assure you that we did not miss the point. We hope that you will appreciate the enclosed poem along with our draft for the payment of your claim.

Sincerely,

G. B. Shaw, Supervisor
Group Claim Department

mk

Exhibit 11–1, *continued*

```
Your wit we can't match
So should we just cry
The booboo was ours
So shouldn't we try

Our question not needed
Our grammar was bad
We asked for a "gotten"
And found we were had

Personal Service our slogan
I guess it's our bag
And since we goofed
We enjoyed your gag

Your humor was great
The point was not missed
The Hornetis Mostmeanest
Is now on our list

The next time you go
On a trip thru the pass
We hope that the stingers
Are all in your glass

But if it should happen
Please turn in your claim
The next time the handling
Will not be the same

Please accept our draft
With apologies plain
Just break your leg
And try us again
```

Exhibit 11–1, *continued*

For example, most small-loan companies begin to follow a set collection procedure five days after an account is overdue:

1. They mail a "late notice" reminder.
2. They follow up by phone three days later—second reminder.
3. They mail an inquiry letter five days later.
4. They phone (one to three calls) stressing urgency of situation within five days of no response to letter.
5. They visit the customer's home with ultimatum—pay or company will take legal action.

These companies, like other creditors, prefer to help the debtor. They are willing to extend the time period of the debt, rearrange payments, accept interest but not principal for several months, or make other concessions. They urge customers to come in and talk over their problems, to explain financial difficulties. The alternatives are unpleasant—garnisheed wages, suits in small claims courts, repossessed merchandise, bankruptcy.

Today all credit accounts are monitored closely, frequently by computer printouts, since finance charges for late payments mount quickly and may engulf and panic the customer. To the four Cs credit guidelines, businesses have added *collection, coverage,* and *caution.* All creditors want their money as quickly as possible but prefer not to lose good will. They want to retain customers and realize that *early and persistent requests for payment may prevent later problems.*

For consumer and business debtor alike, each step in the collection procedure is determined by (1) the reaction of the debtor to the notices and (2) state and federal law. (See the Fair Debt Collection Practices Act of 1978 in Appendix D.)

To keep up with the laws and respond to their own unique needs, many companies train credit managers on the job. These men and women learn the basic principles and specialized applications in short courses and credit/collection seminars run by their companies. The following collection series, therefore, is offered only as a guideline. Individuals may adapt and adjust the series, apply the principles effectively to special requests as well as to collecting debts.

Notification

The regular bill or statement of money due on an account includes notice of the date that payment is required, finance charges, and other pertinent data. (*Assumption:* Customer will pay within the allotted time.)

Reminder

There may be one reminder or several. They may be as simple as a printed sticker attached to a duplicate of the original bill, a page from a snap-apart collection set, or a friendly form letter or personal letter. Whether letter or sticker, and how soon after the due date to send it, depend on the type of account, merchandise or service, customer's past history of payment and purchases. (*Assumption:* Customer has overlooked the bill, will pay if reminded.)

```
Dear Customer:

    There's really no great hurry, but you've been
so prompt in the past, I thought you might do us
the favor of paying the balance of your Clearing
House bill now.

    We'd appreciate it, of course.  And as a way
of saying thanks, we are enclosing a special
reply envelope that needs neither stamp nor
postage.  Just slip your payment and invoice
in the envelope, mail it, and it's done.

Cordially,
```

Inquiry

An inquiry can take the form of a sticker, still another page from a snap-apart series, a friendly form letter, or a personal letter. The creditor is trying to break through the silence, to find out what is wrong. An early and friendly inquiry, approximately two weeks after the last reminder, may prevent serious problems later. (*Assumption:* Customer has a problem; the creditor has a problem. If communication can be established, the problem may be solved.)

```
    Your account for the month of January shows
a balance due of $52.76, covering our invoice No.
14809 of January 14.  Records in our shipping de-
partment indicate that the shipment went to you
by truck on the afternoon of January 14.
```

```
    Your record of prompt payment in the past
causes us to wonder if some problem has arisen.
We would appreciate your verifying this charge
with your records and letting us know if it is
not in line for payment.

    We appreciate your business very much.
Whenever we may be of service to you, we shall
be happy to do so.
```

Appeal

An appeal may consist of a form letter or personal letter, possibly a combination of inquiry, appeal, and urgency. The writer appeals to the customer's pride, honesty, and sense of fair play, pointing out the hazards of a shaky credit rating and subtly suggesting the likelihood of further action. (Special requests for the return of one's property or for an adjustment or the registering of a complaint may *begin* with this stage.)

One or more appeals may be sent, each narrowing the time available to the customer for payment. Timing varies. The first appeal is usually mailed two weeks to a month after the inquiry. (*Assumption:* Customer can still be prevailed upon to pay if a successful appeal to self-interest can be achieved.)

```
    Your account has just been handed to me with
the suggestion that it be turned over to the Credit
Exchange for collection.

    It is our earnest desire to maintain the
pleasant relationship that has existed between us.
Perhaps there is a very good reason for nonpayment
or in this instance we may be at fault.  If such
is the case, won't you please let us know?

    However, if the account is correct, we would
appreciate receiving your remittance so that fur-
ther action will not be necessary.

    Let us hear from you in the next seven (7)
days.
```

A dentist in Waco, Texas, sends out his statements with this sticker added: "When you pay us, we can pay them and they can pay him and he can pay you" (*Reader's Digest*, May 1975, p. 151).

Urgency

A letter expressing urgency is usually signed by a top executive, preferably sent registered mail, return-receipt-requested. It may be preceded by a phone call. The letter emphasizes the alternatives to payment within 5 to 14 days—exact time stated. Such alternatives may include

- reporting the account to a credit bureau
- turning the account over to a lawyer
- turning the account over to a collection agency
- garnisheeing a portion of the salary or wages (applicable only in some states)
- repossessing merchandise

The tone is friendly but firm. This is the last chance for the customer—but there is still time to make arrangements for settling the account. The creditor is very reluctant to take drastic action, has tried courteously and patiently to secure cooperation. It is now up to the customer to act or suffer the consequences.

Indeed, the creditor is very reluctant to use any of the five alternatives, because it would mean losing the customer. Furthermore, collection costs may exceed 50 percent of the debt. It may be more advisable for the creditor to write off the account as a bad debt on income tax returns. Consult a tax accountant or lawyer. (*Assumption:* Customer may be motivated to pay or respond, if faced with drastic, unpleasant action.)

```
    We have tried to collect this account in a
friendly manner, that being part of our credit
policy.  Our efforts, however, have failed to
secure your cooperation.  Therefore, it is now
necessary to place this account with our attor-
neys for collection.

    We dislike to resort to legal services be-
cause of the extra expense and embarrassment to
the customer.

    There is still time for you to make a
satisfactory arrangement with us for the
settlement of the account.  However, unless
we do hear from you within fourteen (14) days,
it will be placed for immediate action.  We
have done our best.  You must now do your part.
```

Ultimatum

The ultimatum may consist of a telegram or last letter reinforcing the urgency of the situation. An urgency ultimatum may close the collection series, or the creditor may send a *final* ultimatum, demanding *immediate* payment, possibly summarizing action to date. (*Assumptions:* Customer must pay immediately; creditor must follow through with promised action or cease dunning.)

```
     This is the last time you'll be hearing from
us.  Just so there is no misunderstanding on your
part, here is a recap of the events to date.

     1.  We shipped merchandise to you in good
         faith, expecting payment within 30 days.
     2.  We sent you several letters requesting
         payment following the due-date.  You did
         not respond.
     3.  Your name has been reported to a national
         credit-reporting agency and future credit
         inquiries will contain information about
         your delinquent account.

     Your account is about to be placed in the
hands of a national collection agency.  We will
instruct them to take whatever steps are neces-
sary to collect the money you owe us.

     This is really your last opportunity to pre-
vent this from happening.  It is imperative that
you send your full payment by special delivery or
even by telegram.  Don't delay a moment longer.
```

Letter from Lawyer, Notice from Collection Agency

The customer is protected against pressure tactics from the collection agency, under law. For example, a bill collector may phone a debtor between 8 A.M. and 9 P.M., at home or at the business location. But if the debtor objects and *puts the objection in writing,* the collector must stop phoning and is permitted only *one* more letter or call, to inform the debtor of further legal steps to be taken.[*]

---

[*]As far as collection practices are concerned, state authorities support any debtor they feel has been subjected to undue harassment. *Once an account is placed with a collection agency or attorney, hands off!* If the debtor contacts the creditor, *the creditor should not make any verbal or written contact with him or her.* When debtors do make contact, the creditor's attorney/collector should be notified immediately.

The lawyer, however, has the same rights as the creditor. Usually, the lawyer will send one letter, asking for immediate settlement of the claim *outside of court*. A compromise of 50 cents or 75 cents on the dollar owed *may be offered.* If the settlement is not made, the lawyer will—depending on the amount owed—(a) file papers with the county sheriff asking the debtor to appear in small claims court or (b) have the debtor served with a summons, requiring appearance in regular court. In either case, a judgment is usually made against the client, forcing payment.

Trying to collect quickly and to prevent an account from reaching this stage are prime goals of a good collection manager. The good collection-letterwriter

- looks toward the future
- knows company collection policies
- knows federal and state laws
- has all the customer's records
- sets up a collection plan for the account
- adjusts to conditions, both the customer's and the company's
- recognizes three different classes of debtors—
    (a) late payers but sound financial risks
    (b) late payers lacking sufficient capital, needing extra time or extra assistance
    (c) late payers deliberately dishonest
- follows up delinquent accounts with increasing insistence
- tries to be helpful and considerate, extending every possible courtesy to keep the customer—within the limits of good business practices

With increasing frequency, business firms are delegating collections and billing to computerized, specialized agencies.

The following assignment will give you practical experience in applying the principles discussed in this chapter. Expect, however, to use the selling pattern for other purposes, too.

ASSIGNMENT: SELLING LETTERS

Because selling letters are so useful in so many business situations, your in-service training director has asked you to respond to any two of the following assignments. As the result of scheduling conflicts, your director has cancelled this week's meeting of your group. Instead, the director will review each member's responses to the assignments and discuss them with you individually.

1. Recall three direct-mail sales letters you have received in the past several months. Identify the appeals. To which, if any, did you respond?

2. Select a product—goods or service.
   a. Conduct a market analysis of your product as directed on pages 209–211.
   b. Compile a mailing list of 10 prospects.
   c. Select the appeals—logical and emotional—most likely to motivate your prospects.
   d. Choose the one offer or proposition most likely to attract your prospects.
   e. Determine the action you desire—order, inquiry, request for demonstration, other.
   f. Using the appropriate attention-getting devices noted on page 215, write a direct-mail sales letter.
   g. Explain your mailing procedures: envelope, stamping, timing.

3. Recall three special-request letters you have received in the past several months. Identify the appeals. To which, if any, did you respond?

4. Using the selling pattern, write a letter to persuade
   a. a teacher to raise your final grade
   b. your employer to raise your salary
   c. your representative in Congress to support a bill you favor
   d. a celebrity to donate an article of clothing to be auctioned off to raise money for your favorite charity.

5. Using the selling pattern, write a letter to persuade a local dealer to make an adjustment or to replace a product (goods or service) that you paid for but that has turned out to be unsatisfactory.

6. Again using the selling pattern, write a follow-up letter to the same dealer (who has not responded to your earlier letter) demanding action and outlining the steps you will take if the dealer does not respond to this, your second, request.

7. Write a progressively sterner series of collection letters to a customer whose payment is overdue without explanation.
   a. reminder (friendly personal letter)
   b. inquiry (friendly personal letter asking if something is wrong)
   c. appeal (firm but friendly personal letter appealing to pride and honesty)
   d. urgency (firm but friendly personal letter emphasizing alternatives)
   e. ultimatum (firm personal letter demanding immediate

payment, summarizing action to date, and stating next action)
8. Explain the differences among the three classes of debtors and state how these differences affect the timing and frequency of collection letters.

FURTHER READING

Avett, Elizabeth M. *Today's Business Letter Writing.* Englewood Cliffs, NJ: Prentice-Hall, 1977.

Butterworth, John. *Debt Collection Letters in Ten Languages.* New York: AMACQM, 1978.

Epstein, David G. *Debtor-Creditor Law in a Nutshell,* 2nd ed. Ann Arbor, MI: West, 1980.

Mager, N. H. and S. K. Mager. *The Complete Letter Writer.* Kaohhsiung, Taiwan: Feng Hsing, 1976.

Marks, Robert A. *Effective Collection System for Delinquent Consumer Accounts.* New York: Pilot, 1979.

McCrimmon, James M. *Writing with a Purpose,* 7th ed. Boston: Houghton Mifflin, 1980.

Pierce, Milton. *How to Collect Your Overdue Bills.* Homewood, IL: Dow Jones–Irwin, 1980.

Pierce, Milton. *How to Manage Accounts Receivable: A Guide to Collection Techniques and Customer Relations.* Homewood, IL: Dow Jones-Irwin, 1980.

Reid, James M. and Robert M. Wendlinger. *Effective Letters: A Program for Self-Instruction,* 3rd ed. New York: McGraw-Hill, 1978.

Saville, Tim and Jenny Saville, *The Complete Letter Writer.* Brooklyn, NY: Beekman, 1980.

Stone, Bob. *Successful Direct Marketing Methods.* Chicago, IL: Crain, 1975.

Weaver, Robert G. and Patricia Weaver. *Persuasive Writing: A Manager's Guide to Effective Letters and Reports.* New York: Free Press, 1977.

CHAPTER TWELVE

Memos

"The horror of the moment," the King went on, "I shall *never* forget!" "You will, though," the Queen said, "if you don't make a memorandum of it."

Lewis Carroll
Through the Looking Glass

Memos are the chief means of written communication within an organization.

From salesperson, to executive to king, memos replace the letter for *internal* (interoffice or intraorganizational) communication. Research shows, moreover, that men and women in professional, technical, and managerial occupations write more memos than any other form of communication.

FUNCTIONS OF THE MEMO

Usually less formal than letters, business memos (1) serve as a reminder by providing a written record—everything from a temporary list to a permanent record of discussions, meetings, policies, changes, procedures; (2) replace or reinforce telephone conversations; (3) carry information *across, up,* and *down* levels or ranks—from one employee to another, from subordinates to management, from management to subordinates (see Chapter 2, pages 31–34, "Organizational Communication").

Memos move up, down, and sideways.

In addition, memos may convey nonverbal implications, establish position (status) through routing, take credit or avoid blame, or avoid confrontations.

Carla Butenhoff, spokesperson for a large midwest corporation, explains that the way a memo is routed indicates who has authority over whom (Butenhoff, pp. 12–13).

. . . What names are on top, which on the bottom to get copies, and whether the names of those getting copies are listed (carbon copies) or not listed (blind or silent copies), makes a great deal of difference.

For example, if I put my immediate supervisor's name AND the vice-president's name on the top, it says I really report to both equally. If the supervisor's name is on top and I send a copy to the vice-president, it means that, though structurally I report to the supervisor, I have direct access to the VP.

If I give the VP a copy, but don't indicate that on the supervisor's memo, I am withholding information from my supervisor and asserting that my "real" boss is the vice-president. If I want to cooperate with my immediate supervisor, I address the memo to him and allow him to route it—he or she, thereby, gets credit for my activities.

. . . it's important not to skip steps in the hierarchy to avoid ruffling feathers. . . . when a company president gets a complaint letter, a memo gets sent to a vice-president who sends a note to an assistant VP, who writes a memo to the director of communication, who gives the letter to a writer. The writer has to send the response back up through the same positions. . . . it allows each person access to all the information possessed by those below and *commentators agree that possession of information equals possession of power in all kinds of situations in and out of business.* [Italics added.]

Similarly, if a vice-president sends a copy of a memo directly to me instead of routing it through my boss, he indicates a higher status for me.

With tongue in cheek, Ms. Butenhoff explains how a writer takes credit:

The simplest way is to attach your memo to someone else's work, saying, "the attached may be of interest to you." A slightly more sophisticated technique is to write a memo attaching your name to the idea of someone else, or, more honestly, write a memo attaching your name to your own idea before somebody else pirates it.

. . . most effective . . . is to simply record everything you do in memos. Rather than just doing your job, you do your job and write a memo. The sheer volume of paper and the repeated appearance of your name convince people that you're working. . . .

If something goes wrong:

. . . quickly fire off a memo reprimanding your subordinate or querying your peer about the matter. You get your licks in first. It is forever recorded as their fault.

To avoid confrontations:

If there is bad news, write a memo and send it in instead of going yourself. The ancient practice of cutting out the tongue of the messenger who brings bad news isn't completely dead. . . .

Professionals will tell you to take seriously Ms. Butenhoff's "humorous" advice. They'll also tell you how both favorable and disastrous first impressions have been created by an employee's first memo.

After you have identified the audience for your memo, put your writing skills to work: determine your pattern of organization (POWER), develop your style, and establish an effective image—appearance.

And *always keep a copy of every memo (and every other business communication that you write.* Forget and regret—you will need the copy for proof, for follow-up, for complaints, for a permanent record.

Keep copies of all your memos—for confirmation, protection, a permanent record.

ORGANIZATION

As the most widely used, most popular form of written communication within an organization, the memo has more than 150 possible applications. It differs from the letter primarily in form and from the report primarily in length.

Like all messages, the memo requires your skill in the use of POWER (Plan, Organize, Write, Evaluate, Revise). Omitting any one of these steps is a mistake, psychologically and professionally, for the memo message flows up, down, and across channels. The memo may have organizationwide exposure and evaluation that can enhance or damage your image.

The memo has two important advantages: speedy planning and organizing. The memo writer usually knows a good deal about the reader(s) (Chapter 4), and a great deal about the five Ws and one H—Who, What, Why, When, Where, and How—(Chapter 6). The writer and reader(s) "speak the same language," have the same or similar business environments.

Memos generally follow the information pattern.

Most memos take the form of the information pattern (discussed earlier in regard to letters), beginning directly with the most important information. You, the writer, know the purpose of the memo and should have the facts directly at hand because most informal memos contain information gathered by the sender.

More formal memos may require your doing research, compiling information from several sources. (See Chapter 13 for reports in memo form.) For such memos, make certain that your information is valid. Cite sources and name names. By means of your access to material; your choice of one source over another; the depth of your research in libraries, in other departments and companies, and with other people, you demonstrate your resourcefulness and objectivity.

Whatever the purpose of the memo, write as well as you can, evaluate carefully, revise if necessary. Maintain the same high standards for writing to colleagues within the organization as you do for writing to clients and others upon whom the organization may depend.

Guard against being sloppy, careless, hurried. Show your concern for *all* readers. Always write with the "you" viewpoint.

STYLE

When in doubt, cut it out. Accuracy, Brevity, and Clarity (ABC) hold for memos as well as letters, reports, and proposals. The technology explosion, including electronic mail and other word processors, may require you to learn several new computer languages. Telex, for example, requires an abbreviated word system. Telegraphese (page 110) is acceptable in some organizations, taboo in others.

Some writers argue that using the telegraphic style for memos carries over to letters and reports. It is like using good English during the week and slang on weekends. You will have to follow the style set down by your organization, adapt and adjust. *Think short for memos,* whatever the message: short words, short sentences, short paragraphs. Get to the point directly, quickly, specifically. Write only what must be included, then stop. Remember KISS!

Make your memos direct, concise, and as short as possible.

IMAGE

Special Forms

Specialized, preprinted, fill-in memo forms are common in business. Sizes vary from 4½ by 5½ inches and smaller (Figure 12–1) to 8½ by 11 inches. Some are single sheets, and others have multiple carbons for speedy replies with instant records. Remember to ask if there is a special form to use if you are asked to write a memo.

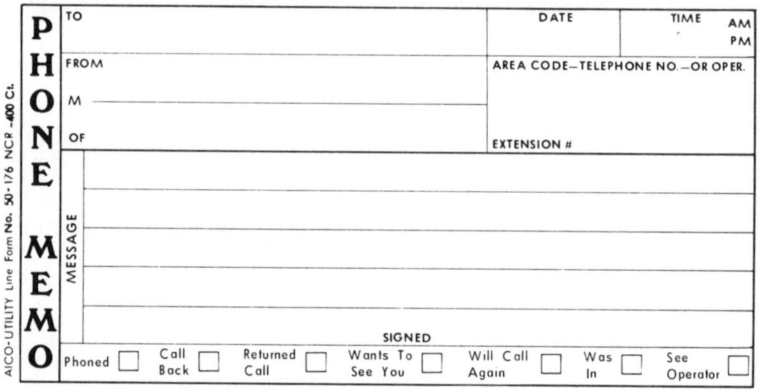

PHONE MEMO

TO | DATE | TIME AM PM

FROM | AREA CODE—TELEPHONE NO.—OR OPER.

M

OF | EXTENSION #

MESSAGE

SIGNED

Phoned ☐ Call Back ☐ Returned Call ☐ Wants To See You ☐ Will Call Again ☐ Was In ☐ See Operator ☐

AICO-UTILITY Line Form No. 50-176 NCR -400 Ct.

Figure 12–1: Specialized Type of Memo

Contemporary or Traditional Format

Use printed memo forms whenever they are available.

Choice of format applies to memos as well as to other kinds of writing. The contemporary format may be a cross between a letter and a memo (Figure 12–2). *Spacing* is more flexible than the *position of elements* in a memo. Standard elements, or parts, usually hug the top of the page (Figure 12–3). Many organizations have these printed on special memo paper. Printed memo parts reduce the time and effort the writer must spend in setting up the message and getting started, the reader must spend in finding information, and the file clerk must spend in filing the memo.

Detailed instructions for military memos leave nothing to chance. A Navy format is illustrated here, but equally exact printed instructions are available for all military services. Applicable to civilian use is the Navy's distinction among three forms:

1. "From-to" memorandum—informal, between subordinates, usually within same activity
2. "Memorandum for" memorandum—more formal, often more official in format, used with high-level officials (see Figure 12–4)
3. Two-way letter/memo—used either as a routine naval letter or as "from-to" memorandum; preprinted, preinserted carbon, two-way communication (reply required)

THE UNIVERSITY OF IOWA

College of Education / Iowa City, Iowa 52240

Date: April 4, 1981

To: Mrs. Dorothy Peterson

From: Joyce Hood

Re: Information on Dyslexia

Dear Mrs. Peterson:

    Dr. Arthur Baxton referred your letter of
March 9 to me.

    I enclose a brochure and a paper that I
hope will help you.

               Sincerely,

               Joyce E. Hood, Director
               Children's Reading Clinic

JEH:gl
encl.

Figure 12–2: A Combination Memo/Letter Format

Memorandum

Domain Industries, Inc.

Date   February 27, 1981

To   All Doboy Dealers

From   Dr. Francis Nelson

Subject   Doboy Baby Pig 5 Promotion

SPECIAL OFFER

During the month of March, Doboy will be giving you, the Dealer, one 50 lb. bag of Pig Pow-R 25 with each 500 lbs. of baby Pig Formula 5.

To help you sell the Baby Pig Formula 5, we are:

1.   Advertising in the National Hog Farmer, announcing the offer of a free bag of Pig Pow-R 25 with the purchase of Baby Pig 5.

2.   Enclosing

    a.   Poster of the Ad
    b.   Two Ad Slicks
    c.   One Radio Script

The tape of the music from the radio ads can be obtained from your Doboy Territory Manager, if you don't already have one.

The Pig Pow-R 25 will be shipped with your order of Baby Pig Formula 5. Indicate if you want code 466 or code 488.

This promotion lasts for the month of March.

Get the baby pigs on Doboy's Baby Pig Program and feed them until they go to market!

vs

Enclosures: 3

Figure 12–3: The Parts of a Memo

(Asterisks indicate items that may not be
required or applicable)

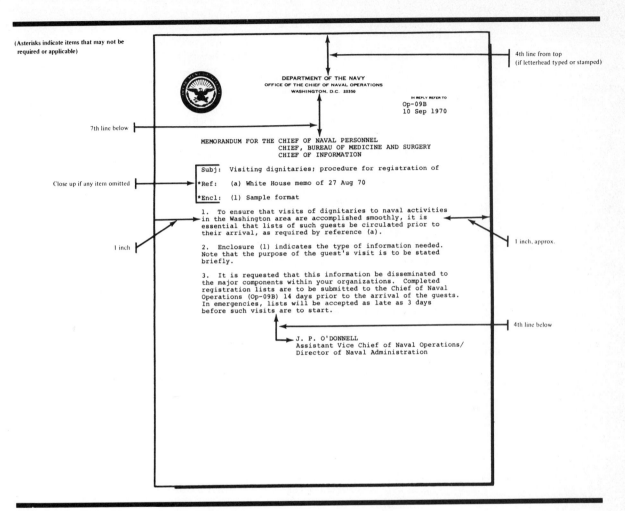

4th line from top
(if letterhead typed or stamped)

DEPARTMENT OF THE NAVY
OFFICE OF THE CHIEF OF NAVAL OPERATIONS
WASHINGTON, D.C. 20350

IN REPLY REFER TO
Op-09B
10 Sep 1970

7th line below

MEMORANDUM FOR THE CHIEF OF NAVAL PERSONNEL
CHIEF, BUREAU OF MEDICINE AND SURGERY
CHIEF OF INFORMATION

Subj: Visiting dignitaries; procedure for registration of

*Ref: (a) White House memo of 27 Aug 70

*Encl: (1) Sample format

Close up if any item omitted

1. To ensure that visits of dignitaries to naval activities
in the Washington area are accomplished smoothly, it is
essential that lists of such guests be circulated prior to
their arrival, as required by reference (a).

2. Enclosure (1) indicates the type of information needed.
Note that the purpose of the guest's visit is to be stated
briefly.

1 inch

1 inch, approx.

3. It is requested that this information be disseminated to
the major components within your organizations. Completed
registration lists are to be submitted to the Chief of Naval
Operations (Op-09B) 14 days prior to the arrival of the guests.
In emergencies, lists will be accepted as late as 3 days
before such visits are to start.

4th line below

J. P. O'DONNELL
Assistant Vice Chief of Naval Operations/
Director of Naval Administration

Figure 12–4: Navy "Memorandum For" Format

Standard Memo Parts

The following memo parts are shown in Figure 12–3.

Heading.   On imprinted stationery, this is identified as "Interoffice Communication," "Memo," "Memorandum," or specialized memo type. It is positioned at the left or right margin or centered, usually with about one-inch top and side margins. Do not settle for "From the desk of" with a place for your name. Your *desk* can't write, and it doesn't want to hear from another *desk.* On unprinted stationery, use the same heading information, following the above content and positioning.

Organization name (part of Heading).   Address and phone number may be included. Or you can place that information on the bottom of the page.

Logo (part of Heading).   This is usually included on all company communications, positioned as it appears on other correspondence forms.

Date line.   The date line is usually located below the heading: marking the left margin; one inch to the left of the right margin; centered beneath the heading; or below the "From" (not preferred). Military style, without commas, is acceptable—27 February 1981. Spell out the month. Writing the date only in figures can cause problems for the reader.

"To" line.   This line is equivalent to the inside address on a letter. It is positioned two spaces below the date. Include name(s), title(s), possibly address(es). Start either two spaces after the "To" or line up with the "From" content (as illustrated in Figure 12–3). Include or omit colon after "To." List multiple names in order of impor-tance. If in doubt about status or ranking, ask someone who knows. (Remember nonverbal implications.) If all the names are at the same level, list them alphabetically. Check off the person's name as you address the envelope or fold the memo for sending. Checking each name on your copy at the same time helps make certain everyone receives the memo.

"From" line.   Include the same type of information as on the "To" line. The writer's signature is not necessary for most internal com-munications. However, initials may be written opposite the "From" line or at the close of the memo. (Opposite the "From" is the pre-ferred position.)

Subject line.   The subject line appears two or three spaces beneath the previous entry, flush with the left margin or indented several spaces for maximum attention. It may be underlined for additional emphasis. "Re:" (in reference to) may be used in place of "Subject." It is shorter, more formal. Remember accuracy, brevity, and clarity as you state the specific purpose of the memo on this line. Subject lines help the writer get started and aid the secretary in filing and retrieval.

Subheadings.   Use subheadings when additional information should be highlighted. They may be centered two spaces above the text, or, more easily, written or typed flush with the left margin.

Body.   Place the body two or three spaces below the subject line, flush (blocked) or indented; single-space with double spaces between paragraphs. Use short words, short sentences, short paragraphs, numerous subheadings, "bullets," itemization, numbers— any device providing fast, easy reading and quick comprehension. Usually informational, memos may convey refusal or selling content. Keep the length of the body to a minimum—one to three pages—the shorter the better. Use plain English, but adapt terminology to the reader.

Special Parts

Initials.   Include initials only if the memo is dictated to and typed by someone else. (Also see discussion of "From" line.) Usually include the typist's initials only (see exception below). Place them two spaces below the last line of the body. They are usually lowercase, but may be in capitals. Omit punctuation.

Signature.   In formal memos from administrators, follow standard letter procedures, omitting the complimentary close but including both typist's and writer's initials *plus* a full signature and title, usually four spaces below the body.

Enclosure.   Place the enclosure line two spaces below the initials or in their place. The word *Enclosure* is usually spelled out in capitals and lowercase letters.

Carbon copy.   Place names in this position rather than listing them in "To" to indicate that you are writing directly to the addressee. You are keeping the other(s) informed as a matter of courtesy, for the record, to protect yourself, or as a way of indirectly asking for a response. List these names in order of importance or alphabetically.

Postscript. Treat as in a letter.

Multipage headings. Treat these as in a letter. For memos sent to groups, omit the name, substitute the subject. Continue the message two to four spaces below the heading. But try to restrict your message to one page, if at all possible.

When mailing a memo (sending it through interoffice mail), include name, department, and, when needed, building, usually typed in the upper-left corner of the envelope. Some organizations have preprinted multiuse envelopes with blanks for data. Seal the envelope if the memo is confidential.

Your response to a memo can be written at the bottom of the page or as a separate communication. Special preprinted carbon or carbonless memo paper provides the possibility for an immediate response.

PAPER AND REPRODUCTION

Memos are frequently written on lighter-weight, less expensive paper than letter stock because they are used internally and in greater quantity. Colors are often distinctive, varied, and coded for quick identification of purpose and source.

Memos may be typed or handwritten. Reproduction for mass distribution follows the methods discussed in Chapter 7.

ASSIGNMENT: MEMOS

Your training and development director has asked your group to meet and discuss the importance of memos in your organization. Prior to the meeting you are to select a subject for a memo and set it up in three different forms: letter/memo, informal, and formal. Bring your three versions to the meeting and exchange them with other members of the group. After everyone has looked over all of the memos, discuss the following topic questions.

Topics

1. What is an internal communication?
2. How does a memo differ from a letter?
3. What are the main uses of a memo?
4. What do we mean when we say that memos "carry information across, up, and down levels"?
5. What are some of the nonverbal implications of a memo? How are these activated? Why is it important to understand these implications?
6. In terms of planning and organization, what are some of the advantages of writing a memo?
7. What are the standard parts of a memo?
8. What are the special parts of a memo?

FURTHER READING

Bentley, Trevor J. *Communication, and the Paperwork Explosion.* London: McGraw-Hill, 1976.

Butenhoff, Carla. "Bad Writing Can Be Good Business." *ABCA Bulletin,* 40, June 1977, 12–13.

Grossman, Lee. *Fat Paper, Diets for Trimming Paperwork.* New York: McGraw-Hill, 1976.

Lee, LaJuana W. *Business Communication.* Chicago: Rand McNally, 1980.

Swindle, Robert E. *Business Communicator.* Englewood Cliffs, NJ: Prentice-Hall, 1980.

Uris, Auren. *Memos for Managers.* New York: Thomas Y. Crowell, 1975.

CHAPTER THIRTEEN

Reports*

"I think I should understand that better," Alice said very politely, "if I had it written down; but I can't quite follow it as you say it."

"That's nothing to what I could say if I chose," the Duchess replied, in a pleased tone.

"Pray don't trouble yourself to say it any longer than that," said Alice.

Lewis Carroll
Alice in Wonderland

Make your reports as concise as possible.

Reports are necessary elements of organizational life. The complexity of a subject and the amount of supporting evidence needed to document a decision may require a report of dozens and even hundreds of pages. Still, a report should never be longer than it absolutely has to be.

The contents of a report may have an immediate value, a future value, or a historical value. As a sales manager, you may want to learn now why people in Peoria have stopped buying parsnips. As the user of computer printouts, you may someday want to know how to get direct access to data. When you are considering moving the corporate headquarters to Dallas, you may want to find out why the present headquarters was moved from Louisville to Atlanta several years ago. In each case, the information you seek will most likely appear in a report.

Reports are more common at lower administrative levels than at the higher levels of an organization. To approve the purchase of new machinery, the board of directors may need to know only that the machinery should cut manufacturing costs by 10 percent. (A memo report, should be prepared to save executives time—see pages 263–264.) Somewhere in the organization, however, someone must have a written record of the basis for that promise.

In deciding whether to adopt a new process, high-level management may wish to know only how well the process will work

---

*This chapter was written in collaboration with Karl E. Gwiasda, Associate Professor of English, Iowa State University. The section on Research was written in collaboration with Alma Jean Walker, Department of English, Iowa State University.

and how much it will cost. They may want a recommendation supported by a summary of relevant data. Intermediate managers, however, need more detailed information supporting the claims made for the process. They base their conclusions on the information gathered through extended research.

Lower-level managers who work closely with the process need the most detailed information of all and frequently do much of the report preparation. Although reports are more common at lower levels, they can have a place anywhere within an organization.

Reports serve a number of functions, such as

- saving people from having to memorize bulk amounts of information
- giving permanence to results of surveys, experiments, field studies, and other investigations
- providing a record of the reasons for starting or stopping an activity
- bringing together information that is useful to or needed by employees, clients, customers, or officials

Like letters, reports may be written for external communication: from one organization to another, from a division or an agency to the general public or some select group, from a consultant firm to a client. Like memos, reports may be written solely for internal communication: from a subordinate to a superior, from one department to another department, from a branch office to the headquarters. Whenever the decision-making activities of business, government, or industry involve large amounts of information, a long report is needed.

Reports may be written for external or internal communication.

Decisions requiring reports occur when

- developing new products
- defining organizational policies
- deciding marketing strategies
- conducting financial analyses
- making design modifications
- detailing matters concerning employee grievances or labor relations
- investigating insurance claims
- comparing and evaluating different options
- describing an organization's past performance and its plans for the future
- establishing fairer hiring procedures
- ensuring safe and healthful operations

During your career, you will probably have to read and write reports. Writing a good report takes time, but it is no harder (or easier) than writing a good letter or memo. Even if the report must be long, you can still make it concise—and simple. The following guidelines will help you.

RESEARCH

Effective reports require research.

Before you can begin to write a report, you must do research. Research is conducted at many levels, for many purposes, with varying degrees of expertise and sophistication. It has been called a science, an art, a technique. It is basic to the holistic approach to good business communication.

Formal research consists of

1. recognizing and defining a problem
2. establishing the purpose for the research
3. reviewing the literature
4. developing the hypotheses
5. designing the investigation
6. writing the proposal
7. collecting, organizing, analyzing, and interpreting the data
8. drawing the conclusions
9. writing the final report

Whatever the problem, whatever the project, there are only two types of research: *primary research*—original, first-hand research; and *secondary research*—research for information already available, published.

Secondary Research

Begin with secondary research, information already available.

To avoid the heartbreak of duplicating someone else's earlier original research and to save time, begin with secondary research. Information located in your library will help you gain an overview of the subject; zero in on a specific area of the problem; find additional means of investigation; and learn specific, necessary data.

Here are some suggestions on how to conduct secondary research.

1. Become acquainted with and use the library staff.

2. Familiarize yourself with the card catalog and the library system of classification.
3. Locate and use the reference section and basic sources:
   a. encyclopedias
   b. yearbooks and almanacs
   c. dictionaries
   d. handbooks
   e. bibliographical dictionaries
   f. business service publications
   g. book guides
   h. periodical and pamphlet guides
4. Use interlibrary loan for access to most public and institutional libraries.
5. Find out where government documents are kept.
6. Use the media center—learn about microforms, video cassettes, slides, film loops, film.
7. Investigate computer research banks and computer search.
8. Collect your material and divide it into these categories:
   a. books (monographs)
   b. serials (periodicals, newspapers, journals, yearbooks, annual reports)
   c. documents and statistics
   d. dissertations
   e. audiovisuals
   (These categories are similiar to the physical division of material in libraries, making it easier for you to find what you need.)
9. Make a bibliographical entry for each source on a 3-by-5-inch card (lined or unlined), using a standardized form for each category (see Figure 13–1, and Exhibit 13–1). You'll want to refer to the secondary research in your report, whether that report is written or oral. Having the exact sources helps establish your credibility, reliability, and scholarship. The card entries will enable you to write footnotes and bibliography quickly and accurately.
10. Check and double-check your information, especially figures.

Primary Research

After you have collected, organized, and analyzed all of the information, you are ready for primary research, if applicable. The combination of secondary and primary research enables you to reach conclusions.

Proceed with primary, first-hand, research.

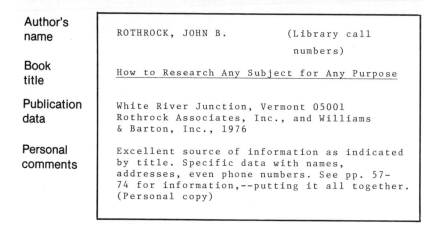

Author's name	ROTHROCK, JOHN B. (Library call numbers)
Book title	<u>How to Research Any Subject for Any Purpose</u>
Publication data	White River Junction, Vermont 05001 Rothrock Associates, Inc., and Williams & Barton, Inc., 1976
Personal comments	Excellent source of information as indicated by title. Specific data with names, addresses, even phone numbers. See pp. 57-74 for information,--putting it all together. (Personal copy)

Figure 13–1: Sample Bibliography Card—Typed or Written by Hand

Here is how to conduct primary research.

1. *Observe.* Keep a detailed daily log of items and events; audit reports; make a content analysis.
2. *Experiment.* Work in the field of the topic under study or in the laboratory. (By law, using human subjects requires special permission from authorities.)
3. *Survey.* Take a sampling; use questionnaires, opinion polls; conduct interviews by phone or in person.

CAUTION

Proceed objectively and logically. This is important in every step of research but particularly when you are drawing conclusions from your total material, using statistics, graphs, and charts.

Endnotes, Footnotes, and Bibliographical Entries: *MLA Handbook* Format

Credit your sources fully and accurately.

When you are writing a report, you should credit your research sources. This not only protects you from claims of plagiarism, but allows others to confirm your findings. Various style guides (see Exhibit 13–1) contain specific directions for writing secondary-research entries. Modern Language Association (MLA) instructions are popular and widely accepted. But ask before you write. A particular organization may prefer one format over another. Many organizations even publish their own guides and demand strict adherence to their rules.

According to the *MLA Handbook,* you should place all references to research papers at the end of the text as *endnotes.* They should appear on a new page, often without a number, with the title "Notes" appearing two inches from the top of the page. Then skip four lines, that is, double-space twice, below the title, indent five spaces, and begin the first line of the first note. Type the note number raised (as a superscript) without punctuation, skip a space, and type the reference. Type notes consecutively, double-spacing within and between notes. Use as many pages as needed. Number any pages after the first.

Footnotes appearing at the bottom of the relevant pages take the same format as endnotes except that entries are single-spaced. In a *bibliography,* however, the entries appear in alphabetical order, last name first, and the second line (not the first) of each entry is indented five spaces.

Exhibit 13–1: Style Guides

A Manual of Style, 12th ed. Chicago: University of Chicago Press, 1969.

CBE Style Manual, 4th ed. Arlington, VA: American Institute of Biological Sciences, 1978.

Clements, Wallace and Robert G. Waite. *Guide for Beginning Technical Editors*. Livermore, CA: University of California, Lawrence Livermore Laboratory, 1979.

MLA Handbook for Writers of Research Papers, Theses, and Dissertations. New York: Modern Language Association, 1977.

Nicholson, Margaret. *A Practical Style Guide for Authors and Editors*. New York: Holt, Rinehart and Winston, 1970.

Publication Manual of the American Psychological Association. Washington, D.C.: APA, 1977.

Style Manual . . . for Guidance in the Preparation of Papers for Journals Published by the American Institute of Physics. New York: AIP, 1973.

Turabian, Kate L. *A Manual for Writers of Term Papers, Theses, and Dissertations*. 4th ed. Chicago: University of Chicago Press, 1973.

Williams, Carol T. and Gary K. Wolfe. *Elements of Research: A Guide for Writers*. Sherman Oaks, CA: Alfred, 1979.

Style guides include examples of almost every type of published and unpublished material with detailed explanations concerning punctuation and spacing. Unfortunately, the explanations are sometimes hard to follow.

The guides listed here are among the most popular in current usage. However, many large public and private organizations (American Oil Company, General Motors, NCR, others), government agencies, and educational institutions compile their own.

If there is more than one author, only the first author's name is reversed. Both footnotes and bibliography contain similar material with some punctuation and spacing changes. Follow these conventions as indicated in the style guide of your choice.

Footnotes or *endnotes* (consecutively numbered) follow this form:

| Indent 5 spaces | Normal order | Comma | Main title | Optional subtitle |

double-space endnotes, single-space footnotes

[1]William Safire, <u>On Language</u> (New York, N.Y.:

Times Books, 1980), p. 134.

| Publishing data in parentheses | Place of publication, publisher, separated by colon | Comma | Period |

Bibliographical entries (secondary-research references) follow this form:

| Reverse for alphabetizing | Three main divisions—author, title, publishing—each ending with a period | Include subtitle |

double-space

Safire, William. <u>On Language</u>. New York, N.Y.:

Times Books, 1980.

| Indent second line 5 spaces | No parentheses around publishing data | No page numbers |

In footnotes, when you need to cite the same source more than once, use a shortened, simplified version of the original. Use either standard abbreviations or Latin terms or—what is even more popular, easier to read—the name of the author(s) and the publication page number(s).

[2]Safire, page 134. or [2]Op. cit., p. 134.

Latin terms traditionally used in the past but some of which are now considered superfluous include

- c. or ca. (*circa*)—approximate date
- et al. (*et alii*)—and others—refers to multiple authors

- ibid. (*ibidem*)—in the same place—refers to immediately preceding footnote
- loc. cit. (*loco citato*)—in the place cited—refers to same page in a previously cited footnote
- op. cit. (*opere citato*)—the work cited—refers to a previously cited footnote followed by at least one other
- pass. (*passim*)—in a number of scattered passages
- q. v. (*quod vide*)—which see
- sup. (*supra*)—above—refers to something discussed earlier

Other popular abbreviations are

- ch.—chapter
- f., ff.—following page(s)
- l., ll.—line(s)
- MS—manuscript
- p., pp.—page, pages
- tr., trans.—translated by

Choose a style and be consistent.

Endnotes, Footnotes, and Bibliographical Entries: Contemporary Format

Text Citations: Endnotes and Bibliographical Entries.   There are two commonly used formats for making citations within the body of the text.

The first format consists of using endnotes. (If you have a choice, use endnotes rather than footnotes. Footnotes distract the reader.) Start with the superscript[1] and continue through the report until the final citation. (Note: Always place the superscript *after* the punctuation.) The endnotes themselves are placed at the end of the report, under the heading "Notes." Observe the following style for endnotes.

1. Match numbers to citations, comments, further information.
2. Follow the superscript number with the author's name for citations—first name first.
3. Underline the title of a book; use quotation marks around the title of an article.
4. Use commas to separate all parts of the citation except the state from the publisher; use a colon following the state's abbreviation; close with a period.

5. Enter the publisher's name as printed on the spine of a book or abbreviate, eliminating "publishing company," "Inc.," or "Press" if the company is well known.
6. Type single-spaced, flush with the left margin; double-space between entries.
7. Include complete addresses, including zip codes if you are recommending readers to write for further information. (Include area codes with phone numbers.)

Notes

[1] William Safire, <u>On Language</u>, New York, N.Y.:
Times Books, 1980, p. 134.

[2] Details of footnotes and bibliography drive people crazy!

The second format for citing within the text consists of briefly citing the reference itself.

"All of life is research. So if R = Research and R^x--the exponential (x) is infinity" (Rothrock, 1976) <u>or</u> (Rothrock, p.1).

Then, at the end of the publication, use the bibliographical form for the complete reference. Observe the following style rules for bibliographical entries.

1. Reverse the author's name for alphabetizing (first author only if there are multiple authors).
2. Use a period after the author's name.
3. Underline the title of the book; use quotation marks around the title of an article.
4. Use a period after the complete title.
5. Follow with the city, comma, state abbreviation, colon, publisher's name (abbreviated), comma, year of publication, period. (If the city is well known, the state may be omitted; but in that case, follow the city with a colon.)
6. Single-space between lines of the same entry, double-space between entries, typing information flush left.

Safire, William. <u>On Language</u>. New York, N.Y.:
Times Books, 1980.

Camelot, Jane. <u>Equal Rights for All</u>. Mount Helena, WA: No Press, 1990.

Footnotes. Footnote only material of *immediate importance* to the text discussion. Use an asterisk in the text to call attention to the footnote at the bottom of that page. (Banish other references to the endnotes.) In typing footnotes, type an approximately 18-character line three spaces below the last line of the text. (Try to keep your pages to the same number of total lines—for good appearance.) Type all lines of the footnote single-spaced and flush with the left margin.

CAUTION

You must follow the style assigned by your instructor or organization. Once you adopt a style, be consistent throughout your writing. Style, too, is part of your image—or that of your organization. (This text uses the contemporary style referred to above.)

VISUAL AIDS

Your research will probably produce a great deal of data. One way of making that data more manageable and presentable to your audience is to use *visual aids*.

To make your data more palatable, use visual aids.

Visual aids within a report

- condense evidence or data for easier reading
- emphasize important material or data
- dramatize major points
- explain complicated or involved relationships
- clarify material otherwise hard to conceptualize

A visual aid within a report is usually identified as either a table or a figure. Tables and figures are numbered consecutively (Table 1, Table 2, Table 3) and are titled (Figure 1: Warehouse Layout; Figure 2: Distribution of Annual Expenses; Figure 3: Crop Yields vs. Annual Rainfalls).

Tables provide convenient, easy-to-read summaries of data. They are especially effective with numerical data but may include brief descriptive phrases (Table 13–1).

Figures refer to all pictorial materials other than tables. The more common types of figures are

- graphs—useful for showing trends, changes, and tendencies
- bar graphs—useful for showing relative magnitudes of compared items (Figure 13–2)

Table 13–1: A Table Summarizing Key Financial Data

Dollar Amounts In Thousands Except Per Share Data **For The Year**	**1979**	1978	1977	1976
Operating revenue	**$115,805**	$104,690	$ 82,448	$ 69,770
Operating expenses:				
Compensation costs	**$ 40,178**	$ 35,648	$ 30,095	$ 25,944
Depreciation and amortization	**6,522**	5,348	4,433	3,600
Other	**38,542**	36,896	27,920	23,523
Total expenses	**$ 85,242**	$ 77,892	$ 62,448	$ 53,067
Operating income	**$ 30,563**	$ 26,798	$ 20,000	$ 16,703
As a percent of revenue	**26.4%**	25.6%	24.3%	23.9%
Financial income (expense), net	**(1,866)**	(2,022)	(85)	114
Income before taxes on income and gain on sale of properties	**$ 28,697**	$ 24,776	$ 19,915	$ 16,817
Gain on sale of properties	**—**	4,590	933	—
Income before taxes on income	**$ 28,697**	$ 29,366	$ 20,848	$ 16,817
Income taxes	**13,304**	13,452	9,178	7,393
Net income	**$ 15,393**	$ 15,914	$ 11,670	$ 9,424
Average number of common and common equivalent shares outstanding (in thousands)	**7,237**	7,371	7,461	7,533
Earnings per common and common equivalent share:				
Net income	**$ 2.13**	$ 2.16	1.56	1.25
Net income, excluding gains	**$ 2.13**	$ 1.81	$ 1.48	$ 1.25
Percent increase	**17.7%**	22.3%	18.4%	30.2%
Working capital from operations	**$ 20,999**	$ 17,054	$ 13,226	$ 11,697
Percent increase	**23.1%**	28.9%	13.1%	36.9%
Dividends per share	**$ .68**	$ .51	$ .40	$ .29
Percent increase	**33.3%**	27.5%	37.9%	38.1%
As a percent of prior year's earnings	**37.6%**	34.5%	32.0%	30.2%

Source: Courtesy of Lee Enterprises, Inc., 1979 Annual Report.

- pie charts—useful for showing proportions among items making up some whole (Figure 13–3)
- drawings—useful for showing what objects look like, how they are put together, how they are used, how they are made
- flowcharts—useful for showing sequence of steps or operations in a process or procedure
- organization charts—useful for showing the functional and administrative relationships among people whose labor and efforts have been divided to achieve some group goal—a flowchart showing paths of authority and responsibility (Figure 13–4)

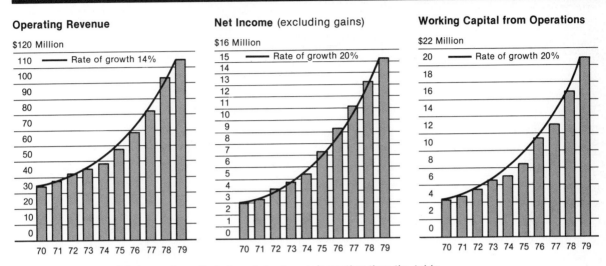

Notice how the graph is more dramatic but contains less information than the table.

Figure 13–2: A Bar/Line Graph of Some of the Data in Table 13–1.

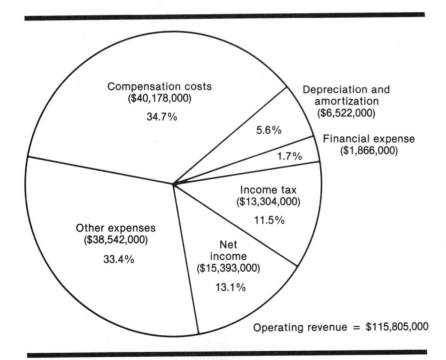

Figure 13–3: A Pie Chart of the Data in Table 13–1.

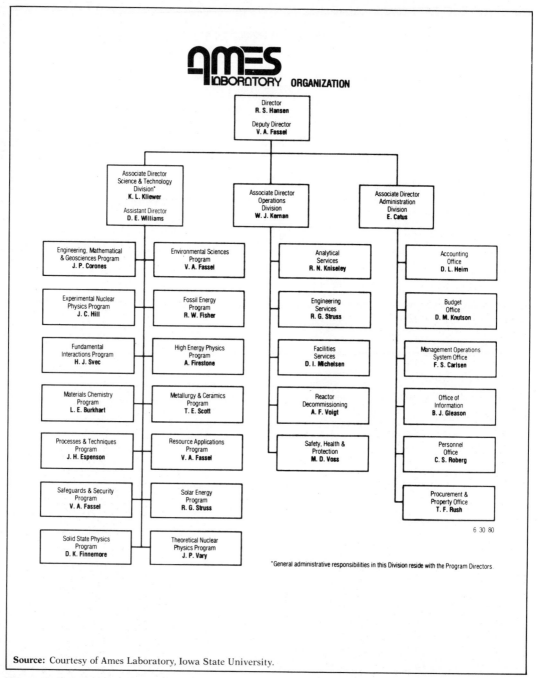

Source: Courtesy of Ames Laboratory, Iowa State University.

Figure 13–4: A Typical Organizational Chart

Other possible figures are schematics, exhibits, layouts, photographs, maps, and reproductions.

Visual aids should never be merely ornamental. They should support or supplement the written text. All such aids should be as simple and uncluttered as possible, professional in appearance. To ensure high-quality visual aids, some writers have them prepared by professional artists, photographers, or draftspersons. (For a discussion of visual aids in presentations, see Appendix B.)

Visual aids should support your text.

MEMO REPORTS

The short report displays the writer's ability to distinguish between unimportant and important details. Usually written for someone within an organization, it is used when the reader's time is limited and full detail is not needed. It can summarize a long report or it can alert its reader to take needed action.

Use the memo report when full detail is unnecessary.

The *memo report* follows the same basic format as the memo (Chapter 12). In addition to "Date," "To," "From," and "Subject" lines, most memo reports include, centered or flush with the left margin,

- Introduction, purpose, or problem
- Conclusion(s), solution(s) (including costs, if any)
- Recommendation(s) or alternate ways of handling the problem, and action requested

Immediately following the subject line (two or three spaces below) or after the conclusion(s), centered or flush with the left margin, in semiformal reports the following may appear:

- Summary of Results
- Discussion
- Tables

Still another possible organization consists of the following steps: purpose, conclusion, recommendation, advantages, disadvantages, cost. Informal or semiformal reports may also be written in letter form. Your purpose is to have the message read quickly. Plan, organize, and write for your reader and purpose. Keep it simple. Figures 13–5 and 13–6 show variations of the organization and content of the memo report.

LONGER REPORTS

Planning

Plan carefully before you write a long report.

There are four helpful rules for planning a long report.

1. Visualize your reader(s).
2. Identify your purpose.
3. Assemble the contents.
4. Determine the pattern—IRS or combination.

Suppose the company you work for makes leather buggy whips. Not only do your suppliers of leather keep raising their prices, they are unreliable in their shipments. You think you can use a vinyl to make buggy whips just as good as the leather ones. Your employer thinks rubberized fabric would work better. So you run tests on samples made from each material to compare them for strength, durability, and cost. You get your results, and you're ready to report them.

In this case, you know your reader. And you've assembled the contents for a report in one or more forms, such as data sheets, file cards, computer printouts, company records, and publications.

Now, what is your purpose? There are different possibilities:

• To report the results
• To make a recommendation based on the results
• To identify the advantages and disadvantages of the options

The purpose you select will determine the material you include, the emphasis you give to different parts of that material, and the arrangement of the material. Time and effort are often wasted because a writer ignores the purpose or identifies a purpose different from the one that suits the reader's needs.

Reports are always informational. When your purpose includes making recommendations, you want your reader to be persuaded that the recommendations are logical and based on sound conclusions. To that extent, such reports involve selling. If your buggy whip tests show that vinyl is superior to rubberized fabric, the information or the recommendations in your report will disappoint your employer, will not meet his or her hopes or expectations. Then the report involves the possibility of refusal.

The information comes from your research:

• tests or experiments
• surveys or questionnaires

```
Date:

To:

From:

Subject:


1.  Problem:          Define the problem in one or two
                      sentences.  (Why the report?)

2.  Solution or
    Recommendation:   Begin with "I recommend"; state in one
                      sentence.

3.  Facts:            List objective facts in descending
                      order of importance (most important
                      first).

4.  Discussion:       Explain reasons for recommendation,
                      including subjective information.  List
                      in descending order of importance, one
                      paragraph for each reason, each para-
                      graph beginning with a topic sentence.

(Value:  saves reader's time--presents information quickly,
completely.)
```

Figure 13–5: Suggestions for Organizing Semiformal Memo Reports (Limit to 1¼–1⅓ pages)

- field studies
- publications (professional journals, books, government documents, and so on)
- observation
- interviews
- personal experience

Be sure that your sources are reliable and the information is relevant to the report. *Above all,* double-check the information for accuracy. Even minor errors can weaken a reader's confidence in what you say and can discredit the work you put into the report. Pity the engineer who exclaimed, when the bridge collapsed, "I guess I did misplace that decimal point after all!"

Problem

Recommendations
Facts

Discussion

```
ACME TRACTOR COMPANY

TECHNICAL MEMO

    DATE:  May 23, 1981

    TO:    R. A. Smith, Engineering
           J. A. Morris, Technical Center

    FROM:  J. L. Jones, Engineering

    SUBJECT:  Evaluation of New Anti-Wear Oil #SL-1

    Introduction:  Research and Development recently sent
                   #SL-1 Oil for field testing on latest
                   model tractors.  Nature of test is to
                   determine if #SL-1 improves MPG.

    Recommendations:  I recommend #SL-1 go into production.

    Summary of Results:  1.  Average MPG improved by 10%
                             over standard detergent oils.

                         2.  Engine starting temperature
                             flexibility identical.

                         3.  Corrosion and wear resistance
                             not significantly different.

    Discussion:  15 model 2604 Acme Tractors were used in
                 tests that totaled more than 1,500,000....
```

Figure 13–6: A Sample Memo Report

Name your sources. Where did that population figure come from? The report of the latest U.S. Census? The Chamber of Commerce?

Be specific. How many questionnaires were sent out and how many were returned? In what ways is the inventory control system "inefficient"?

Avoid irrelevancies. Maybe Millard Fillmore once slept in Smithville. But does that fact help explain why Smithville is a better site for a new warehouse than Cranbury?

Organization

Some writers compose a report by putting down their first thought and then adding sentences to it until they run out of things to say. That's the hard way—to write and read.

If you organize first, writing your report will go more easily. Developing a *topic outline* is a simple but effective way to give order to your report. To develop a topic outline, first identify the major ideas or topics; then break up your material by grouping the separate points into apropriate topics or ideas.

Organize a long report by preparing a topic outline.

Traditionally, major ideas are assigned roman numerals, groupings under a major idea uppercase letters, smaller groupings arabic numerals, and so on. This system is rapidly being replaced by the *decimal* or *scientific, system.*

Decimal System	*Roman*
1.0. Leather Buggy Whips	I. Leather Buggy Whips
1.1. Strength Test	A. Strength Test
1.1.1. Subjective Tests	1. Subjective Tests
1.1.2. Objective Tests	2. Objective Tests
1.1.2.1. Absorption	a. Absorption
1.1.2.2. Heat Dispersion	b. Heat Dispersion
1.2. Durability Test	B. Durability Test
1.2.1. Tearing	1. Tearing
1.2.2. Wear	2. Wear
1.2.3. Discoloration	3. Discoloration
1.3. Cost	C. Cost
2.0. Vinyl Buggy Whips	II. Vinyl Buggy Whips
2.1. Strength Test	A. Strength Test
2.1.1. Subjective Tests	1. Subjective Tests
etc.	etc.

Note that in every roman notation, every A division requires at least a B, every 1 requires a 2.

Consider using an idea grid to order your outline.

The decimal system enables a reader to know the exact state of a report. The decimal system may be indented, but not indenting saves time, space, and energy. Variations of the *alphanumeric system*—a combination of the decimal and roman—are used worldwide by librarians, statisticians, and museum curators.

The *idea grid* is a device to help you prepare your material for outlining. David Radloff of the Western Wisconsin Technical Institute explains the advantage of this technique:

> The idea grid is based on the principle of "divide and conquer." That is, while nearly any significant writing project can seem monstrous when viewed as a totality, the same project, if broken down into components, can be comparatively easy (Radloff, 1979).

Here is how the idea grid works. You write each idea or topic on a sheet of paper and identify specifics that apply. Now the material is in manageable portions. Your single lengthy message is now a series of short messages or units. You can deal with those units much as you would handle a letter or short report. You can begin writing the sections in any order.

The best sequence of sections can be decided by arranging and rearranging the idea sheets. Radloff suggests placing the sheets on a table or the floor. Select the sequence that best matches your purpose and pattern (IRS).

Choose the organizational pattern that best fits your audience and purpose.

Writers are often tempted to arrange materials in a chronological order. Such reports become logs of what the writer did rather than announcements of what the writer found out. Frequently, the reader is forgotten.

Suppose, for instance, to use the buggy whip example, your purpose was to recommend the better substitute for leather. Chronologically, the report sections appear in this order:

1. Background
2. Tests run (method)
3. Results (data, evidence)
4. Discussion of results (conclusions)
5. Recommendations

Such an arrangement is serviceable, in fact, almost standard, for technical reports. For our buggy whip report, however, this inductive arrangement (see Chapter 11) hides the most important material behind less significant content. Your report might be more helpful to your boss arranged this way:

1. Recommendations
2. Background
3. Tests run
4. Results
5. Discussion of results

In outline form, such an arrangement might look like this:

1.0. Recommendations
1.1. Begin production of vinyl buggy whips
1.2. Retain limited production of leather buggy whips
2.0. Background
2.1. Costs and unreliable sources of leather
2.2. Possible benefits of vinyl
2.3. Possible benefits of rubberized fabric
3.0. Tests Run
3.1. Strength Test
3.1.1. Subjective Tests
3.1.2. Objective Tests
3.1.2.1. Absorption
3.1.2.2. Heat Dispersion
3.2. Durability Test
3.2.1. Tearing
3.2.2. Wear
3.2.3. Discoloration
3.3. Costs
4.0. Results
4.1. Leather is stronger than vinyl
4.2. Vinyl is stronger than rubberized fabric
4.3. Vinyl is more durable than leather or rubberized fabric
4.4. Vinyl is less expensive than leather and the same price as rubberized fabric
5.0. Discussion of Results

There is yet another way to organize your report: in a deductive arrangement (see Chapter 11). Suppose tests show vinyl is a better substitute than rubber. The boss thought rubber would be better. You might then want to arrange your report persuasively:

1. Summary of results
2. Recommendations
3. Background
4. Tests run

5. Results (in full)
6. Discussion of results

The summary of results would report your conclusions, namely, that the test results show vinyl to be superior to rubber as a substitute for leather. The recommendations would identify the action to take, namely, to replace the leather with the vinyl.

Of course, not all reports include the results of tests. Not all include recommendations. You must think about the special factors and conditions that apply to each report you prepare. But if you remember your audience and the purpose and pattern of the report, then you can prepare a successful report.

Once you have carried out planning and organization, you are ready to write, evaluate, and revise. These last applications of POWER can be made just as they are for other kinds of writing. However, since a report can be considerably longer than most letters, it is helpful to organize your writing time. One way to plan any complicated task is to make a PERT chart (Program Evaluation and Review Technique). Applied to your report writing, it might look something like the one in Figure 13–7. You'll find this technique equally helpful in writing proposals (Chapter 14).

Style

Use a simple, direct style; adapt word choice to your audience.

In any report, long or short, use simple sentences and the active voice wherever possible. Although reports are usually less personal than letters or memos, use the "you" viewpoint whenever it is appropriate. The most formal or most technical report is still a communication between or among human beings.

Try to use everyday language in your reports. If you must use terms unfamiliar to your reader, be sure to explain them.

F. A. Upson, Manager of Engineering for AMOCO Chemical Corporation, offers this advice: "In any report, choice of words is of utmost importance. The words need not be fancy, but they must be used correctly. An otherwise good report can be completely ruined by loose terminology." See Chapter 6.

Image

Some recurrent reports, although not strictly "long reports," may be standardized by means of preprinted forms filled in by the report writer. Examples include quality-control reports, accident reports, inventory reports, and insurance claims.

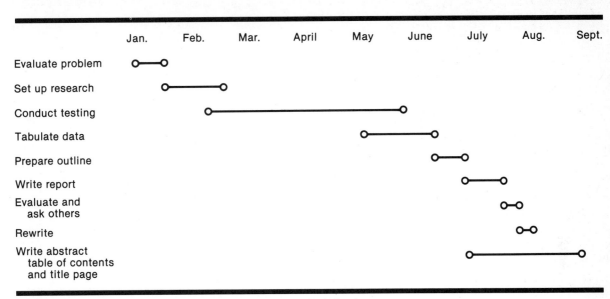

Figure 13–7: A PERT Chart (Program Evaluation and Review Technique)

Formal and semiformal reports tend to follow a traditional format: indented paragraphs, lines of page width, symmetrical layout, and so on. Single-spacing is common, usually with extra space between paragraphs. Manuscripts to be typeset by a compositor, however, are usually double-spaced for the printer's convenience.

Headings and subheadings are used to identify major and subordinate topics. They help readers find material of special interest or importance. Sections may be as short as a paragraph or extend over several pages. In general, the longer the report, the greater the extent of division into sections and subsections. (Note the use of headings—chapter titles—and subheadings in this text, see Figure 13–8.)

Adopt a traditional format, and use headings to guide your audience.

Components

The usual components of a long report are

- title page
- letter of transmittal (see Chapter 9, page 174)
- authorization (optional)
- table of contents

page 2.

SPECIFICATION HIGHLIGHTS

1. New Classes, though listed are not necessarily available. (Explain)

2. Label Color Code, Proof Test Voltages, and Nominal Maximum Use Voltages:

ANSI/ ASTM Color Code	ANSI/ ASTM Class	ANSI/ASTM Proof Test Voltage		ANSI/ASTM Nominal Max. Use Voltage—AC		Conventional Work Position
		AC	DC	Ph to Ph	Ph to Grd	
Red	0	5,000	20,000	1,000	600	Structure or Basket
White	1	10,000	40,000	7,500	4,400	
Yellow	2	20,000	50,000	17,000	10,000	Electrically Isolated Basket or Platform
Green	3	30,000	60,000	26,500	15,000	
Orange	4	40,000	70,000	36,000	20,000	

3. Classification:

   Class 0, 1, 2, 3 & 4
   Type I Non-resistant to ozone - Natural rubber.
   Type II Ozone resistant such as Salisbury Salcor.

IN SERVICE OR RETEST SPECIFICATIONS:

A. Rubber Gloves - Test interval shall not exceed 6 months.
B. Rubber Sleeves - Test interval shall not exceed 12 months.
C. Rubber Blankets - Test interval shall not exceed 12 months.

   A "Designated Person" shall visually inspect rubber gloves at least every six months. Electrically tested gloves and sleeves which have not been issued cannot be put into service unless they have been electrically tested within the previous 12 months.

   NOTE: Definition - "Designated Person" - "An individual who is qualified by experience or training to perform an assigned task". FOREMAN, SUPERVISOR, SAFETY INSPECTOR, but NOT THE USER HIMSELF UNLESS HE IS IN AN ISOLATED LOCATION.

   There is no retest requirement for covers, i.e., hoods, connectors, dead-end protectors and other special coverup devices and line hose. However, the In-Service Specifications emphasize the importance of inspection, performed by the individual, as a requirement in providing PROTECTION FROM ELECTRICAL SHOCK.

   Any cover or hose that upon inspection is found to have punctures, deep cuts, severe corona or ozone cutting, contamination from injurious materials or has lost normal elasticity, shall be rejected.

Source: Courtesy of Paul E. Skarshaug, Skarshaug Testing Laboratory, Ames, Iowa.

Figure 13–8: Sample Page Layout for a Formal Report

- summary or abstract
- body
- conclusions
- recommendations
- appendix (optional)

Special sections are discussed under "Other components."

Title page.   The title page states the report title, the writer's name, and the date. It may also identify the recipient of the report and the place of origin and may possibly include a file number and space for signatures. Some organizations have preprinted forms for use as title pages or as combination title pages and covers.

Authorization.   The authorization consists of a letter, memo, or other document requesting the writer to do the work documented in the report and specifying what is to be done. Authorization pages appear in government and military reports more often than in business and industrial reports. In some instances, an authorization may be a copy of a proposal just initialed as "OK."

Table of contents.   The table of contents identifies the major subdivisions (topic headings) of the report and the pages on which they begin. The headings shown on the contents page(s) must agree with the headings that appear in the report. When a report has only a few divisions (major headings and subheadings), list all of them; when a report has numerous levels of division, you may list only the major divisions. The table of contents helps a reader to see quickly the general structure of a report and the range of topics or information within it.

Summary or abstract.   The summary or abstract restates concisely the report's central ideas or content, rarely exceeds one page, and is best if less than that. (Write it *after* you complete the main body of the text.) A good summary or abstract will save the decision maker from reading every page of the report. The pages must be there, however, just in case the reader needs more detail and in order to keep the historical record complete.

Body.   The body contains the "guts" of the report. The body typically includes

- background
- theory, assumptions made

- statement of problem
- methods, procedures
- sources
- description of study or investigation
- data, evidence, the "facts"
- results (often as tables, charts, graphs)
- conclusions
- recommendations
- suggestions for further inquiries

Conclusions.   Conclusions identify the meaning or significance of the data and results. The conclusions are generalizations drawn from the evidence.

Recommendations.   Recommendations identify the steps or actions to take in light of the conclusions. Writers sometimes confuse recommendations with conclusions. A simple example shows the distinction. Suppose you put a bottle of milk on the table and leave the room. When you come back, you find the bottle broken on the floor and see a cat lapping the milk. You *conclude* that the cat knocked over the bottle to get the milk. You *recommend* that bottles be put where the cat can't get at them in the future.

Appendix.   The appendix adds material relevant to the report but not essential to it. Many reports have no appendix. Materials typically included are

- data sheets
- calculations
- examples of questionnaires or other forms used in gathering evidence
- graphs, charts, maps, tables, and other visual aids
- brochures, sales bulletins, and other published documents pertaining to the report

Other components.   You may need to include these additional components:

- list of figures—"table of contents" for the visual aids in the report
- list of symbols (or abbreviations)—"shorthand" devices used in a report

- computer index—list of key words used to cross-reference the report in a computerized indexing system
- glossary—minidictionary, defining technical or specialized terms used in the report; helpful for nonspecialist readers
- list of references—identification of the sources used in the report; used mostly in scientific or research work
- bibliography—list of published works consulted, whether or not they include materials specifically used in the report, or a list of works the reader may consult for more information
- acknowledgments—expression of thanks to people or organizations who have helped the writer

Printed reports may, like books, include still other components, such as a preface, copyright page, dedication, and index.

Paper, Reproduction, and Binders

Reports are usually typed on an 8½-by-11-inch white letter stock, especially when the report is an external communication. Charts, tables, graphs, and other visual aids often require larger paper. Such items are usually folded to conform with the report page size. Also, colored paper is occasionally used to identify special sections of a report or to distinguish certain kinds of reports.

Strive for an appropriate image and attractive appearance.

Reports are sometimes reproduced for mass distribution. The method of reproduction will depend on the quantity of copies needed, quality required, and cost factors. See Chapter 7.

Report binders for long or semiformal reports can be cover stock or plastic in a variety of colors. Many organizations imprint covers with their name, logo, or other identifying marks (Figure 13–9). Opaque covers may have windows or openings for reading the report title on the title page.

Sundstrand Hydro-Transmission

world's most complete family
of hydrostatic transmissions and control systems

division of Sundstrand Corporation

FORM NO. 700076

REPORT NO. _____

PROJECT NO. _____

PAGE _____ OF _____

DATE _____

REVISION DATE _____

ENGINEERING REPORT

TITLE _____

_____

_____

_____

APPROVAL AND CLASSIFICATION

INTERNAL DISTRIBUTION	Chief Engineer	Date	Prepared By	Date
CUSTOMER DISTRIBUTION	Chief Engineer	Date	Group Engineer	Date
DISTRIBUTION PROHIBITED	Chief Engineer	Date	Section Manager	Date

Source: Report Cover Courtesy of Sundstrand Corporation.

Figure 13–9: A Report Cover

ASSIGNMENT: REPORTS

You will spend several weeks practicing writing reports of various lengths and various degrees of formality. Your in-service training director asks that you first write a memo report on one of the following topics and then develop it into a semiformal or formal report. Each member of your group is to present an oral report of the semiformal or formal written report, explaining how the material was researched and developed.

Topics

1. Select about 20 items frequently purchased by students at your school or by workers in your office. Check the prices of these items at three or more stores in your community. Write a report to explain your investigation and present your findings.
2. The author of a textbook you have used plans to publish a revised edition of the book. As a guide to the author, you have been asked to identify the strengths and weaknesses of the book. Write the report you wish the author to see.
3. Write a report to explain to beginners what they should look for when they buy the equipment needed in some sport, hobby, or other activity you know.
4. Choose similar items manufactured by at least three different companies and compare them for construction, design, durability, cost, and so on. Write a report to present the results of your comparison.
5. While you were working on some project or at some job, you observed certain procedures and practices that were not as efficient as they could be. Write your supervisor a report to explain the changes or improvements that should be made.
6. Write a report summarizing and evaluating the activities at some meeting or conference you attended.
7. Choose three or more journals or magazines in your field. Compare them for content, style, use of illustrations, and so on. On the basis of your comparison, decide what class of reader would be best served by each journal. Write a report that presents your conclusions.

FURTHER READING

Barzun, Jacques and Henry F. Graff. *The Modern Researcher,* 3rd ed. New York: Harcourt Brace Jovanovich, 1977.

Bates, Jefferson D. *Writing with Precision: How to Write So That You Cannot Possibly Be Misunderstood.* Washington, D.C.: Acropolis, 1978.

Freeman, Joanna M. *Basic Technical and Business Writing.* Ames, IA: Iowa State University, 1979.

Guidelines for Research in Business Communication. Prepared by the Research Committee of the ABCA. Urbana, IL: American Business Communication Association, 1977.

Houp, Kenneth W. and Thomas E. Pearsall. *Reporting Technical Information,* 4th ed. Encino, CA: Glencoe, 1980.

Keithley, Erwin M. and Philip J. Schreiner. *A Manual of Style for the Preparation of Papers and Reports,* 3rd ed. Cincinnati, OH: South-Western, 1980.

Lesikar, Raymond V. *Report Writing for Business,* 5th ed. Homewood, IL: Irwin, 1977.

Persing, Bobbye Sorrels. "Search and Re-search for Solutions to Communication Problems." *The Journal of Business Communication* 16, Winter 1979, 13–25.

Radloff, David. "Replacing Some Assumptions in the Teaching of Technical Writing." *Journal of Technical Writing and Communication* 9, 1979, 2.

Rothrock, John B. *How to Research Any Subject for Any Purpose.* White River Junction, VT: Rothrock Associates, 1976.

CHAPTER FOURTEEN

Proposals

Merely suggesting an important project, a good product, or a low price does not assure a proposal's success; the project, product, or price must be well presented.

David Fear
Technical Writing

A *proposal* is (1) an offer to perform some service or (2) a request that some service be performed. In the first situation, an individual or organization usually makes the offer of service to another company, foundation, or agency. In the second situation, a company, foundation, or agency usually requests that someone else (an outsider—individual or organization) perform the service.

Proposals are offers of or requests for service.

Proposals are written to initiate all sorts of programs and projects. Whatever the reasons—to obtain cooperation, use of resources, financial support, and so on—proposals are basically persuasive communications. Although the purpose of a proposal may be similar to that of a report, there is also a crucial difference. A report states what you have learned, what you have done, what you have concluded. A proposal, on the other hand, states what you would like to do (or what someone else would like you to do)—why and how.

Proposals are either *solicited* (requested) or *unsolicited* (not specifically requested) and, in terms of structure, either formal or informal. Sales proposals, for example, may range from a formal, elaborate multimedia presentation prepared for a prospective client either by invitation (solicited) or on speculation (unsolicited) to an informal telephone call urging renewal of a magazine subscription (unsolicited). Whether spoken, written, or visual, formal or informal, solicited or unsolicited, however, proposals require the selling pattern of persuasion and the selling organization of attention, interest, conviction, and action.

Proposals require the selling pattern of persuasion.

279

SOLICITED PROPOSALS

Requests for Proposals

Requests for Proposals invite proposals to accomplish a specific task.

Requests for Proposals (RFPs) are invitations by government agencies, public or private foundations, and so on to prepare and submit proposals to accomplish a specific type of work. See Figure 14–1. The details and specifications of the requests must be matched exactly, but the *ideas for acccomplishing the work are originated and defined by the applicant—the proposal writer.* Expertise in initiating, preparing, and presenting successful proposals—*grantsmanship*—is needed.

RFPs are usually advertised. For example, the requests shown in Figure 14–1 were published in *The Chronicle of Higher Education.* Every government RFP exceeding $5,000 is published in the *Federal Register* and the *Commerce Business Daily,* as well as in other publications. Some agencies also send the announcement to favored bidders or contractors (proposal initiators) and to people listed from earlier inquiries. Theoretically, everyone has a chance to send for detailed information and forms, prepare a proposal, and be awarded a contract or funding. But in reality, agencies have a number of ways of screening out various potential bidders.

Even before an advertisement is released, professionals carefully read the *Federal Register* for announcements of legislation: (1) proposed rules, (2) comment periods of 60 to 90 days, (3) final rules and closing dates. Even before money is appropriated for the legislation, these "grant experts" are calling and visiting Washington to discuss possible proposals with agency members, making preliminary investigations and plans, asking for technical assistance. (Late summer is a good time.)

Some RFPs include a deadline that must be met. Others accept proposals at any time. Because the RFP is released months before a response is due, proposals may be in preparation for several months, in evaluation for six months to a year; and after acceptance, funding may take even longer.

Some companies regularly search for RFP announcements. After a preliminary inquiry, the company may send the details of an RFP to its research and development staff. The corporate technical staff will work out several approaches and submit the best one to its management. Management then makes the final decision on whether to respond to the RFP.

Assess potential profit, time, and use of personnel and equipment before you prepare a proposal.

Profit potential, time, and the best use of personnel and equipment are all important in the decision. In addition, a company or individual must consider the percentages—the chances of being

Deadlines

THE CHRONICLE OF HIGHER EDUCATION

July 21, 1980

August 12—Gerontology: Nominations for Brookdale Awards for Research in Gerontology. Contact: Chairperson, Brookdale Awards Screening Committee, Gerontological Society, Suite 305, 1835 K Street, N.W., Washington 20006; (202) 466-6750.

August 15—Geography: Applications for grants for projects in geography and regional science. Contact: Barry Moriarty, Division of Social and Economic Science, National Science Foundation, Washington 20550; (202) 357.7326.

August 15—Oceanography: Applications for grants for projects in oceanography. Contact: Robert Wall, Division of Ocean Sciences, National Science Foundation, Washington 20550; (202) 357-7924.

August 15—Science: Formal proposals for grants for public-service science centers. Contact: Public Service Science Centers, Office of Science and Society, National Science Foundation, Washington 20550.

August 15—Social sciences: Applications for grants for projects in law and social sciences. Contact: Felice Levine, Division of Social and Economic Science, National Science Foundation, Washington 20550; (202) 357-9567.

August 15—Sociology: Applications for grants for projects in sociology. Contact: Roland Liebert, Division of Social and Economic Science, National Science Foundation, Washington 20550; (202) 357-7802.

August 18—Local schools: Applications for grants for research on the organization of local schools and school systems. Contact: Gail MacColl, Program on Educational Policy and Organization, National Institute of Education, Mail Stop 16, Washington.

August 19—Mathematics education: Proposals for prototypes in mathematics education using information technology. Contact: Dorothy Deringer, Development in Science Education, National Science Foundation, Washington 20550; (202) 282-7910.

August 25—Aging: Applications for grants under the program for model projects on aging. Contact: Model Projects Program Guidelines, Administration on Aging (MPD), Washington 20201.

September 1—Data and measurement: Applications for grants for research on measurement methods and data resources. Contact: Murray Aborn, Division of Social and Economic Science, National Science Foundation, Washington 20550; (202) 357-7913.

September 1—Economics: Applications for grants for research in economics. Contact: James Blackman, Division of Social and Economic Science, National Science Foundation, Washington 20550; (202) 357-9674.

September 1—Humanities: Applications for grants for research in state, local, and regional history. Contact: Division of Research Programs, National Endowment for the Humanities, 806 15th Street, N.W., Washington 20506.

September 1—Science: Applications for grants for projects on science in developing countries. Contact: Gordon Hiebert, Division of International Programs, National Science Foundation, Washington 20550; (202) 357-9700.

September 1—Science: Applications for grants for projects on the history and philosophy of science. Contact: Ronald Overmann, Division of Social and Economic Science, National Science Foundation, Washington 20550; (202) 357-7617.

September 1—Science: Proposals for seminars under the U. S.-Japan cooperative science program. Contact: Stephen Mosier, Division of International Programs, National Science Foundation, Washington 20550; (202) 357-9537.

September 1—Science: Proposals for long-term research visits under the U. S.-Australia cooperative science program. Contact: Alan Milsap, Division of International Programs, National Science Foundation, Washington 20550; (202) 357-9558.

September 1—Social policy: Papers on leadership in social policy and reform in Western society for a new journal, *Studies in History and Politics.* Contact: The Editors, *Studies in History and Politics,* Bishop's University, Lennoxville, Quebec, Canada, J1M 1Z7.

September 1—Spanish: Papers for possible presentation at a conference on Spanish in the U. S. setting, to be held in October in Chicago. Contact: Lucia Elias-Olivares, Department of Spanish, Italian, and Portuguese, University of Illinois at Chicago Circle, Box 4348, Chicago 60680; (312) 996-2278.

September 4—Medicine: Applications for grants for faculty development in family medicine. Contact: Division of Medicine, Bureau of Health Professions, Health Resources Administration, Center Building, Room 3-22, 3700 East-West Highway, Hyattsville, Md. 20782; (301) 436-7350.

September 5—Arts: Applications for participation in the National Endowment Fellowship Program, during spring, 1981. Contact: Fellowship Program Office, National Endowment for the Arts, 2401 E Street, N.W., Washington 20506.

September 15—Administrators: Applications for participation in the institute for academic deans, and business and advancement officers to be held in December in Arizona. Contact: Harry A. Marmion, Director, Institute for College and University Administrators, American Council on Education, One Dupont Circle, Washington 20036; (202) 833-4780.

September 15—Science: Applications for grants under the U. S.-India exchange-of-scientists program. Contact: Hildegard Kramer, Division of International Programs, National Science Foundation, Washington 20550; (202) 357-9550.

September 30—Biology: Applications for grants for biological instrumentation. Contact: Larry Faller, Division of Physiology, Cellular and Molecular Biology, National Science Foundation, Washington 20550; (202) 357-7656.

September 30—Children's literature: Applications for Children's Literature Association fellowships for scholarly or critical work in children's literature. Contact: P. F. Neumeyer, Department of English and Comparative Literature, San Diego State University, San Diego 92182.

October 1—Faculty development: Applications for faculty-development awards from former Woodrow Wilson fellows teaching in New England and the Mid-Atlantic states. Contact: Woodrow Wilson National Fellowship Foundation, Box 642, Princeton, N.J. 08540.

October 1—Historical records: Applications for grants for the preservation, arrangement, and description of historical records and archives. Contact: Records Program, National Historical Publications and Records Commission, National Archives and Records Service, Washington 20408.

October 1—Humanities: Applications for grants for basic archaeological projects. Contact: Division of Research Programs, National Endowment for the Humanities, 806 15th Street, N.W., Washington 20506.

October 1—Humanities: Applications for grants for pilot programs in the humanities. Contact: Division of Education Programs, National Endowment for the Humanities, 806 15th Street, N.W., Washington 20506.

October 1—Humanities: Applications for grants for reference works and tools and editions. Contact: Division of Research Programs, National Endowment for the Humanities, 806 15th Street, N.W., Washington 20506.

October 1—Medical education: Applications for grants for innovative programs in medical education. Contact: National Fund for Medical Education, 999 Asylum Avenue, Hartford, Conn. 06105; (203) 278-5070.

October 1—Medical research: Applications for awards to senior medical-school faculty members concentrated research and study. Contact: Faculty Scholar Award Program, Josiah Macy, Jr., Foundation, One Rockefeller Plaza, New York 10020.

October 1—Piaget: Proposals for possible presentations at the international conference on Piagetian theory and the helping professions, to be held in January in Los Angeles. Contact: J. Magary, University Affiliated Program, Childrens Hospital of Los Angeles, P.O. Box 54700, Los Angeles 90054.

October 1—Science education: Applications for grants under the program for pre-college teacher development in science. Contact: Theodore Reid, Faculty Oriented Programs, National Science Foundation, Washington 20550; (202) 282-7795.

Figure 14–1: Newspaper Ad Showing Government Requests for Proposals.

funded against the time and effort it takes to prepare and submit the proposal. Sometimes there may be three RFPs for the same project: a call for formulating a concept, an award for producing a prototype, and a final award for full-scale production. The RFP may not indicate this fact. (An excellent source of insider's information and a blueprint for preparing proposals is *The Grantsmanship Workplan,* The Eckman Center, 8399 Constanza Blvd., Canoga Park, California 91304.)

If the company decides to submit a proposal, they will find that help varies from agency to agency, foundation to foundation. Some organizations will critique a typed proposal before it is submitted officially. Certain federal educational agencies are mandated to provide assistance. It is up to each proposal applicant to ask. Many organizations will not volunteer assistance, but all are approachable.

Invitations for Bids, Requests for Quotations

Invitations for Bids and Requests for Quotations solicit proposals that involve government contracts.

There is business to be had and money to be made by submitting solicited proposals to state and federal agencies. (Depending upon the agency, and the unit within the agency, purchases over $300 to $500 must be open to competitive bid.)

Government solicitations for proposals that involve contracts are known as Invitations for Bids (IFBs) or Requests for Quotations (RFQs). These invitations or requests clearly define the quality, type, and specifications of the project, and the proposal writers, or bidders, must be prepared to prove that they can meet all requirements, including national standards and "specifications as necessary for local conditions."

In addition to providing detailed information on the service or product, proposals may include special provisions and supplementary specifications. A bidder may, for example, be required to carry particular types of insurance; show equal employment opportunity/affirmative action compliance; hire on-the-job trainees; provide financial statements, professional résumés of the principals involved, and certification of equipment availability. Regular bidders on engineering projects may be allowed to file some of this information only once a year, thus eliminating duplication time.

A bid, or proposal, is evaluated on the basis of cost, facilities, personnel, and past history with the government agency.

Formal proposals submitted to government agencies are returned to the initiating agency in sealed envelopes. All those who have made a bid or proposal may be present when the bids are opened at the prespecified time and day. The "winner," the lowest and best bid, is chosen on the basis of cost, facilities, qualification of personnel, and previous history with the agency.

A contractor may win a bid and then solicit bids from sub-contractors, all based on the rigid requirements of the initial government request. In the near future, however, it may be necessary for the prime contractor to list all subcontractors in the initial proposal.

Informal government invitations are usually sent to at least three vendors (those who submit the proposal or bid) by an agency buyer, with a request for a reply within a stated time—usually two to three weeks. The buyer selects the vendors from an alphabetized vendor index compiled by the agency over the years, from the yellow pages of a telephone directory, or from the *Thomas Register of Manufacturers*. (You can request that your name or company be included on the vendor index.) Your proposal, or response to the invitation, is confidential until the award is made. At that time, all the proposals become a matter of public record.

Formal government invitations are advertised in local newspapers, in the *Commerce Business Daily* (Superintendent of Documents, Washington, D.C. 20401), and in publications such as the Department of Transportation (DOT) *Weekly Letting Report*. Formal announcements give only the most general information. Those interested in submitting a proposal or bid must write for plans and specifications and then fill out the various forms *exactly as required* and return them within two to four weeks of the advertisement. (Bids have been discarded because of one unmarked box or omitted date.)

To give themselves more time to prepare the bid, contractors and other vendors frequently drive or fly to the source of the information, pick up the necessary bid package, and then deliver the proposal by hand to meet the deadline. (The Education Research Funding Council even sponsors a special VIP Proposal Delivery Service which guarantees hand-delivered mail to any federal agency in Washington from airports, trains, and bus lines.)

UNSOLICITED PROPOSALS

Unsolicited proposals, those not specifically requested, are initiated by someone who has a project or program he or she wants to do. As noted earlier, these proposals may be as informal as a phone call urging a subscription renewal or as formal as multimedia sales presentation that you or your company initiates. A project may involve just one individual, many people, or an entire company, but one person is usually responsible for starting the whole process.

Before submitting an unsolicited proposal, find out who might be interested, what funding is available, how to apply, and how to prepare an effective proposal.

Your chances of success increase dramatically when you know how to find out who might be interested in the project or program you are proposing, what grant money is available, how to apply, how to be competitive, and how to prepare and package an effective proposal. The rest of this chapter will help you to accomplish these objectives.

"Success" is the acceptance of your proposal, the opportunity to put your project or program into action. It means to be awarded a share of the $100 billion-plus annually available to assist with research projects and educational, cultural, and social programs sponsored by government agencies, foundations, and business and industrial organizations.

PREPARING AND WRITING PROPOSALS

Remember the selling pattern of persuasion and the selling organization of attention, interest, conviction, and action.

All proposals, solicited and unsolicited, demand the selling pattern of persuasion and the selling organization of attention, interest, conviction, action. However, because most solicited proposals (with the partial exception of Requests for Proposals) involve set procedures and the completion of established forms, and because you already know where you will submit a solicited proposal, much of the following information pertains to unsolicited proposals.

Preapplication Phase

Step 1: Decide to make a proposal.

Before initiating a proposal, *ask and find answers to a number of questions.*

1. How much training and experience do I have in the proposed subject? (Will my credentials indicate my qualifications to complete the project satisfactorily?)
2. How much help will I get from my department, institution, organization, associates?
3. How adequate are the present facilities?
4. Is the project possible with reasonable financing?
5. How clear and measurable are the objectives?

Step 2: Look for funding.

Once the decision is made to go ahead, *look for possible funding sources.* Three types of money may be obtainable:

1. *Entitlement* money—made available on a federal, state, local basis from public and private sources. Awarded on a "formula" basis—a portion of the total funds based on some need factor: population, level of unemployment, birth defects, enrollment, others. Applicants write application rather than proposal, showing justification for funds, proof of entitlement or qualification. Flexible use and local administration of funds.
2. *Categorical* money—made available on a federal, state, local basis from public and private sources. Awarded for a particular activity—providing access for handicapped, school buses, library out-reach programs, others. Awards are locked in for a particular use, cannot be jumped between categories for other purposes. Grantees chosen on entitlementlike system with a funding agency attempting to balance giving pattern, not quality of activity. Variable administration of funds.
3. *Grant* money—made available from public and private funds to individuals, organizations, and agencies for a particular project, either solicited or unsolicited. Money given in regular, periodic payments or in lump sum. Sponsor concerned that money is spent, not how it is spent.

The following list offers suggestions on how to find out about available funding, using an educational project as an example.

1. Write or call agencies at the federal, state, and local levels:
   - local educational agencies
   - area educational agencies
   - Department of Public Instruction
   - special departments—Career Education, Special Needs, Title IV–C, Title II, others
   - U.S. Department of Education
   - State Arts Council
   - State Board for the Humanities
2. Write, call, and see friends, professional colleagues, legislators, lobbyists. (Cultivate the "old boy–old girl" networks.)
3. Write or call professional organizations:
   - fraternal societies
   - professional honoraries
   - professional associations
4. Write or call foundations:
   - state foundations
   - university foundations
   - professional foundations
   - national/international foundations
   - private foundations

5. Read and search through magazines, newspapers, books, brochures, trade journals (publications sent by foundations, others):
   - *Federal Register* (daily)
   - *Commerce Business Daily*
   - *DPI Dispatch* (Department of Public Instruction, monthly/bimonthly)
   - *198_ Federal Funding Guide* (annual)
   - *198_ Catalog of Federal Domestic Assistance* (annual)
   - *Foundation News* (bimonthly)
   - *The Foundation Directory* (updated periodically)
   - *Grantsmanship Center News* (bimonthly)
   - *Education Funding News* (weekly)
6. Check EDGAR (Educational Division General Administrative Regulations). Every federal grant must comply with EDGAR—for the *general* regulations and *special* regulations for a particular program. Every applicant must check the codes of federal regulations. When a notice or RFP appears in the *Federal Register,* it is compiled into a code for the related department—Labor, Health, Education, other. (Since April 3, 1980, all codes are written in simplified language.)
7. Attend workshops, seminars, lectures on proposal writing.
8. Get names of project directors of funded proposals from *Commerce Business Daily, Federal Funding Guide,* other sources. Write them for information. (*Guide* contains criteria for grants, names of contacts; separate volumes for education, other areas.)
9. Run a computer search using key words or phrases.

Next *make a list* of all potential funding sources, including oganizations that have previously demonstrated an interest in your proposed activity or field. Omit organizations with special requirements that you cannot meet: location, affiliation, academic credentials, race, sex, age, health, income, future obligations, deadlines, others.

Step 3: Prepare an outline.   With the possibility of funding, *prepare an outline or abstract* of the proposed activity. (Some people prefer to reverse steps 2 and 3. Follow whichever sequence you prefer.)

In the preapplication phase, the outline can be quite informal. It should include

1. what is to be done
2. why it is worth doing
3. how it is to be done
4. how long it will take
5. approximate cost

6. updated résumés of principal investigator or project director and other participants
7. literature review
8. evidence of credibility (endorsements or supporting evidence for the program or organization in letters or memos from other agencies, organizations, clients, key figures in the field, administration/management; newspaper clippings or other published material)

For a more sophisticated planning outline, see the exhibit on pages 288–289.

With a well thought-out proposal, a good idea of potential funding sources, a basic outline, and a rough budget, you should *ask for reactions.*   *Step 4: Ask for reactions.*

Consult people within and outside the program area, from department administrators or supervisors to grant and office personnel. Find out as much as possible about the funding sources, their personalities as organizations, their personnel, their likes, dislikes, current funding capabilities, and priorities. (Consult annual reports, Standard and Poor's *Register of Corporations, Directors and Executives,* other grantees, library files, publications. Get the *exact* names, addresses, and phone numbers of people you will want to contact.)

If possible, visit the source(s) in person, so they can see you as an individual instead of a signature. If such visits are impractical, send a letter of inquiry, asking for information on other researchers, additional references to the literature, and specific comments on your enclosed three- to four-page outline. Here is one possible approach to follow before preparing the final application.

1. Consult organizational representatives to determine if the project is acceptable to the administration.
2. Write funding source(s) for information, application forms, and a possible appointment for an interview, addressing the letter to the specific program director or office head *by name.* An exploratory letter should briefly state (1) objectives of the project, (2) the sponsoring organization, and (3) the qualifications of personnel involved.
3. Send the program director a letter with a three- to four-page summary of the project, objectives, problem(s) to be studied, description of expected results or brief 250- to 300-word abstract along with three- to four-page proposal summary.
4. Phone or visit the program director to discuss comments, revisions to the proposal. (Get to know the grants management officers.)

A BASIC PLANNING FORMAT FOR PROPOSALS
Norton J. Kiritz

Norton J. Kiritz, president of the Grantsmanship Center, recommends the following proposal format.

1. Introduction
2. Problem statement or assessment of need
3. Program objectives
4. Methods
5. Evaluation
6. Future funding and alternative sources
7. Budget

Kiritz states that proposals are frequently funded on the basis of reputation, personal "connections," or key personnel rather than on the basis of the program content alone. (Knowing men and women who are in key positions or who know others in similar positions in funding agencies is helpful—especially if the investigator has made a favorable personal impression. "Old boy-old girl" networks are notorious in federal government funding.) Thus, the *introduction* should include information to establish credibility of the investigator and/or the organization he or she represents. It should contain a brief history pointing out distinctive characteristics, significant accomplishments, organizational goals, and support from others.

The problem statement or assessment of need should make a logical connection between the background information and the problems and needs with which the investigator proposes to work. It should support the existence of the problem with evidence—statistically, through endorsements from others, and with publications. Here is the place to define the problem in a simple statement.

Program objectives should be specific, measurable outcomes of the program. The objectives should offer relief from the problem, a solution to the problem.

Methods should describe the activities needed to accomplish the objectives.

The evaluation should be both subjective and objective with emphasis on the latter. The evaluation should be built into the program from the beginning, Kiritz says.

Future funding sources should be presented to show how a new program will be maintained after the initial grant has run out. Assuring a funding source that there will be continuation for the program without outside grant support can be extremely helpful in being selected.

The budget may include direct cost items and indirect costs or personnel and nonpersonnel. The categories depend on the funding agency.

Personnel includes wages and salaries, fringe benefits, consultants, and contract services. *Nonpersonnel* includes space costs, rental, lease, or purchase of equipment, consumable supplies, travel, telephones, and other costs.

Direct cost items cover a wider range: salaries and fringe benefits of the investigators, their clerical and technical staff and assistants, expendable supplies and equipment, permanent equipment, travel expenses, publication costs, computer costs, and miscellaneous items such as postage, phone calls, consultant fees, subcontracts, books and films, equipment rental, temporary secretarial assistance, and machine maintenance and repair.

Indirect costs are usually prorated for general and administrative expenses, research administration costs, departmental administrative expenses, building use charges, equipment use charges, library costs, student services, operation and maintenance of a physical plant, and improvements other than on buildings. Each institution carrying out research and seeking outside support is authorized to use a predetermined rate to cover indirect costs. This rate is referred to as the *negotiated indirect-cost rate.* Knowing it helps simplify preparing the proposal budget.

Most grant-making organizations prefer to make awards to institutions rather than individuals because of an Internal Revenue Service ruling (The 1969 Tax Reform Act) that made granters responsible for seeing that funds are used correctly. Thus, although the principal investigator is usually the catalyst, the instigator, that person usually serves as a go-between for the institution and the funding body.

Kiritz suggests dividing an 8½-by-11-inch sheet of paper into several columns, beginning with "Problem," then "Objectives," next "Method," and finally "Evaluation."

If you list all your objectives separately in the second column, you can then identify the problem it relates to, the specific methods in your program that deal with the objectives, and the criteria of success in reaching the objectives as well as the method of evaluation (Kiritz, 4).

Thinking through the various components, Kiritz says, will enable an investigator to develop a logical way to approach planning the project. Thinking through the various sections will disclose everything a private or public fund source is likely to ask.

See Norton J. Kiritz, *Program Planning and Proposal Writing*, Los Angeles, CA: Grantsmanship Center, 1978.

5. Revise, if necessary, and send the program director the updated proposal.
6. Send thank-you letters to everyone assisting in the preapplication phase. Write the program director, reconfirming your commitment to meet the project deadline.
7. Set up a timetable three to six months before the deadline, allowing several months for finding sources, writing the abstract/summary.

Consulting the funding source director is frequently overlooked. He or she can be very helpful by indicating immediately that the proposed project does not fit the agency's priorities or guidelines, or by offering encouragement and suggestions.

Proposal Application Phase

Planning, researching, and consulting can take several months or several years. The actual writing of the proposal can be relatively easy. Some funding sources have detailed application forms; others send general instructions to follow and ask for a formal letter of intent. Here are some broad guidelines that will help you be competitive in your application for the grant.

1. Know as many people as you can in the chain of the organizational entities dealt with—funding sources and personnel group.

2. Know the requirements of the law and your funding source, as well as other regulations.

3. Know the required format (if any), number of copies requested, names and addresses of persons to receive copies, and related details for submission such as deadlines.

4. Be current—aware of present and future trends.

5. Be well researched—on top of literature and activities in the field.

6. Be persuasive—convincing proposal reader to want to fund your project out of his or her pocket.

7. Be communicative—using simple and direct language.

Step 1: Write the proposal.

Using basic persuasive writing skills, hand-tailor the proposal for each funding organization. In short proposals, you may abbreviate information and combine some elements under one heading. In lengthy proposals, organize the information as follows:

1. Frontmatter: letter of transmittal (see Chapter 9), cover, title page, abstract, table of contents, statement of assurances.
Title page includes project title, date of submission (completion), person or organization to whom submitted, person or organization preparing proposal, program funds applied for, dates of project operation, restrictions.
Statement of assurances anticipates questions of compliance with restrictions such as hiring minorities, using human or animal subjects, financial responsibility. Offers brief, signed statements.

2. Project rationale: introduction, statement of need, ideal project goals, realistic project objectives.

3. Procedures: workable step-by-step plan to get job done. Particular techniques to be used, training programs, timetables, equipment, other details. The who, what, when, where, why, and how of the activity.

4. Evaluation: measurement procedures, tabulation and analysis of data, distribution of evaluation results, third-party evaluation/audit, other means.

5. Project personnel: vitae. Some agencies require full vita of principal investigator, brief résumés of other personnel.

6. Budget: current support, pending applications, future funding. Include expected income from other grants, sales, dues, fees, and contributions such as furniture, free printing, bookkeeping advice, volunteer help, donations of time and material, matching funds.

7. Appendices: supportive material such as letters and press clippings; statistical tables, questionnaires for use in procedures, charts, graphs; copy of tax-exempt classification letter if applying to a foundation.

At this point, knowing why some proposals are rejected may be helpful in suggesting how you can avoid certain pitfalls. Dr. Ernest M. Allen, Chief of the Division of Research Grants, National Institutes of Health, conducted a classic study in 1960, which was published in *Science* that same year. Table 14–1 summarizes his findings.

Following this advice from Jeffrey Simering may make the difference between success and failure for a project. At a Washington, D.C., Education Funding Research Council seminar, he offered a number of suggestions for helping harried proposal reviewers. These suggestions apply to proposals of any kind.[*]

1. Keep the proposal organized. A concise abstract, detailed table of contents, and a running cross-reference between the proposal and the evaluation criteria can be of immense aid. . . . Some proposal writers include a "reviewer's guide," which lists the evaluation criteria in one column and the relevant proposal passage in the other column.
2. Be as specific as possible. . . . Tell the reviewer exactly what you are going to do. . . .
3. Coin high-sounding terms. Call everything an "approach" or a "strategy." . . . Be wary of going overboard.
4. Build your credibility. If your program is endorsed by high-ranking state authorities, emphasize it. . . . Borrow components from other successfully funded . . . projects. . . .
5. Play to the reviewer's expectations. (Possibly) stress the government's neglect . . . your creative use of limited resources.
6. Use charts and diagrams to explain and expand your text. . . . The diagram may simply repeat the text, but it leaves a double impression in the reviewer's mind.

"Basic persuasive writing," says Simering, "may be the heart of any good proposal, but with today's intense competition for grants, it takes more than that to get federal funds. If you were going to a bank for a $100,000 loan, you would have to go through all sorts of activity to prove you could pay the bank off. It's the same thing with the federal government. They're making you jump through a few hoops."

[*]*Education Funding News*, November 7, 1979.

Table 14–1: Why Applications Are Disapproved

Area of Application Found Deficient		Frequency	Shortcoming
The problem	*The question the proposed research seeks to answer*	**58%**	Problem is of insufficient importance; is more complex than the investigator realizes; warrants only a pilot study; research proposed is overly involved; description of research is without clear research aim.
The approach	*The means by which the answer is to be sought*	**73%**	Proposed methods and procedures are unsuited to the objective; are too unclear to permit adequate evaluation; overall design not carefully thought out; statistical aspects not given sufficient consideration; controls inadequate; material proposed for research is unsuitable.
The person	*The scientific and technical competence proposed toward pursuit of the research*	**55%**	The investigator does not have adequate experience or training; appears to be unfamiliar with recent pertinent literature or methods in his or her area; the investigator's previously published work in *this field* does not inspire confidence; investigator proposes to rely too heavily on insufficiently experienced associates; investigator is spread too thin; needs more liaison with colleagues.
Miscellaneous	*Nonscientific aspects*	**16%**	Equipment and/or personnel proposed are unrealistic; other responsibilities would prevent devoting sufficient attention to the proposed project; there is an unfavorable institutional setting for the proposed research.

From Ernest M. Allen, *Science* 132, November 25, 1960.

Step 2: Package.

    After you have planned, organized, and written the proposal you must package it. Here are some suggestions.

1. Proposal cover: use heavy-weight, possibly colored cover stock with appropriate artwork if desired. Include project title and logo/seal of submitting organization. Duplicate on offset or at local copy center where binding is available. (Examine agency annual report for style and quality; then follow its lead.)
2. Content: must have perfect typing, proofreading, printing, consistent format, footnotes. Use good-quality bond paper.
3. Physical arrangement: follow agency guidelines but consider using index tabs or different colored paper for ease in finding sections. Try submitting proposal in two sections: first containing project description, second containing budget information. (Some agencies evaluate each individually.)
4. Field reader's guide: add a separate index, following similar guide used by agency readers and reviewers. (Each agency has one or more. Ask for a copy, and then organize material to follow.)

Once the proposal is properly signed and sealed, it is ready to be delivered to the funding organization. Here adequate timing is essential. Since agencies sometimes change the terms and conditions of their projects, it is advisable to check periodically with the agency contact person. (Expect something to go wrong. Allow extra time.)

Step 3: Deliver.

To make sure the package is delivered safely, send it by first-class special-delivery, registered mail, return receipt requested; air freight; courier pick-up; or UPS. Better yet, deliver it in person. If you cannot deliver it in person, enclose a self-addressed card and ship two sets by different carriers or send one to a friend in the same city as a back-up. Then, five days later, telephone the person you shipped it to, just to make sure it arrived.

Yes, it is permissible to send the same proposal to several organizations. But the wise submitter will change the proposal to suit each organization's priorities and guidelines. Private and public funding agencies have high regard for multiple submissions. They indicate seriousness, enterprise, and depth of research. If and when funding is awarded, several agencies may join to support the proposed project.

Step 4: Submit to several agencies.

Postapplication Phase

How proposals are reviewed depends on the size of the organization and its source of funding. Many have peer reviews in study sections or review committees. Both consist of experts in a particular field

NATIONAL SCIENCE FOUNDATION
Information for Reviewers of Proposals

Mail reviews play a key role in the National Science Foundation's evaluation of the scientific merit of proposals. Please provide both written comments and a summary rating using the definitions provided.

Written Evaluation
Quality of the Research
Be candid in your assessment of the proposed research; point out strengths and weaknesses in the approach and content of the proposal. Please comment on the originality and creativity of the proposed research. Be as specific as possible.

Qualifications of Principal Investigator(s)
Please comment on the principal investigator(s)' recent research record or other evidence of research potential. Does the record suggest that the principal investigator(s) are likely to make an important and original contribution? Evaluate recent research accomplishments, or, especially for younger scientists, other evidence of potential.

Budget and Institutional Capability
Comments on the reasonableness of budget requests for particular items, such as instruments, computer time, research assistants, travel and other factors, will be helpful. If appropriate, also comment on the research environment, including equipment, and other resources that are available to accomplish the proposed work.

Summary Ratings
On the basis of your written comments, please check one of the summary ratings. In making the selection, keep in mind both the quality of the proposal and the principal investigator(s)' recent research record.

Excellent: Probably will fall among top 10% of proposals in this subfield; highest priority for support. This category should be used only for truly outstanding proposals.

Very Good: Probably will fall among top ⅓ of proposals in this subfield; should be supported.

Good: Probably will fall among middle ⅓ of proposals in this subfield; worthy of support.

Fair: Probably will fall among lowest ⅓ of proposals in this subfield.

Poor: Proposal has serious deficiencies; should not be supported.

Length of Proposal
Because scientists are increasingly concerned about the length of research proposals, the National Science Foundation is encouraging brief and concise proposals. The Foundation has established 15 single-spaced typewritten pages as a normal limit for the project description portion of research proposals. Somewhat greater length may be appropriate for proposals with multiple investigators or for proposals of unusual complexity.

Conflict of Interest
If you have an affiliation or financial connection with the institution or the person submitting this proposal that might be construed as creating a conflict of interest, please describe those affiliations or interests in your own words on a separate piece of paper and attach it to your review. Regardless of any such affiliations or interests, unless you believe you cannot be objective, we would like to have your review. If you do not attach a statement we shall assume that you have no conflicting affiliations or interests.

Confidentiality of Proposals & Peer Review

The Foundation receives proposals in confidence and is responsible for protecting the confidentiality of their contents. For this reason, please do not copy, quote, or otherwise use material from this proposal. If you believe that a colleague can make a substantial contribution to the review, please consult the NSF program officer before disclosing either the contents or the proposal or the applicant's name. When you have completed your review, either return the proposal to the program officer or destroy it.

Verbatim copies of reviews, ratings, and any other evaluative comments will be sent to the principal investigator/project director. The copies will *not* contain your name or the name of your insti-

tution, or names which might constitute an invasion of the privacy of others. Subject to this Foundation policy and applicable laws, including the Freedom of Information Act, 5 USC 552, and formal requests from chairpersons of congressional committees having responsibility for NSF, your participation as a reviewer and the content of your review will be given the maximum protection from disclosure.

The Foundation will publish annually a list of names and addresses of persons who have reviewed proposals. Individuals will not, however, be identified with specific proposals. In this way, the Foundation can publicly acknowledge your services as a reviewer and at the same time protect the confidentiality of your comments.

Figure 14–2: Field Reader's Guide. In 1978, the National Science Foundation (NSF) revised its Form 1A. This sheet accompanies proposals it sends to outside referees for peer review. The form is reproduced here as a reminder to NSF grant seekers of the criteria by which their proposals will be judged and how the Foundation attempts to assure confidentiality—both of the proposed research and the identity of the reviewer.

who review all proposals related to that field. But before the committees receive the proposal, it will have passed several other hurdles.

On receipt, each proposal is checked in and reviewed for completeness. If it is incomplete, it is returned to the applicant.

Step 1: Receipt.

If the proposal is complete, it is assigned a number and sent on to be examined to make sure it fits the organization's guidelines, or to see if more information is needed. (If the applicant has previously contacted the agency, chances are good that the proposal will proceed to the next stage.)

Step 2: Examination.

Frequently, at this point, staff workers prepare a summary of the proposal: of the budget and general content. (By preparing your own proposal summary, you will save the organization's staff time and ensure that particular details of your proposal will get attention.)

Step 3: Summarization.

Peer reviews follow, with each expert seeing both the summary and the original proposal. If there is a committee, a primary reviewer is selected. That person is responsible for preparing a written report and recommendation for approval or disapproval after group discussion. (If review is by mail "from the field," the organization staff compiles the report. Figure 14–2 contains one

Step 4: Review.

such directive.) Occasionally, before the written proposal is completed, a committee or investigator may make an *on-site visit* or ask for a *meeting* with the proposal writer.

Step 5: Ranking.

If the proposed project is recommended, it is ranked according to the organization scoring system. Scores from various readers are tallied and averaged, giving the proposal its *priority score.*

Step 6: Final summarization.

Proposals with the highest scores are sent on to an executive secretary or similar administrator, who prepares a *summary statement,* including a summary of the experts' comments, recommendations, suggestions, and the priority score. (All this information is available to the proposal writer on request.)

Step 7: Advisory council examination.

Depending on the organization and the size of the funding request, the summary statement may then be sent along with the proposal to an advisory council. With requests in the $50,000-plus range, a council usually makes the final decision.

Like review committees or study sections, the council meets two or three times a year, spending several days holed up in a hotel or office, comparing notes and passing final judgment on proposals. The advisory council, however, is primarily concerned with controversial or particularly large requests. They check on the initial review to make certain all eligible proposals have been given a fair hearing.

Even with approval and a high priority score, a proposal must still pass one final hurdle—the amount of money available and the agency's current priorities. After the advisory council meets, or after the final field reports have been tallied, the agency staff must

Step 8: The "pay list."

develop a "pay list." If the proposed project fits within this pay list—that is, if it is related to the agency's priorities—it will be funded. If not, it will be considered for at least a year, in most cases, and sometimes longer. Chances of its being funded are poor, however, unless more money becomes available or the organization's priorities change. (Preapplication research on the funding source may reveal these priorities.)

Step 9: Funding.

If the proposal makes the pay list, the organization's grants management staff negotiates the specific amount and conditions of the grant. This staff usually consists of two people: a grants management officer, who deals with administrative matters relating to the grant, and a program officer, who provides technical guidance and watches the progress of the project. Notification of acceptance usually comes at this time with a letter, or a phone call followed by a letter.

Step 10: Reporting procedures.

Following funding, depending on the funding source, agency, and type of money, you may be required to submit any number of reports: progress reports concerning the current status of the project; trip reports, justifying charges; laboratory reports, including reasons for tests, procedures, recommendations; an annual, a semi-annual, and a final report. Such reports may be in memo form or formally constructed. (Guidelines appear in Chapter 13.) The funding source may have its own formats and schedules for reporting. The grants management officer will supply this information. (Still other means of evaluation may include conducting workshops, writing papers or books, and creating audiovisual material for presentation.)

ASSIGNMENT: PROPOSALS

In preparation for your future formal proposal writing, your in-service training director has asked you to respond to all of the following topics. You and the other members of your group are to bring your written responses to this week's meeting and read them to your colleagues. A three-minute critiquing period will follow each reading.

Topics

1. Your company research and development director has an idea for a new kind of energy. You are asked to search for possible outside funding sources. Do so, and include a list of sources in a memo to your director.
2. As superintendent of schools, you read about the government's plans for giving local high schools word-processing hardware for vocational training. Prepare a letter of inquiry with an application showing your entitlement.
3. Think of a program or project you would like to initiate. Prepare a preapplication-phase outline according to the eight steps suggested on pages 286–287.
4. Write an informal unsolicited proposal to your department head, stating how you would like to go about saving the department money. Be persuasive!

FURTHER READING

DeBakey Lois and Selma DeBakey. "The Art of Persuasion: Logic and Language in Proposal Writing." *Grants Magazine* 1, March 1978, 43–60.

"Grantsmanship: How to Get the Competitive Edge." *Education Funding News*. Washington, D.C.: Education Funding Research Council, Nov. 7, 1979.

Grantsmanship Workplan. Eckman Center, Washington, D.C.: Capitol, 1974.

Hall, Mary. *Developing Skills in Proposal Writing.* Portland, OR: Continuing Education Publications, 1977.

Kiritz, Norton J. *Program Planning and Proposal Writing.* Los Angeles, CA: Grantsmanship Center, 1978.

Lerner, Craig Alan. *Grants Register: 1981/1983.* 7th ed. New York: St. Martin's, 1980.

Margolin, Judith B. *About Foundations: How to Find the Facts You Need to Get A Grant.* New York: The Foundation Center, 1977.

The Process of Grantsmanship and Proposal Development. Washington, D.C., Education Funding Research Council, 1979.

White, Virginia P. *Grants: How to Find Out About Them and What to Do Next.* New York: Plenum, 1975.

CHAPTER FIFTEEN

The Telephone

The telephone has become one of the nation's chief time-savers and is on its way to becoming the nation's number one marketing tool. An estimated $50 billion dollars a year is spent on goods and services that are marketed by telephone or by telephone combined with other marketing methods.

Charles Bury
Telephone Techniques That Sell

More and more business is being conducted over the telephone. Using the telephone saves time and money—and can also make money. It can establish good will, sell an idea or service or product, answer questions, clear up confusion or misunderstanding. Effective use of the telephone requires many of the listening and speaking skills discussed in Chapter 3. It also requires many of the writing skills discussed in chapters 4 through 14 because whenever possible you should confirm or reinforce an important phone call with a letter, memo, or other appropriate written communication.

To save time, save money, and make money, use the telephone.

GROWING BUSINESS USE OF THE TELEPHONE

Selling—persuasion—by phone is becoming increasingly popular. Olan Mills Portrait Studio uses the phone exclusively; Wilson Foods Corporation sells meat wholesale primarily by phone; stockbrokers sell stocks, bonds, and commodity futures, transacting the majority of their business by phone; Dr. Pepper Company reduced returns of unsold bottles by use of Tel-Sel, estimating orders for delivery before loading delivery trucks; magazine and newspaper companies contact new subscribers and urge old customers to renew over the phone. The list is endless.

With the increased cost of fuel and services—an estimated $40 to $80 for each personal prospect/customer-in-person visit versus $10 or less using a Wide Area Telecommunication Service (WATS) line—more and more marketing will be done by phone. The phone is an efficient vehicle for many purposes. Among the many business uses of the telephone today are the following.

Selling by telephone is increasingly popular and economical.

- To sell existing accounts
- To sell on the service call (suggest new models, other products)
- To qualify prospects and to make appointments
- To stretch sales "reach" to distant markets
- To increase frequency of customer contacts
- To automate repeat orders
- To sell real estate and follow up on unsuccessful presentations
- To convert a prospect into a customer
- To collect overdue accounts
- To find out customer's reason for not paying
- To work out plan to keep account current
- To seek information for research, development, and publication
- To measure sales results (phone-sample market area)
- To check distribution (has advertised product arrived?)
- To pretest an ad campaign
- To coordinate a test market
- To reactivate old accounts
- To open new accounts (follow-up coupons, other inquiries, trade lists)
- To introduce new products
- To recruit a sales force (immediate feedback)
- To conduct surveys (market research, opinion polls, political trends)
- To appeal for funds, memberships, time, goods (for charity, social service, community activity)
- To retain customer good will

In the following selection, D. David Dahl of the Northwestern Bell Telephone Company discusses the subject of telecommunication, or communication at a distance by means of cable, radio, satellite, and so on. In addition to briefly tracing the history of telecommunications, Dahl outlines various types of voice communication equipment and their myriad applications in business and explains voice network services available to most consumers.

TELECOMMUNICATIONS
D. David Dahl*

Since its birth in 1877, telecommunications has been growing and changing. Originally, telephone communication took place only over two-way lines on a one-to-one basis. Then came the manually operated

*D. David Dahl is marketing industry manager, Northwestern Bell Telephone Company.

switchboard, making it possible for an individual to talk with anyone having a phone connected to that board. Still later, switchboards became interconnected with electromechanical circuitry.

Today, switching is computerized, with stored program control. Input is received as dialed or punched phone numbers; output consists of switching instructions. Interconnecting central offices in communities all over the United States create a giant telecommunications network. This network links over 110 million telephones and handles more than 20 million long-distance messages per day, including

- voice communications—telephone
- data communications—business machines
- video communications—television relays
- facsimile communications—photocopy machines

VOICE COMMUNICATIONS EQUIPMENT

Electronic switching enables organizations to adapt the telephone to their specialized needs. A *PBX* (Private Branch Exchange) is similar to a telephone company central office. Within the organization it enables the forwarding of private calls, inward dialing, call detail recording, automatic wake-up (for hotels/motels), energy control, bed census, and other services. Modern PBXs are programmed individually to meet the customer's needs.

The telephone is adaptable and versatile.

Centrex/Essex is much like the PBX. However, unlike the customer-premise-located PBX, Centrex/Essex is located at the local phone company. Electronically, these systems provide internal communication among the telephone stations within a customer's organization, as well as the facilities for connecting these sets to the telecommunications network.

Multiline or "key" systems enable a customer to place and receive telephone calls on more than one line on a single telephone. Such systems generally handle between two and 29 lines. Buttons or "keys" permit signaling, switching, intercom use, and line holding.

Intercoms allow stations within a system to communicate with each other without going through a central office. Intercoms require one- to four-digit codes for connections.

Paging equipment permits the broadcast of messages to various locations on the customer's premises by means of loudspeakers. Paging may be by voice or by coded beeps or tones.

Other special equipment includes the following:

1. Standard telephones, wall phones, concealed phones—nondial, rotary dial, or pushbutton for residential and business use.

2. Multibutton telephones with a row of pushbuttons on the set to permit line selection.

3. Outdoor phones enclosed in weather-resistant housing—for construction sites, forestry stations, highway emergency locations.

4. Explosive-atmosphere telephones encased in cast iron or a high-strength aluminum alloy housing designed to limit the possibility of explosions—for grain elevators, flour mills, nuclear power plants, chemical plants, smelting mills.

5. Handicapped services:
   - speech and hearing amplification
   - artificial larynx to produce audible speech for individuals whose vocal cords have been removed or paralyzed
   - set converting sound signals into visual signals for the deaf
   - set converting sound signals into vibrating, tactile signals for the deaf-blind
   - set with a sending key for the mute

6. Automatic dialers with capacity to record frequently called phone numbers and automatically dial those numbers. Numbers are stored on punched cards or are recorded on a solid-state memory and played back at the touch of a button.

7. Recording equipment that automatically answers incoming calls, presents a prerecorded message to the caller, records the caller's message, and disconnects.

8. Amplifiers that enable groups of people to listen to conversations.

9. Conference equipment that uses amplifiers in two-way group conversations and uses microphones for responses.

10. Alarm-reporting equipment for fire (temperature) alarm or burglar alarm.

11. Automatic call sequencers that answer high volumes of incoming calls in the order received, play a recorded message to the caller, and then forward the call to the first available operator—for airline and other reservation systems.

12. Message-waiting services that provide users a lamp console, LED (Light Emitting Diodes) or LCD (Liquid Crystal Diodes) flashing light while the user is away, indicating message being held.

13. Mobile telephone in car or truck for originating or receiving calls.

14. Remote access to enable subscriber to dial an access code and get into a PBX network—usually a very large business or government agency private line. Once into the network, the caller can dial anywhere in it. Reduces charges, offers bulk calling service.

15. Facsimile telecommunication that transmits reproduced images, photographs, or other types of graphics over the network.

16. Electronic blackboard that combines graphics and voice communication at any number of remote locations connected to a given call.

VOICE NETWORK SERVICES

Private lines connect telephones at separate locations or may connect two or more PBXs, creating a private-line network for voice or data telecommunication. In addition, *switched-service* networks are available for customers requiring extensive private-line communications. In this system all stations associated with the network may dial each other regardless of location and without using exchange and toll facilities.

DDD (Direct Distance Dialing) or *MTS* (Message Telephone Service) provides service almost anywhere in the United States for voice and data. *IDDD* (International DDD) allows business and residential customers to call countries outside the United States. As of 1979, 74 countries were able to be direct dialed.

Reverse charge and *no-charge*-to-caller services include Enterprise, Zenith, and WX numbers listed in local phone books for distant organizations. *FX* or Foreign Exchange Service gives the customer representation in a potential market area without the expense of operating a branch office. A telephone number from a distant city automatically rings in the company's office, providing toll-free telephone access to clients. *WATS* (Wide Area Telecommunication Service) provides for the *origination* of calls from a station with a WATS access line to stations in a designated service area. An *800* service provides the *reception* of calls from stations in a designated service area to a station associated with an inward WATS access line.

Both WATS and 800 programs are bulk-calling plans that are available for a set monthly fee. WATS customers have a choice of seven interstate service areas and one intrastate service.

Teleconferencing or *video teleconferencing* between two or more locations, among three or more people, can substitute for face-to-face meetings, saving travel time and energy. Teleconferencing offers audible, visual, and graphic communication capabilities. These conferences are routed through a simplified dialing procedure as part of the customers' PBX, Centrex, or ESSEX system. Currently, the video linkup is between remote conference locations on telephone company property or on leased premises.

Multiperson telephone conferences are becoming routine.

DATA COMMUNICATION EQUIPMENT

Data communications transport encoded information from one point to another without change or processing. This data may start out as voice information spoken into a special recorder or as some other form of recorded information. The sound is converted into an electrical signal for transmission. The signal can assume an almost infinite number of values during any specified time; this signal is called *analog information*.

Most computers, however, perform calculations using *binary digital data.* Calculations occur in codes where the code is either on or off. A *data set* or *modem* enables data communication terminals to be reached over the telephone. The data set converts the digital signals used in data terminals and computers to analog signals suitable for transmission over telephone lines. The analog signals are received and reprocessed into digital signals suitable for reception by a particular computer system.

(The telephone company is developing a *packet-switched network* to enable any computer to talk with any other computer or terminal via the public-switched network. This will reduce costs to users by eliminating the need for communications *processors.*)

Data communications occur terminal to terminal, terminal to computer and vice versa, and computer to computer. A *terminal* is the point where data can enter or leave a communication network. *Data entry* is called *input; data results* are called *output.* Sophisticated terminals can edit, display (on a CRT—cathode-ray tube), and print data. The most complex terminals are called "smart" terminals or "intelligent" terminals, for they have the capacity to perform some data processing functions on their own without totally relying on the host computer. See Figure 15–1 for the possible components of an office automation system.

TRANSMISSION MEDIA

Telecommunications are transmitted through various media, including open wire pairs of copper or steel suspended by insulated cross arms on telephone poles; insulated wire cables; coaxial cables—a single wire conductor surrounded by a hollow, insulated copper cylinder, bundled together into large cables; fiber optics and millimeter waveguides (fiber optics are thin tubes of transparent plastic—a waveguide is a method for transmitting very high-frequency radio waves); submarine cables; microwave towers; and communication satellites.

Obviously, the present technology is awesome. It is up to you, the *human* communicator, to use it effectively. Here are some suggestions.

SELLING BY TELEPHONE

For selling, getting the other person to like you is the most valuable thing you can do. But first *you* must like people—and show that you like them by the tone of your voice, by your consideration, and by the things you say and do.

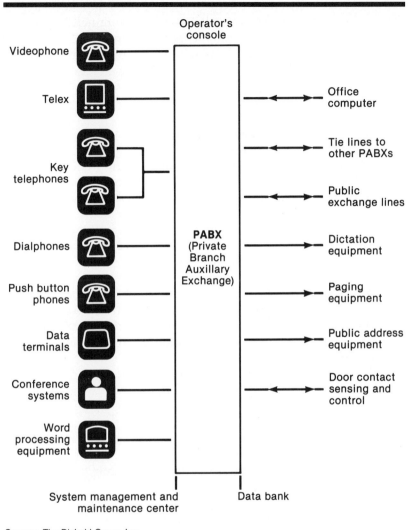

Source: The Diebold Group, Inc.

Figure 15–1: Schematic of an Evolved Office Automation System

George C. Combe (in Black, 1973) advises: "Before you pick up the telephone, smile. Don't talk with marbles in your mouth, don't use curse words, and don't hang up the phone with a bang." In other words, remember that the telephone leaves your listener with the impression of the kind of person you are and that this impression frequently determines whether he or she wants to do business with you. This positive decision is the basis of successful selling.

Combe and other experts on selling by telephone suggest "Phone Power," similar to the steps already recommended for persuasive written communication. (AT&T offers specific Phone Power publications for various types of selling. Ask for the free series as a customer service.) A general approach would include the following (Ben Berman):

Plan each telephone call ahead of time.

1. Know exactly what you are going to say.
2. Have appropriate material at hand.
3. Assume a confident attitude.
4. Verify—make sure you are talking to the right person.
5. Identify—introduce yourself and the company.
6. Tell—explain the reason for your call in terms of benefits to the prospect.
7. Ask—give your prospect a choice between something and something.
8. Thank the prospect for his/her time.

Put a smile in your voice.

In addition, the salesperson is reminded to smile when talking, speak about 140 words per minute, offer an excuse if leaving the phone for more than 30 seconds, allow the customer to hang up first, and *take readable notes.* Unless the conversation is being taped, with the permission of the customer, the salesperson should take thorough notes. Recording customer reactions and other vital data can help with future selling. Figure 15–2 shows a few selling dos and don'ts.

Planning is the first step in telephone selling, just as it is for selling by written communication. You must know your company, know your needs (see Chapter 5), know your audience and their needs and wants. You must research and search for prospects, learning as much as possible about each one.

You can compile your own or purchase or lease a mailing list (Appendix C). Telephone directories sometimes show different areas of the city, always have yellow or white business pages; Reuben H. Donnelley Corporation (in Florida, Hill Donnelley) publishes city directories including address, phone numbers, and occupations; the *Thomas Register* lists manufacturers; ethnic lists and other special groups are available from publications—magazines, newspapers, newsletters; voting registration lists are open for inspection.

Remember your audience, the person you are calling.

You must form a visual picture of the person you are calling so that you can speak a common language. You should line up prospects in advance, preferably on 3-by-5 cards, with all the available information written on the card: full name, address and zip

Do	Don't
1. Smile	Frown
2. Speak clearly and concisely	Mutter
3. Be enthusiastic	Sound tired
4. Lower the pitch of your voice for friendly conversation	Speak in a shrill voice
5. Talk in a positive mood	Be negative
6. Be prepared to answer objections	Be overconfident
7. Come to the point	Ramble
8. Do something *for* the customer	Do something *to* the customer
9. Discuss	Argue
10. Politely thank the customer for listening	Hang up abruptly if refused

Source: Ben Berman, Furst and Furst.

Figure 15–2: Telephone Selling Dos and Don'ts

code, telephone number with area code, gender of decision maker, title of business person, name of his or her secretary, working hours—any and all information to help form a picture in your mind of the *person* and *place* you are calling.

Again, it is wise to remember that few if any services or products are sold on the first call. Any contact provides information for future use.

Organizing the telephone selling campaign begins with drawing up the list of prospects and includes developing a sales script or working notes, preparing answers for most common objectives, creating a comfortable and efficient work area, and determining the best hours of the day to call your prospects.

Bury (1980) recommends calling business concerns from 9 A.M. to 5 P.M. and residences from 9 A.M. to 9 P.M. Morning seems to be better than afternoon for catching business executives in their offices. Another good time is between 4 and 4:30 when they return to their offices to clear off the work on their desks.

Place your telephone calls at an appropriate time.

Contractors should be called before they leave for their job sites, between 7 and 8 A.M. Homemakers are usually at home from 9 A.M. to 1 P.M. and again from 3 to 5. The best evening hour for calls, Bury concludes, is from 7 to 8, after dinner.

Ben Berman (1979), veteran debt collector, points out the time and frequency restraints built into the Fair Debt Collection Practices Act of 1978 (Appendix D). In addition, he says, "A good telephone collector must be a good actor who can change roles quickly. . . . A good telephone collector is both diplomat and super salesperson. He or she adapts to the differences in individuals and knows how to make tactful and motivating appeals to the customer to bring results."

Develop a telephone "script."

These appeals are built into a "sales script." Such a script may be written or memorized. After repeated use, certain practices will become automatic. You should, for example, call ahead for an appointment for an initial selling situation. Ask for the person to whom you wish to speak, then give your name. "May I speak to Mr. Jones, please? This is Mary Smith of Acme Company." If you give your name first, the secretary may not get it, particularly if it is unfamiliar or unusual. You will be asked to repeat it, giving the secretary a chance to quiz you about why you want to talk to the boss. If you tell first that you wish to speak to Mr. Jones, the secretary will be alerted and will get your name, know why you are calling. (It is smart to enlist the secretary's cooperation, even on the phone. Secretaries, like all of us, respond to courteous and complimentary treatment.)

Another "script" includes writing first, offering to show something of benefit to the prospect, and then following up with a phone call. "I believe Marianne McManus, our sales manager, wrote you a week or so ago about our No. 99 Scanner that will cut down your office expenses. Do you recall the letter?" The salesperson should pause and then proceed, no matter what the reply. "Well, I'm here now and would appreciate 10 to 15 minutes of your time. Is it possible for us to get together this afternoon?" This is a low-key conversation between two business people. The prospect has a chance to speak, but the reply is almost certain to be affirmative, particularly if the salesperson offers to *show* benefits to the customer.

Get to the point quickly.

The telephone approach must move rapidly; the subject of the call must be introduced quickly. The opening should be only one or two short sentences and should end in a leading question inviting the reply, "Yes." The salesperson must get to the objective of the call quickly. Brevity is permissible in the call more so than in the personal interview.

Once you've tried several scripts, you can refine, evaluate, and revise their content and your techniques. The same techniques are useful for selling products and services and for finding a job ("Career Search," Chapter 18).

TELEPHONE ETIQUETTE

In business and in social life, effective telephone behavior can help you win friends and create good will. The person you are talking to can't see your facial expressions; thus your personality can only be judged by how you sound. (Many telephone companies offer free instructions, films, and other aids to teach proper telephone behavior.)

Be courteous, tactful, and accurate.

When the telephone rings:

- Answer promptly—indicate friendly efficiency.
- Identify yourself—personalize the call.
- Listen carefully—eliminate the need for repetition.
- Be considerate—concentrate attention on the caller; include explanations for delays; ask if the person wishes to wait; check back every 30 seconds; thank the caller for waiting when you have the information; hang up quietly *after* the caller.
- Transfer a call only when necessary—ask the caller's permission.

When you answer for a co-worker:

- Identify yourself—it's helpful to have people know your name: "Miss Elkin's office, Mr. Hansen speaking."
- Be helpful—offer what information you can.
- Be tactful—use a noncommittal explanation for co-worker's absence: "Mr. Jones is away from his desk."
- Take accurate messages—include name, time, date, telephone number for speedy reply, your name for reference.

When you need to phone:

- Determine and plan objective of call.
- Be sure of the number—check the directory.
- Place your own calls—save time, show your interest.
- Let the phone ring up to ten times—give person time to answer.
- Identify yourself—establish rapport and get off to a good start.
- Ask if it is a convenient time to talk.
- Remember time differences—check for time zone on directory map.
- Space calls—someone may be trying to reach you.
- Return calls promptly.
- Give sense of urgency to long-distance calls—identify such calls immediately.

When you answer for your employer:

- Be alert, friendly, and helpful (as above).
- Screen calls only if requested (screening irritates some callers, so it is not recommended)—identify yourself to encourage caller to do the same; avoid "Who is calling?" and respond with "Yes, he (she) is in but is in another office right now. May I take a message?"
- Verify spelling of a name and the exact telephone number.

In general:

- Greet callers pleasantly and sincerely.
- Address the caller by name.
- Treat every call as important.
- Apologize for errors or delays.
- Use common courtesy words: *please, thank you, you're welcome.*
- Be tactful, particularly when refusing a request—create "buffers" by using words people like to hear, saying what you can do rather than what you can't (positive approach).
- Keep your promises—follow through with a reply at the time agreed upon.
- Suggest an appropriate time for calling back.
- Show co-workers the same courtesy you show your customers and personal friends.

ASSIGNMENT: THE TELEPHONE

This week's training session will be devoted to the telephone as a major means of effective business communication. Come prepared to lead a round-table discussion on any two of the following topics.

Topics

1. Ten of the many business uses of the telephone.
2. Three voice communication equipment systems and their business applications.
3. Six kinds of special telephone equipment and their uses.
4. Dos and don'ts of telephone selling.
5. The planning stage of selling by telephone.
6. The organizing stage of selling by telephone.
7. Etiquette in answering any telephone call.
8. Etiquette in initiating any telephone call.

FURTHER READING

Berman, Ben. "Using the Telephone to Improve Collections." *Construction Equipment Distribution,* October 1979.

Black, George. *Sales Engineering, An Emerging Profession.* Houston, TX: Gulf, 1973.

Brody, John H. *How to Be a Successful Telephone Persuader.* Alexandria, VA: Phoenix Press, 1980.

Brown, M. T. *Making Money with the Telephone: The Complete Handbook of Telephone Marketing.* Camarillo, CA: Future Shop, 1977.

Bury, Charles. *Telephone Techniques That Sell.* New York: Warner, 1980.

Collier, Lisa. *Telephone Tactics That Make You a Winner.* New York: Rawson Wade, 1979.

Ortland, R. J. *Handbook of Professional Telephone Selling.* Reading, MA: Addison-Wesley, 1980.

Peterson, Ken T. *How to Sell Successfully by Phone.* Chicago, IL: Dartnell, 1975.

The Phone Power Way. New York: AT&T, 1971.

Roman, Murray. *Telephone Marketing Techniques.* New York: American Management Association, 1979.

Taraba, Tibor, *How to Turn Telephone Inquiries into Sales.* New York: Reuben H. Donnelley, 1979. (Free)

CHAPTER SIXTEEN

Meetings

Middle managers in industry may spend as much as 35 percent of their work week in meetings. That figure can be as high as 50 percent for top management.

David R. Seibold
"Making Meetings More Successful"

Meetings require the entire range of communication skills.

Business meetings take time—frequently too much time—but decision by consensus (group agreement) helps gain cooperation. In a democratic organization, people meet to discuss mutual problems, to study alternatives, to reach conclusions. Each person has a chance to speak out. Business meetings can serve as a showcase for ambitious executives and other employees. For more information on the interpersonal dynamics of meetings, see pages 27–30.

In addition to requiring the listening, speaking, and reading skills described in Chapter 3, successful meetings also require effective planning, organizing, writing, evaluating, revising (POWER).

Plan:
- Determine the purpose of the meeting.
- Select appropriate participants.
- Determine the most suitable date, time, place. (Before lunch or before going home, attendees are especially time-conscious.)

Organize:
- Make out an *agenda*—list of topics for discussion.
- Establish the order and priority of topics.
- Follow *Robert's Rules of Order* for formal meetings. (Variations are accepted, but the *Rules* is the oldest and most frequently used standard of procedure.)

Write:
- Notify attendees by memo, letter, electronic mail.
- Include *agenda* with notification.

312

- Record the meeting actions in *minutes.* (Appoint or bring along a secretary. A tape recorder is useful for verification.)
- Distribute the minutes.

Evaluate:

- Determine whether goals were accomplished—chairperson's duty.

Revise:

- Reschedule, replan—if necessary—on the basis of outcome.

INFORMAL MEETINGS

Here are some guidelines.

1. Call meetings only when absolutely necessary, when you cannot write, phone, or handle the situation yourself.
2. Call the meeting by phone, memo, or electronic mail; try to arrange a time convenient for all involved. (Sometimes it helps to collect schedules earlier, blocking off times of regular commitments, meetings, trips, and so on.)
3. Invite only those directly concerned with the subject—to gain more information or to alert them to what you know, what they need to know.
4. Draw up an informal agenda including items of interest to everyone. Items with specialized appeal should be discussed with individuals at another time.
5. Distribute the agenda, if there is time, or keep it to yourself. Some chairpersons bring out the "hidden" items at the meeting without previously having given others an opportunity to prepare a defense or attack. They consider the surprise element valuable.
6. Conduct the meeting according to the agenda but without following *Robert's Rules of Order.* Most informal meetings are for exchanging ideas rather than for voting to reach decisions—although voting may follow later.
7. If applicable or advisable, call for reports or assign areas of research to be reported on at a later, stated time.
8. Stop possible confrontations by seating potentially argumentative members side by side rather than across from each other. Closeness discourages verbal abuse.
9. Control long-winded speakers or unnecessary interruptions tactfully by interrupting to wrap up the statement.
10. Send a memo summarizing results of the meeting to all the participants. Include

Most informal meetings involve an exchange of ideas rather than a final decision.

a. the date, time, place
b. names of participants
c. itemized list of topics and conclusions

Try to keep the format consistent, easy to read, easy to find. A written record, even in memo form, will establish sequence of events and actions.

However, it is also possible that you may want to keep the informal meeting confidential, off the record. Tape-recording the proceedings for yourself can serve the same purpose as a written memo—and can be equally useful as evidence.

FORMAL MEETINGS

Here are some guidelines.

1. A quorum of more than one-half the membership must be present or the meeting is unofficial. (In its constitution, an organization may set another figure for the quorum.)
2. The meeting should start at a preset, scheduled time.
3. The presiding officer opens the meeting with the traditional "The meeting will please come to order."
4. The meeting proceeds following the *agenda*, usually
   a. roll call—recording of those present
   b. reading of the *minutes* of the previous meeting (If distributed earlier, these need not be read. Some organizations save expense by including *minutes* with *agenda* and other relevant material, such as treasurer's report, communications, preprinted forms for motions, in one early mailing. This enables participants to review, research, prepare intelligently for the meeting.)
   c. approval of the minutes
   d. communications
   e. committee reports (Each person reporting should know sequence of appearance and time allotted.)
   f. unfinished or old business
   g. new business
   h. adjournment

Formal meetings are highly structured.

This order may be altered—for example, new business before old—but the chairperson must notify attendees of the change and may request approval of the change prior to the meeting.

5. Members wishing to speak address the chairperson as Madam Chairperson, Mr. Chairman, Madam President, Mr. President, or less formally by name.
6. The officer recognizes the individual by name, thus indicating his or her right to speak.

7. The member offers opinions, statements concerning the subject. If a *motion—a suggested course of action*—is to be made, the member says, "I move that. . . ." If the preceding speaker's statement covered the problem, the member could say, "I so move."

8. Someone else must second the motion to make it valid. The chairperson usually says, "Do I hear a second?" or "Is there a second?" Recognition is not necessary, only the statement, "I second." (Without a second, the motion "dies.")

9. The chairperson calls for a *discussion* following the second— "Is there any discussion?" Members should address remarks to the chairperson, not to other members, should limit remarks, speak no more than twice on the subject. But every official attendee has a right to speak although the maker of a motion may not speak against it (but may vote against it).

10. The chairperson or a member may close the discussion. The chairperson may ask, "Are you ready for the question?" or a member may call out, "Question." This signals a call for a vote on the motion.

11. Voting may be by
    a. general consent—"I ask for general consent to. . . ."
    b. voice—"All in favor say 'aye'—opposed say 'no.'"
    c. standing—"In favor, please stand; opposed, please stand."
    d. raising hands—"In favor, raise right hand; opposed, raise right hand."
    e. roll call
    f. written ballot

12. A motion may be "tabled" or someone may call for adjournment to prevent a vote (see *Rules* for finer points of procedure).

13. A pending motion must be disposed of before a second motion may be introduced. If an amendment is made to the original motion, the amendment must be voted on before the main motion may be considered.

14. The chairperson or a member may call for adjournment when the agenda material has been completed or time has run out. Usually the chairperson says, "A motion for adjournment is in order," or, "Is there a motion for adjournment?" This motion, too, must have a second and must be voted on—usually by voice.

15. *Formal minutes,* or the record of the proceedings of a meeting (see Figure 16–1), include
    a. the kind of meeting (regular or special)
    b. the name of the organization or group
    c. the date, time, place

MINUTES OF THE SCIENCES AND HUMANITIES
REPRESENTATIVE ASSEMBLY MEETING

October 10, 1981

1. The meeting was called to order at 4:10 P.M. by Dean Wallace A. Russell, Chair.

2. The Chair asked that the agenda be modified to include under New Business possible action on a report from the Committee on Instruction pertaining to plus-minus grading. The modification was accepted and the agenda was approved.

3. The minutes of the meeting of September 12, 1981 were approved.

COMMENTS BY THE DEAN ON THE STATUS OF THE BUDGET

Dean Russell's comments are attached to the minutes as Appendix I.

COMMITTEE REPORTS

4. John R. Clem, Chair of the Executive Committee, presented the Executive Committee report and called attention to paragraph A.4. of the report. The Executive Committee noted that the Assembly's usual meeting day in November is during final examination week but nevertheless recommended making no change in the schedules date unless it becomes clear that extensive conflicts would result. A shown of hands at the meeting confirmed that in fact there would be few conflicts.

5. Fred Brown, Chair of the Committee on Instruction, presented a report from that committee on plus-minus grading. This report was prepared as a result of a motion passed at the January 10, 1981 meeting of the Representative Assembly, by which the Assembly went on record as favoring a grading system that would provide faculty with a plus-minus grading option in undergraduate courses. At that time the Assembly also requested that the Committee on Instruction draft a specific plan by which such an option might be accomplished and bring the recommendation to the Assembly for further action.

Brief discussion of the report followed.

NEW BUSINESS

6. John R. Clem and George H. Bowen presented the following motion regarding plus-minus grading:

(a) that the Representative Assembly approve the October 10, 1981 recommendations of the Committee on Instruction regarding a plus-minus grading option for the College of Sciences and Humanities, and

(b) that the Assembly recommend that the College administration take the necessary steps to implement these recommendations.

Figure 16–1: Typical Minutes of a Meeting

2

7. The motion was seconded. Brief discussion followed. During the discussion period the Chair explained that if the Assembly approves a plus-minus grading option, the College will need to obtain a waiver from the all-university regulations regarding grades stated in the General Catalog. Probably this matter would be taken to the General Faculty through the University Academic Standards Committee or the University Council on Instruction.

8. John R. Clem moved to postpone action on the motion until the next meeting. This motion was seconded and passed. Copies of the report of the Committee on Instruction will be circulated as soon as possible to all faculty so that Assembly members may obtain reactions to the proposal in time for the November meeting.

9. Assembly members agreed not to change the date of the next meeting from the regularly scheduled date, Wednesday, November 14.

10. The meeting adjourned at 5:10 P.M.

Submitted by

Millard R. Kratochvil
Recording Secretary

Permanent copy: S&H Dean's Office--A-15

    d. the names of the official members present or their sub-stitutes

    e. the names of the regular chairperson and secretary or the names of their substitutes ("Chair" may be used to refer to the chairperson)

    f. reference to the minutes of the previous meeting—whether read and approved as read or as corrected

    g. a separate paragraph for each subject discussed, including motions, actions, names of members involved

    h. the hour of adjournment

Copies of the minutes are prepared soon after the meeting and distributed to the individuals who attended. The minutes become a chronological history of the meeting activities and the final word in future discussions related to the topics covered.

16. *Notice* of most formal meetings should be posted where easily seen or printed in organizational publications for the information of the employees. *Notice of public and governmental agency meetings* must be posted and published at least 24 hours ahead of time. The notices should include date, time, place, agenda.

17. *Closed sessions* require specific procedures now that most states have open-meeting laws.

    a. Board, council, trustees, others convene in open meeting.

    b. Chairperson accepts a motion for a closed session with the reason(s) stated and allowed under the law.

    c. Roll-call vote for the closed session is made and each member's vote is recorded in the minutes.

    d. Meeting goes into closed session—no outsiders permitted.

    e. Secretary *tape-records* and keeps detailed written minutes of all closed-session discussion.

    f. Minutes and tape recordings are sealed and retained (for one year, in many states).

    g. Members reconvene in an open meeting.

    h. Members *vote* on actions resulting from closed-session discussions.

(For implications of open-meeting laws to your organization, get a legal opinion.)

AD HOC MEETINGS

Ad hoc meetings deal with a single topic.

Ad hoc meetings are called for one special purpose. Such meetings may be formal or informal. In general, ad hoc meetings take precedence over other activities except for high-level, regularly scheduled formal meetings.

MAKING MEETINGS MORE SUCCESSFUL*
David R. Seibold

At one time or another we may all have sat in a meeting and wished we could break an unproductive group deadlock by personally initiating conclusive action. Meetings, both small-group sessions and larger conferences, have become a major and often frustrating part of our lives. We seem to be attending more of them than ever before. Too frequently, our assessment of a meeting is, "What a waste of time; nothing was accomplished."

Meetings probably *are* held more frequently nowadays. A study sponsored by the 3M Company revealed that the number of meetings and conferences in industry alone nearly doubled during the past ten years, while their cost tripled. Estimates suggest that most organizations devote between 7 and 15 percent of their personnel budgets to meetings. One large California-based corporation figures that almost $30 million of its $350 million personnel budget is spent on meetings. At the individual level, middle managers in industry may spend as much as 35 percent of their work week in meetings. That figure can be as high as 50 percent for top management.

Why do we hold such an extraordinary number of meetings? Perhaps because in every field, whether it's industry, government, legal and civic circles, or academia, meetings are essential if organizations are to function effectively in our increasingly complex and interdependent world. They are a major means by which groups of people receive or gather information about their environment, arrive at collective orientations toward that information, jointly utilize these interpretations to solve problems, and simultaneously recognize their unity as a purposeful, functioning group. Meetings may be convened for any or all of these purposes: to inform members; to solicit opinions and request guidance from members; to promote unity and cohesiveness among members; to solve problems, make decisions, or recommend policy.

Meetings may be called to inform members, solicit opinions, promote unity, solve problems, make decisions, recommend policy.

But meetings need not be a waste of time. Proper planning for a meeting, as well as judicious selection from among alternative problem-solving formats and procedures, are preliminaries that will ensure the success of any session.

Thoughtful preparation for a meeting is a must, and the chairperson should:

- Determine that a meeting is *necessary.* If matters can be handled just as readily by means of personal memorandums, a conference phone

*Abridged version from *The Best of Business,* vol. 2, no. 1, Spring 1980. Knoxville, TN: 13–30 Corporation, pp. 49–53. Annotated, original article available in American Business Communication Association *Journal of Business Communication,* Summer 1979.

Proper planning can help ensure a successful meeting.

call, or individual meetings with selected group members, a formal face-to-face meeting is unwarranted.

- Identify the specific *purposes* of the meeting and delineate its goals. Is the meeting being held to disseminate information, bolster morale, solve problems and make decisions, settle grievances, or stimulate involvement? What are the desirable outcomes? The chairperson should be prepared to state the purposes and goals of the meeting in an agenda, and should be ready to restate them if members digress too much during the meeting.

- Decide on the *composition* of the group for the meeting. If the group is an established one, such as a standing committee, will outsiders be invited to observe and participate? If attendance will not be settled by de facto membership, who will be asked to take part in the meeting or conference? How will the participants differ with regard to their power, status, experience with the issue under discussion, concern about the problem, relationships with other group members, hidden agendas (that is, personal goals for the session), and communication skills?

- Settle the *logistics* of the meeting. Where and when will the group meet? Determine how long the meeting should last and abide by the time limit. All the details of arranging the meeting, including the use of audiovisual equipment and visual aids, the seating arrangement, and the reproduction and distribution of written materials, should be considered and planned for well in advance.

- Delineate appropriate group *roles,* assign responsibility, and delegate authority where necessary. Certain members may be asked to act as group recorder, to prepare a special presentation, to introduce an invited expert, to make room arrangements, or perhaps to lead a portion of the meeting. When possible, you should have these group members report that they have carried out their responsibility or are prepared to do so during the session.

- *Brief* all members on their roles in the meeting by means of an agenda, identifying the particular issues for which each individual member will be responsible in an accompanying memorandum. If members can anticipate the purposes, goals, and issues that form the basis of their meeting, as well as their own responsibilities for its conduct, they are likely to come better prepared and more motivated.

- Try to form a *mental picture* of how the meeting will proceed. Will anyone make opening statements? What are the major themes and issues to be discussed during the meeting? Will you impose time limitations? Have you chosen a format and problem-solving procedures? Do you anticipate any problems (for example, one member dominating discussion time or an unclear presentation by another member)? Once you have envisioned the meeting, you can plan how to expedite the good passages and how to manage potential problems. The chairperson's job before, during, and after meetings is demanding—an amalgam of planning, promoting, leading, directing, informing, interpreting, encouraging, stimulating, refereeing, judging, moderating, and conciliating.

One of the major elements in the chairperson's mental picture of a meeting is its format, or the general structure for organizing the session and facilitating discussion. Many alternatives are available, especially for larger conferences:

Meeting formats include media presentation, presentation by one person, panel discussion, format discussion, and unstructured discussion.

- Begin the meeting with a *media presentation* (videotape, film, slides) to present information to members and stimulate concern about the problem they face. Then initiate a collective problem-solving discussion with the group.
- Start with a *presentation by one person,* such as an invited expert, and follow it with a problem-solving discussion.
- Open the session with a *panel discussion* (interrelated, brief, and informal presentations by several persons from within the group or by invited panelists) or a *symposium* (formal statements by experts), then begin joint group questioning (forum discussion) and problem solving.
- Adopt a *format discussion* plan in which all participants jointly discuss topically or sequentially related issues that have been identified by the chairperson and distributed as questions in outline form, a procedure analogous to following a general agenda.
- Plan for open, *unstructured discussion* at the beginning of the meeting, followed by summarization and further, more focused problem solving thereafter.

To complete the mental picture of a meeting or conference, the chairperson must decide which *problem-solving procedures* can be suggested to members during the session. These procedures can serve as vehicles to systematize a group's discussion and decision-making efforts. Both research and common experience suggest that when organizing schemes are not applied, group members tend to be haphazard and disorganized in the discussion process and in attempts to come to a decision.

Problem-solving procedures help circumvent inefficiency, delay, confusion, redundancy, and occasional frustration by coordinating members, focusing their attention on common issues, and guiding them through problem diagnosis, solution selection, and implementation. Among the many group and conference procedures that the chairperson may wish to utilize are the following techniques, which have been

Problem-solving procedures help to eliminate inefficiency, confusion, and frustration through problem diagnosis, solution selection, and implementation.

selected for their focus on problem-solving procedures rather than selection among alternative solutions:

Problem census determines participants' opinions about issues to be considered.

Problem census. The chairperson systematically polls all members at the meeting about items that should be discussed, or parameters of a problem under consideration, or alternative issues that have not been considered to that point in the deliberations. The purpose is to obtain a "census" of members about issues that should be considered. Results are posted for all to see. They can be used to guide further discussion at the present meeting or to set a future agenda. Whether introductory or interim, this technique helps draw all members into the discussion.

Rational reflection involves a thoughtful, methodical approach to a specific aspect of an issue.

Rational reflection. Participants attempt to solve a problem by proceeding through a comprehensive series of predetermined "reflective" phases intended to address specific aspects of a problem in rational and methodical fashion. Discussion at any time is limited to the particular phase of the problem under consideration. The phases, in order, require discussion of these questions:

1. What *is* the problem? (How can it be stated? What are its relationships to other problems? What are our assumptions about the problem as stated and isolated?)
2. What are the *causes* of the problem and why do we need to solve it? (What is the origin and history of the problem? What is the significance of the present harm? How persistent is the problem?)
3. What are the minimal *criteria* necessary for an adequate solution?
4. What are all the *possible solutions* of the problem as analyzed? (What are the data supporting each proposed solution? Have all possible solutions been considered?)
5. What is the *best solution*? (Does it minimize the significance of the problem? Does it alleviate the persistence of the problem? Is it workable? Do the advantages of the solution outweigh disadvantageous consequences?)
6. How should the chosen solution be *implemented*?

If they are adhered to, these phases can facilitate thorough and efficient small-group problem solving.

Brainstorming generates creative ideas.

Brainstorming. This technique promotes creativity in discussion groups by reducing some of the inhibitory aspects of group problem solving, especially criticism and evaluation. The sole concern of members taking part in a brainstorming session should be idea generation, not idea evaluation. To this end, the chairperson should tell members that criticism of any contribution must be withheld until later. The chairperson should also suggest that they strive to come up with as many ideas as possible in the time available—the wilder the better, since it is easier to "tame down" than to "think up."

Members should be given some time alone to record their ideas before joint brainstorming is begun. The chairperson should also be prepared to contribute ideas, to "prime the pump" when discussion slows, and to have a recorder present to note all contributions. When criticism is scrupulously avoided, members usually relax, generate a longer list of contributions than they would have otherwise, and often come away from this portion of the meeting invigorated.

Buzz groups.   Participants at the meeting are divided into subgroups and given a brief period of time to discuss a specific aspect of a problem or solution. Each buzz group may focus on maximizing the number of ideas generated (as in brainstorming), or, conversely, on evaluating and discussing an item in more detail than the larger group might be able to go into. Each "caucus" then reports back to the main group.

Buzz groups brainstorm or discuss and evaluate a particular item more thoroughly than the larger group might be able to do.

As in brainstorming, members often get more involved in the problem when this subgroup procedure is used, and a wise chairperson can breathe life into a stagnant meeting by suggesting that members break into buzz groups. Buzz groups are also an especially effective means of reducing the anonymity and cumbersomeness of very large meetings, since members can be grouped with the four or five persons seated around them. Reports from each of these buzz groups may then indicate the issues where consensus exists and those that require further discussion by all present.

Nominal group technique.   This procedure is so called because members are really a group in name only. During most of the process, they work individually. The chairperson directs each member to create separate lists of the advantages and disadvantages associated with the proposition under discussion (for example, unionization, shift changes, worker layoffs). After 20 minutes, members are sequentially polled and a master list of all advantages and disadvantages is posted on a flipchart or blackboard visible to all.

Then members are directed to work alone again for ten minutes, this time ranking all advantages and all disadvantages from highest priority to lowest priority. Members privately submit their priority lists and an "average" master list is compiled while all adjourn temporarily. When the meeting resumes, the rank-ordered tabulations provide the basis for collective discussion of the issue. The nominal group procedure thus generates a basis for group discussion that reflects all members' views.

The nominal group technique involves individuals working alone on a proposition and eventually forming a master list to generate group discussion.

Delphi method.   Like the nominal group technique, the Delphi method severely restricts interaction among group members. The procedure is especially useful when the meeting is an ad hoc conference of experts. To minimize overcommitment to previously expressed personal views, domination by the most vocal experts or those with the highest status, and the tyranny of majority opinion, the experts' opinions are pooled as the participants work alone and anonymously. The procedure calls for participants to answer an initial questionnaire designed to elicit their expert opinions about some problem, issue, recommendation, or policy. After an intermission, all group members receive a second questionnaire listing others' contributions and are asked to evaluate each idea by several specified criteria. During the following session, a third questionnaire reports the second-round rating, a mean rating, and any consensus. Members are asked to revise their earlier ratings in light of the average or consensual view, or to justify their deviant position.

In the Delphi method, participants individually answer a series of questionnaires that culminate in data on which the participants or an independent body strive to make a final recommendation.

A final questionnaire includes all ratings, the consensus, and remaining minority opinions. Members are given a last chance to revise their original positions. Depending on the nature of the conference, these final data may be forwarded to an independent body of decision makers, or the experts may be directed to initiate face-to-face discussion and strive for a final recommendation. The difficulties associated with gathering experts, administering questionnaires, collating results, writing opinions, and dealing with lack of interaction obviously limit the applicability of this problem-solving procedure. The Delphi method has been employed widely and successfully, however; a recent international conference on solutions to world hunger is one example of its use.

Listening teams.   When media presentations, panel discussions, symposia, or guest lectures are used to start a meeting (that is, before group discussion of the problem takes place), there is always the possibility that information will be lost by the time it is needed for the discussion session or sessions that will follow. This loss may occur because too much information is set forth, because information is given in too much detail or is otherwise poorly presented, or because participants are distracted or attend only to certain aspects of the presentation.

Much of the preliminary information presented can be retained through the use of "listening teams," especially when the discussion group is large. Before the presentations, subgroups of audience members are formed and assigned a particular listening task. For example, one group may be asked to listen for the causes of the problem, another for the solutions suggested, a third for the consequences of each solution, and so forth. Each subgroup is then given time to codify its recollections before the group convenes to discuss the problem. Then, regardless of which problem-solving procedure is utilized by the entire group, these members can serve as resources when the aspect of the problem to which they paid special attention is discussed.

Experimental research suggests that people attend to, comprehend, and recall more of a message when they are cued to the fact that they will be asked to recollect and restate it. The same principle may make listening teams an advantageous bridge between informational presentations and problem-solving discussions.

Listening teams are assigned a specific listening task and act as a bridge between presentations and problem-solving discussions.

Role playing. In some group meetings, the problem at issue is a human relations one. A church group may meet to consider how to improve family relations among congregants. A work unit may be called together to settle grievances with their supervisor. Top management may undertake an analysis of their interpersonal relations. Role playing is often a helpful technique for presenting, analyzing, and remedying problematic human and management relations.

In essence, participants are asked to play a known or unknown role based on their perceptions of how another person acts or should act. Members may first be supplied with a case study similar to their own for warm-up purposes. Then they may be asked to jointly construct a case/script that includes all the roles relevant to the problem they are discussing, the interrelationships of the different roles, and the specific situation in which the problem has arisen. Participants are then asked to act out the roles they have been assigned. Discussion among all group members follows, focused on an analysis of the reasons for and remedies of the difficulty.

Role playing requires participants to assume a role based on their perception of how another person acts or should act in a certain situation.

Role playing is usually directed by a qualified trainer and probably should not be undertaken by the chairperson alone. Good role playing requires motivation on the part of members, careful introduction into the meeting or conference, considerable time, and full discussion afterward. Bad role playing can become unwieldy, damage the momentum of the conference, or adversely affect the image that group members have of the role players. Qualified role-playing trainers increase the probability that the results will be positive.

Two-column method. According to Norman R. F. Maier, "The two-column method is designed to deal with controversy constructively and to lead to an appreciation of the fact that each position has merits as well as weaknesses." Like the problem census procedure, the two-column method requires that the chairperson poll all group members and post their reactions in a visible place, as on a blackboard or flipchart. Members express arguments over why position X is better than position Y, and the chairperson lists all contributions in the appropriate columns.

The two-column method requires participants to express a position on a controversial subject. Positions are recorded for all to see, and their merits are then discussed.

The chairperson should attempt to elicit as many listings as possible in the shortest time possible. Then discussion turns to consideration of the merits of each column, the ways in which differences can be resolved, the advantages and disadvantages of both, and so forth. The controversial dimensions of the issue become objectified during this procedure, and members do not become divided around each position. And once the two lists are completed, both sides of the issue can be more realistically and cooperatively appraised.

In the risk method, participants individually list what they consider the major risk involved in the preferred solution, and the entire group addresses all fears, or considered risks.

Risk method.   After group members have decided upon a solution to the problem under discussion, the chairperson may wish to employ the "risk" procedure. Participants are asked, one by one, to list what they view as the major risk involved in the adoption and implementation of the preferred solution. These "second-chance" concerns then receive the attention of the full group. At the least, each member's unwarranted fears can be allayed once and for all. At best, risks that appear serious and insurmountable may signal reservations about the chosen solution and suggest a need for further discussion. This technique helps to reduce the chance that false consensus about the solution exists or that members will adopt a solution hastily or uncritically.

PERT is a method of reviewing the steps of a complex plan; their timing and order; and resources required.

PERT.   Once a group has identified a solution to the problem under discussion, the details of implementing that solution must be discussed. PERT (Program Evaluation Review Technique) is a procedure well suited to a systematic review of all the steps needed to carry out a complex plan, the order in which each should be performed, the length of time each will take, and the resources and materials that will be needed during the entire process. PERT may be performed in a small-group meeting as follows:

1. Determine the final step (that is, the form the solution should take when fully operational).
2. Enumerate any events that must occur before the final goal state is realized.
3. Order these steps chronologically.
4. If necessary, develop a flow diagram of the process and all the steps in it.
5. Generate a list of all the activities, resources, and materials that are needed to accomplish each step.
6. Estimate the time needed to take each step, then add all the estimates to get a total time for implementation of the plan.
7. Compare the total time estimate with deadlines or expectations and correct as necessary (by assigning more persons or less time to a given step).

8. Determine which members shall be responsible for each step.

A final caveat is in order. In lieu of a participant-oriented, group-centered approach, this essay has emphasized the chairperson's preparation and orchestration in making meetings a success. Too, the focus has been on procedures to the exclusion of process—that is, the interactive, dynamic, emergent aspects of task groups' problem solving and decision making. Both these emphases are on but one side of the small-group coin. The success of a meeting obviously depends on more than the skill of the chairperson. The leader shares the leadership role and the responsibility for a successful meeting with all the participants.

The success of a meeting depends not only on the chairperson but on all the participants as well.

ASSIGNMENT: MEETINGS

Your next in-service training session will be an informal ad hoc meeting. Its purpose is to make employees aware of the importance and procedures of effective business meetings. Participants are the members of your study group. The group is to meet at its usual time and place. The agenda, which has been distributed to all members, consists of the topics listed below. You have been asked to prepare a report on one of these topics and to be ready to contribute to the panel discussion following the other topic reports. After the session, write a memo summarizing the results of the meeting; distribute the memo to all participants.

Topics

1. Differences between informal and formal meetings.
2. Reasons for growth in the number of business meetings held.
3. The problem-solving procedures of problem census and rational reflection: What they are and what their advantages are.
4. The problem-solving procedures of brainstorming and buzz groups: What they are and what their advantages are.
5. The problem-solving procedures of the nominal group technique and the Delphi method: What they are and what their advantages are.
6. Listening teams and role-playing techniques: What they are and when they should be used.
7. How the risk method is used after a solution has been reached.
8. Steps in the Program Evaluation Review Technique (PERT).

FURTHER READING

Guth, Chester and Stanley Shaw. *How to Put on Dynamic Meetings.* Reston, VA: Reston, 1980.

Jones, Martin. *How to Organize Meetings: A Handbook for Better Workshop, Seminar, and Conference Management.* New York: Beaufort Books, 1981.

Meyer, Herbert E. "The Meeting-Goer's Lament." *Fortune*, October 22, 1979, pp. 94–102.

Robert, General Henry M. *Robert's Rules of Order.* Glenview, IL: Scott, Foresman, 1970.

Seekings, David. *How to Organize Effective Conferences and Meetings.* London: Kogan Page, 1980.

Sponberg, Harold. *The Meeting Will Come to Order.* East Lansing, MI: Ext. Bulletin #294, Cooperative Extension Service, Michigan State University.

Stewart, Wilbur F. *Helps in Mastering Parliamentary Procedure.* Zanesville, OH: G. A. Biery, 1976.

Part Four

Communication and Careers

CHAPTER SEVENTEEN

Career Research[*]

If you are to successfully deal with the stiff competition in the job market, you will have to use innovative job research and interview techniques so that you will stand out in a crowd.

Ray Shaw
President, Dow Jones

Before examining the elements of self-evaluation, analysis by others, and job opportunity resources that you will consider in your career research, it may be helpful to examine the ways in which most job openings are created and filled.

The Creation of a Job

A job is created when a manager decides there is more work to be done than can be physically or economically accomplished by the worker or workers presently on the payroll. The decision may result from a series of events:

A job is created when an employer is willing to pay for some kind of work to be done.

- failure to meet deadlines because of personnel shortages
- overtime work regularly required
- individual overload
- new area of activity

A newly created job may include anything that needs to be done, and it may occur at any level within an organization. The list of tasks assigned to the job, the *position description,* may be varied or may consist of a single task repeated again and again.

A position description outlines the requirements of the job.

---

*Written in collaboration with Mary C. Thompson, Alumni Relations and Communications Coordinator, Purdue University, School of Nursing, West Lafayette, Indiana.

331

The employer considers the task(s) so necessary that he or she is willing to pay to have the work done.

In large organizations, where an individual or a department is assigned to handle employment details, there is usually a procedure for filling a newly created position or an already existing position that is vacant. The personnel staff may be requested to initiate a new position or may be notified of an impending vacancy. A standard form is often used at this stage.

The personnel staff may interview the job supervisor and perhaps members of the work group to determine what tasks will be assigned to the position. Work requirements are specified and may cover:

- education required/desired
- work skills required/desired
- hourly requirements (full- or part-time)
- work location
- work period (yearly, summer, seasonal)
- salary range

Companies bidding on government contracts are subject to specific employment regulations. The personnel departments of such companies must follow *affirmative action* programs that commit them to aggressively seek and hire members of certain minority groups. With affirmative action guidelines, these organizations are required to advertise jobs for a designated period of time, usually 30 days. You've undoubtedly seen such advertisements in newspapers; most end with the statement, "Equal Opportunity Employer."

Union officials may also be involved in the review of new position descriptions and vacancies. Union contracts often contain detailed requirements for hiring *blue-collar employees.* These workers are directly involved with the manufacture of a product. They are line employees earning an hourly wage. These jobs are referred to as *nonexempt,* with the employee usually being paid weekly or twice a month and receiving overtime pay for all hours worked beyond the 40-hour work week. In some cases, entry-level administrators and clerical workers may also be nonexempt.

Exempt positions are *salaried* jobs that are often paid on a monthly basis. The exempt employee usually does not receive additional compensation for hours worked beyond the established work week. The employee is considered available at any time and is expected to be on the job 40 to 44 hours each week. Such employees usually have more freedom to come and go during a work-

Nonexempt employees are usually paid an hourly wage and receive overtime pay for working more than 40 hours per week.

ing day and receive other compensations in place of overtime pay for overtime hours. These compensations may include a company car, "first dollar" medical insurance, sabbaticals, relocation aid, financial counseling, home financing, stock options, club memberships, and other perquisites, depending on the employee's status. An exempt position may be directly related to the organization's product line or it may be labeled a *staff* position.

Exempt employees are paid a salary and generally do not receive overtime pay. Instead, they may receive other compensations not available to nonexempt employees.

    Staff positions are the supporting jobs necessary to operate a business. These positions include administration, accounting, research, management information, public relations, and so on.

The Hiring Process

Announcement of the job.   Once a job vacancy is listed with the personnel department and the position description is prepared and approved, the position is posted. Some organizations place strong emphasis on promotion from within. In such instances, in-house employees may be told of a job opening one to two weeks before it is advertised to the general public—locally, regionally, and nationally.

Announcements for newly created or vacated jobs are usually posted in the organization and advertised in newspapers and with agencies.

    Advertisements that appear in newspapers and with agencies usually do not list the job responsibilities in detail. Instead, they give the job title, the minimum amount of education required, and the number of years of work experience desired. You, the candidate, must determine the generally accepted responsibilities for that job title and evaluate your background to see how well you can fit that position. (In some cases, you may want to ask for the position description.)

Candidate selection.   Employers seek the best-qualified candidate for the job. The position description will often state the desired attributes for the job, but the employer usually accepts the candidate who has the greatest number of desired characteristics. (In certain instances, a job is created for an individual with special skills needed by the organization. The posted position description may actually describe the qualifications of that specific individual. Thus job applicants for that vacancy are competing with an ideal candidate and are therefore rarely selected for such a position.)

    The interview is the most widely used selection device for hiring. Employers try to attract a large number of applicants from which to select those to be interviewed. Jobs are advertised where the best-qualified candidates are most likely to see or hear about the position, usually in specialized magazines, newspapers, and

In most cases, the best qualified candidate is selected on the basis of résumé, interview, and, less frequently, tests.

journals. Candidates with minimal qualifications are screened by agencies or personnel departments. Letters and résumés of promising candidates are forwarded to the hiring supervisor. Depending on the expense involved, three to five candidates are usually invited to take part in on-site visits for professional jobs. With local vacancies, the number may be much higher.

For some jobs, applicants may be asked to take a test. However, the use of tests—commonly administered in the past to determine math skills, aptitude, IQ, and work skills—has been reevaluated to avoid unfair discrimination. The courts have ruled that any test given must have a direct relationship to the job to be considered a legal discriminator. Commonly accepted tests are those that measure clerical skills and the manual dexterity needed for assembly-line work.

The job offer. The final hiring decision is made by the supervisor. The selected individual is usually the one whose personality and job skills seem to be best suited to the needs of the specific job, the supervisor, and the work group.

A job offer is not usually made until all candidates have been interviewed and evaluated.

A job offer is sometimes made to an outstanding candidate during the interview. More frequently, however, an individual is not selected or notified until after all the interviews have been conducted and evaluated. (Ask about the usual notification time.)

The personnel staff makes a salary offer that fits the company salary structure and determines the benefits the new employee is entitled to receive.

The last step in the hiring procedure may be to pass a company physical examination.

ANALYZING YOURSELF

In *"The New York Times* National Recruitment Survey" (October 12, 1980, p. 71), David Sanger made the following observation:

> For decades the accepted wisdom has been that job-seekers should first prepare an attractive résumé and then work on refining their interview technique. But now increasing numbers of job counselors are urging applicants to set aside the mechanics of the process temporarily and concentrate on the mental preparation they say most people entering the job market lack. A job hunter, they say, must first develop in his own mind a clear picture of what he wants to do, what skills he possesses, and what working environments he finds most suitable.

People get satisfactory jobs because they

- know what they want to do
- are qualified for the job they think they want
- know how to sell themselves
- have a job campaign strategy
- have the courage or determination to overcome almost prohibitive odds to reach their objective

Before persuading someone to hire you and pay you a substantial salary, you must know what you have to offer. You must analyze yourself to determine your assets and liabilities in the employment market. In other words, you must do a market analysis (see Chapter 11); you must concern yourself with a *prime product—* yourself. Whether seeking an entry-level position or making a mid-life career change, you'll find this analysis invaluable in preparing for your job search. The information you select from your analysis forms the basis for this search:

When seeking a job, think of yourself as the "prime product" and analyze your marketability.

- the application letter
- the résumé
- the interview

With these tools, you market yourself to your *prime prospects*, the employers.

Being objective about oneself is very difficult. One way to do this is to adapt the market analysis (Table 17–1). Only some of this material will appear in your application letter and résumé. All of it, however, will help you form your career objectives. You should begin with some basic facts about yourself, including your physical description:

Take stock of yourself: physical characteristics, psychological factors, strengths and weaknesses, education, work experience, activities, and special requirements.

- birthdate
- height
- weight
- skills
- military status
- address
- health factors
- marital status
- dependents
- phone number

Table 17–1: Market Analysis (Adapted for Use with Products or People)

	Product	Person
Résumé/Letter Information	1. Name	1. Name
	2. Where located	2. Address
	3. Picture of product	3. Photograph
	4. Physical description	4. Physical description
	5. Uses of product	5. What you can do (skills)
	6. Psychological description	6. Psychological description
	7. Service facilities	7. Education
	8. Method of operation	8. Work experience
	9. Distinctive characteristics—how product is unique, differs from competition	9. Distinctive characteristics—activities, hobbies, interests, accomplishments
Strategy Development	10. How sold—direct mail, door to door, wholesale, retail, and so on	10. How marketed—direct mail, door to door, advertising
	11. Selling price	11. Salary desired/acceptable
	12. Purchase terms—prepaid, credit, C.O.D., and so on	12. Wage package—health insurance, retirement, vacations, sick leave, and so on
	13. Method of distribution	13. Car, bus, taxi, plane, train
	14. Prime buyers or prospects	14. Employers, recruiters, agencies
	15. Users (if different from buyers)—include as many demographic variables as possible	15. Supervisors, peers
	16. What is users' buying power?	16. Employment opportunities
	17. What do users want? Under what circumstances?	17. Job description

Everyone has strong preferences, goals, even limitations—psychological factors. List yours:

- geographical location
- working with abstract ideas/working with tangible objects
- hobbies
- indoor/outdoor activities
- recreation
- working in the private/public sector
- rural/urban living
- organizational/cultural ties

List your strong dislikes. For example:

- cold weather
- sales work
- lazy people
- large groups

- owing money
- physical labor
- people who can't make up their minds
- travel
- desk jobs

List your personal strengths. For example:

- sense of humor
- attentive to detail
- well organized
- self-motivated
- responsible
- leadership experience
- creative
- honest
- work well under pressure
- flexible

List your personal weaknesses—honestly. For example:

- always late
- can't write/spell
- need deadlines
- borrow things
- stubborn
- poor educational background

Remember, *this inventory is for your own information.* You will list facts about yourself that perhaps only your closest friends or family know about. Next, analyze your educational background, an area in which you are continually compared with others.

Education

Rarely do two people have exactly the same study program even if they are working toward the same college degree. You have selected distinctive electives. You differ from the competition in many ways. Certainly your education is one area you can market productively.

You selected a major in college because you liked the subject area and expected to be successful. Evaluate the strengths and weaknesses of your classwork since high school. For example, consider your

- major area of concentration
- grade-point average (GPA)
- electives
- functional areas: technical, scientific, liberal arts, business
- changes of major (include number of credit hours in each)
- poorest subject areas
- hours carried per quarter or semester
- favorite teachers

Some employers weigh education and grades heavily. They place a great deal of emphasis on your grades because your GPA is your "track record." Grades indicate how your teachers evaluated you and your work in comparison with your peers and their work.

Other employers, seeking applicants for sales, manufacturing, and teaching, for example, emphasize work experience, personality, activities, and the ability to get along with people.

Work Experience

Your job experience—any job, regardless of whether it is related to your career interest—is marketable. It provides insight into your character. In the long run, you benefit from everything you do. Include in your self-analysis what you can do and what you can't do or don't want to do. List your work experience, including

- full-time work
- part-time work
- summer jobs
- co-op employment
- working for relatives

Include volunteer work. For example:

- shoveling snow for a neighbor
- collecting for the Community Chest
- raising money for a school activity
- acting in community theater

Specifically note jobs requiring responsibility for

- meeting a schedule
- making deadlines
- work habits
- leadership
- routine tasks
- multiple requests
- budgeting time and money
- working independently

Write down each employer's or supervisor's name if you can re-member it. Under each name, list your major responsibilities. For example:

```
Kenneth Freeland, Supervisor

Pizza Supreme

Worked part time, 20 hours per week, after
school (Sept. 19__ to June 19__). Prepared
and served pizza. Responsible for inventory,
cleanup, and closing three nights each week.


Hazel Hammer, Director

ACTORS

For three months (Sept. 19__ to Nov. 19__)
spent 3-4 hours per day, three days per week,
preparing for lead role in community theater
play. Built sets, sold tickets, distributed
posters.
```

When you begin the job search, you can draw on this expe-rience to demonstrate your work skills and activities.

Activities

Your activities are important in your self-analysis. Employers are interested in what you do with your free time. Of particular interest is evidence of leadership and initiative. As you review your activ-ities and hobbies, consider, for example, whether you have ever

- belonged to a professional organization
- started a club or group

- organized an activity—a team, an interest group
- been treasurer of an organization, handled other people's money in a responsible way
- served as a volunteer for a charitable organization
- built things—furniture, models, electronics
- designed things—clothing, games, mechanical gadgets

This information may help a prospective employer compare your interests with those of other employees, to evaluate how well you would fit into an assigned work group.

Your market analysis can include any other information you wish. For example, indicate if you have ever

- received a scholarship
- won a competition—bowling, marksmanship, sports
- received recognition for community activities such as scouting
- won a prize for special skills—music, writing, photography
- served in the armed forces or reserves

Vital and Special Needs

Your market analysis should include salary requirements, housing requirements, and special needs—such as the location of elementary or secondary schools, colleges for continuing education for yourself or your family.

Here's another suggestion. Federal legislation has designated certain categories of employees as protected groups:

- certain minorities
- females
- the handicapped/disabled
- veterans
- people over 45 years of age
- legally immigrated aliens (LIA), holders of "green cards" or work permits

If you fit into one or more of these categories, include that information in your analysis.

When you have finished compiling the data, you can begin to evaluate the kind of position you are best suited for. You will have at least half of the information you need to write an application letter and will be ready to answer any questions that you may be asked during an interview. You will have all of the information you need to prepare your résumé.

If you cannot draw conclusions from your self-inventory about the kind of job you would like and are qualified for, you can seek assistance from other people.

ANALYSIS BY OTHERS

Schools

When you were in high school, you probably took one or more interest-inventory tests. Common tests are the

- Kuder Occupational Interest Survey and Person Match
- Iowa Basic Skills Test
- Strong-Campbell Inventory
- Holland's Self-Directed Search
- Guide for Occupational Exploration

The tests were interpreted by counselors trained to assist you in choosing a career path or paths.

When you enrolled in college, your choice of curricula may have been based on suggestions by your high school teachers or counselors. They may have said that you would be very good at math, science, English, engineering, or liberal arts. Perhaps, however, after a year of exposure to a variety of courses and career possibilities, you, like many other students, changed majors. Experts estimate that more than half of all college students change majors at least once.

College counseling personnel and college placement counselors are prepared to help you evaluate your strengths and weaknesses in relation to a career. They offer you an opportunity to retake tests and receive another evaluation of your responses.

Consult your college counseling and placement services.

Agencies

A number of employment agencies offer counseling and interest-inventory tests. Your state employment agency or job service offers counseling free of charge. Private agencies often charge a fee for testing and counseling.

Investigate state and private employment agencies.

Publications

Check libraries and bookstores for information on getting a job.

There are a number of excellent books on the market to assist you in analyzing your skills and "selling" yourself to an employer. They are available in college and city libraries and most bookstores. (See Further Reading at the end of this chapter.)

JOB OPPORTUNITY RESOURCES

Most individuals, regardless of age or experience, momentarily panic when faced with finding a job. What jobs are available? Where do you go to look for a job? How do you find job leads?

People

The best place to start is with your

- friends
- relatives
- neighbors
- teachers
- business acquaintances

Ask them about job openings in your general career area.

A majority of jobs are filled through personal contacts.

Personal acquaintances. Research indicates that 75 percent of all jobs are filled through personal contact—people you know. Many companies invite employees to submit names of job candidates when an opening occurs. Some even offer "finder's fees" for hard-to-fill vacancies, payable when the applicant begins work. Recommended applicants must apply and compete for positions, of course, but the recommendation of a satisfactory employee carries a great deal of weight with the hiring supervisor.

Professors and counselors. Many organizations maintain contact with college campuses. They depend on recommendations from the faculty to help them select outstanding students. Become acquainted with your professors. If they are aware of your career plans, they will be able to recommend you when an appropriate position comes to their attention.

Professional meetings.   If you belong to a professional organization, the annual national meeting is a good place to contact employers in your career area. Also attend and get to know people at the regional and local meetings of the organization. There are always discussions of job openings during the course of these meetings.

College placement staff.   Most knowledgeable of the current job market for professional careers, your college placement staff will assist you in selecting job areas and companies hiring in specific job areas. Contact your placement office early in the year you plan to graduate to take full advantage of the services they offer. These services include

- counseling
- assistance in preparing letters and résumés
- employment library
- company literature
- on-campus interviews
- recommendations
- trip interview information
- *College Placement Annual*
- alumni placement assistance
- reciprocity (use of the placement facilities at another school—ask your placement counselor)

Agencies

State employment agencies.   Local employment opportunities, as well as openings throughout the state, are listed with the state job service. The listings cover a wide variety of jobs, from lower-level to professional positions. There is no charge for this service. The agency also provides counseling and other assistance.

Private employment agencies.   Many private employment agencies specialize in placing persons in specific career areas. A number of these agencies operate branches throughout the country. You can apply at one location and receive multiple listings or referrals to jobs elsewhere.

Computers are being used more and more frequently, especially by private firms, to help match job applicants with job openings. The Harvard Business School is trying out a job-match

COMMUNICATION AND CAREERS

program that will allow users to search for openings on the basis of industry, job function, and geographic area.

Many private agencies provide assistance with résumés and application letters and forms. *Caution:* Before you fill out forms of any kind, inquire whether the firm (1) charges you a fee, (2) requires a contract for a specified period of time, and (3) charges additional fees for counseling.

Some agencies do not require fees from job seekers. Instead they receive "finder's fees" from employers for assisting them with their employee search. Other agencies charge the employees a fee for assisting them with their job search. The fee rates vary from agency to agency and range from a flat charge to more than your first month's salary in the new job. The fee is usually payable in advance, but terms can sometimes be arranged.

As hiring practices become more and more regulated, many companies are turning to *executive search firms* to assist them in finding employees. They find it less costly and more efficient than maintaining their own recruiting staff.

Compare services and fees before choosing an employment agency.

Compare services before agreeing to work with a specific agency. Be sure to ask for exemption of a fee should you find employment on your own. Discuss with your agency counselor the names of companies they expect to contact about your employment, and keep a copy of your personal correspondence with prospective employers. If you are paying an agency a fee for their assistance, and you are hired by a company as a result of a letter and résumé you submitted prior to your contact with the agency, you may still be required to pay the finder's fee under certain circumstances. Read your contract carefully.

Publications

For information on organizations and job openings and requirements in your field, consult The College Placement Annual, *journals, directories, newspapers, and government publications.*

Job research means finding out about organizations and job openings—doing your homework. Information is readily available from bulletin boards, trade journals, newspapers, libraries. Prepare a card file with information about companies and organizations that interest you. The file will provide your mailing list and background information for interviews.

The College Placement Annual.   Published annually and indexed alphabetically, geographically, and by occupation, *The College Placement Annual* is probably available free of charge at your college placement office. It provides information about approximately

1500 companies, including names and addresses of corporate personnel, and uses codes to identify degree areas regularly of interest to the company. Organizations pay to advertise in this book; it is an excellent resource.

Journals. Your professional organization's magazine and many trade journals offer a personnel section. There may be space for advertising your availability; there will probably be a section devoted to job vacancies. Check the journals in your field.

Directories. Your college or university library and your city library have a large number of publications to aid you in your job research and search.

- *Dun and Bradstreet—Million Dollar Directory* and *Middle Market Directory*—Lists United States companies with a net worth of $500,000 or more. Lists officers and directors, products and services, approximate dollars in sales, and the numbers of employees. Indexed by both geographic location and industry.
- *Thomas Register of American Manufacturers*—Lists manufacturers by specific product. Products listed alphabetically, usually with an address, branch offices, subsidiaries, assets classification, and a list of leading trade names.
- *Standard and Poor's Corporation Reports*—Includes companies having both listed and unlisted securities. Has well-indexed daily news sections. Includes addresses, state of incorporation, officers, history, property, provisions of bylaws, and financial statements.
- *Encyclopedia of Associations* (vol. 1, National Organizations of United States, Gale Research Company, Detroit, MI)—Lists all types of national organizations. Arranged by broad classifications with alphabetical key, word index, list of chief officers. Contains brief statement of activities, number of members, names of publications.
- *Manufacturing directories* (available in many states)—List state manufacturers alphabetically, by location, and by classification. Have an alphabetical list of products and employment range. Check with your local library reference desk.
- *Directories of companies with overseas branches* (available in business reference sections of your library)—List United States headquarters and overseas offices. Alphabetized by company, location, and product.
- *City directories*—List names, addresses, and telephone numbers of business firms. City telephone directories have classified sec-

tions identifying local firms in any industry. If you have a specific geographical preference, both types of directories are especially useful in your job search.

Newspapers.   Newspapers are a good source of local job openings ranging from blue-collar to professional occupations, from entry-level to upper-level openings. Affirmative action programs include advertising job openings. Many of those listed in the newspapers are also listed at state employment agencies. The *Wall Street Journal* lists job openings one or two days each week, primarily for persons with prior work experience. This newspaper offers business and financial news, company news, and a digest of earnings, commodity prices, stock market price quotations, and Dow Jones averages.

The Dictionary of Occupational Titles (D.O.T.) and the Standard Occupational Classifications Manual (S.O.C.).   These publications provide descriptions of hundreds of jobs. The D.O.T. includes listings of education, skills, and ability requirements for each job. The descriptions are necessarily brief but offer an overview of many different job categories.

Occupational Outlook Quarterly and the Occupational Outlook Handbook.   Both the *Quarterly* and the *Handbook* are published by the Bureau of Labor Statistics. The Bureau projects employment outlooks through a broad range of occupations (Figure 17–1). The *Handbook* contains information to help you match your employment goals, education, and skills with opportunities in several hundred occupations and 35 industries. These publications are usually available in libraries and school guidance and placement offices.

BEGIN THE SEARCH

The information you have gathered will form the basis of your résumé and job application letter.

Let us take stock. You have seen how most job openings are created and filled. You have analyzed yourself and know where to look and whom to see in order to help crystallize your career qualifications and goals. You know how to find out what kinds of jobs are available and where to look for job leads. This information will form the basis for your job search documents: the application letter and résumé.

In earlier chapters, you learned how to write selling letters, memos, and reports. The application letter is similar to the selling

Fastest Growing Jobs, 1978-90[1]

Occupation	Annual openings
Bank clerks	45,000
Bank officers and financial managers	28,000
Business machine repairers	4,200
City managers	350
Computer service technicians	5,400
Construction inspectors	2,200
Dental assistants	11,000
Dental hygienists	6,000
Dining room attendants and dishwashers	37,000
Flight attendants	4,800
Guards	70,000
Health service administrators	18,000
Homemaker-home health aides	36,000
Industrial machinery repairers	58,000
Landscape architects	1,100
Licensed practical nurses	60,000
Lithographers	2,300
Nursing aides, orderlies, and attendants	94,000
Occupational therapists	2,500
Occupational therapy assistants	1,100
Physical therapists	2,700
Podiatrists	600
Respiratory therapy workers	5,000
Speech pathologists and audiologists	3,900
Teacher aides	26,000
Travel agents	1,900

[1]**Note:** For these occupations, employment in 1990 is projected to be at least 50 percent higher than it was in 1978.

Jobs with the Most Openings, 1978-90[2]

Occupation	Annual openings
Secretaries and stenographers	305,000
Retail sales workers	226,000
Building custodians	180,000
Cashiers	119,000
Bookkeeping workers	96,000
Nursing aides, orderlies, and attendants	94,000
Cooks and chefs	86,000
Kindergarten and elementary teachers	86,000
Registered nurses	85,000
Assemblers	77,000
Waiters and waitresses	70,000
Guards	70,000
Blue-collar worker supervisors	69,000
Local truck drivers	64,000
Accountants	61,000
Licensed practical nurses	60,000
Typists	59,000
Carpenters	58,000
Industrial machinery repairers	58,000
Real estate agents and brokers	50,000
Construction laborers	49,000
Engineers	46,500
Bank clerks	45,000
Private household workers	45,000
Receptionists	41,000
Wholesale trade sales workers	40,000

[2]**Note:** Replacement needs and growth are projected to cause these occupations to offer the largest number of openings. Competition for openings will vary by occupation.

Figure 17–1: Recent Projections from the *Occupational Outlook Quarterly*

letter; it helps persuade an employer to hire you. The résumé is similar to the short report in that it contains the information the reader needs and it is concise, direct, to the point.

You have the tools and resources. Now you are ready for the next step—the actual job search.

ASSIGNMENT: CAREER RESEARCH

1. If you have not already done so, complete in writing a market analysis of yourself as outlined on pages 334–341.
2. Visit your college counseling center. Find out what kinds of career research services it offers. Does the center provide help in evaluating students' job strengths and weaknesses? Does it have any brochures or other printed information to help in job research? Does the center permit students to retake any tests? Write a memo summarizing your findings.
3. Go to the local office of your state employment agency. Check current job listings. Analyze the available job openings in terms of location, type of job (manual labor, professional, clerical, and so on), and industry (agricultural, automotive, construction, energy, and so on). What conclusions do you draw from your analysis?
4. In your college library or guidance office, examine a copy of the *Standard Occupational Classifications Manual.* Select three jobs you think you might be interested in. Jot down a description of each, including education, skills, and ability requirements. Compare the three descriptions. Does one job seem to fit your career goals and qualifications more than the others? Explain your answer in a short report.

FURTHER READING

Bolles, Richard N. *The Three Boxes of Life and How to Get Out of Them.* Berkeley, CA: Ten Speed, 1976.

——— . *The Quick Job-Hunting Map, Beginning Version.* Berkeley, CA: Ten Speed, 1977.

——— . *What Color Is Your Parachute?* Berkeley, CA: Ten Speed, 1980.

Holland, John L. *Making Vocational Choices: A Theory of Careers.* Englewood Cliffs, NJ: Prentice-Hall, 1976.

Kesselman, Judi. *Stepping Out, A Guide to Leaving College and Getting Back In.* New York: M. Evans, 1976.

Lathrop, Richard. *Who's Hiring Who.* Berkeley, CA: Ten Speed, 1977.

Powell, C. Randall and Donald K. Keits. *Career Services Today: A Dynamic College Profession.* Bethlehem, PA: College Placement Council, 1980.

Ritti, R. Richard and G. Ray Funkhouser. *The Ropes to Skip and the Ropes to Know.* Columbus, OH: Grid, 1977.

Shingleton, John and Robert Bao. *College to Career—Finding Yourself in the Job Market.* New York: McGraw-Hill, 1977.

Weiler, Nicholas W. *Reality and Career Planning.* Reading, MA: Addison-Wesley, 1977.

(Also see Chapter 18, "Career Search.")

CHAPTER EIGHTEEN

Career Search*

A career file, a well-planned résumé, and a carefully written cover letter are the tools you need. Careful research and study will help you locate the job. Employers favorably impressed by your résumé and cover letter will ask to interview you, and eventually your career will be under way.

S. Bernard Rosenblatt, Robert L. Bonnington,
Belverd E. Needles, Jr.
Modern Business

To begin your career search

- select a career objective
- compile a prospect list
- make a company research file
- make up a mailing list
- prepare your résumé
- write your application letter
- interview on campus or on site
- respond with an appropriate letter
- follow up

This chapter examines the first six of these steps; Chapter 19 examines the last three.

JOB CAMPAIGN STRATEGY

Searching for the position that best fits your career goals requires a plan. You have analyzed your qualifications and decided what type of individual you are, where you can be most useful, and how you work. You know how to develop a marketing strategy (Table 17–1).

---

*Written in collaboration with Mary C. Thompson, Alumni Relations and Communications Coordinator, School of Nursing, Purdue University, West Lafayette, Indiana.

Choose your *prime prospects.* Select approximately one hundred organizations that hire people in your area of specialization. A good way to organize your job search is to use file cards to list

- the name and address of the organization
- the name of the personnel director or another individual in the organization
- data about the organization's location(s), number of employees, whom they hire, products or services
- financial standing
- three reasons why the organization appeals to you

In seeking a job, determine which organizations appeal to you and why.

Designate those organizations you plan to reach by mail. Excellent prospect letters sent to one hundred organizations may result in replies from 85. Some companies do not respond unless they have an opening. Others will send a form letter stating that they have no openings at this time but will keep your letter and résumé on file. Organizations that are seriously interested in your qualifications and those that are seeking to increase their applicant pool will send you an application form.

If you receive six or seven invitations to interview for a job in response to one hundred over-the-transom (unsolicited) letters and résumés, consider your campaign successful. From six or seven interviews, you can expect to average two or three job offers. Of course, there are exceptions. The highly qualified individual in a high-demand field such as mechanical engineering or computer science may do much better. Candidates with lesser skills and a low-demand specialization will have to work harder to find employment.

Your job strategy will be based primarily on direct-mail and door-to-door sales techniques. But you may also use the campus placement office or agencies to make appointments for interviews without the use of a letter. You may respond to advertisements with a letter and résumé.

Caution: Do not quit a job before accepting another, no matter how fed up you are. Being without a job puts you in a weaker negotiating position. Furthermore, you will be tempted to accept your first offer. Try to be patient. Haldane Associates, executive-search firm, figures a month of searching for every $10,000 increment of desired salary.

Once you have decided on the organizations you are interested in and have determined how you will contact them, you are ready to compile your search documents—the résumé and application letter. Your goal will be to get and schedule as many job interviews

The résumé and application letter are your job search documents.

as possible. The more interviews you have, the more experienced you become in interviewing and the greater the possibility that you will be selected for a job.

The résumé and application letter describe your life in capsule form. They provide pertinent information in short, descriptive terms. From your market analysis, you have the vital statistics needed to compile the résumé. You have 90 percent of the material you need to write the application letter.

Your résumé and application letter should be presented as a package. Because there are as many different kinds of employers as there are applicants, no one can advise you with complete accuracy as to how you should present these. Nevertheless, the following suggestions should be helpful.

THE RÉSUMÉ

The résumé is a brief history of your life.

Although many "gimmicks" have been recommended and eager candidates have submitted résumés written with crayon on paper bags or enclosed in bottles, as a general rule, beware of gimmicks.

There are instances, however, when a contemporary (creative) résumé is appropriate. Using an appealing ad format when applying for a position in advertising might indicate creativity in writing and layout. An architectural student might use a blueprint format to demonstrate drafting skills and design concepts along with a statement of job qualifications. The computer science major might use a program format for his or her résumé.

The majority of you will probably select a more traditional approach in preparing an application package. But even with a traditional approach, there are different ways to present the data you wish an employer to have.

Format

The chronological format lists the items in your résumé in reverse chronological order, most recent activity first.

Select the résumé format most flattering to your data, most acceptable to future employers. The *chronological approach* begins with your most recent activity (Figure 18–1). With this approach, you would arrange the items in each section of your résumé in reverse chronological order, that is, list the most recent event first. You would include dates showing the length of each experience. Until recently this was by far the most common approach, and it still fits best with employment application forms.

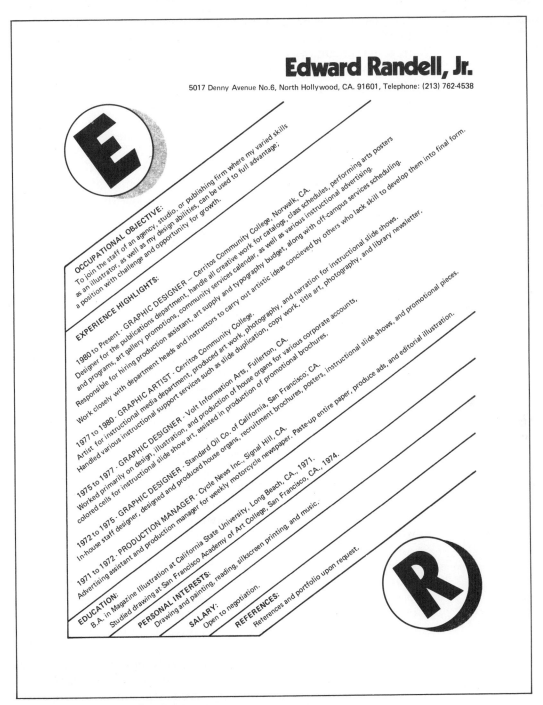

Edward Randell, Jr.

5017 Denny Avenue No.6, North Hollywood, CA. 91601, Telephone: (213) 762-4538

OCCUPATIONAL OBJECTIVE:
To join the staff of an agency, studio, or publishing firm where my varied skills as an illustrator, as well as my design abilities, can be used to full advantage; a position with challenge and opportunity for growth.

EXPERIENCE HIGHLIGHTS:

1980 to Present - GRAPHIC DESIGNER – Cerritos Community College, Norwalk, CA.
Designer for the publications department, handle all creative work for catalogs, class schedules, performing arts posters and programs, art gallery promotions, community services calendar, as well as various instructional advertising.
Responsible for hiring production assistant, art supply and typography budget, along with off-campus services scheduling.
Work closely with department heads and instructors to carry out artistic ideas concieved by others who lack skill to develop them into final form.

1977 to 1980 - GRAPHIC ARTIST - Cerritos Community College.
Artist for instructional media department, produced art work, photography, and narration for instructional slide shows.
Handled various instructional support services such as slide duplication, copy work, title art, photography, and library newsletter.

1975 to 1977 - GRAPHIC DESIGNER - Volt Information Arts, Fullerton, CA.
Worked primarily on design, illustration, and production of house organs for various corporate accounts, colored cells for instructional slide show art, assisted in production of promotional brochures.

1972 to 1975 - GRAPHIC DESIGNER - Standard Oil Co. of California, San Francisco, CA.
In-house staff designer, designed and produced house organs, recruitment brochures, posters, instructional slide shows, and promotional pieces.

1971 to 1972 - PRODUCTION MANAGER - Cycle News Inc., Signal Hill, CA.
Advertising assistant and production manager for weekly motorcycle newspaper. Paste-up entire paper, produce ads, and editorial illustration.

EDUCATION:
B.A. in Magazine Illustration at California State University, Long Beach, CA. 1971.
Studied drawing at San Francisco Academy of Art College, San Francisco, CA. 1974.

PERSONAL INTERESTS:
Drawing and painting, reading, silkscreen printing, and music.

SALARY:
Open to negotiation.

REFERENCES:
References and portfolio upon request.

Figure 18–1: A Chronological Résumé

The functional format emphasizes the functions or titles of jobs you have held, with the function most important to the job you are seeking listed first.

The *functional approach,* which is gaining in popularity, highlights the job function, or titles of the jobs you have had, with the most significant work experience listed first (Figure 18–2). With this approach, you would list other titles and responsibilities that support your qualifications for the specific area you are seeking. In this case, names of employers and dates of employment are subordinate to function.

The *analytic approach* emphasizes particular vocational skills or specialized knowledge (Figure 18–3). With this approach, you would group your training and experience to show their applicability to your career goal. This approach is most helpful if you have changed jobs frequently, had numerous part-time jobs, or are changing careers.

Most job application forms follow the education, work experience, activities format (Figure 18–4). Therefore, if your résumé is arranged chronologically, you may be able to attach it to the application without filling in all the blanks on the form. That is the concept on which the following résumé format is based. However, if you have extensive work experience, you will probably want to emphasize that fact before presenting your educational experience. Decide what arrangement will work best for *you.*

Regardless of the format you choose, be sure to include all pertinent information in your résumé: name, address, telephone number, job objective, education, work experience, references.

Begin with your name.   Use all capital letters or boldface type. Center it on the page unless you plan to use a photograph. With a photograph, place your name to the left of the picture. Remember the nonverbal aspects of your résumé.

Use a photograph if you wish.   Organizations cannot request a picture because of a variety of interpretations of the affirmative action guidelines. However, a photograph may help some employers visualize you as a "real person" as they review your application. If you decide to include a photograph, choose a clear black and white glossy print that will reproduce well.

Give your current and permanent addresses.   An organization will contact you at your school address until the date you give for graduation. If the organization does not have an immediate opening that fits your qualifications, your résumé may be held on file for up to three years so be sure to also give your permanent address.

Include your social security number if you wish.   Some companies like to have your social security number because the code gives some information about your background. Others require it on their application form but do not look for it on the résumé.

ADELE SCHEFF	80-25 Parsons Blvd. / Jamaica, N.Y. 11432 / (212) 953-4520 (Business)
Career Objectives	Graphic Design, Filmmaking
Experience	Doubleday & Company, Inc., New York, N.Y. Junior Designer February 1978 - Present
	New York State Research Institute on Alcoholism, Buffalo, N.Y. Photography and Illustration Department July 1976 - August 1977
	S.U.N.Y. at Buffalo, Buffalo, N.Y. Undergraduate Teaching Assistant Introduction to Serigraphy and Photoscreenprinting January 1976 - August 1977
Job Description	Design, layout and paste-up of children's books, photographic inserts, in-house publications. Book dummying, scaling, extensive typography. Medical illustration, photoreproduction, photography and slide production. Silk screen preparation, use of films and various stencil materials, color mixing and ink chemistry. Photoscreenprinting processes.
Equipment Skills	Varityper, phototypositor, poloroid reproduction system, horizontal and vertical cameras, darkroom procedures, photoprocessors, manual and automatic screenprinting press, vacuum and exposing tables, 35 mm, 8 mm, and 16 mm cameras, projectors and editors.
Freelance Work	Mean Alice's Restaurant, Buffalo, N.Y. Designed and constructed life size puppet and costumes for stage shows. July 1977
	S.U.N.Y. at Buffalo, Buffalo, N.Y. Division of Undergraduate Studies Designed logo and letterhead. November 1977
	Buffalo Philharmonic Orchestra, October 1976. Sunshine House Crisis Center, December 1976. Designed and printed posters. Buffalo, N.Y.
	S.U.N.Y. at Buffalo, Buffalo, N.Y. Biological Illustration, Biology Department. 1974 - 1975
Exhibitions	S.U.N.Y. at Buffalo, Buffalo, N.Y. Senior Communication Design Exhibition, May 1977. Creative Craft Center, March 1976.
	Syracuse University, Syracuse, N.Y. Contemporary Printmakers, 1977.
	University of Michigan, Ann Arbor, MI Student Print Show, 1976
	Union Carbide Gallery, New York, N.Y. Nationwide Competition, 1973. First Prize, Graphic Arts Category.
Education and Honors	S.U.N.Y. at Buffalo, Buffalo, N.Y. B.F.A. Communication Design, May 1977 Graduated Magna Cum Laude Second Major: Biology.
	High School of Art and Design, New York, N.Y. June 1973 Valedictorian
Personal	Born 6/7/55; single; excellent health. Have travelled extensively throughout major European countries, U.S. and Canada. Outside interests include the biological sciences, medical illustration, screenprinting, music.
References	Professional and personal references available upon request.

Figure 18–2: A Functional Résumé

David Hall
P.O. Box 2494
Mission Viejo, California 92690

OBJECTIVES   A strong position in Graphic Communications with a firm seeking the expertise, versatility and experience I possess.

EDUCATION   AA in Technical and Scientific Illustration
San Diego State University.

Bachelor of Arts
Graphic Communications
San Diego State University
San Diego, California

STRENGTHS   Ten years experience in Graphic Communications. Expertise in technical as well as asthetic aspects with design layouts and type, choosing type fonts and materials to complete mood of given assignments. Directing art departments and selling new ideas. .
Handling complaints from clients, and training new personnel.

EXPERIENCE   Communicating with client and salespersonnel on particular accounts.
OUTLINE   Selling ideas and handling complaints.
Work out new ideas for improved production.
Executing special assignments for particular clientele.
Producing ad presentations for prospective clients.
Professional photographer.
Calculating enlargements and/or reductions for cameraperson.
Operating horizontal and vertical copy cameras, when necessary for halftone and line shots.
Producing illustrations of any subject matter.
Complete technical illustrations from multiview projections and translating them into isometric drawings.
Cut color seperations.
Designing of brochures, pamphlets and any aspect of materials for marketing, logos, letterheads, and business cards.
Paste-up artist.
Conceiving and producing slide shows.
Designing training programs.
My experience also includes newspaper advertising, paging and paste up.

I will be interested in discussing the details of my backround and will supply references upon request at a personal meeting.

Very Truly Yours.

David Hall

Figure 18–3: An Analytical Résumé

Richard E. Robinson
15436 Laurel Drive
San Diego, California 92021

OBJECTIVES & BACKGROUND

Career Objectives   To work in the graphic communications field
with a high level of responsibility and challenge.
   Position Desired: Art director and/or graphic designer.

General Background   Seven years experience in graphic design
emphasizing visual communication problem solving in education
and training, public relations, and identity and promotion packaging.
   Skills and Qualifications:
● Management skills necessary to operate state-of-the-art graphics
facility and coordinate production personnel.
● Working knowledge of graphic design principles and methods,
specifically; layout and composition, typography, photographic
processes, mechanical preparation, printing processes, and
technical and general illustration.
● Working knowledge in the production of audio-visual programs,
video graphics, printed publications, exhibits, and wall graphics.

DICK
ROBINSON
DESIGNER
ILLUSTRATOR

15436 Laurel Drive
San Diego, CA 92021
714/532-1080

EXPERIENCE

Publications Designer	**District Artist/Illustrator**	**Illustrator**
1979 to present	1977 to 1979	1974 to 1977
University of California,	*Grossmont Union High School*	*Fleet Combat Training Center,*
San Diego La Jolla, CA	*District La Mesa, CA*	*Pacific San Diego, CA*

Publications Designer — Responsible for design and production of all official UC San Diego publications. Independently developing page layouts, publication formats, logotypes, illustrations, and campus identity and promotion packages.

District Artist/Illustrator — Served as art director for the District Instructional Media Center. Responsibilities covered:
● Designed and produced visual presentations and instructional programs.
● Coordinated production personnel.
● Consultant for administrators and teachers on visual communication problems.
● Coordinated production efforts between clients and printing personnel.
● Furnished cost and date of completion estimates for clients.
● Conducted inservice workshops for teachers.
● Gave on campus lectures of graphic design principles and methods to students.

Illustrator — Responsible for design and production of artwork to support naval education and training programs. Worked directly with instructors to assess their graphic needs.

Education	**Personal Data**	**References/Portfolio**
B.A. degree, 1973	Birthdate: August 14, 1951	Available on request
University of California,	Married	
San Diego		
Major: Visual Arts		

A.A. degree, 1971
Mesa College, San Diego
Major: fine arts
Minor: mathematics

Figure 18–4: A Contemporary Résumé that Emphasizes Educationally Relevant Courses

Include both home and business telephone numbers. Tell the employer where you can be reached between 8 A.M. and 5 P.M. each day. If that is not appropriate or possible, ask a friend or relative to take messages and relay them to you. In that case, include that number on the résumé. Or indicate the hours you can be reached at a particular phone number—and be there. There is enough competition for most jobs that if an employer tries to phone you four or five times and doesn't receive an answer, another individual will be given the job opportunity.

State your job objective. It helps an employer to know what type of position you are seeking and your general qualifications for that position. Use short summary phrases:

```
JOB OBJECTIVE: mechanical engineer with
emphasis in machine design. Long-range goal
--management.
```

```
CAREER OBJECTIVE: a position utilizing my
education and experience in marketing and
sales, with special emphasis in computer
technology.
```

```
CAREER GOAL: accountant with industrial or
other private-sector firm. Progress toward
the C.P.A. and supervisory responsibilities.
```

Employers who review large numbers of résumés are often frustrated by job objectives stating that the writer seeks "a challenging position leading to management." You should describe as concisely as possible your career area, although it is not necessary to specify a job title. Review the D.O.T. and the S.O.C. described in Chapter 17 for assistance in composing an appropriate job objective. (If you believe that including an objective will limit your choice of jobs, save it for your application letter.)

Review your education—a major asset. Give your educational history, most recent first. Include undergraduate history—associate degree, B.S., or B.A.—and advanced degrees. Refer to your high school education only if you have less than two years of college or if it strongly supports your job objective. Be specific. List

- years attended, year diploma received
- diploma, degree, certificate
- name and address of colleges, universities, technical schools attended

You may want to provide additional information to indicate

- specializations—major areas of study
- minors
- grade-point average (GPA) if B– or better
- the name of your major professor/teacher
- change of major and credit hours completed before transfer
- percentage of expenses you earned while in school

Changes of major could show up as credit hours in a minor and indicate another area of strength in your program. Instead of GPA, you can use class rank, GPA in your major (MGPA), or GPA for the last two years. Be sure to qualify the grade statement by detailing what area or time period you are using.

Supplying the name of a major professor (for graduate students), teacher, or advisor who knows you is a good way to provide employers with a quick contact to substantiate school information. Including the period of time you spent acquiring the degree tells the employer that you

- completed your degree within an average time period
- took more than the usual time, but persisted
- had grade difficulties but overcame them
- changed majors
- had a double major

You may want to cover some of these details in your application letter.

Review and evaluate your work experience—another major asset
You may want to group your experience according to full-time, part-time, and volunteer work; functional area; or chronological order. Help the employer evaluate your skills fairly. Provide, in reverse chronological order,

- the names and addresses of all previous employers
- the inclusive dates of employment
- job titles
- summaries of assigned responsibilities

Stress your accomplishments. Omit references to salary history. (Salary discussions come later.)

Describe specific skills and abilities that apply to your job objective, using these terms as they fit:

Personal Attributes
- analytical
- creative
- decisive
- flexible
- independent
- innovative
- responsible
- well organized
- stress tolerant

Experience In
- budgetary accountability
- quality control
- supervision
- organization
- communication
- evaluation
- teaching/training
- risk taking
- leadership

Select from your list of activities those compatible with your job objective. Include

- professional contacts
- leadership positions
- special skills
- areas of expertise

Employers and supervisors use this information to find commonality with their own interests. Membership in common groups, recreational activities enjoyed by the work groups—these are factors in matching employees to work groups. Reaction to individual activities depends upon the interviewer's age, sex, and personal interests. You may include honors, awards, and hobbies in this section or in a separate section.

Include personal data if you wish. It is helpful to the employer to know as much as possible about you, but laws prohibit personal questions that might be used to discriminate. Any information you include on your résumé can be discussed during an interview. However, the good interviewer will quickly turn the conversation away from subjects that might lead to charges of discriminatory hiring practices. Some of this information is required when you are hired, however, in order for the company to calculate your take-home pay and benefits. You may include the following on your résumé:

- birthdate
- marital status
- number of dependents
- citizenship

Other items sometimes included under the personal information section are your

- sex, if you have a name used by both males and females and you do not include a photograph
- height and weight
- geographical preference
- willingness to travel, relocate
- health factors (If you are visibly handicapped, say so. Some companies actively recruit handicapped individuals.)
- military or veteran's status

These factors occasionally influence employment, for example, when corporate officers designate certain groups for preferential hiring.

Refer to or include references.   The statement "References are available upon request" is an acceptable way to conclude your résumé. It is also acceptable to include the names of three individuals who are willing to vouch for your character. Impressive references include professors and teachers; administrators in business, industry, government, and education; and personal friends with high status. Employers, former employers, and educators are the ones most frequently contacted.

Teaching positions, as well as certain other jobs, require reference letters from specific individuals. The letters are expected to describe both the applicant's strengths and weaknesses. To allow the letterwriters to express their opinions freely, the applicant may agree not to read the letters (a "closed file"). The letters, along with the applicant's signed waiver form and a form authorizing their release to employers, are usually held on file in the college placement office. At the student's request, the credentials are mailed to prospective employers. A reference file may or may not be required. Signing the waiver is optional.

Use date compiled if you wish. The résumé becomes out of date almost before it is prepared, in terms of present employment, activities, or current address. Providing the date your résumé was compiled helps the employer account for and ask questions about the intervening time between compilation and the present. It also enables an aggressive candidate to update the résumé when the employer doesn't respond favorably or when the candidate wants to keep the application active with an employer. The update can be handled as a letter or as an addendum to the résumé if the additional information is significant.

Finally, you may want to attach a copy of your *transcript* to the résumé. You can purchase a certified transcript from your school registrar and then have uncertified copies made. Some companies ask for the transcript when they are seriously interested in an applicant. Most employers appreciate this additional document.

Review

Be sure that your résumé is accurate and complete.

Be sure that the information you provide in the résumé is accurate. Falsification or omission of relevant information is grounds for not hiring or for immediate dismissal following hiring. Ask someone you trust to react to the presentation before you have the résumé typed or printed. Remember, however, that other opinions are just other points of view. Use your own judgment regarding suggested changes.

Image

Try to keep your résumé to one page.

Now that you have compiled and reviewed the information in your résumé, you must consider matters of image, or appearance. Résumés may be typewritten or typeset (printed). Whichever method you select, keep the résumé to one page if at all possible. Most important, your résumé should be pleasing in appearance; free from errors in spelling, grammar, and fact; and concise.

Typewriting is appropriate for any résumé and application letter. When you select this method, be sure that the type on your typewriter is clean, that the letters do not fill in, and that any corrections are not smudged or obvious. Typewritten copy, especially when prepared with a carbon ribbon, provides excellent "camera-ready" copy for use with electrostatic copiers or offset printing.

Before your résumé is duplicated, proofread the original carefully. It is a good idea to have someone else proofread it, too. Make any necessary corrections neatly and carefully.

Ensure that your résumé is attractive and free of errors. Proofread it to eliminate errors in grammar, spelling, and punctuation.

Whenever possible, try to use the same paper for both your résumé and letter of application. Mail the letter and résumé in a matching envelope. (You may want to include a self-addressed, stamped envelope to encourage an early reply.)

Generally, you should select a 20- or 24-pound bond paper. Choose a businesslike color—white, natural, ivory/cream, or pale gray.

THE APPLICATION LETTER

A good application letter gets the writer an interview. Although there are rules for good application letters, there is no one form to be used without variation. Your letter communicates your unique qualifications and background—your education, work experience, and activities. Of course, some type of form letter will develop if you write to 10, 20, or more organizations, but its basics will be uniquely your own.

The effective application letter conveys your uniqueness, complements your résumé, and gets you an interview.

The application letter, sometimes called a *transmittal* or *cover* letter,

- introduces you to the employer
- provides specific details not covered in your résumé
- describes contributions you believe you can make to the organization
- allows you to describe how you can apply your education and skills to the employer's needs
- requests an interview

The job application letter is a selling letter that requires persuasive writing (Chapter 11) based on your self-analysis (Chapter 17). Design your letter to meet the criteria for the position you are seeking.

The application letter is a selling letter; use persuasion to sell yourself.

The letter should be an original document addressed to a specific individual within an organization. Keep a copy of each letter you send for your personal file as a record of your correspondence. Copies are especially useful in cases where

- the original is lost in the mail
- you need to correspond further with the same organization
- you make certain commitments and must follow up

Use any format you wish, but be consistent throughout the letter. Remember, you are selling something. You must convince prospective employers that your product—you—is the best that money can buy.

Personnel people must select job candidates for an interview on the basis of the material presented in letters and résumés. Many times letterwriters omit the name of the position they desire or they forget to mention any relationship between their education, work experience, and activities and the position they are seeking. They sometimes simply refer the reader to their résumé, where their career objective is stated as being a challenging position leading to management responsibility. Avoid these pitfalls!

As a rule, there are two or more career paths within a given professional area. In most cases, individual letters should be developed for each. For example, an engineer may be qualified to work in the fields of engineering design, manufacturing, and technical sales. A management major may want to consider administrative positions in both retailing and manufacturing. A home economics major may be considering positions as a buyer and as a clothing designer.

As a job applicant, you have three major areas of emphasis—your education, your work experience, and your activities. Your background in these three areas is a matter of record. Only the presentation of these facts can be altered.

Organization

Using the concepts of organization described in Chapter 5, you should

- capture the reader's *attention* immediately
- continue with details of specific *interest*
- *convince* the reader to become involved
- call for specific *action*

When personnel people review application letters, they are looking for specific information. They are trying to fill specific openings in the organization. To expedite their work, you should open your letter with attention-getting information:

- position sought/job title
- education—degree, major
- date available for employment

- "outstanding" qualifications—GPA, co-op, honors
- who recommended the company

For example:

```
     Please consider me for a position as a
production foreman with your company.

     I will receive a B.S. degree in indus-
trial engineering on June 1 from the Univer-
sity of Illinois, with a 5.2 grade-point
average (A = 6).  I have been a co-op student
and have two years of work experience.  Pro-
fessor Herbert Harmison suggested I contact
you.
```

```
     Please review my qualifications as an
accountant with your company.

     I have completed all the accounting
courses offered at Western Illinois Univer-
sity and will graduate in August with honors.
I have a minor in computer science and wish
to work with management information systems.
My advisor, Professor Daniel Wayne, suggested
I write to you about employment.
```

This information allows the reader to sort your application quickly into the correct category for consideration.

The rest of your letter should show, specifically, what you have gained from your education, work experience, and activities. One way to prepare your letter is to write a series of paragraphs about your qualifications. Describe

- specific classes and projects
- each job you have held
- activities in which you excelled or led
- honors

Arrange the paragraphs so that your strongest qualifications appear first. If you have appropriate work experience in your career area, place that first. If not, describe your education first. Use transition sentences between paragraphs.

COMMUNICATION AND CAREERS

Begin your application letter with attention-getting information, proceed with items of interest to the reader, and close with a call to action.

As you review my résumé you will note that I have participated in the engineering co-op program. I was assigned to work with an engineering group designing. . . .

This work experience was especially helpful when I studied hydraulics in ME 408. We designed a. . . .

For an assignment on design simulation in a computer science class, I modeled a Mercury 318 c.i.d. engine in a program to test energy efficiency. . . .

Both my education and work experience reflect my career goals in retailing. While enrolled in the management curriculum, I have gained first-hand knowledge of retailing by working part time at The Weathervane, a clothing store catering to college students and staff.

Classes in marketing taught me to analyze trends and customers. Electives in logic and persuasion helped me to communicate with people.

Special reasons for locating in a particular geographic area, such as spouse employment, health requirements, or recreational preferences, may be included in your application letter.

I am committed to finding employment in New York because my wife will be working for Arthur Andersen. Your company has been highly recommended by our faculty because of its integrity, benefits, and transfer considerations.

For health reasons--a mild asthmatic condition--I am eager to locate in the Southwest. Although I have missed only four days of work in the last two years, I have been advised I would be free of symptoms in a dry climate.

Along with your reasons for relocating, you should express a specific interest in the company you are writing to and offer a feeling of permanency if employed.

The last paragraph of your application letter is a request for *action*. You must tell the employer what you want done. You will probably want the employer to review your résumé and supporting credentials. You may want an interview. Give specific times when and where you will be available to take a phone call (between 8 A.M. and 5 P.M.). You may state a preference for interview dates, such as during school vacations or periods between examinations.

```
    After you have reviewed my qualifications,
please contact me about when we can meet.  I
can come for an interview at your convenience,
and a Tuesday or Thursday fits my schedule
best.  I am eager to hear from you soon.

    Please review my qualifications with your
supervisory personnel, and then contact me to
talk about career opportunities with your com-
pany.  I am available for an interview during
the second week in April and the first week
in May or at another time more convenient for
you.  I am eager to hear from you soon about
when we can meet.
```

Format

Your letter may be several paragraphs long. It may even extend onto a second page. But it is extremely important that every paragraph provide the employer with another convincing reason why you should be selected for the job you desire. Figure 18–5 illustrates a classic employment letter.

There are times when a creative or contemporary letter is especially effective in a job application situation. Such letters have special appeal for positions in artistic careers or those requiring strong communication skills—for instance, writing, drama, public relations, art, and advertising. There is an element of risk in writing an innovative or humorous job application letter, but when the reader is empathetic, an excellent job match may result (Figure 18–6).

November 6, 1981

Dr. LaNelle Geddes
Head, School of Nursing
Purdue University
West Lafayette, IN 47907

Dear Dr. Geddes:

Please consider me for the position you have available for
a coordinator of alumni relations and communications. I
have enclosed my résumé, my college transcript, and a copy
of a publication I edited.

Briefly, my college work was intended to prepare me to work
in the area of public relations--in the fields of communications and/or personnel administration. My degree is inter-
disciplinary and allowed me the utmost freedom in selecting
courses specific to my employment goals.

You will see, as you review my transcript, that I have
completed a wide variety of communications courses: writing,
media analysis, communications law, and television ethics.
I have some experience with newspaper work, television special events, and a radio show. I included courses in reporting, editing, and public relations in my program of study.

I have been active in community affairs. I have worked as
a volunteer with the Boy Scouts, 4-H, the Band Club, and my
church. In several of these organizations, I was responsible for public relations activities.

I believe my major strengths are strong communication skills,
an ability to meet and relate to people, the ability to accept an assignment and carry it out with a minimum of supervision, and a career orientation that is not confined to an
eight-to-five time schedule.

After you have reviewed my résumé, transcript, and the
publication I have enclosed, I would like to have the opportunity to talk with you about job specifics--your needs, and
my qualifications. I can come for an interview at your convenience, and am looking forward to hearing from you when
you begin interviewing for this position.

Sincerely,

Mary C. Thompson
2511 Raintree Drive
West Lafayette, IN 47906

Enclosures

Figure 18–5: A Classic Application Letter

3506 Lincoln Way, #8
Encino, California 91316
October 28, 1981

Dave Nixon, News Director
KABC-TV
4151 Prospect Avenue
Los Angeles, California 90036

Dear Mr. Nixon:

A few years ago a college degree was a precious commodity.
A few years ago a college degree was a ticket to a job.
A few years ago a college degree meant prestige and status.

But that was a few years ago.

Today a lot of people have college degrees. And a lot of them
hold degrees in journalism. And a lot of those journalism grads
want jobs.

I'm one of them. But I think I'm a little different from the
rest of them.

I'm different because I've got more than just a college degree.
I've got experience--four years of it in college and commercial
newspaper work and broadcasting. I think that experience can
help KABC-TV maintain their number one rating in the Los Angeles
news market.

May I get together with you at your convenience in the near
future? A videotape of my airwork is available on request.

I'd appreciate hearing from you soon.

Sincerely,

J. C. Kain

J.C. Kain

1 enc.

Figure 18–6: A Contemporary Application Letter

Be sure that your application letter directly applies to the position you are seeking.

Once again, the employment letter may exceed one page *as long as the content is directly applicable to the job.* Personnel officers are trying to make successful placements. Their job depends on it. The more appropriate "job-match" information you provide, the better the chance that an interview will result.

Review

Be sure that your application letter follows the principles of the persuasive selling letter. Have you written it from the "you" point of view? Have you combined the reader's (employer's) benefits with the writer's (your) wishes? Will your letter attract the reader's attention and maintain his or her interest? Have you used convincing logic and requested an action from the reader?

See that your application letter is persuasive, attractive, and error-free.

Ask an instructor or peer to critique your letter. Incorporate appropriate suggestions. Be sure that your grammar and spelling are correct. After the letter is typed, proofread it carefully. Have someone else proofread it. Make any necessary corrections neatly, and check to see that the overall appearance is attractive.

ASSIGNMENT: CAREER SEARCH DOCUMENTS

Following the guidelines presented in this chapter, prepare a résumé and application letter that will get you an interview.

FURTHER READING

Austin, Michael J. *Professionals and Paraprofessionals.* New York: Human Science, 1978.

Catalyst, Inc. *Marketing Yourself: The Catalyst Women's Guide to Successful Résumés and Interviews.* New York: Putnam, 1980.

Feingold, S. Norman. *Careers for Today and Tomorrow.* Washington, D.C.: B'Nai B'rith Career and Counseling Service, 1977.

Figler, Howard. *The Complete Job Search Handbook.* New York: Holt, Rinehart and Winston, 1979.

Hall, Francine S. and Douglas T. Hall. *Two-Career Couple.* Reading, MA: Addison-Wesley, 1979.

Irish, Richard. *Go Hire Yourself an Employer.* Garden City, NY: Anchor, 1978.

Jackson, Tom and Davidyne Mayleas. *The Hidden Job Market.* New York: Quadrangle/The New York Times, 1977.

McLaughlin, John E. and Stephen K. Merman. *Writing a Job-Winning Résumé.* Englewood Cliffs, NJ: Prentice-Hall, 1980.

Powell, C. Randall. *Career Planning and Placement Today,* 2nd ed. Dubuque, IA: Kendall/Hunt, 1978.

Stanat, Kirby W. and Patrick Reardon. *Job Hunting Secrets and Tactics.* Chicago: Follett, 1977.

Strauss, Anselm L. *Professions, Work and Careers.* New Brunswick, NJ: Transaction, 1975.

CHAPTER NINETEEN

The Employment Interview*

An application letter and a well-written personal data sheet [résumé] get you off to a good start. If effective, they will result in an interview. But as most employers point out, it is the personal interview that often determines who gets the job.

Charles R. Hopkins et al.
General Business in Our Modern Society

T he interview gives you the opportunity to meet face to face with a representative of the organization you are interested in working for. The interviewer will have in hand a summary of your life obtained from your letter and résumé or from an application form that you completed on your arrival. (See Figure 19–1.) You, on the other hand, will probably be meeting a total stranger.

The employment interview is a face-to-face exchange of information to fit the right person to the right job.

The employment interview is a conversation with a purpose—a purpose that has been determined in advance—to exchange information that will help the interviewer select the right person for a position that will provide satisfaction for both employer and employee.

TYPES OF INTERVIEWS

Interviews range from completely structured to completely unstructured. They may be conducted by college recruiters, personnel people, and/or supervisors.

The Structured Interview

In the *structured interview*, you are asked a predetermined list of questions. Your responses may be checked against a pattern of responses prepared by the personnel department and ranked for

---

*Written by Mary C. Thompson, Alumni Relations and Communications Coordinator, School of Nursing, Purdue University, West Lafayette, Indiana.

372

EMPLOYMENT APPLICATION

FOR OFFICE USE
Appl. Filed_____ To Begin_____
Appl. Accepted_____ Dept. _____
Clock No. _____ Position_____

Date_____

Print Name in full_____ S.S. No._____

Address_____ Tel. No. _____

City_____ State_____ Zip_____

Kind of work desired? _____ Salary Expected?_____

What other lines of work in your experience? _____

Have you ever been apprenticed? _____ How long?_____

When apprenticed?_____ What Company?_____

Are you a Citizen of U.S.? _____

Have you any relatives or friends   Name _____ Relationship?_____
employed by this Company?

EDUCATION	Name & Location of School	No. of Years Attended	Course of Study General Special	Did You Graduate?	Date of Leaving Mo. Yr.
Grammar School					
High School					
Night School					
Correspondence School					
College or University					

In case of accident notify_____
                                                         Telephone

Address   City   State
_____

Figure 19–1: A Typical Employment Application Form

acceptability. Your selection for an employment offer will be based on your numerical score (Figure 19–2).

The Unstructured Interview

In the structured interview, you are asked a number of predetermined questions in a specific order, and your answers are graded and ranked. In the unstructured interview, you may be asked a variety of questions in any order, and you are expected to do most of the talking. Most interviews fall somewhere between these two extremes.

In an *unstructured interview*, there is no predetermined list of questions. The interviewer has a basic series of questions to determine your skills, but these questions may be asked in any order and adjusted to meet a particular situation. In the unstructured interview, you are encouraged to do most of the talking.

The unstructured interview is most commonly used during counseling sessions. Conversation is directed by the interviewer's use of techniques of nodding, one-word replies, mirror questions, and pauses to elicit conversation from the interviewee after the initial greetings have been conducted.

Most interviews are neither completely structured nor completely unstructured, but fall somewhere in between.

The Stress Interview

The stress interview is designed to determine how well you cope with pressure and personally threatening situations.

The *stress interview* is rarely used for initial employment. It is significant to mention, however, because interviewers have borrowed questions from that type of interview for occasional use during employment interviews. The stress interview is justified on the grounds that there will always be occasions when employees must function under stressful conditions. Employers may feel it important to know how you react in such situations. Interviewers may ask,

- What is your worst habit or trait?
- What is your poorest subject?
- Have you ever failed to accomplish something you started? What was it?
- What was your most embarrassing moment?

The questions are used to determine how well you cope under pressure and handle situations that are personally defeating or embarrassing. Should questions like these be asked in your interview, keep cool and answer honestly. Preparation of a market analysis should aid you in supplying an answer and give you an opportunity to demonstrate preparedness.

Candidate's Name _____

Reviewed by _____

Date _____

Entry Level

Score 1–10

1. Image   _____

2. Communication skills   _____

3. Leadership and responsibility level (nonwork)   _____

4. Career goals (ambitious, but realistic)   _____

5. Judgment and common sense   _____

6. Personal impact   _____

7. Enthusiasm and energy level   _____

8. Maturity   _____

9. Preplanning and organizational ability   _____

10. Knowledge of sales   _____

                                  Total _____

Image—general appearance: dress, hair style, personal grooming.

Communication skills—ability to communicate ideas clearly, proper use of vocabulary.

Leadership and responsibility level—active leadership in groups, organizations, athletics; self-sufficient, not passing blame.

Career goals—setting goals that are ambitious, but realistic.

Judgment and common sense—logical reasoning for doing things, not emotional.

Personal impact—air of confidence, commands respect and attention.

Enthusiasm and energy level—active and optimistic.

Maturity—logical, not emotional; confident, poised, secure.

Preplanning and organizational ability—time utilization, foresight, detail oriented.

Knowledge of sales—overall insight into structure of sales force, opportunities by industry, difficulties encountered in selling, prior exposure.

Figure 19–2: Interview Rating Sheet

The Campus Interviews

Many organizations send recruiters to college campuses to seek applicants for certain jobs.

A variety of organizations send recruiters to college campuses to meet and interview job applicants. The recruiters are responsible for seeking the applicants that seem to fit specific job requirements. Selected applicants are later invited for on-site visits, where the actual job selection is made by the supervisor of a specific work group. Campus interviewers often work in teams or units and are assigned specific campuses to visit, often schools from which the interviewer graduated.

You may or may not be offered an application form during your campus interview. You may occasionally be invited for an on-site visit during the campus interview; however, most organizations do not permit campus recruiters to offer applications and trips during the initial contact.

The Personnel Office Interview

Most organizations initially have a personnel officer interview and screen applicants. Applicants are screened on the basis of submitted résumés and application letters or on the basis of "walk-in" interviews. Those who fit the specifications for posted openings are referred to the supervisor who is seeking to fill a vacancy. As a rule, only three or four persons actually reach the hiring supervisor for each opening. The choice of applicant, at that point, can be made on the basis of best fit for the work group because the personnel office has certified that each candidate is relatively equally qualified.

The Supervisory Interview

Usually a personnel officer of an organization first interviews the job applicant. However, in some cases, the supervisor with a position to fill conducts the interview.

In some instances, the supervisor with a vacancy to fill is responsible for the screening and the selection. Supervisory interviews tend to be more unstructured than personnel office interviews, with fewer constraints on time and the variety of questions. Selection is likely to be heavily weighted on personality factors and less precise qualifications. This situation most often occurs in consulting businesses and organizations hiring less than 50 people, or where professional positions are being filled.

PREPARING FOR THE INTERVIEW

There are a number of guidelines you can follow to prepare for the employment interview. Although they may not guarantee you a job, these steps will certainly help your chances and ensure a more productive exchange between you and the interviewer.

In preparing for an interview, learn all you can about the organization, confirm any necessary travel arrangements, dress in a businesslike manner, arrive promptly with a copy of your résumé and a pen and notebook.

Learn about the Organization

Once an interview has been scheduled, find out as much as you can about the organization. Be familiar with the products or services that it offers. Know where its headquarters and branch offices are located. Check on

- the number of employees in the organization
- the length of time it has been in business
- its reputation in the industry
- the price of its stock, if listed

Consult your job research file and make inquiries. Review your reasons for being impressed with the organization.

Your knowledge of the organization will impress the interviewer. It will show that you are well organized, that you take initiative and have serious interest in the job and organization. Questions, too, can be helpful in this regard. You might ask the interviewer about

- job-related responsibilities
- promotion policies
- hiring policies—employment of relatives, for instance
- company benefits
- growth rate of the organization
- travel requirements
- training programs

Travel Arrangements

Out-of-town interviews may require travel by car or plane. You may be instructed by the organization to

- make your own travel arrangements

- follow prearranged travel schedules
- pay your own out-of-pocket expenses
- fill out an expense form for reimbursement (save all receipts)
- meet a member of the organization at the airport, at a motel, or at the office
- follow a prearranged schedule of meetings for part or all of a day

Some organizations arrange for a spouse to accompany you. You will need to mention that you are married if you wish such consideration.

If any arrangements are not clear or if you have questions, ask. Failure to follow instructions or communicate adequately can be damaging to your application.

Dress

Dress appropriately for the interview. For women, a blue or gray suit or skirt and jacket is often recommended. For men, a dark suit or conservative jacket and trousers is preferred. The rule is to dress in a businesslike manner. Do not wear an excessive amount of jewelry. If you fly to the interview, your luggage may not arrive when you do. Therefore, consider carrying your basic grooming needs, the paperwork required for your interview, and other necessary items in a handbag or briefcase. Wear an outfit that *could* be worn appropriately for the interview. In your luggage carry the outfit you *would like* to wear.

Arriving for the Interview

Carry an extra copy of your résumé and any other required forms, such as an application blank and referral forms, with you to the interview. Also, be sure to have a notebook and pencil to write down the names and titles of the people you meet during your visit.

Plan to arrive in plenty of time so that you do not appear rushed. Allow sufficient time to cope with traffic, parking, and finding the person you are to see.

After you arrive at the office, identify yourself and the person with whom you have the appointment. When your name is called for the interview, stand promptly and greet the interviewer by name if you are sure of the correct pronunciation. If you are not, wait until the interviewer introduces himself or herself and repeat the name for clarification. Be prepared to shake hands firmly. No one likes a limp handshake. Wait until a chair is offered before you sit down, and don't smoke unless you are invited to do so.

During this introductory period, a great deal of nonverbal communication takes place. The interviewer makes mental notes regarding your dress, your manner, your personal grooming. The way you sit, the amount of eye contact you maintain, your sub-conscious energy level all become factors in your interview.

Your nonverbal communication is extremely important in the initial stage of an interview.

ORGANIZATION OF THE INTERVIEW

Most screening interviews are structured—comprised of an open-ing, a body, and a close. In a typical 30-minute interview (Figure 19–3), the first 5 minutes are devoted to making you comfortable. The interviewer may chat about the weather, a ball game, your background in order to make you feel at ease.

The next 13 minutes are designed to give you a chance to "sell yourself." The interviewer's questions give you an opportunity to discuss your strengths and goals as they relate to the job and the organization.

Another 7 minutes of the typical interview are usually allotted to provide you with additional information about the organization. The interviewer answers questions and briefly describes some of the job opportunities available for you with the company. During this time, you are also told about follow-up procedures. Then, in most cases, the interviewer stands and indicates the termination of the interview. The last 5 minutes of the 30-minute period take place after you leave the room. The interviewer uses this time to make notes and recommendations about you before he or she sees the next applicant.

If the interviewer's schedule is not filled, you may be given more time. However, surveys of practicing interviewers reveal that the average interviewer makes a screening decision within the first 4 minutes of the 30-minute interview.

Most interviews consist of an opening, which is designed to put you at ease; a body, which allows you to answer questions and "sell" yourself; and a conclusion, which provides you with additional information about the organization and follow-up procedures.

QUESTIONS TO EXPECT DURING THE INTERVIEW

Each interviewer's aim is to elicit information about how your education, skills, and career objectives match the needs of the or-ganization, to assess how well you handle oral communication,

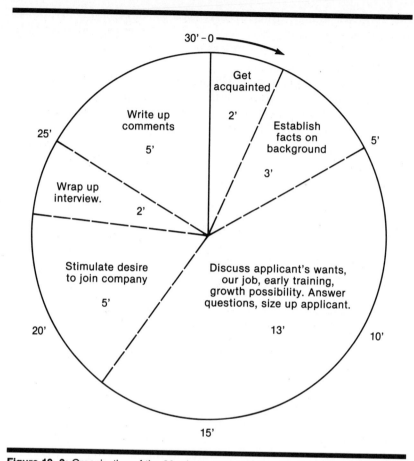

Figure 19–3: Organization of the 30-minute Interview from the Interviewer's Viewpoint

how well you respond to direct questions, and how well you anticipate the unexpected. The interviewer works closely with the supervisors and knows the work that needs to be done, as well as the image the organization seeks to achieve. The interviewer selects candidates who seem likely to stay with the company, who fit well in the work environment, and who will achieve regular advances in the organization's hierarchy. The selection decision is based on observations made during the employment interview.

Some of the questions you are asked in an interview are open-ended; such questions allow you great latitude in a response. Other questions will require only a yes or no answer.

During an interview you may be expected to respond to open-ended questions, mirror questions, probes, and pauses. Your responses should present your best image and your qualifications for the job.

Mirror questions restate your reply with the intent of soliciting additional information. For example, in response to your answer that you grew up on a farm, the interviewer might respond with, "You say you grew up on a farm." You are thus encouraged to continue to talk about that aspect of your life.

Probes may be used during an interview to encourage you to continue talking on the same subject. They are stimulated by your responses to open-ended questions. "Why?" "How?" "When was that?" are examples of probes that are used to help you remember or to draw additional information from you.

The *pause* is another commonly used interview technique to encourage you to continue talking on the same subject. This technique can be very effective when used by a skilled interviewer. Unprepared interviewees usually perform poorly when long pauses occur during an interview.

You are given the opportunity to present your strongest qualifications and supporting skills when you are asked such questions as the following:

- What can you tell me about yourself?
- Why do you want this job?
- What do you want to be doing ten years from now?
- Can you sell me something?
- What extracurricular offices have you held?
- Do you prefer working with others or by yourself?
- Why do you think you would like this particular type of job?
- Have you ever changed your major field of interest while in college? Why?
- How do you spend your spare time?
- Do you have an analytical mind?
- What are your own special abilities?
- Do you like to travel?
- Do you have any questions you would like to ask?

Selection factors include personality, poise, initiative, and appearance. You may also be asked some personal questions:

- Is your home life happy?
- What is your father's occupation?
- Are you from a large family?
- What is the source of your spending money?
- Do you have any debts?
- Which of your parents had the most profound influence on you?
- Do you date anyone regularly? Is it serious?

If you prefer not to discuss personal matters, you can avoid questions by asking if they are job related. In many instances, however, job candidates feel pressured to respond in some way. For some occupations, the questions may be pertinent; on some occasions, they may be asked by inept interviewers. Table 19–1 indicates the kinds of inquiries that can be made lawfully in one state and that are common in most states.

Finally, refrain from criticizing former employers, teachers, or acquaintances. And don't be afraid to apologize during the interview, if an apology is indeed called for. Assume responsibility for your errors. Everyone makes mistakes; not everyone can admit them (see "Interpersonal Communication" in Chapter 2).

FOLLOWING UP ON THE INTERVIEW

At the end of your interview, you will be told to expect a response within a given time period. You will probably be invited to call, collect perhaps, if you have further questions after you leave.

At the end of the time you were told to expect a response, follow up by writing a brief note or making a telephone call asking about the progress of your application. As long as you are not a pest, your initiative will be appreciated. Applications occasionally get sidetracked or buried on a desk. Your reminder indicates your interest and enthusiasm about a position with the organization.

Thank-you Letters

Follow the interview with a short good-will letter if you are especially impressed with the organization and the interviewer.

Many organizations prefer that you not send follow-up thank-you letters after an initial interview. If, however, you are very interested in a particular company and very impressed by the recruiter, it is appropriate to send a short good-will letter thanking the interviewer for the time spent with you, reiterating your interest in the company, and repeating your eagerness to hear soon about a follow-up interview.

After an on-site visit, you will want to write a short letter to people you met. Thank them for their time and for the opportunity to visit. Restate some significant impression from your visit and mention your appreciation of their interest in you. In a letter to the personnel department, send your expense record and receipts. Then wait.

Your chances of being offered a job after the on-site visit are quite good, probably better than 50–50. Most companies limit the

Table 19–1: Michigan Pre-employment Inquiry Guide

Subject	Lawful Pre-employment Inquiries	Unlawful Pre-employment Inquiries
Name	Applicant's full name.	Original name of an applicant whose name has been changed by court order or otherwise.
	"Have you ever worked for this company under a different name?"	Applicant's maiden name.
	"Is any additional information relative to a different name necessary to check work record? If yes, explain."	
Address or duration of residence	"How long have you been a resident of this state or city?"	
Birthplace		Birthplace of applicant.
		Birthplace of applicant's parents, spouse, or other close relatives.
		Requirement that applicant submit birth certificate, naturalization or baptismal record.
Age	"Are you 18 years old or older?"*	"How old are you?" "What is your date of birth?"
Religion or creed		Inquiry into an applicant's religious denomination, religious affiliations, church, parish, pastor, or religious holidays observed.
		An applicant may not be told, "This is a Catholic (Protestant or Jewish) organization."
Race or color		Complexion or color of skin.
Photograph		Requirement that an applicant for employment affix a photograph to an employment application form.

*This question may be asked only for the purpose of determining whether applicants are of legal age for employment.

Table 19–1: Michigan Pre-employment Inquiry Guide, *continued*

Subject	Lawful Pre-employment Inquiries	Unlawful Pre-employment Inquiries
		Request an applicant, at his or her option, to submit a photograph.
		Requirement for photograph after interview but before hiring.
Height		Inquiry regarding applicant's height.
Weight		Inquiry regarding applicant's weight.
Marital status		Requirement that an applicant provide any information regarding marital status or children. "Are you single or married?" "Do you have any children?" "Is your spouse employed?" "What is your spouse's name?"
Sex		Mr., Miss, or Mrs. or an inquiry regarding sex. Inquiry as to the ability to reproduce or advocacy of any form of birth control.
Health	"Do you have any impairments, physical, mental, or medical, which would interfere with your ability to do the job for which you have applied?"	"Do you have a disability or handicap?" "Have you ever been treated for the following diseases?" "Do you use any adaptive device or aid?"
	Inquiry into contagious or communicable diseases which may endanger others. "If there are any positions for which you should not be considered or job duties you cannot perform because of a physical or mental handicap, please explain."	Requirement that women be given pelvic examinations.
Citizenship	"Are you a citizen of the United States?"	"Of what country are you a citizen?"

Table 19–1: Michigan Pre-employment Inquiry Guide, *continued*

Subject	*Lawful Pre-employment Inquiries*	*Unlawful Pre-employment Inquiries*
	"If not a citizen of the United States, do you intend to become a citizen of the United States?"	Whether an applicant is naturalized or a native-born citizen; the date when the applicant acquired citizenship.
	"If you are not a U.S. citizen, have you the legal right to remain permanently in the United States?" "Do you intend to remain permanently in the United States?"	Requirement that an applicant produce naturalization papers or first papers.
		Whether applicant's parents or spouse is naturalized or native-born citizen of the United States; the date when such parents or spouse acquired citizenship.
National origin	Inquiry into languages applicant speaks and writes fluently.	Inquiry into applicant's a. lineage b. ancestry c. national origin d. descent e. parentage f. nationality
		Nationality of applicant's parents or spouse.
		"What is your mother tongue?"
		Inquiry into how applicant acquired ability to read, write, or speak a foreign language.
Education	Inquiry into the academic, vocational, or professional education of an applicant and the public and private schools he or she attended.	
Experience	Inquiry into work experience. Inquiry into countries applicant has visited.	

Table 19–1: Michigan Pre-employment Inquiry Guide, *continued*

Subject	Lawful Pre-employment Inquiries	Unlawful Pre-employment Inquiries
Arrests	"Have you ever been convicted of a crime?" "If so, when, where, and what was the nature of the offense?" "Are there any felony charges pending against you?"	Inquiry regarding arrests.
Relatives	Names of applicant's relatives, other than a spouse, already employed by this company.	Address of any relative of applicant, other than address (within the United States) of applicant's father and mother, husband or wife, and minor dependent children.
Notice in case of emergency	Name and address of person to be notified in case of accident or emergency.	Name and address of nearest relative to be notified in case of accident or emergency.
Military experience	Inquiry into an applicant's military experience in the armed forces of the United States or in a state militia. Inquiry into applicant's service in particular branch of United States Army, Navy, etc.	Inquiry into an applicant's general military experience.
Organizations	Inquiry into the organizations of which an applicant is a member, excluding organizations the name or character of which indicates the race, color, religion, national origin, or ancestry of its members.	"List all clubs, societies, and lodges to which you belong."
References	"Who suggested that you apply for a position here?"	

NOTE:

1. The Pre-employment Inquiry Guide is based on the provisions of Public Acts 220 and 453 of 1976. Employers who are subject to Public Act 453 may apply to the Michigan Civil Rights Commission for an exemption on the basis that religion, national origin, age, height, weight, or sex is a bona fide occupational qualification essential to the normal operation of the business or enterprise. Upon sufficient showing by the employer, the Commission may grant an exemption. An employer may have a bona fide occupational qualification on the basis of religion, national origin, sex or marital status, height and weight without obtaining prior exemption from the Commission, provided that an employer who

Table 19–1: Michigan Pre-employment Inquiry Guide, *continued*

does not obtain an exemption shall have the burden of establishing that the qualification is reasonably necessary or essential to the normal operation of the business. In the absence of *business necessity,* a selection criterion should not be used if it has a disproportionately burdensome effect, or disparate impact, upon those of a particular race, color, national origin, sex, age, marital status, height, weight, or the handicapped.

2. Exceptions to the list of unlawful questions are permitted by applicable federal *law* or by rules promulgated by the Michigan Civil Rights Commission, including rules relating to affirmative action plans if approved by the Commission. Upon application to the Commission, employers may be permitted to make pre-employment inquiries prohibited by Public Acts 220 and 453 for purposes not inconsistent with the Constitution and Statutes.

3. It is unlawful to make or use a written or oral inquiry or form of application that elicits information concerning the handicap of a prospective employee for reasons contrary to the provisions or purposes of Act 220.

Source: Michigan Department of Civil Rights, State of Michigan Plaza Building, 1200 Sixth Avenue, Detroit, Michigan 48226

number of on-site interviews because of expense. You will probably be one of three to five persons being considered for an opening.

Letters are appropriate for

- confirming plans for an on-site visit (Figure 19–4)
- declining an on-site visit
- acknowledging an on-site visit (Figure 19–5)
- acknowledging a job offer (Figure 19–6)
- accepting a job offer (Figure 19–7)
- declining a job offer

Keeping an Application Active

Someone must be rejected when two or more people compete for the same job. If you do not receive a job offer after one or more interviews with an organization, and you are still interested in working for that organization, let the personnel people know. Ask them to keep your application in their active files. They have already certified you as being the kind of person they want to hire. It is just a matter of finding the right place for you.

That may take time, however, and you may make another choice before that opening occurs. Upon accepting a job, you should

If you do not receive a job offer but are still interested in the organization, ask that your application be kept in their active files.

Date

Individual's Name
Title
Organization
Street
City, State, Zip Code

Dear (Name):

Thank you for your ____(date)____ letter offering me a
plant/office visit. You suggested that 8:00 a.m. on March
27, 28, or 29, or __(date)__ would be most convenient for
you.

Friday, March 29 is the best day for me. I am looking
forward to seeing you at your office at 8:00 as requested.

(Include any other information about the visit that is
appropriate, such as details about tickets, enclosed
application, requests for other details.)

I am eager to learn more about career opportunities at
_____and look forward to meeting with
you.

Sincerely,

(Written signature)

(Typed Signature)
Address

Figure 19–4: On-site Visit Arrangements

September 20, 1981

H. A. Birkness, Project Engineer
Amoco Chemicals Corporation
200 East Randolph Drive
Chicago, IL 60680

Dear Mr. Birkness:

Thank you for the opportunity to visit Amoco to discuss
company activities and my qualifications. I'm tremendously
impressed and eager to hear your decision.

As you requested, I have enclosed a record and the receipts
for my visit on _____(date)_____.

The building is magnificent--its architecture, location,
facilities. But even better are the people. Dave Mergler
and John Moser shared their enthusiasm for Amoco and made
me feel at home. They convinced me that Amoco is a great
place to work. I know now I'd like to be involved in the
energy research.

I certainly appreciate the visit. It has convinced me to
place Amoco first on my career list. I look forward to
your reply.

Cordially,

John R. Culligan
828 Sunset Drive
Oshkosh, ID 83544

Enclosure: Incidental travel expense receipts

Figure 19–5: Site Visit Acknowledgment and Reinbursement for Expenses

Date

Individual's Name
Title
Organization
Street
City, State, Zip Code

Dear (Name):

Thank you very much for your letter of ____(date)_____
offering me employment as _____(state title and terms).

I am very interested in your offer, and I appreciate your
giving me time to consider before I make my decision. I
want to make a choice that will be most beneficial to both
of us and I will respond on or before __(date mentioned in
employer's letter__.

Your confidence in me and my ability is very much appreciated.

Sincerely,

(Written Signature)

(Typed Signature)
Address

Figure 19–6: Thank-you Letter for Job Offer

```
Date


Individual's Name
Title
Organization
Street
City, State, Zip Code

Dear (Name):

I am pleased to accept your offer for employment as (state
position offered    .  I am pleased with the terms outlined
in your letter of    (date)   , (describe the rest of the
terms).

(Describe any enclosures, application blank, employee forms,
expense account forms, or other comments.)

Your company/organization offers excellent opportunities in
my area of interest, and I am looking forward to the chal-
lenges of beginning a career with    (organization)   .

Sincerely,

(Written Signature)

(Typed Signature)
Address
```

Figure 19–7: Employment Acceptance

contact any organization that is considering your application, informing them of your employment decision. Maintain as much good will as possible. Five or ten years from now, you may again want to be considered for work with that organization.

ASSIGNMENT: THE EMPLOYMENT INTERVIEW

1. Review the questions that you should expect to be asked during an employment interview. (See pages 379–381.) In writing, briefly and succinctly answer each question. In some cases, you will have to invent an answer. Do so with an eye toward getting the job.
2. What should you say to the interviewer if
   a. you prefer not to answer a personal question
   b. there is a pause in the conversation
   c. you are asked your opinion of a former employer
   d. you realize you have answered a question incorrectly, made a mistake?
3. Write a confirmation letter to the person in an organization who has invited you for an on-site interview.
4. Write a letter accepting a job offer.
5. Suppose that after two interviews you are turned down for a position in an organization that you would still like to work for. Write a letter asking that your application be kept in their organization's active file.

FURTHER READING

Benjamin, Alfred, *The Helping Interview.* Boston: Houghton Mifflin, 1974.

Conducting the Lawful Employment Interview. New York: Executive Enterprises, 1979.

Downs, Cal W. et al., *The Organizational Communicator.* New York: Harper & Row, 1977.

Downs, Cal W. et al., *Professional Interviewing.* New York: Harper & Row, 1980.

Fear, Richard A. *The Evaluation Interview,* 2nd ed. New York: McGraw-Hill, 1978.

Gorden, Raymond L. *Interviewing: Strategy, Techniques and Tactics.* Homewood, IL: Dorsey, 1975.

Maier, Norman R. *The Appraisal Interview: Three Basic Approaches.* San Diego, CA: University Associates, 1976.

Stewart, Charles J. and William A. Cash, Jr. *Interviewing Principles and Practices.* Dubuque, IA: Wm. C. Brown, 1974.

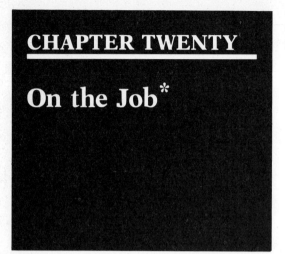

CHAPTER TWENTY

On the Job*

"The brain is a wonderful organ; it starts working the moment you get up in the morning and does not stop until you get into the office."

Robert Frost

When you report for work to begin your new job, you may have an opportunity to participate in an orientation program, also called vestibule training. The program may last only an hour or so, or it may cover a week or several months, with your being moved from department to department or branch to branch.

During your orientation, or soon after you begin work, someone—the supervisor or an employee from the personnel department—will describe company policies, programs, performance appraisal, probation and evaluation periods, and other services and benefits.

BENEFITS

Because benefits cost the employer money, the number and scope of benefits vary widely from organization to organization. Benefits are figured as part of your wage, even though you may not take advantage of all of them. The benefits offered by most companies are equal to an additional 35 to 40 percent of an employee's annual gross pay.

Standard benefits offered by your employer may include

• retirement programs—social security and/or other pension plans

*Written in collaboration with Mary C. Thompson, Alumni Relations and Communications Coordinator, Purdue University, School of Nursing, West Lafayette, Indiana.

- paid holidays—federal and state
- sick leave—varying lengths, paid and unpaid
- insurance programs—medical, maternity, dental, eye, major medical; paid by company or partially paid or at rates lower than individual policies
- vacations—length based on tenure with company
- funeral, military, jury duty leaves

Other benefits may include

- education—reimbursement for classes related to your work and/or leave, paid and unpaid
- personal leave without pay—for extended absences but with job retention
- incentive pay for performance
- stock options
- credit unions
- travel allowances
- expense accounts
- housing allowances
- bonus programs
- company vehicles for employment and personal use
- cafeterias
- day care
- free parking
- employee lounges, recreation areas, recreation facilities
- tools
- eye glasses
- counseling—financial, family, alcohol, and drug related

These benefits are often described in a policies and procedures manual, sometimes called the "company bible." You may be given a copy of this manual, which may also contain samples of organizational forms with instructions on how to fill them out and submit them. The manual may define company policy on vacation and sick leave, as well as provide other often requested information. The policies and procedures manual serves as a rule of reference when questions arise regarding employment, and it allows the personnel department to offer uniform responses to employees throughout the organization.

Employee benefits are often explained in an organization's policies and procedures manual.

Payroll accounting is regulated by federal and state requirements. Federal and state taxes are automatically withheld from your paycheck on the basis of the gross amount of your annual pay and your tax-filing status. Before you receive your first check, you

Federal and state income taxes are withheld from the employee's salary.

will be required to complete a W-2 form stating the number of dependents you claim for income tax purposes.

Social Security Benefits

Social security payments are also withheld from the employee's salary, and equal amounts are paid by the employer.

Federal law also requires that employers withhold a percentage of your wage to cover your social security benefits. An equal amount is paid directly by the employer. Social security benefits are intended to provide you with income after you retire. Since the enactment of the social security system, many other benefits have been added. The benefits now include monthly payments to spouses and dependent children in the event of your death before retirement, disability pay if doctors certify that you are unable to work, extended medical benefits after retirement, and others. However, these benefits are available only after you have fulfilled the minimum work period requirements set by the Social Security Administration. They are not automatically yours.

Pension Plans

Most companies have their own pension programs.

The federal social security system is not the only pension or retirement plan available. Government and state employees and most other organizations have additional pension plans. You may have the option, too, of participating in both the social security system and another pension plan outside your organization. You may be eligible to receive retirement benefits from tax shelters such as *individual retirement annuities* (IRA) or *Keogh* plans if you are self-employed or work for an organization that does not withhold retirement benefits from your wage.

These tax shelters allow you to deposit up to 15 percent of your gross income not covered under a pension plan into a tax-exempt savings account or insurance plan. You will, however, have to pay income tax on the money when it is withdrawn from the plan upon your retirement. The Keogh plan is designed specifically for self-employed persons or persons who are partners or principals in organizations. IRA programs are for people who work part-time or have a second income not covered by retirement benefits. These programs do not provide the supplemental benefits available under the social security program.

Caution: Be sure to inquire about your "vested" interests in a company pension plan. *Vesting* is defined as "the retention of an entitlement to money you and/or the employer have contributed to a retirement fund." Funds may "vest immediately" or be subject to "delayed vesting."

With immediate vesting, you retain this entitlement from the very first time you contribute to a program. With delayed vesting, you must fulfill certain service/age requirements, depending on the company, before you are entitled to the employer's contribution. Service requirements range from one month to many years. Age requirements are equally diverse.

Counseling Services

As part of their benefit programs, some organizations offer a variety of counseling services. You may seek counseling for financial planning, marital problems, or alcohol- or drug-related problems.

The counseling or "helping" interview is designed to help you define your difficulties and review alternatives to solve problems. Trained counselors discuss options at your request; they should not advise or direct you to take a specific course of action. They serve as confidential listeners to help you weigh the consequences of each alternative and support your course of action.

Some companies offer the employee a number of free counseling services.

PERFORMANCE APPRAISAL OR REVIEW[*]

On the job, you will probably receive regular performance appraisals. New employees are sometimes reviewed at the end of 90 days, after six months, and then annually. Depending on organizational policy, promotion and pay increases may be based entirely or in part upon the supervisor's evaluation of your work determined by performance appraisal.

The performance appraisal interview is difficult for most supervisors to conduct satisfactorily and in an objective way. Appraisal forms have been developed to help keep the evaluation job related and focused on employment objectives. The interview is usually scheduled in advance and held behind closed doors. How long the interview lasts will vary, depending on work relationships.

Your performance may be evaluated on the basis of production units, preestablished objectives or goals reached during a predetermined time, or on the basis of specific improvements in skills or additional educational experience. A good appraisal interview

The performance appraisal is a review of how well the employee is doing his or her job.

*We are indebted to Donna Stine, Assistant Professor of English, Iowa State University, for assistance and research on performance appraisals and evaluations.

centers around job performance. Your supervisor may describe areas in which your performance is above average, average, and below average.

During this interview, you should have an opportunity to discuss your supervisor's expectations, your employment concerns, suggestions for improving your personal performance and goals and timetables for accomplishing those goals. The interview should be future oriented, motivating you to become a better employee.

Management by objective is a technique that allows the employee and supervisor to set mutually agreed upon goals for the employee.

The performance appraisal technique known as *management by objective* is widely used in many different forms by trained management personnel. Commonly referred to as M.B.O., the technique allows the supervisor and the employee to set mutually agreed upon goals and objectives. A timetable for accomplishing the goals is also agreed upon. The goals are reviewed periodically and adjusted if appropriate. This appraisal method is intended to be less threatening than one in which the employee is measured against a uniform organizational standard without appropriate input from the employee.

At the conclusion of most performance appraisal interviews, you, the employee, are asked to review any evaluation forms and notes made by your supervisor. You may be asked to sign the evaluation sheets(s) to indicate that you have seen the material that will be held in your personnel file. Your signature does not necessarily mean that you agree with your supervisor's evaluation. If you feel it does not fairly represent your performance, you have the option of requesting another review within a short period or instigating grievance procedures. Information about this is usually available in your company procedures manual. Appraisal evaluations are confidential, seen only by your supervisor and authorized administrators. Figure 20–1 illustrates one performance appraisal form.

Should your performance appraisal result in your receiving a written reprimand for any reason, usually for violation of company policy or failure to perform, the information is held in your personnel file. The number of reprimands necessary for dismissal varies from organization to organization.

Termination can be the result of reprimand, or it can result from an employee's misrepresentation, giving of false information, theft, sexual misconduct on the job, or physical assault of another employee. Termination can also result from the elimination of the position you hold, layoff, or other business reasons. Most employers are very reluctant to fire an employee. Documentation made during performance appraisals is used to support cause of dismissal to avoid legal consequences.

**HYDRO-TRANSMISSION
SUPERVISORY/MANAGEMENT
EMPLOYEE PERFORMANCE APPRAISAL**

NAME: _____ CLOCK #: _____ DIVISION: _____ DEPT.: _____ DATE: _____

PRESENT CLASSIFICATION: _____ TYPE OF APPRAISAL: ☐ SEMI-ANNUAL ☐ SPECIAL
☐ ANNUAL

PART I. Job Performance-Indicate Appropriate Response and Explain Reasons for each Rating.

OVERALL EFFECTIVENESS: Consider ability to achieve results and meet predetermined goals.		
Has not met goals established and results achieved are unsatisfactory.	Has met the various goals established and overall results are satisfactory.	Has surpassed goals established and results have exceeded expectations.

Describe for the rating period this employee's objectives, degree of completion and effectiveness of results:

NOTE: Use additional sheets if necessary.

PLANNING AND ORGANIZING: Effectiveness in achieving maximum utilization of time and assets considering the impact of schedules, deadlines, priorities and outside pressures.				
Is disorganized; has difficulty planning even routine activity.	Generally effective in planning routine activities; has difficulty organizing new or varied activities.	Plans most activity well; may require assistance on new or unusual assignments.	Consistently able to plan and organize all activities assigned.	Displays exceptional ability to plan and organize all activities assigned.

Comments: _____

LEADERSHIP—Effectiveness in bringing a group to accomplish a task and in getting ideas accepted.				
Sets a poor example; lacks enthusiasm and interest; has difficulty inspiring subordinates.	Often exhibits lack of enthusiasm and interest; has difficulty inspiring subordinates.	Generally sets a good example; may have difficulty sustaining subordinate interest.	Consistently generates and sustains interest and enthusiasm in subordinates	Sets an excellent example; displays an exceptional ability to generate interest and enthusiasm.

Comments: _____

USE OF DELEGATION—Ability to effectively use subordinates and to understand where a decision can best be made.				
Seldom delegates; tends to do the work himself.	Reluctant to delegate other than minor responsibilities.	Normally effective in delegating responsibilities.	Consistently delegates well and utilizes subordinate talent.	Displays exceptional ability to delegate and fully utilize subordinate talent.

Comments: _____

Heuss Printing--80024A

Figure 20–1: Performance Appraisal Form

There is a direct cost to employers who fire employees. Unemployment insurance is available to workers who are dismissed or laid off jobs. The cost of unemployment benefits is usually borne by the employer in a ratio dependent on the number of employees, the number of claims, and other state requirements. It may run between 1 and 5 percent of the employer's wage total, and the money is paid to the state and held for claim by former employees. *Employees who resign voluntarily are not eligible for unemployment benefits.*

In some organizations, the supervisor is asked to make pay raise recommendations based on merit, while the personnel department at the same time establishes a base, across-the-board rate increase for all employees. The increases may be tied to government cost-of-living indexes with a small percentage of total available wage funds designated for merit increases. To avoid discrimination, many organizations offer annual announced percentage increases for all employees. Increases or decreases above and below the announced percentage are used to inform the employees about how their personal performance is viewed by the supervisor.

Salary increases may be based on merit, across-the-board raises, cost-of-living indexes, or a combination of these.

A wide variety of incentive pay plans are used by organizations to increase productivity, improve quality control, and increase personal achievement. These incentives include *annual bonuses, sales commissions, production quotas*, and *reimbursement for educational achievements* obtained away from the job.

CHANGING JOBS

Statistics indicate that you may change jobs three times within the first five years after you leave school. Recent research shows the crossing of occupational boundaries—even by those technically trained—occurs with greater ease than customarily thought. Skills and abilities acquired through higher education and work experience have many applications beyond those initially perceived.

Today's employees are changing jobs more frequently and easily than ever before.

Many personnel departments conduct termination interviews when you resign or accept employment elsewhere. Turnover rates among corporate personnel indicate the amount of employee satisfaction or dissatisfaction. High termination rates may be the result of low pay scales, bad company policy, poor location, or a variety of other factors. Exit interviews are used to locate areas of discontent and alleviate problems.

As you progress in your career, you'll find that some companies always try to fill their top executive positions by promotions from within the firm. Others advertise and have executives talk to friends in other companies.

Increasingly, however, large organizations turn to *professional executive search firms* (*MBA*, pp. 17–27). These are either branches of management consulting or accounting firms or independent operations. In either case, the search firm works for the company doing the hiring and not for the candidate. It is not an employment agency. Search firms charge a fee plus expenses for each assignment—as much as 25 to 30 percent of the successful candidate's total first-year salary.

Executive search firms are being used by many organizations to fill upper-level job openings.

People who call or write to inquire about possible openings rarely match the exact requirements of any search in progress. However, the search firm usually puts the "transom" candidate's résumé into its research file, pulling it when a search calls for someone with those particular talents. ("Transom" or "over the transom" refers to unsolicited material of any kind—résumés, articles, books—sent to an *agency* for consideration without a previous letter of inquiry. "Cold turkey" is another popular term referring, in particular, to résumés and applications sent to possible *employers* for consideration without a previous interview or similar contact.)

Computers may be used for both a talent search and a job search. Registering your combination of talents, experience, and education in a computer bank will make you eligible for consideration.

PROFESSIONAL RÉSUMÉS

The résumé you prepare for your initial employment may be used, with your permission, by the company personnel department for a variety of purposes after you begin your employment. It may be included with contract proposals, requests for bids on construction, architectural and engineering contracts, and to document other professional activities.

Many companies use an employee's résumé to support their strength when seeking contracts.

Your résumé may also be used as the basis for introductions for speaking engagements, news releases, training sessions, and other public or community functions. Although the content will not change, the format may be altered for specific needs.

Business résumés are intended to demonstrate teamwork and group strength among the people who will be responsible for projects. Effective résumés, attached to government or industry Requests for Proposals (RFPs) (Chapter 14) in the fields of engineering, architecture, and technology, are presented on the organization's letterhead stationery. They are designed to be persuasive, to support the organization's strengths. They include

- person's name, title, company, location
- person's experience
- person's education

Experience is the most important feature of the professional résumé, which should be updated regularly.

Experience is considered the most important feature of the professional résumé. Begin with the most recent, relevant work and include similar jobs and specialized knowledge. Update your résumé regularly to include significant recent professional achievements.

LOOKING TOWARD THE FUTURE

As you gain experience and tenure in the employment world, you may become a supervisor, possibly an employer. You may be called upon to interview, to evaluate, to hire, and to dismiss employees. You may be required to communicate orally and in writing the results of your decisions. You may spend your days learning and using many of the applications noted by the writers of the following diaries.

Knowing and practicing the principles of good business communication will help you become a more productive, more confident professional.

COMMUNICATION DIARIES

Someone has written, "An experience to be experienced must be experienced, not just read about." But with these diaries, you will look into the daily lives of men and women working in many occupations. You will "meet" busy administrators and conscientious professionals. You will see how varied are their communication experiences—and how vital.

How do these logs apply to you?

If you are a student or a professional you can compare and contrast your expectations with reality. Reading the dairies may tilt your interest away from one profession and toward another. Reading them may suggest a new direction or new activities. Most of all, you will recognize the importance of the individual and of communication in business.

Public Relations Director—Insurance

```
Marjane Cloke
Director of Public Relations
MONY (Mutual of New York)
1740 Broadway
New York, NY  10019
```

Here's a "day in the life of Marjane," and it was kind of fun, not only doing it...but seeing how many crazy things I can get involved in in one day. Funny, you know you do these things, but never actually put it down in black and white to take a look at....In just that day I made use of my knowledge of

- newspapers--layout and art
- figures in establishing the yearly budget
- public speaking--in two fields--letter writing and secretarial science
- scholarship program for coporation--and art competition
- printing--and what's involved in producing material
- contribution program and how it's administered
- handling a golf tournament
- writing job descriptions
- dealing with TV networks
- community programs that MONY might become involved in
- selecting gifts for management
- heading up a women's organization

TODAY

8:00 a.m.   Meeting with Editor of MONY News (employee newspaper) to discuss layout, art, and captions for special supplement announcing results of Employee Opinion Survey.

8:30   Worked on figures for 1979 budget request to Management.

9:45   Dictation--

            Accepted invitation to speak at Life Underwriters' Convention in Honolulu

in March 19__--subject, "Modern
Business-letter Writing."

Confirmed by letter, phone conversations agreeing to give two talks
for Sales Executives Club in Lansing, Michigan, in May--subjects,
"Modern Business-letter Writing"
and "The Boss and His Secretary."

Wrote to 19 members of MONY Scholastic Art Awards advisory board,
setting up meeting in Syracuse
in October to prepare for 19__
competition.

Acknowledged requests from three
organizations that were requesting
monetary contributions from MONY.

9:55   Telephone call interruption. Call
        from advertising agency in New
        York, requesting historical infor-
        mation about the American Council
        of Life Insurance.

10:00   Back to dictation--

        Congratulatory letters to three
        students (children of MONY employ-
        ees) who have just been named semi-
        finalists in the National Merit
        Scholarship Program. Reminded them
        of qualifications to be met in or-
        der to qualify to receive MONY-
        sponsored scholarships--if they
        become finalists.

10:02   Telephone call interruption. Call
        from Assistant to President to dis-
        cuss request from Boy Scouts to
        print their campaign material.

10:05   Visit from Director of Consumer Re-
        search to discuss changes in art in
        the MONY News supplement of Employee
        survey results.

10:10   Back to dictation--once more--

Memo to Chairman of the Board, giving facts and figures on producing fund-raising material for Boy Scouts.

Memo to Executive Vice-President concerning amount of purse for the 19__ MONY Tournament of Champions. (Golf tournament held at La Costa, California, sponsored by MONY-- supervised by Director of Public Relations)

Memo to Personnel Director re writing a job description for new Public Relations Assistant in Syracuse office.

10:30   Discussion with PGA (Professional Golfers Association) official, Publicity Director, Advertising Agency Vice-President concerning change in telecast network from ABC to NBC for the 19__ MONY Tournament of Champions.

11:30   Meeting with couple from Massachusetts who are looking for help from a corporation in establishing a home for juveniles (14 to 18 years of age) who are minor offenders-- but who, without suitable accommodations, are put in with hard-core criminals. They are asking MONY to consider putting up money for a down-payment on farm property-- plus a yearly stipend to complement funds provided for each child by the state.

12:30 p.m. Lunch with MONY officers to select woman executive at MONY to be honored by the YWCA Academy of Women Achievers.

1:00   Dictation--

Invitations to MONY Officers to
attend 4-Day Letter Writing Seminar in November.

Reply to Advertising Manager of
British Airways for samples of letters used in my talks.

Letter by YWCA nominating our second Vice-President--Actuary (MONY's
first woman executive) to Academy
of Women Achievers.

Analysis of request from National
Choral Council to sponsor "Sing-
Ins" around the country.

1:30   Went to Tiffany & Company to select gifts for Chairman of Board
to present to the chairmen of his
United Way committees.

2:15   Phoned Account Executive at public
relations agency in Syracuse that
handles MONY account, to discuss

possible use of Charles Ives (com-
poser) film at Syracuse University

developing four-page newspaper to
go to all junior and senior high
school students in Central New York
--entirely devoted to the 19__ MONY/
Scholastic Art Awards

details of Syracuse Volunteer Fair
to be held at MONY Plaza in October, including TV and newspaper
coverage

possible MONY sponsorship of New
York State High School Soccer com-
petitions to be held at Syracuse
University in late November

2:55   Telephone call with Sister Francis
Agnew, Chairwoman of Advisory Committee for MONY/Scholastic Air Program, concerning resignation of one

member of Committee and possible
replacement.

3:10   Editor of "The Actuary," monthly
         newsletter of the Society of Actu-
         aries, stopped by to leave material
         for next issue. (Production of
         publication is handled through me.)

3:20   Call from Director of Personnel in
         Syracuse office concerning new
         article on possible "merger" of
         Carrier Corporation and United
         Technologies...and its effect on
         the city of Syracuse.

3:30   Met with Senior Vice-President--
         Mass Marketing re possible invitees
         to the 19__ MONY Tournament of
         Champions.

3:45   Completed copy and layout for invi-
         tations to be sent to New York
         Executives to attend dinner party
         being given by New York Chapter,
         Executive Women International.
         Sent to printer to set.

4:30   Prepared this agency for Professor
         Feinberg.

5:30   Chaired monthly dinner/business
         meeting of New York Chapter, Exec-
         utive Women International, of which
         I am President.

10:30   HOME!

Communications Include

layout, art, captions for employee newspaper
data processing
letters (all kinds)
board meetings
memos
newspaper releases
job descriptions
public speaking

```
financial planning
dictation
telephone
agenda
reports
TV releases, planning
interviewing
community relations
policy making/planning
```

Electrical Engineer

```
Wayne L. Moser
Senior Project Engineer
Amoco Chemicals Corporation
200 E. Randolph Drive
Chicago, IL  60680
```

I. Business Communication Areas

    A. Contractors

        1. Write specifications describing work contractors are to perform. Specifications should be clear and concise and not subject to various interpretations.

        2. Provide written comments pertaining to engineering drawings prepared by contractor, including deviation from the specifications.

        3. Oral discussion with contractor's engineers, relating to job requirements.

    B. Manufacturers

        1. Write specifications for the purchase of equipment.

        2. Provide written comments relating to proposals and drawings, indicating deviation from the specifications.

3. Oral discussion with manufacturer's engineers, relating to specific equipment requirements, problems with equipment already provided, and technical merits of new or improved products.

C. Amoco Manufacturing Plants

1. Prepare memorandums relating to plant technical problems.

2. Oral discussion by phone or in personal meetings with plant engineers relating to technical problems.

D. New employees

1. Check letters, specifications, and drawings for technical content and clear expression.

2. Oral discussion of job requirements

E. Institute of Electrical and Electronic Engineers (IEEE)

1. Write letters to technical paper authors relating to paper content and rules for preparation and presentation.

2. Prepare meeting minutes and written comments on various documents such as bylaws.

3. Write letters to IEEE headquarters about operations in my area of responsibility.

4. Oral discussion with authors, IEEE officers, committees.

F. Manufacturing Chemists Association (MCA)

1. Work with the National Electrical Code (NEC) Task Group of the MCA

to prepare written proposals for
NEC revisions and written comments
of NEC proposals by others that
affect the chemical industry.

2. Represent the MCA at meetings of
the NEC Committee to present oral
arguments relation to MCA positions on NEC proposals.

Communications Include

specifications for contractors
comments on engineering plans
purchasing specifications
memos
staff conference
client conferences
personnel relations
technical papers
proposals
speeches
professional conferences
letters:
   inquiry
   comment
   disappointing
   persuasive
   instructional
meeting minutes
agenda
professional editing

Executive Secretary

Betty Wooden, CPS (Certified Professional
   Secretary)
PSI Publications Review Representative
Professional Secretaries International
440 Pershing Road
Kansas City, MO 64108

Typical Day of a Secretary
in a Regional Sales Office

1. Check "to do" list made previous evening.

2. Cross-check appointment calendars of
    executive, assistant, and secretary.
    Ensure that executive's desk is out-
    fitted with working materials needed
    for the day--pens, clips, paper, spe-
    cial files, etc. Review important
    appointments, phone calls, and reports
    of the day with executive.

3. Open mail; distribute to executive and
    assistant. If answer required, attach
    files.

4. Check computer reports on inventories
    and sales of new product; prepare com-
    parative analysis for executive's re-
    view; type master and run copies for
    distribution to interested departments.

5. Discuss sales contest with executive;
    transcribe (rough draft) shorthand notes
    on proposed contest rules; double-check
    with executive and make necessary
    changes. Type master and run copies
    for all sales managers.

6. Transcribe machine dictation; make
    photocopies of data to be attached.

7. Call Houston office manager regarding
    late reports!

8. Remind executive of luncheon appointment
    with Mr. Anderson.

9. Analyze sales records for each branch;
    establish sales forecast for next year
    (by months); prepare master sheet for
    executive and self. Write individual
    letters to each sales manager, request-
    ing that he acknowledge receipt and ad-
    vise his plans for meeting the forecast.

10. Remind managers (by letter) of due date
    for submitting expense budgets.

11. Check airline schedules for executive's
    trip to Chicago; call airline and make

reservations; TWX Chicago manager to make hotel reservations and meet executive at airport.

12. Call hotel and make arrangements for sales meeting on the 20th; select menu; arrange for audiovisual equipment to show film; type list of attendees; reproduce copies for each; print name tags; type executive's speech (from machine dictation, handwritten notes, etc.). Type agenda and mail copies to each who will attend.

13. Prepare voucher and request accounting office to issue expense check.

14. Process employment papers on new sales trainee in Dallas.

15. Check data on salary request form for sales representative in Phoenix; make necessary corrections; have executive sign and forward to personnel department.

16. Phone call from St. Louis office manager--he is confused regarding budget data and productivity reports; explain correct procedure.

17. Phone call from unhappy customer--refer to Distribution Manager.

18. Write note to Tulsa manager requesting explanation for unusually high expenses on repairs to delivery equipment.

19. Call florist to order flowers for Joe Smith's wife (in hospital for surgery).

20. Type up purchase order for new company car for executive (check with dealer on optional equipment, colors available, probable delivery date, etc.)

21. Ask Sam Jones to pick up samples of new competitive product; have shipping clerk

pack and mail to Marketing Department in headquarters.

22.   Read and annotate trade publications (newspapers, magazines, journals). Call executive's particular attention to article in Wall Street Journal concerning financial difficulties of XYX Company. Call accounting department to find our account's current balance due us; request them to keep a close watch to minimize possible losses if account files bankruptcy.

23.   Check executive's calendar to see if he will be available Friday for luncheon with his broker; call broker's secretary to confirm time and place.

24.   Compose letter to Austin sales manager congratulating him for exceeding quota on special promotion.

25.   Call PSI Attendance Committee chairperson to make reservations for dinner meeting next Wednesday evening.

26.   Place outgoing mail in envelopes; run through postage meter.

27.   File material accumulated during day from executive's outbasket and from the day's business. Sort other material for routing or further action.

28.   Make "to do" list for next day.

Communications Include

transcribing shorthand notes, handwritten
  notes, machine dictation
sending teletype (TWX) messages
receiving and placing phone calls
analyzing sales records
abstracting publications
organizing sales meetings
processing employment papers
interpreting computer printouts

personal (executive) services--liaison
  between executive and public staff
letters
vouchers
purchase orders
memos
agenda
preparing reports (typed or handwritten,
  using calculator/adding machine
typing duplicator masters

Attorney

Robert L. Byman
Jenner & Block
One IBM Plaza
Chicago, IL 60611

As an attorney specializing in commercial litigation, it is impossible to define a "typical" day. Moreover, it is difficult to even generalize, since every case required different functions, skills, and activities, and I may be working on as many as two dozen matters contemporaneously. It is fair to say, however, that nearly me entire practice involves the art of communication, by face-to-face contact, telephone, and the written word.

My job is to assimilate facts and legal principles (through communication from others) and communicate that data to a judge or an adversary to reach a solution to a problem.

Following is a list of the types of tasks I might generally perform in a year, with an approximate number of hours assigned to indicate the relative time devoted to each general category. In a typical year, my hours would total between 2,100 and 2,500.

1. Trials (50 hours)
    a. Jury trials
    b. Bench trials

2. Immediate Preparation for Trial
    (250 hours)

a. Preparation of witnesses
b. Draft of arguments; rehearsal
c. Legal research; review of other
    attorney's research
d. Interviews with clients, potential
    witnesses
e. Office conferences with other
    attorneys and paralegals
f. Communications with opposing coun-
    sel (telephone, correspondence,
    personal meetings)
g. Organization and review of
    documents
h. Preparation of exhibits
i. Preparation of jury instructions,
    legal memorandums, briefs
j. Reports to clients

3. General Pretrial Preparation
    (1,200 hours)
    a. Interviews with potential
        friendly witnesses
    b. Physical inspection of
        facilities
    c. Conferences with clients;
        reports to clients
    d. Depositions of adverse and
        third-party witnesses
    e. Preparation and defense of
        client depositions
    f. Other discovery
        (1) Interrogatories
        (2) Production and review of
             documents
    g. Argument of pretrial motions,
        status calls, pretrial confer-
        ences, other court appearances
    h. Draft and review of briefs,
        pretrial orders
    i. Conferences with opposing
        counsel
    j. Interoffice conferences with
        attorneys, paralegals
    k. Legal research; review of other
        attorneys' research
    l. Correspondence

4. Appellate Practice (200 hours)
   a. Draft and review of briefs (including research)
   b. Preparation for argument
   c. Oral argument

5. Office Practice (200 hours)
   a. Client interviews
   b. Correspondence
   c. Draft of contracts, other documents
   d. Preparation of opinion letters, memoranduma

6. Miscellaneous (400 hours)
   a. Administrative duties
      (1) Assignment of young lawyers for research, cases
      (2) Organization of firm parties
      (3) Interviews with law students
      (4) Office meetings
   b. Bar Association activities
   c. Continuing legal education
      (1) Attendance at seminars
      (2) Writing of articles; speaking at seminars
   d. Travel

Communications Include

briefs
depositions
memos
interviews
client relations
writing instructions
journal articles
travel
telephone
letters
research reports
staff meetings
contracts, wills, etc.
speeches
consulting with other attorneys and
   paralegals

Financial Specialist

```
Lloyd A. Bettis
Financial Services Officer
The Northern Trust Company
50 South La Salle Street
Chicago, IL  60675
```

Daily Activities, October 23, 19__

1. Morning Coffee: Discussion with farm man-
    agers (Trust Department) regarding near-
    term outlook for cattle market.

2. Phone: Returned call to broker at Paine,
    Webber, Jackson and Curtis. Discussed
    details of a new agricultural leasing
    corporation he was familiar with in North
    Dakota that is looking for a relationship
    with a larger bank. I committed to fol-
    lowing up with company directly on Octo-
    ber 24.

3. Financial Analysis: Completed financial
    analysis of company where we have an
    $8,000,000 commitment. Overall operation
    of company looks good. Liquidity, capi-
    talization, and coverage of debt are ade-
    quate. Analysis forwarded to my depart-
    ment head.

4. Luncheon: Discussion centered around the
    coordination of agriculturally related
    activities between Banking Department and
    Trust Department. The lack of proper com-
    munication in the past has resulted in
    lost new business opportunities for both
    departments. As an officer of the Banking
    Department, I am to serve as a liaison be-
    tween the Banking Department and the Trust
    Department and am to explore ways to im-
    prove on the exchange of leads and ideas.

5. Budgeting of Expenses: Reviewed budget
    with department head for special events
    (luncheons, conferences, etc.) on an
    actual-to-budget basis. Since I was over
    the budget, I had to justify the addi-
    tional expenses to be sure Northern was

getting its money's worth. Task accomplished.

6. Meeting Schedules: At the request of a new Trust executive, I scheduled a meeting with one of his customers to discuss his farming situation and areas of mutual interest.

7. Personal Dinner Engagement: Called Kathy (wife) to determine whether we were free to join a new Trust executive and his wife for dinner on Saturday night at their home. Received go-ahead.

8. Material Mailed: Sent information on hedging feeder cattle requested by young farmer in Iowa that works with one of our correspondent banks.

9. Financial Analysis: Initiated an analysis of another borrowing customer. Gathered information using our business files and our corporate library. Actual analysis will span three to five days.

10. Evening Meeting: Attended Chicago Farmers' dinner meeting. Program featured marketing experts who spoke on "The Importance of Understanding BASIS." During the dinner, I visited with a present bank customer regarding our overall commitment to the Agri-Business Industry.

Job Description

The primary responsibility of a credit analyst is to monitor the financial status of corporations that are borrowing customers. The purpose is to assure that a company remains financially sound and is in a position to honor terms of their loan agreement. In this regard, the financial reports of the company, along with other information, is analyzed to determine the income-generating capacity of the company, their liquidity position, and the level of capitalization.

The analysis is utilized by the account officer and loan committee in determining our
future commitment to the company.

In addition to credit responsibility, the
Financial Analysis Division (Credit Department) serves as the training and development
area for new account officers. In my case,
this is an interim assignment in preparation
for a career as an account officer with primary responsibility in the agricultural lending area. Once assigned, I will be working
with both our commercial accounts as well as
our correspondent banks in the Midwest.

Job History

Following graduation in 1970 from Iowa
State University, I joined Jewel Companies,
Inc., headquartered in Chicago. Working in-
itially in sales and then in sales management,
I found my responsibilities required my mov-
ing to Los Angeles, Chicago, Denver, and San
Diego. These moves were over a period of
4½ years.

My career was moving along well at Jewel
and I really had no desire to leave. However,
early in 1975 a fraternity brother employed by
The Northern Trust Company called and asked
that I consider a career with Northern. After
completing the interviewing process, I decided
to accept a position as Trust Officer. In this
capacity, I solicit the farm management business of absentee landowners in the Midwest for
the Trust Department. I accepted the position
because I thought I would enjoy the reassocia-
tion with agriculture and was sufficiently impressed with the commitment Northern had made
to the area.

After 3½ years in the Trust Department, I
was approached by a senior member of the Banking Department regarding their interest in expanding their agricultural lending area. Because of the opportunity to become involved on
the ground floor of an expanding area, I transferred to the Banking Department on June 1,

1978. My training program will include time
in financial analysis, cash management, operating, and bond departments.

Communications Include

client conferences
financial analyses
liaison work
staff meetings
new employee orientation
training and development
telephone
budget preparation
memos
letters:
  promotion
  information request
  goodwill
  credit
  persuasion
lunch/dinner meetings
inquiry responses

Hospital Dietitian

Patricia Rua, R.D.
Director of Dietary Services
Mary Greeley Memorial Hospital
Ames, IA 50010

Hours

8:00 a.m.-4:30 p.m. (or as needed, till 6:30
p.m. for monthly medical staff; on call for
emergencies

Duties

  1. Meetings:
      a. Staff
            cooks
            food service workers
            supervision
            dietitians

2. Prepare budget and submit it to administration

3. Planning for department

4. Assist with interviewing

5. Sign purchase orders for food, direct purchase requests for equipment

6. Evaluate dietitians and supervisors

7. Attend meetings to keep up-to-date in dietetic field and to summarize meetings

8. Communicate needs of department to administration

9. In-service for employees

10. Approve all menus

11. Responsible for food service to patients and employees

12. Responsible that department conforms to:
    a. State Department of Health regulations
    b. Joint Commission on Accreditation of Hospitals

13. Direct activities with students:
    a. Coordinate Undergraduate Program at Iowa State University
    b. Dietetic Technician Program at Des Moines area Community Colleges

14. Meetings--In-house
    a. Management once a week
    b. Safety once a month

15. Responsible for:
    a. Safety
    b. Infection control
    c. Sanitation
    d. Preventive maintenance
    e. Inspection: receiving and storage of food

16. Time cards signed

17. Develop policies for other departmental
    relationships:
    a. Nursing
    b. Occupational therapy
    c. Social services
    d. Physical therapy
    e. Housekeeping/laundry

Communications Include

staff meetings
employment interviews
policy planning, decisions
agenda
reports
meetings with vendors
inspection (reports/counseling)
personnel relations
telephone
orders
data processing
budget and financial planning
evaluations
teaching/lecturing
memos
research
decision making
counseling
public relations
inventory
letters:
   complaint

Author

Robert Orben
1200 North Nash Street
Arlington, VA 22209

[Bob Orben is editor of "Orben's Current
Comedy," published 24 times yearly, and
"Orben's Comedy Fillers," published 12 times
yearly, as well as 43 books of professional
humor material. (Subscribers to his services

use the material as their own.) He is an active lecturer, and he conducts humor workshops
for corporate speakers, writers, and communicators, teaching the basics of how to make
people laugh.

He's written material for Jack Paar, Red
Skelton, and Dick Gregory and served as a
speechwriter for business and political figures. In January 1976, he was appointed as
Special Assistant to Gerald R. Ford and Director of the White House Speechwriting Department.]

A Typical Work Day

6:00– 8:00 a.m.	Get up. Stagger out to kitchen to plug in electric percolator. Make half-real-half-decaffinated coffee. With first cup, get spurt of crea-tive energy. Revved up. Start reading 40 different newspapers, magazines, and other publications for subject matter. (<u>Washington Post</u>--intensely--<u>U.S. News & World Report</u>, <u>Wall Street Journal</u>, etc.) Feel the flow--write down key words to remember joke. Write it down immediately or it's gone.
8:00	Quick breakfast.
8:15– 11:00	Write jokes for two services, speech, article, or lead-in for speech, using pencil and 8½-by-11 pad. (Electric typewriter upsets creativity--seems to say, "Do some-thing.") Creative energy lasts two to three hours.
11:00– 12:30	Feel ebb of creative energy. Han-dle more immediate correspondence, phone calls.
12:30 p.m.	Lunch
1:15–	More routine writing. Type of

3:15   morning material on IBM electric
        (sometimes dictate). Use quality
        letterhead stationery. Get sen-
        suous pleasure from weight, tex-
        ture of paper. If working with
        client, use audio/videocassette
        to get speech pattern.

5:00   Correspondence, paperwork, phone
        calls. Clear desk daily.

5:00-   Relaxed reading over food (partic-
6:00   ularly Polynesian nibbles) and
        drink. Read books--current, busi-
        ness, economics, etc.

6:30   Watch television network news.

7:30   Dinner out. Movie, theater, PBS
        (Public Broadcasting System)
        afterward.

10:00- Bed. I'm a routinized person.
11:00   Must have seven hours of sleep min-
        imum, eight maximum, or I don't
        function well. Different story
        during White House service!

Communications Include

writing for publication
memos
telephone
instructions
public relations
travel
financial planning
reports
letters (all kinds)
speeches
video/audiocassettes
editing
seminars/workshops
agenda
outlines
dictation

Medical Social Worker

Kay Berger
Mary Greeley Memorial Hospital
Ames, IA 50010

I am a medical social worker in a hospital Social Services Department, sometimes referred to as the Family Counseling Service. Our department consists of a director and two full-time social workers, three part-time social workers, and sometimes as many as three students doing their university practicums.

Physicians send us written referrals. These referrals are often suggested by nurses or others involved with a patient. Services requested vary, usually for "discharge planning" or "support" or (for the Mental Health Unit) "social history." Invariably, the job entails much more than requested on the referral note.

Discharge planning. A social worker takes a record sheet or "fact sheet" and a pink carbon blank, the "consultation note," and goes to the patient's floor. There the worker goes over the patient's chart, noting down on the fact sheet the following: pertinent statistics, address, telephone number, insurance; medical diagnosis, previous medical (mental and surgical) history; social service background. Next follows a visit to the patient.

More information is gathered and documented on the fact sheet: the patient's situation, problems with discharge, significant people in the individual's life. Often the person is elderly; sometimes there is no one of any significant relationship. Sometimes the patient has a family unable to make decisions or understand what is happening. Sometimes, too, the patient must face a nursing home move for the first time.

Whatever the discharge problem, it is seldom simple to the patient.

As a medical social worker, I have to be knowledgeable concerning Medicare, Medicaid, Meals-on-Wheels, Social Services for all counties, Visiting Nurse, Homemakers, and many other services. I explain these to patients and their families and, many times, these make the difference between their going to a nursing home or returning to the family home. All such activities/information from the Social Services Department social worker are noted on the consultation sheet and a copy is placed with the patient's chart as a permanent record.

Support. Referrals vary; many are for terminal cancer or seriously ill patients. Thus support involves family counseling, patient counseling, and a great deal of a social worker's experience and education in dealing with a "death and dying" situation.

Social histories. A referral from the Mental Health Unit requires my contacting the family, usually a cooperative experience. Occasionally, however, patients have to supply these themselves.

With each referral comes a great deal of patient and family contact. Though the referral may state specific problems, a social worker will see the patient daily to talk, care, and act in many helpful ways--for the individual and the family.

Follow-up. Calls or contacts continue after discharge--all noted on the pink permanent record sheet. Sometimes the patient will return in a few days, weeks, or months. The same social worker receives another referral note and continues on the case.

Laws/services. Medicare and Medicaid laws keep changing. Services to alcoholics, mentally retarded, physically and emotionally handicapped, elderly, and drug dependents keep changing. Laws are different in different counties and states. We constantly update our knowledge and services.

Surgical information. The social worker is
permitted to go into the recovery room and
keep track of every person being operated on
the the family that does with each patient.
Thus I, for example, keep the family informed
of the surgical patient's progress, from the
recovery room to the return to his or her
floor. (We take turns on this service although a part-time social worker has the main
responsibility.) While my job is very emotionally and physically taxing, to me this is
one of the most satisfying, most immediately
rewarding of a medical social worker's many
activities. We are "patient advocates"; we
work for each patient without charge. We believe completely in the value of service to
human beings.

Communications Include

notes
evaluations
case histories
consulting
travel
referrals
lunch meetings
client relations
counseling
reports
charts
schedules
legal procedures
financial planning
letters
instructions, oral and written
telephone

ASSIGNMENT: ON THE JOB

1. From friends, relatives, or personnel departments, obtain policies and procedures manuals of three different organizations.
Compare the three in terms of insurance programs, pension

plans, and vacations and sick days. How do these employee benefits differ among the three organizations? Are the differences substantial? What does this comparison tell you about the importance of investigating employee benefits before you decide on a position and an organization?

2. Check on current social security regulations to answer the following questions.
   (a) What percentage of an employee's wage is withheld for social security?
   (b) What is the maximum yearly amount of an employee's wage on which social security is withheld?
   (c) What is the minimum retirement age at which an individual may collect social security?
   (d) At what age may an employee retire and collect the maximum social security retirement benefits?

3. Explain at least five grounds for employment termination. Why are most employers reluctant to fire an employee?

4. Discuss the pros and cons of changing jobs. Why do you think more people are changing jobs more often today than they did in the past?

5. After reading the eight communication diaries in this chapter, have your ideas on your own career changed? Which diary appealed to you the most? Why?

6. After reading the diaries, have your thoughts about the importance of communication in business changed in any way? If so, how? If not, why not?

FURTHER READING

Batten, Joe D. *Tough-Minded Management*. New York: AMACOM, 1979.

Buskirk, Richard H. *Your Career: How to Plan It—Manage It—Change It*, 2nd ed. Boston, MA: CBI, 1980.

Dauw, Dean C. *Up Your Career*, 3rd ed. Prospect Heights, IL: Waveland, 1980.

"An Executive Search," *MBA*, 11, June 1977, 17–27.

Figgins, Ross. *The Job Game: Playing to Win the Job That's Right for You*. Englewood Cliffs, NJ: Prentice-Hall, 1980.

Figler, Howard. *The Complete Job Search Handbook*. New York: Holt, Rinehart and Winston, 1980.

Ginzberg, Eli. *Good Jobs, Bad Jobs, No Jobs*. Cambridge, MA: Harvard University, 1980.

Glueck, William F. *Personnel: A Diagnostic Approach*. Dallas, TX: Business Publications, 1978.

Jackson, Tom and Davidyne Mayleas. *The Hidden Job Market*. New York: Quadrangle/The New York Times, 1977.

Killian, Ray A. *Managers Must Lead!* New York: AMACOM, 1979.

Maccoby, Michael. *The Gamesman: The New Corporate Leaders*. New York: Simon & Schuster, 1977.

Moore, Charles G. *The Career Game*. New York: Ballantine, 1976.

Pollock, Ted. "Mind Your Own Business." *Supervision*, 40, November 1978, 24–26.

Stickney, John. *Self-Made: Braving an Independent Career in a Corporate Age*. New York: Putman, 1980.

Whalen, Tim. "The Proposal Résumé: A Study of Styles in Business and Industry." *Journal of the Society of Technical Communication*, Third Quarter, 1980, pp. 26–29.

Epilogue

Changing Technology

CHAPTER TWENTY-ONE

Communications Systems—Present and Future

Consider this imaginary scene from the 1980s:

An executive wants some information on a project. A computerized information system provides instant data, then prints it out in a standard report format, complete with colored graphs and charts. The report is completed and on the executive's desk in less time than it would have taken for a junior staff person to collect the information and write it up.

Technological change is going to be a major factor in determining the types and number of jobs available in the white-collar category, which takes in technical and professional jobs, managers and administrators, sales and clerical workers.

Not only will there be many new jobs in fields related to developing technologies, such as computers and genetics, but some changes also have the potential for changing the way existing jobs are done.

Karen W. Arenson
"White Collar Sets the Style for the 80s"

In the following selections, several experts examine developing technologies and the implications of their impact on the future of the business community.

INFORMATION SYSTEMS
William J. Lord, Jr.[*]

To understand information systems and the impact of the computer, we have to look back to the 1960 computer boom or even earlier. In 1960, some organizations made the mistake of acquiring a computer before they had systematized their work. Prior to computers, people thought of data processing as clerical-level record keeping or bookkeeping usually carried out in the accounting department.

That situation has changed dramatically. Now, virtually everyone recognizes the important role data processing plays in an information system that affects every aspect of modern business.

Leslie H. Matthies has probably done as much as anyone to bring order and understanding to systems study. He defines a *system* as the means for accomplishing some purpose or set of objectives—a device by which men and women manage and by which operating personnel get work done. The system can be simple or complex. It is the *coordinating element* of management, getting results at the working level.

*William J. Lord, Jr., is Professor and Head of Information Systems, University of Texas, Austin.

CHANGING TECHNOLOGY

The effective manager must have accurate information about an organization's resources: human energy, machines, materials, methods, and money.

An *information system* may be defined as a combination of people, data-processing equipment, input-output devices, and communication facilities. Success or failure depends on how the boundaries between humans and machines are joined. The interface (connecting parts) depends more on experience with people or particular groups of people than it does on technology. The computer enters the picture only as a means of improving the effectiveness of information systems.

An organization's success depends on how well managers balance the mix of five resources: human energy, machines, materials, money, and methods. Current and accurate information about these resources is the bottom line of a manager's success in directing the organization to accomplish its objectives.

An information system = people + data processing equipment + input-output devices + communication facilities.

Today, all of us are users of computer data. We put information/data into the system or we receive information/data from the system's data bank (stored data). *Users* include supervisors, managers, and operating people—everybody working in the organization. In every organization, successful management occurs when data has been turned into information, interpreted correctly, and acted upon. *Data* refers to one or more facts, not necessarily meaningful for the recipient. *Information,* on the other hand, is always meaningful. Data needs to become meaningful to be used.

Data are facts that may or may not be meaningful to the recipient. To be meaningful, data must be turned into information that the recipient can use.

There are some problems. Computers manipulate data using specialized code symbols referred to by a variety of language names. Some common languages are FORTRAN, PL/1, and COBOL. The data is frequently generated in one place and sent via telephone to another location for processing—much different from the time all record keeping was centralized within each operating unit.

These specialized languages have increasingly stifled the smooth flow of information between untutored users and the data-generating sources. All too frequently when users and data processing personnel don't speak the same language, stacks of computer-produced data are ignored. Without some in-house training, intended users may rig their own reporting system. Thus the computer may create new problems by dumping data into the information system:

- data so excessive as to be useless
- data of no significance to the recipient
- data merely "recitals" of activity
- data coverups for a group, division, department—to show "it's doing okay."

Work goes on, stops, or changes depending on whether the data reaching individuals really is meaningful. Each person needs specific information to carry on assigned tasks. Thus every user needs to understand what a system is and what it is not. But the system is invisible until it is studied, until you or someone gives it tangible form.

The person with the title of *systems analyst* knows the *equipment* needs of an organization but often doesn't know the needs of the system's *users*.

The *information specialist* bridges the communication gap between system designers and system users. That person is an individual (1) trained to know both the user's needs and the system's capability of supplying information, and (2) skilled in the art of effective human communication.

An information specialist knows the user's need and the information system's capability.

Today, the information specialist with knowledge of word processing, telecommunications, and data base management is assuming a major role in managerial systems. Analysts and programmers know how to make the computer perform. The information specialist combines technical knowledge with the user's expert knowledge of his or her own work to create a functional information system.

A successful system is one that operates smoothly between the programmer, processor, and user to do the job for the organization and for its staff and clients/customers.

THE AUTOMATED OFFICE
*William R. Feeney**

INFORMATION REVOLUTION

The information revolution is changing our society. Over 50 percent of employees in the United States work with information processing as opposed to providing services, manufacturing products, or growing food. (See Figure 21–1.) Using information networks, machines perform accounting functions, write memos and reports, take orders for goods, gather news, and do many other kinds of information-related activities.

More than half of all employees work with information processing.

There is a real parallel between the Industrial Revolution of two hundred years ago and the information revolution starting now. During the Industrial Revolution, products formerly handcrafted were produced by machines. For the product user, there were two major benefits: the quality of the produced items could be closely controlled and presumably improved, and, most important, products became less expensive to buy.

*William R. Feeney is Assistant Professor, Department of Information Systems, at San Diego State University.

CHANGING TECHNOLOGY

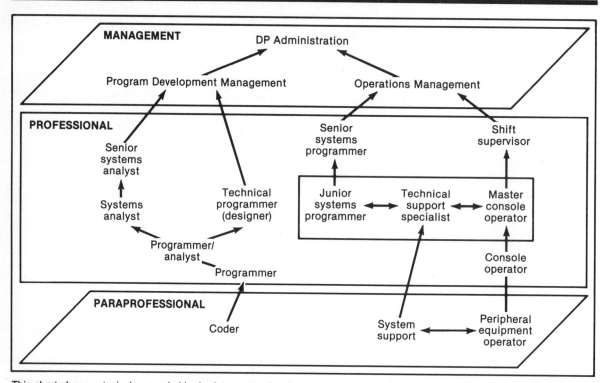

This chart shows a typical career ladder in data processing. Its progression is similar to word processing in that personnel start as equipment operators and progress to analyzing the work and designing solutions before going into management. (**Source:** Courtesy, Word Processing Systems.)

Figure 21–1: Data Processing Career Ladder

Today, office information processing is moving from an essentially hand/mechanical function to an electronic function. This not only dramatically increases the speed of information processing and transmission, but makes managing huge amounts of information relatively simple. The *automated office* is the result of this revolution in information processing.

The automated office incorporates a collection of technologies, techniques, and functions normally separated in a nonautomated office environment. The automated office integrates all of these with the help of a central office computer and with microprocessor circuitry built into the office machines.

From another point of view, the automated office is a new communications medium enhancing, through electronic means, the flow of information in a single office environment and between offices. This can be done by providing the people who work in the office—secretaries, managers, professional people—with automated office workstations and other equipment.

The automated office is a new communication medium based on an electronic flow of information within and between organizations.

The automated office has been called the "office of the future" and the "paperless office." This first label is already disappearing as the automated office becomes practical in terms of cost and available personnel. The second label emphasizes the diminished need for the large quantities of paper now used. While it is true that offices using electronic equipment need less paper, it is still impossible to function in business without hard-copy records.

Automated office technology increases efficiency within a particular room or building and ties together individual offices geographically remote from one another. Office computers tied together in networks quickly convey messages and other kinds of information across the nation and around the world.

COMPONENTS OF AN AUTOMATED OFFICE

Most of the components found in the automated office are also found in the traditional office: telephones, typewriters, calculators, files, dictation machines, copiers, and facsimile machines. In the automated office these machines are tied together by electronic circuitry. The circuitry enables these machines to communicate with the central office computer and with each other to perform additional functions.

The automated office integrates traditional office machines by means of electronic circuitry and a central office computer.

Office practices can be divided into five major functions:

1. Input
2. Process
3. Storage
4. Output
5. Distribution

In the traditional office, separate pieces of equipment perform these functions; in the automated office there is similar equipment, but it is integrated informationally with a computer. Figure 21–2 illustrates the components of an automated office and shows how these parts are connected to a computer.

Inputting, or getting information into the automated office computer, is done in three ways. First, the equipment has a standard keyboard that permits keying information into the computer system. The operator looks at a cathode-ray tube (CRT), or televisionlike screen, rather than inserting a piece of paper in a typewriter. The operator sees

Inputting is placing data in the automated office computer.

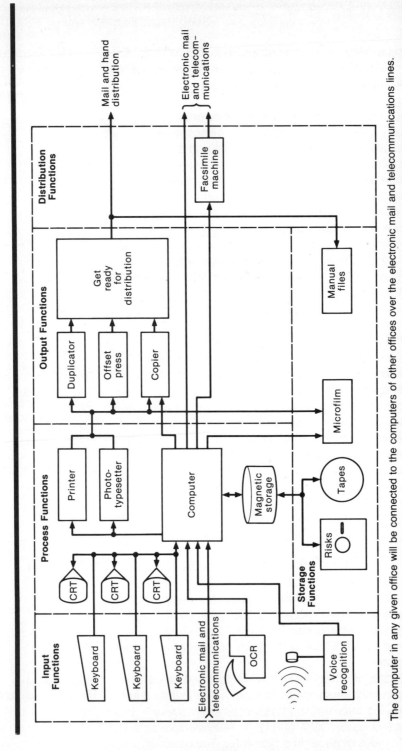

Figure 21–2: General Diagram of Automated Office Functions Tied to a Central Computer.

The computer in any given office will be connected to the computers of other offices over the electronic mail and telecommunications lines.

electronically produced images of what he or she is keying. The computer system "remembers" or magnetically stores, what is keyed in.

A second input method is optical character recognition (OCR) in which a reader unit directly inputs information to the computer from a printed or typewritten page by actually "reading" the printed characters. OCR units are common in newspaper offices and print shops and will be even more common in the future.

Voice recognition, the third method, is not yet well developed and has some severe limitations for office use. At present, most commercially available devices recognize less than one hundred spoken words. Future units, however, hold the promise of being able to interpret large vocabularies.

Processing information in the automated office involves not only data manipulation and computation but also making information contained in the system available for review and change. This necessitates producing images of information, either in words or pictures, for the operator to work with. The images are produced either as electronic images on a screen or as hard copy imprinted on paper.

Processing is making data in the system available for review and change.

The screen images are needed for review or updating—for only a short time. Thus screen images are useful for editing a section of a page. Paper copies are needed for storage or more often for distribution to people who may not have automated office functions.

Storage, in the traditional office, refers to retaining information (hard copies) for a definite period in files of some kind. In the automated office, storage again refers to hard-copy files, but also to the retention of information on either magnetic media or microfilm.

Storing is holding data on magnetic media or microfilm.

Magnetic media consist of either small disks or magnetic tapes. There are two kinds of disks: floppy (flexible) disks, with a capacity to hold one million or fewer characters; or rigid disks, with capacities ranging from 10 million to 900 million characters. Magnetic tapes are stored as reels, cassettes, or cartridges, each holding 50 million characters or less.

Microfilm, many experts think, will continue to be used in the future, but with some changes. Computers can now printout, or output, microfilm for storage and distribution. Future computers, through optical character recognition techniques, will also read microfilm as input.

Still another medium coming over the technology horizon is *bubble memory*. Bubble memory will replace disks, tapes, drums—all types of nonalterable large banks of static memory. This innovation will make possible sizable storage capability. In addition, the use of semiconductors—large-scale integration (LSI) chips or very large scale integration (VLSI) chips—will enable smaller-size, high-performance computers to function far faster than large ones do today.

The office computer system *output* uses three basic methods to put information onto paper:

1. A printer interfaces with the computer and produces hard copy on command.
2. A microprocessor-controlled copier, sometimes called an "intelligent" copier, accepts information in the form of digital signals from a computer or in the form of printing on another piece of paper to be copied directly, just as ordinary copiers do now.
3. A master sheet is produced for duplicating machines and offset presses. The masters have phototypeset quality and, in the more expensive units, are able to reproduce excellent graphics as well as text.

Once the output from the automated office has been printed or duplicated, it can be automatically collated, bound, folded, labeled, and stamped, ready for mail or hand distribution.

Distributing is getting data where it needs to go.

The final function in the automated office is *distribution*—in the traditional manner or over phone lines or other communication links using digital signals. In the future, computers will be sending messages to one another, instead of involving people in the transmission and reception of messages.

THE AUTOMATED OFFICE WORKSTATION
Marjorie M. Leeson*

PROBLEMS OF TODAY'S COMMUNICATION NETWORK

According to Dave Reynolds of IBM, it is projected that by 1985, 40 percent of the work force will be involved in some type of office work—much of which will involve some type of communication. A 14-month study of the "office" conducted by IBM brought forth the following:

1. There were unequal work loads. Often the amount of work assigned to employees depended on the person for whom they worked.
2. Excessive administrative "float" often existed.

*Marjorie M. Leeson is Professor and Chair of the Data Processing Discipline of Delta College, University Center, University of Michigan.

3. The available information was incomplete and/or inaccurate.
4. The same data was stored in multiple files.
5. Archaic methods were being used for creating text (letters, memos, and other types of reports).
6. The communication costs were far greater than necessary.
7. The data stored in files that could be used with EDP methods was usually only a very small portion of the total data available within the organization.
8. Much of the data was stored in more than one file, which resulted in higher costs than were necessary.

The study revealed that the average document is copied 19 times. Often missing from any type of formal documentation is a write-up regarding how the computer is utilized to provide better communication. It was found that the average secretary spends

- 19 percent of the time communicating (by phone or in person)
- 24 percent of the time away from his or her desk copying material, storing material, or retrieving material from files
- 18 percent of the time waiting for work

Modern electronic data processing concepts could be applied, improving the secretary's efficiency, and perhaps making the secretary more of an administrative aide. This would, in turn, increase the productivity of the executive (top management). It was also found that top management spends

- 19 percent of the time writing
- 6 percent of the time dictating
- 9 percent of the time reading
- 14 percent of the time on the phone
- 22 percent of the time in meetings

Sixty-one percent of the time, managers are engaged in some type of communication. They are judged by the way they communicate through writing and speaking.

IMPROVING EFFICIENCY

The automated office will make possible a more efficient and coordinated use of time and information. Among the more important characteristics we can look forward to are the following:

1. Everyone will have a workstation that consists of a CRT (cathode-ray tube), a keyboard for entering data, and the availability of a printer.
2. The workstation will interface to a computer.
3. Programmable terminals will often be part of the employee's workstation.
4. Query languages will be used, enabling the user to abstract data and summarize data stored in the data base.
5. A vast amount of online data will be available in an online data base by keying in a request for the information from the workstation.
6. The system will improve the productivity of both the secretary and the executive.
7. Use of the workstation will reduce the amount of time the secretary will be away from his or her desk, since less material will need to be copied, filed, or retrieved from conventional files.
8. The quality of the information will be improved, since it will be more timely and more accurate.
9. Better information will be available for management to utilize in the decision-making process.
10. The executive will communicate more directly with other members of the organization, since it will be easier to input information directly into the system by using the workstation than it will be to dictate messages to a secretary.
11. The new applications for which the computer will be utilized in the area of communication will result in twice as much information being processed electronically than is now being processed in what is currently thought of as electronic data processing.
12. Most of the computer systems will be real-time systems and the data will be processed as it is entered from the workstation.

How will the use of computerized workstations, or terminals, enhance communication? Let's consider a few examples.

Scheduling a Meeting

If a secretary tries to schedule five busy executives for a meeting, it may take as many as 50 phone calls—perhaps more. The secretary feels elated after calling the first three individuals on the list, since they can all attend a 4 P.M. meeting on Tuesday. Then the fourth phone call is made and the secretary finds out that the last individual on the list is not available on Tuesday. The only solution is to pick another time and start all over again. After a great deal of frustration, the meeting is finally scheduled. How might the meeting be scheduled if a computerized workstation, or terminal, is used?

To begin with, each executive's schedule is already in the data base. The secretary sits down at the workstation and signs on to the system. The dialogue may go something like this:

COMPUTER:	Good Morning. What program do you wish to run?
SECRETARY:	Schedule-ex.
COMPUTER:	Please enter the names of the people who are to attend the meeting.
SECRETARY:	(Enters all five names.)
COMPUTER:	Please enter the purpose of the meeting.
SECRETARY:	(Enters a one- or two-line statement regarding the purpose of the meeting.)
COMPUTER:	Please enter the agenda.
SECRETARY:	(Enters the agenda.)
COMPUTER:	Is there anything that people should bring with them to the meeting?
SECRETARY:	Yes. A copy of last week's minutes.
COMPUTER:	Please order both tea and coffee since Mr. Smith drinks coffee rather than tea.

COMPUTER:	Your meeting is scheduled for
	    Wednesday at 10:00
	    Boardroom A
	Everyone who will be attending the meeting has been notified. Do you have another program to run?

SECRETARY:	No.
COMPUTER:	Good afternoon. Have a pleasant day.

The entire process may have taken only one or two minutes. The secretary is relaxed, has enjoyed the task, and does not feel frustrated. A message regarding the meeting will be displayed on each participant's CRT. On Wednesday, when the participants sign on to the system, they will again be reminded of the meeting. By their replying "Yes" to the question, "Do you want a copy of the agenda?" the printer will print a handcopy of the agenda.

Sending a Memo

A memo is to be sent to all of the district salespersons. Since each salesperson also has an online workstation, this is no problem. Mr. Executive may wish to compose the text of the message. This is easy since corrections can be made before the text goes into the data base. His secretary then indentifies the group to whom the memo is to be sent. Within a second or two the message is displayed upon each salesperson's CRT. Each salesperson has the option of having a copy of the memo printed. If anyone's workstation is being used for another purpose, the message is held in a queue (temporary storage area) until the CRT is free.

SKILLS OF THE FUTURE

As more companies develop new applications such as the ones described, there will be more direct communication between individuals. Often there will not be the middle-person (the secretary or stenographer) to put the message into a different form or format. A far greater emphasis will be placed on communication skills. In the office of the future, which has no walls and can be anywhere, everyone will need to know how to construct correct and meaningful messages. Good grammar, spelling, and punctuation will be considered essential.

Although corrections will be easier to make than when they are made on a standard typewriter, it is assumed that most people will have a reasonable amount of skill in using the keyboard of their workstations. It is also assumed that individuals working in the office of the future will have a good command of the English language. By using a query or natural language, these office workers will be able to retrieve and manipulate vast amounts of information merely by communicating in Englishlike statements with the computer.

TODAY OR TOMORROW

Systems such as the ones described here are already available and are being used by some of the more progressive companies today. As the cost of computing and storing data in online data bases continues to decrease, exciting applications that merge data processing and word processing concepts will continue to be developed.

WORD PROCESSING*
Larry D. Hartman

Doctors, lawyers, and other professionals have found that word processing (WP) enables them to use their time and resources far more efficiently than they ever did before.

More and more individuals and organizations are depending on word processing to help them do their work more efficiently.

With WP, for example, insurance companies (Massachusetts Mutual Life, Springfield, Massachusetts; Fireman's Fund American Life Insurance Co., San Rafael, California; American Republic, Des Moines, Iowa; and many others) are able to get out policies, monitor deadlines and cancellations, and correspond with clients quickly, with far smaller staffs than would otherwise be required.

Since 1976, the National Association of Accountants (NNA) New York City headquarters has maintained computerized membership files, organized continuing education courses, and provided top-level administration coordination using word processing. Other national organizations with other needs use similar methods.

The University of Cincinnati's alumni association office is only one of thousands using word processing to send out mass mailings of brochures for fund-raising, class reunions, and homecoming events.

One of the largest lobbying forces in the State of California, the California Medical Association (CMA), uses word processing to oversee membership, committees, legislation, and publications. The American Bar Association (ABA) national headquarters in Chicago uses word processing to aid the administrators' work with memorandums, agenda, research for speeches, reports, and letters to the membership.

More and more organizations and individuals are using word processing. And, almost daily, word processor capabilities are increasing, incorporating data processing and other management information systems in a single, compact, comfortable workstation. See Figure 21–3.

WHAT IT IS AND WHAT IT DOES

Word processing is a method of producing written communications at top speed, with great accuracy, little effort, and low cost. It is a system involving the coordination of people, procedures, and automated business equipment "in an environment of job specialization and supervisory controls for the purpose of producing typed documents in a routinized, cost-effective manner" (Dartnell, p. 54).

Word processing is a method of producing typed communications easily, quickly, and inexpensively.

---

*Adapted in part from *Business Education into the Eighties,* Illinois Business Education Association, Dr. Larry D. Hartman, Liaison Editor, 1979.

CHANGING TECHNOLOGY

Figure 21–3: Typical Word Processing Workstation

Word processing operators type correspondence and related material on a machine resembling a standard typewriter. But refinements of the machine enable operators to make corrections, shift words and paragraphs, add and delete at will—in other words, edit the original text.

The text may appear on a TV-like screen large enough to show an entire page or a short paragraph. Or it may appear on the typing page. When the typed or viewed copy is exactly as wanted, the operator can enter it into a memory (storage) unit by using a special code symbol key. This memory may be on magnetic cards, in a direct-linked computer, or on paper or magnetic tape. Depending on the equipment, the memory can store characters equal to several pages or even a short book. The memory stores the material until it is erased.

When the operator wishes to reproduce the document, he or she activates a printing code key. The machine itself or a connected printer prints out the material at from 180 to 500 or more words per minute. The completed copy can be produced with a variety of typefaces, with ragged right or right-justified (even right) margins, and camera-ready for offset printing. Some word processors are even tied in (interfaced) with optical scanners (OCRs) for instant phototypesetting or for laser printing.

Where there was once a secretary equipped only with a typewriter, paper, and an eraser, there is now a rapid electronic transfer of information—and a rapid increase in equipment—revolutionizing office efficiency. And word processing is but one component of information management. Other key components include data processing, records management, reprographics, micrographics, electronic mail, dictation equipment, and forms of telecommunications. All may be interrelated.

SYSTEMS

Amy Wohl, word processing editor for *Datapro*, divides word processing systems into four categories, each having specific characteristics and uses:

1. *Mechanical standalone word processors:* This equipment is "blind" (meaning without video display) and includes all types of less sophisticated, less expensive products for use in automated correspondence, short document revision, and other relatively uncomplicated applications.

2. *Display standalone word processors:* These word processors are equipped with a video display (usually gas plasma or cathode-ray tube) to permit the word processing operator to see the text as it is entered or edited (Figure 21–4). These systems often employ diskette (floppy disk) media and may offer sophisticated routines to automate pagination, hyphenation, and global changes. [The message is recorded on a flexible disk similar to an audio record.]

3. *Shared-logic word processing systems and/or distributed logic systems:* These systems have some intelligence at the individual stations but allow several word processing stations to share computer power, storage, and such peripherals as printers. They can also interface for communications, photocomposition, and optical character recognition scanners (OCRs).

4. *Time-shared services:* These services allow a user with a terminal or communicating word processor access to the power of the time-shared service's computer, which is typically a large-size mainframe. Users are billed only for the time they actually use (Wohl 1977).

Users should try to match their equipment needs with product features. In addition, they should consider cost, service, and repair, systems support by the manufacturer, training of personnel, appearance

CHANGING TECHNOLOGY

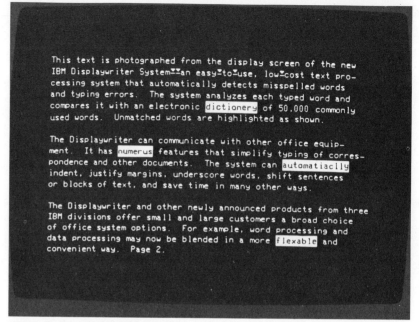

This text is photographed from the display screen of the new IBM Displaywriter System——an easy-to-use, low-cost text processing system that automatically detects misspelled words and typing errors. The system analyzes each typed word and compares it with an electronic dictionary of 50,000 commonly used words. Unmatched words are highlighted as shown.

The Displaywriter can communicate with other office equipment. It has numerus features that simplify typing of correspondence and other documents. The system can automatiaclly indent, justify margins, underscore words, shift sentences or blocks of text, and save time in many other ways.

The Displaywriter and other newly announced products from three IBM divisions offer small and large customers a broad choice of office system options. For example, word processing and data processing may now be blended in a more flexable and convenient way. Page 2.

Figure 21–4: A Sample Word Processor Screen **(Source:** From the IBM Stockholder's Quarterly Report, July 11, 1980.)

and ease of operation, standardization of equipment, the effect of obsolescence, and the reputation of the manufacturer.

Most of all, users should choose a flexible system, one able to meet the ever-changing needs of business and the ever-changing capabilities of equipment. This caution is emphasized for, more and more, the line between data processing and word processing is blurring.

PERSONNEL

Increased use of word processing equipment is changing the role of office personnel.

Equally dramatic but less discussed than the word processing equipment explosion is the change in the traditional role of office personnel (Figure 21–5).

Traditionally, a secretary performs a wide range of duties. In the office using word processors, the work is performed by specialists. Traditionally, a secretary works for only one employer, is physically located near that person, and is supervised by that individual. In the word processing system, all the secretarial work is divided into two functional areas: (1) typing/keyboarding/correspondence (WP—word processors), and (2) nontyping or administrative (AS—administrative

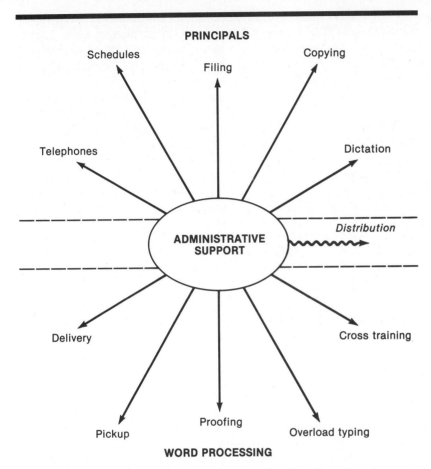

PRINCIPALS

In providing a liaison between principals and word processing operations, administrative support secretaries relieve executives of routine tasks and help word processing operators prepare and distribute correspondence.

Figure 21–5: The Role of Office Personnel in Word Processing Systems

support). The secretary usually works for many managers rather than one individual and is directly supervised by professional word processing or administrative support managers or supervisors.

These managers or supervisors have determined acceptable work standards, created appropriate record-keeping systems, determined priorities, and established effective procedures to meet the secretarial needs of the organization.

Work is distributed to the word processing employee(s) most capable of completing the work properly.

CHANGING TECHNOLOGY

New job descriptions and job titles are constantly updated.

Of course, in some offices secretaries are trained to serve in both administrative and correspondence roles. In addition, in some organizations, top management executives continue to employ private secretaries who work only for them and who are only indirectly involved with word processing.

The change, however, has resulted in new job titles and descriptions that are constantly updated. The International Word Processing Association in its publication, *Job Titles on Description of Word Processing Personnel,* in 1979 listed the following:

1. *Word Processing Trainee:* Entry-level position for those having 0 to 12 months word processing experience. Must have adequate typing skills, good knowledge of grammar, punctuation, spelling and formatting, the ability to use dictionaries, handbooks, and other reference materials, and be oriented toward teamwork and the use of machines. A Trainee's functions include routine transcription and manipulation of text from various types of source information (dictation, handwritten, etc.). Maintains own production records and may be required to proofread own work.

2. *Word Processing Operator:* The next level up from WP Trainee for those having 6 to 24 months word processing experience. In addition to having all the qualifications and functions of a Word Processing Trainee, a Word Processing Operator handles special documents, meets established quality standards, uses all of a machine's text-editing functions, and is familiar with department terminology and company practices. (Other titles for this position include: Correspondence/ing Secretary; Document Specialist; Magnetic Keyboard Specialist; Power Typist; Management Support Specialist; Word Processor, etc.)

3. *Word Processing Specialist I:* A Word Processing Operator with a minimum of 18 months experience who can format, produce, and revise complicated documents, such as lengthy technical and statistical reports, from complex source information, including the retrieval of text and data from electronic files. Exercises independent action when interpreting instructions to produce a quality document, understands proofreader marks, and assumes full responsibility for document accuracy and completeness. Has thorough knowledge of Center procedures and maintenance of records. May operate word processing equipment in the telecommunications mode. (See "Word Processing Operator" for additional titles used.)

4. *Word Processing Specialist II/Assistant Supervisor:* A person at this level exercises all of the competencies of Word Processing Specialist I and may act as Assistant Supervisor. A Word Processing Specialist II is able to operate all the information-processing functions within the installation. Responsibilities include coordinating and assigning work, analyzing requirements for specific projects, communicating with users, compiling production statistics and recommending changes in Center procedures. May also assist in training personnel. (See "Word Processing Operator" for additional titles used.)

5. *Phototypesetting Specialist:* A Word Processing Operator who enters special codes while keyboarding and revising text that is to be output on a photocomposition system. Has knowledge of points, picas, typefaces, leading, and other aspects of typesetting and printing. (Other titles for this position include: Reprographics Specialist; Reprographics Operator; Phototypesetting Operator; Graphics Processor, etc.)

6. *Word Processing Trainer:* Someone with a minimum of 24 months experience operating word processing systems who spends much of time training new operators. May also be responsible for instructing users in dictation methods and other procedures to ensure maximum utilization of a Word Processing Center. Should make recommendations to management with regard to new equipment purchases from the standpoint of ease of use.

7. *Proofreader:* Proofreads typed copy for text contents, spelling, punctuation, grammar, and typographical errors. May be responsible for setting grammar and format standards, guidance and/or training of secretaries and users.

8. *Word Processing Supervisor:* With all the competencies of a Word Processing Specialist II, a Supervisor is responsible for the operation of a Center (or section within a large Center). Schedules and coordinates work flow, assists word processing personnel in document production and in establishing and maintaining quality standards. Also analyzes production data and procedures, identifies potential improvements, and may be responsible partially for budgets and equipment recommendations. Reports to Word Processing Manager. (Other titles for this position include: Secretarial Supervisor; Office Supervisor; Supervisor of Correspondence Center.)

9. *Word Processing Manager:* Responsible for the overall operation of a Word Processing Center, including the guidance of Supervisors, personnel administration, staff requirements, user liaison, and evaluation, design, and implementation of future word processing systems. Also is responsible for budgets, overall production reports, and coordination of services with administration support. May also manage the operation of photocopying, printing, mailing or graphics services. In larger organizations, the Word Processing Manager reports to Director of Secretarial Support Systems. (Other titles for this position include: Coordinator, Word Processing; Supervisor, Document Production; Manager, Correspondence Center; Manager, Communications; Manager, Information Services; Manager, Office Systems.)

An administrative secretary usually works for three or more executives in a word processing system. As a member of the support team, this person, too, has several career paths, job titles, and job descriptions.

1. *Administrative Secretary:* Someone who works for a group of principals (users) as part of a team under the direction of an Administrative Support Supervisor or Manager. Responsibilities include the support

functions such as filing, photocopying, maintaining calendars, records, and lists, and providing special secretarial services, etc. (Other titles for this position include: Administrative Assistant; Administrative Support Specialist; Executive Assistant; Management Support Specialist; Management Support Secretary.)

2. *Senior Administrative Secretary:* Has a record of exceptional performance. At times may act as Assistant to Supervisor of an administrative team, and is qualified to compose and edit documents for principals (users), provide research support, and perform other paraprofessional duties. Handles special projects and is fully aware of company standards and practices. (See "Administrative Secretary" for additional titles used.)

3. *Administrative Support Supervisor:* May have the responsibilities of Senior Administrative Secretary in addition to scheduling and administering work flow to a team of Administrative Secretaries. Responsible for liaison with and training of users who benefit from administrative support. Evaluates staffing requirements, prepares management reports, recommends new methods of handling Administrative Secretaries. Reports to Administrative Support Manager.

4. *Administrative Support Manager:* Has full responsibility for developing, maintaining, and evaluating all service structures under administrative support within an organization, such as filing, telephone, mail, and paraprofessional support. Monitors the success of the administrative support group and is familiar with the company's goals and objectives. Works closely with the Word Processing Manager to ensure cooperation of the two functions. May manage other major administrative duties such as records and retention, microfilm, print shop, purchasing, etc. Reports to Director of Secretarial Support Systems (in large organizations). (Other titles for this position include: Administrative Coordinator; Manager, Administrative Services; Office Manager; Supervisor, Secretarial Services.)

5. *Staff Analyst:* Responsible for consulting with and assisting Word Processing and Administrative Support Supervisors and Managers. Conducts studies, reviews operations, and determines and recommends appropriate staffing, procedures, and equipment. Reports to Director of Secretarial Support Systems or Word Processing Manager or Administrative Support Manager.

6. *Director of Secretarial Support Systems:* May be Vice-President or Assistant to Vice-President in some organizations. Has total responsibility for all aspects of an organization's office system, including word processing, administrative support, and other information processing. Ensures the collaboration of all support functions. Reports to a chief executive officer. (Other titles for this position include: Manager/Director, Office Systems; Manager/Director, Information Services; Manager, Information Systems; Manager, Communication Services.)

Other career opportunities available for competent and knowledgeable word processing personnel include positions as marketing and/or sales support representatives for word processing and data processing equipment manufacturers; systems analysts; in-house office education directors; sales or training representatives of word processing software-oriented companies; publishers; and other closely related occupations.

Increasingly, professional support personnel are being promoted to management positions. Nevertheless, despite the lure of higher salaries, there will be a shortage of qualified secretaries well into the eighties. It is predicted that the demand may exceed the supply by as many as 250,000 trained men and women (*Forbes*, p. 61).

Many career opportunities in the word processing area lead to management positions.

TRAINING

Correspondence and administrative personnel must be able to communicate well both orally and in writing. They must have complete command of English usage including grammar, spelling, and punctuation. In addition, they need basic skill proficiency in

- typing (both speed and accuracy)
- the use of available business machines
- office telephone techniques
- the use of business terminology
- efficient organization of work

Furthermore, they should have a basic knowledge of the concepts of word processing, the various career areas in word processing, the work flow for processing information in the office, prevailing office standards. Depending on their support function, they should be able to follow through on assignments, as well as compose, format, and proofread memos, letters, and other documents under pressure and deadlines.

Formal instruction is available at various levels: in secondary schools, community colleges, four-year colleges, continuing-education classes, minicourses, and business schools. Employee-training programs and special short courses supplied by manufacturers to purchasers of equipment offer additional opportunities for on-the-job training.

Successful word processing personnel must have a good command of the English language, a basic knowledge of word processing concepts, and, for advanced positions, training in administrative skills.

Most office procedure courses include training in basic administrative skills. Training in advanced skills, those needed by administrative supervisors and managers, is found in courses offered by departments or schools of business education, business or industrial administration, industrial education, and industrial engineering. Continuing-education short courses and seminars offer a wide variety of related topics, techniques, and skills, including

- effective supervision and evaluation of employees
- dealing with all levels of personnel, including top management
- time and motion studies
- preparing instructional material
- conference leadership
- public relations
- techniques of teaching
- occupational analysis
- human resource management
- financial information systems
- interpersonal problems in management

Professional Secretaries International, The International Word Processing Association, Toastmasters International, and International Toastmistress Clubs, Inc., provide opportunities for personal and professional development. The rapid, continuous technological changes in equipment demand constant re-education—either through the numerous books, pamphlets, manuals, and audiovisuals available or through day or night classes.

Certificates and degrees plus team and individual performance result in higher-level jobs, higher-level salaries. Word processing is an exciting profession with a great many challenging opportunities.

ELECTRONIC MAIL
*J. Morgan Smythe**

Information is transmitted by telex, telephone, or hand-delivered mail, depending on its urgency and nature.

Today there are basically three ways to transmit information from one place to another: *telex* (wireless transmission), *telephone*, and *hand-delivered mail*. The last two methods are used extensively by almost everyone. Telex, although rarely utilized by the public in general, is used as the telecommunications vehicle for world business and commerce.

Each medium is employed on the basis of the urgency of the message and the nature of the information. Obviously, hand-delivered mail takes longer to reach its destination than does telex. And telex, in turn, takes longer than a telephone call. The trade-off in each case is cost. Telephone calls are the most expensive, followed by telex, then hand-delivered mail. If the message is not urgent, then use mail.

*J. Morgan Smythe is branch manager, I.P. Sharp Associates Limited, Toronto, Ontario, Canada.

But some messages must be sent by one medium, or else the value of the message will be greatly reduced. For instance, if you wanted the receiver to have a schematic of a certain operation, you would probably use the mail service. It would be almost impossible to convey your meeting over the telephone or via telex. In other cases you must use the telephone, or else the "flavor" of the message will be lost. The receiver may arrive at a totally different interpretation of your message, depending on the medium selected. Therefore, the method used is usually determined by both the cost and the nature of the message.

Each of the three methods has served us well over the years. But lately a strain is being placed on them all, a result of the sheer volume of information being sent. More and more people and industries are transmitting and receiving more and more information. Therefore, all three methods are changing to try to cope with this ever-increasing volume.

All three methods of transmittal are changing in an effort to handle the increasing flow of information.

The telephone system, for instance, is changing from the analog method of transmission to the more efficient digital method and is also introducing fiber optics into its networks. Telex is attempting to improve its transmission speeds in order to remain competitive. The mail system has begun to introduce "electronic mail." As a result, a significant portion of the correspondence that is currently being delivered by hand will soon be transmitted *electronically*.

According to Tom Alexander in *Fortune* (June 1979, p. 92):

Computers can not only replace the expensive human sorting operations in post offices, but can also perform other chores. For example, a business mailer might prepare only one master version of, say, an invoice. He or she could then send that version, together with a list of addresses and other individual details, via magnetic tapes or phone lines to a local post office. It would then either transmit copies of the invoice electronically to those addresses who had a telex printer, word processor screen, or facsimile receiver—or else print the copies out, fold them into envelopes, and hand them to human letter carriers.

Facsimile mail is already being used by a number of companies. The result is that the *users have a transmission facility similar to telex and the versatility of mail*. They can transmit sketches, charts, or whatever into the receiver's hands in a matter of minutes.

Another facet of electronic mail is being developed around computers. Here messages are transmitted to a central computer facility and kept until the intended receiver(s) "reads" them. The sender enters the text via a remote computer terminal that is connected to the computer by means of the telephone system. Once the text is entered, it

CHANGING TECHNOLOGY

is sent over the telephone wires to the central computer, where it awaits the intended receiver.

At any time during the day or night, from virtually any location in the world, the receiver literally telephones this same computer and instructs it to print out mail on his or her terminal. The main advantage of this system over all the others is that neither senders nor receivers have to be at specific geographic locations at specific times to send or receive their mail. They merely telephone the computer from wherever they are; and most of these calls are local calls, so no long-distance charges are involved. No longer do messages and correspondence have to "chase" after people as they move from department to department, or city to city. In addition, the same message can be sent to several receivers at once without additional cost.

Electronic mail marks a significant breakthrough in our mail service. Traditionally, the delivery of mail has met with varying degrees of success. But with this new method, recipients must "pick up" their own mail. This change will allow postal organizations to simplify many of their past logistic problems and to vastly increase the transmittal of mail.

TRADITIONAL SPEEDY COMMUNICATIONS

Teletype networks: Carry messages between company locations via telephone lines

Telex and **TWX** (trade names for two similar systems of Western Union): Carry messages to company locations not on the teletype network or to noncompany locations subscribing to Telex or TWX facilities.

Mailgrams: Transmitted directly or indirectly to Western Union by computer-generated magnetic tape from a customer's computer (messages are similar to hard copy of electronic mail).

Western Union telegrams: Used when other telegraphic methods are not available or fast enough.

FAX or **facsimile:** Reproduce graphically complex data in tables, charts, graphs, maps, and other materials difficult to explain, type, or redraw. Facsimiles are transmitted via telephone lines to special receiver/transmitter equipment.

The above messages frequently use company codes. They also convey emphasis and urgency, and supply proof of sending and receipt.

Fast delivery of mail is available to almost everyone today through privately owned and bonded courier services. Slower and less dramatic than electronic mail, courier services use trucks, motorcycles, bicycles, and planes for fast local and national delivery of letters and packages. Consult the yellow or business pages of your telephone directory for "Delivery Services."

FURTHER READING

Information Systems

Asten, K. J. *Data Communications for Business Information Systems.* New York: Macmillan, 1973.

Booth, Grayce M. *Functional Analysis of Information Processing.* Huntington, NY: Krieger, 1980.

Chacko, George K. *Management Information Systems.* Princeton, NJ: Petrocelli, 1980.

Gessford, John E. *Modern Information Systems: Designed for Decision Support.* Reading, MA: Addison-Wesley, 1980.

Kleinjnen, Jack P. *Computers and Profits: Quantifying Financial Benefits of Information.* Reading, MA: Addison-Wesley, 1980.

Martin, J. *Principles of Data Base Management.* Englewood Cliffs, NJ: Prentice-Hall, 1976.

Matthies, Leslie H. *The Management System: Systems Are for People,* Wiley Series on Systems and Controls. New York: Wiley, 1976.

(Numerous newspapers, magazines: *Electronic Buyers' News, Electronic Engineering Times, Computer Systems News, Information Systems News, Word Processing Systems.*)

Word Processing

Bergerud, Marty and Jean Gonzalez. *Word Processing: Concepts and Careers.* New York: Wiley, 1978.

Business Education into the Eighties. Illinois Business Education Association Publication Committee, Wilma Jean Alexander, Project Director. Dr. Larry D. Hartman. Liaison Editor. Dept. of Business Education and Administrative Services. Illinois State University, Normal, IL 61761, 1979.

Cecil, Paula B. *Word Processing in the Modern Office,* 2nd ed. Reading, MA: Addison-Wesley, 1980.

Dartnell Corporation. *Dartnell's Glossary of Word Processing Terms.* Chicago: The Dartnell Corporation, 1977.

Ganus, Susannaha. "Word Processing—Books and Periodicals." *ABCA Bulletin,* 42, June 1979, 23–25.

"The Secretary Is Becoming an Endangered Species." *Forbes,* December 11, 1978, p. 61.

Wohl, Amy D. "Reporting the Equipment Explosion." *Words, the Journal of the International Word Processing Association*. Summer 1977, in *Business Education into the Eighties*.

Word Processing Systems. New York: Geyer-McAllister Publications, Inc., 51 Madison Avenue, New York. Monthly publication.

Electronic Mail

Alexander, T. "Postal Service Would Like to Be the Electronic Mailman, Too." *Fortune*, 99, June 18, 1979, 92–94.

Anderson, J. and K. Willenson. "Electronic Mail Hits a Glitch." *Newsweek*, 94, December 31, 1979, 59.

Clines, F. X. "Leapfrogging Hand Deliveries, Your Mail Is Going Electronic." *Science Digest*, 85, January 1979, 57–60.

Harris, Kathryn. "Private Firms, U.S. Agencies May Stay Electronic Postman." *Los Angeles Times*, April 20, 1980.

Sirbu, M. A. "Automating Office Communications: The Policy Dilemmas; Electronic Mail." *Technology Review*, 81, October 1978, 50–57.

Appendices

Appendix A

DICTATION
*Lois W. Sears**

PRINCIPLES OF EFFECTIVE DICTATION

Dictation is speaking converted by someone into writing. It is sometimes called voice writing. The dictator speaks

- to a person who takes notes, later transcribed into a written message
- to a person who simultaneously produces (types) the written message
- to equipment storing the spoken message for *transcription* into the written message

Most business people originate their written messages by dictation. Thus it is important to learn how to compose orally. In addition, because there is an intermediary—the person converting the spoken message into the written message—there is a possibility for a breakdown in the communication process.

Here are some practical rules for effective dictation:

1. An effective dictator knows and uses the principles of good business writing (such as the material previously presented).

*Lois W. Sears is Assistant Professor of Business Education at Delta College, University Center, Michigan.

461

2. An effective dictator visualizes the receiver of the written message and considers that person first and always, throughout the dictation.

3. An effective dictator recognizes the importance of timing and organization. Timing—acting upon information promptly—often results in clearer communication. Organization means the person prepares before dictating:
   - reads every message carefully
   - assembles all necessary information
   - pencils notations on letters or memos for replies
   - constructs a rough outline of key words or phrases, mentally or on the message itself
   - numbers questions for answers and identifies them in the dictation
   - responds to most urgent mail first

4. An effective dictator selects a regular and appropriate time and place for dictation, free from distractions.

5. An effective dictator considers the person receiving the dictation, anticipating this person's needs. The dictator and transcriber should work as a team. The dictator should speak in a normal voice, concentrating on dictating, setting up the purpose in the first paragraph, then developing each point. The transcriber should feel free to offer suggestions and ask questions. The dictator must remember to supply supporting documents used for reference.

In face-to-face dictation, the dictator has immediate feedback on any points unclear to the transcriber. This opportunity decreases in machine dictation, particularly in large systems where the dictator sends the message to be transcribed to any one of a group (pool) of transcribers. Listening to the recorded material can help a beginning dictator improve this skill.

MACHINE DICTATION

Although the most common type of dictation has been face-to-face dictation, the use of machine dictation is growing in popularity. The equipment used for recording and transcribing is being constantly improved. Equipment that utilizes electronic chips is very compact. Various companies manufacture battery-operated hand units small enough to fit into a pocket. With these units, a business person can dictate anywhere, at any time—in the evening, between calls to customers, and while traveling. These recording units utilize standard or micro cassettes, which can then be given to a transcriber during normal work hours.

Cost factors also have increased the use of machine dictation. When a business person dictates to a secretary, two people's salaries are involved. With dictating equipment, only the dictator's salary and the cost of the equipment are involved. Furthermore, instead of hiring people skilled in both taking dictation and transcribing, the employer can hire people who can simply transcribe. As the cost of the equipment becomes more competitive with the cost of labor, *economy justifies the use of machine dictation.*

In machine dictation, the dictator must be thoroughly familiar with the equipment. Various types of equipment are available and each contains special features. The equipment may be visible to the dictator, such as with desk or handheld recording units. In other systems, the equipment is not visible; the dictating is done on special telephone lines connected to the recording equipment. In machine dictation, understanding the scope and limitations of the equipment is a key factor in successful dictation.

THE DICTATION PROCESS

The dictation process described here is for machine dictation. It may be modified for face-to-face dictation. When dictating, the dictator should give the information for each item in order. The dictator should talk to the transcriber by name or simply say "transcriber." The dictator should speak at such a rate that every word is audible and clearly enunciated. Dictation may follow this pattern:

Preliminary Instructions

1. Identify yourself by name and department.
2. Specify the type of document (letter, memorandum, report), case or code number, and priority. Start with high-priority items and specify the completion time (when due).
3. Specify if the item is to be in rough draft form, and whether it is to be held or returned for revision.
4. Specify the type of stationery or form, number of copies (beyond the file copy), and envelope requirements. Dictate form responses from left to right, top to bottom.
5. Specify letter and punctuation style or report style, indicating any special features.
6. Indicate date and inside address or report title.

Good Dictation Techniques

1. Back up and redictate areas to be corrected, or preface corrections by the word "Correction."
2. Spell out proper names and foreign, technical, or unusual words.
3. Indicate capitalization by "All Caps" or "Initial Cap" before the word(s).
4. Indicate paragraphing by a slight pause and the statement "Paragraph."
5. Indicate special preferences on punctuation and unusual punctuation. Normal voice inflection usually is used to indicate periods and commas.
6. Dictate long or unusual figures by digits.

Closing Instructions

1. Dictate the name and title to appear at the end of a letter.
2. Specify enclosures or attachments.
3. Indicate distribution of copies.
4. Specify "End of Dictation" or "End of item 1."
5. Thank the transcriber.
6. Send reference material with the recorded message.

Final Responsibilities

1. Proofread the transcribed document carefully before signing it.
2. Check enclosures.
3. Indicate corrections, if any, on the document, or revise the document so that it will have to be retyped only once.
4. File appropriate copies.

Appendix B

AUDIOVISUAL MEDIA RESOURCES
*Robert B. Lindemeyer**

In 1911, International Harvester produced a film called *Back to the Old Farm.* Recognized today as one of the earliest applications of audio-visual media to business communications, this melodrama told the story of how the gasoline tractor was revolutionizing agriculture.

Today's corporate communicators are applying audiovisual media with a variety of sophisticated technology and techniques to a host of communication needs including

- marketing
- consumer education
- corporate training
- point-of-purchase selling
- management communications

Proven to be highly cost effective, audiovisual media can add impact, flexibility, and drama to virtually every area of business communications. Corporate use of audiovisual media providing effective communications—both internal and external—is a key part of business activity. And today's successful business people know how to communicate.

*Robert B. Lindemeyer is the Director of Media Development at Iowa State University, Ames, Iowa.

Following are brief descriptions of a variety of audiovisual media devices and applications, proceeding from the simple and inexpensive to the complex and sophisticated.

Mini cassette.   Pocket-portable audiocassette recorder provides dictation, note-taking, briefings, or training anywhere. Available from Sony, Norelco, Dictaphone, and others from about $100.

Instant pictures.   For the appraiser or investigator, the sales or service person, an instant picture camera, for use on location can save time and capture important details. Available from Polaroid and Kodak from about $50.

Overhead.   Long a standard in the classroom, the overhead transparency projector is now widely used in the sales conference, training session, and boardroom. Whether you write directly on the clear acetate transparency or use prepared visuals with color overlays and animation, leave the room lights on, face your audience, the flexibility of the overhead projector is a natural for effective communications. Available from 3M, Bell & Howell, American Optical, and others from about $180.

Pocket camera.   Easy to carry, simple to shoot, these miniature, cartridge-load, high-speed color or black and white film cameras can make slides or prints. While they don't provide instant pictures, most cities have overnight processing available. Available from Kodak, Minolta, and others from about $30.

Rear-screen filmstrip/cassette.   Music, other sound effects, and narrative, paced and synchronized with a strip of 35mm colored visuals, are all self-contained in and with presentation screen. The rear-screen filmstrip/cassette presentation package is a low-cost audiovisual system limited only by its lack of motion and the creativity of those producing the program. Widely used today for individualized training with applications from assembly-line skills to selling bonds and all you can imagine between. Available from Dukane, Singer, LaBelle, and others from about $275.

Standard audio cassette.   Developed by Phillips/Norelco in the 1960s, this is the audiotape cassette everyone knows. From the basic portable recorder by Panasonic, Sony, and others at under $50 to the ultra stereo Dolby hi-fi deck—they all use the same standard cassette.

Self-contained slide/tape.   Looking like a square TV set with a slide tray on top, the self-contained, rear-screen, slide/tape projection box works well for individualized or small-group instruction or point-of-sale display. Available from Kodak, Bell & Howell, Singer, and others from about $375.

Microfiche individualized instruction.   Compact in size, inexpensive to duplicate, a single 4-by-6-inch color microfiche card can hold 98 visual images. Viewable on any microfiche machine, these cards can be reproduced in quantity for a few dollars each from slides or hard copy and thus provide wide distribution at low cost. Contact Kodak or your nearest microform service laboratory for this service.

35mm SLR camera.   The workhorse camera for advanced amateurs through professionals, the 35mm single-lens reflex is a must for anyone requiring quality color or black and white slides or prints for publication. The array of films and lenses plus such features as built-in automatic exposure systems make the SLR truly versatile. Look to Canon, Pentax, and others for good basic SLRs starting at about $275.

Super 8mm loop projector.   Ideal for point-of-sale demonstrations and individualized instruction, these cartridge-loaded loops of color motion picture film provide the impact and versatility of more expensive 16mm film and videotape systems at considerably lower cost. Loop projectors available from Kodak, Technicolor, and others from about $300. Cartridges loaded with your film program from about $30 by numerous motion picture service laboratories.

Half-inch videocassette.   Rapidly growing in popularity for home video recorder applications, the ½-inch videocassette is widely used in industry for point-of-sale demonstrations and internal communication systems. Up to six hours of high-quality color video is provided from a $15 cassette the size of a paperback. Two totally incompatible formats continue to struggle for market supremacy. Whether you choose Beta or VHS, the recorder/player costs around $750, but shop around.

Portable color TV camera.   Electronic miniaturization is producing a real revolution in TV cameras. Today, educators and corporate trainers are "making TV" with battery portable color mini-cams that weigh only a few pounds and cost less than $1,000. But you will still need the recorder, TV sets, tapes, and so forth. Unless yours is a straightforward and proven application, get some professional advice before you start purchasing problems. Sources include Panasonic, Hitachi, and JVC.

Large-screen TV.   We've all experienced the frustration of trying to see and hear a normal-size TV set from the back of the room. The costs and complications of cabling together several TVs to cover a group of viewers can be just as bad. Major advances in brightness and picture quality of large-screen TV projectors now warrant a closer look by anyone who needs to play back TV to a *group* of viewers. Sony, Panasonic, and Advent are producing excellent 4- to 6-foot color images for about $3,500.

Multi-image presentation. The multiscreen, multiprojector extravaganza is best left to those with high budgets. But for long-running applications or to kick off a new product sales presentation, the spectacular impact of multi-image is worth considering. There's a tremendous array of equipment available for multi-image from Spindler & Sauppe, Audio-Visual Labs, and others, for a few to many thousands of dollars. Start with professional production assistance—the hardware comes later.

Whether it's a big media or little media event you are thinking about, the best advice you can receive is to study the communication problem you are up against before you purchase or produce anything. Who *is* your target audience? What do you want them to do, learn, or become as a result of experiencing your message? For instruction, public relations, sales, management, and a host of applications, audio-visual media can provide highly successful communication.

FURTHER READING

Audiovisual Market Place 1980: A Multimedia Guide, 10th ed. New York: R. R. Bowker, 1980.

Blythe, Hal T. et al. *Competencies in Materials Development and Machine Operations: Self-Directive Activities, A Functional Approach.* Boston, MA: Americas, 1979.

Gerlach, Vernon S. and Donald P. Ely. *Teaching and Media.* Englewood Cliffs, NJ: Prentice-Hall, 1980.

Kemp, Jerrold E. *Planning and Producing Audiovisual Materials,* 4th ed. New York: Harper & Row, 1980.

Roberts, Elizabeth A. "Advice for the User of Visual Aids." *Technical Communication,* 26, no. 4, 4th Quarter, 1979.

INFORMATION SOURCES

Audio-Visual Communications. Published 12 times a year. Leading periodical of the AV field. Specializes in business-related AV communications. $13.50/year. Write: United Business Publications, 475 Park Ave. S., New York, NY 10016.

Audio Visual Equipment Directory. Published annually by the National AV Association. 500-plus page directory—pictures, detailed specifications, prices of AV hardware. $24.50. Write: National Audio-Visual Association, 3150 Spring St., Fairfax, VA 22031.

Instructional Innovator (Previously *Audiovisual Instruction.*) Published 9 times a year. Official magazine of the Association for Educational Communications & Technology. Principle publication and professional organization in field of AV media. $18/year to nonmembers. Membership ($50/year) includes magazine, other services. Write: Association for Educational Communications & Technology, 1126 16th Street N.W., Washington, D.C. 20036.

1982 Publications Index. Comprehensive listing of 250-plus Kodak publications on materials, equipment, production of AV media. No charge. Write: Eastman Kodak Co., Motion Picture and AV Markets Division, Rochester, NY 14650.

Videocassettes, floppy disks, audiocassettes and films (super 8mm and 16mm) are available from many companies. Send for free catalogs, listing titles in distribution, marketing, management, training, communication, and other business- and industry-related topics: BNA Communications Inc., 5615 Fishers Lane, Rockville, MD 20852; Roundtable Films, Inc., 321 S. Beverly Dr., Beverly Hills, CA 90212; Time-Life Video, Dept. 32-37, Time-Life Bldg., New York, N.Y. 10020.

ADVICE FOR THE USER OF VISUAL AIDS*
Elizabeth A. Roberts

The effective use of visual aids by a speaker is vital for the success of any presentation. Research in sensory reception has repeatedly shown that material that is seen is remembered 55 percent better than material that is only heard. Visual aids enhance audience understanding of ideas, heighten audience interest in a subject, and increase audience retention of material.

Before wholeheartedly embracing visual aids for use in every presentation, however, the speaker should note that certain materials found in speeches or technical reports lend themselves especially well to the use of visual aids. Those materials deal with appearances, functions, statistics, and major ideas. In other words,

- show what it looks like
- show how it works
- show the data
- show the main points or topics

*From *Technical Communication*, Fourth Quarter, 1979, pp. 15–17.

If the visual aids selected can respond to these directives, the aids benefit both the listener and the speaker. The former is provided with visual reinforcement of the spoken message, the latter with memory cues, as well as freedom from lectern notes.

REQUIREMENTS FOR VISUAL AIDS

If visual aids are to enhance these materials in a technical presentation, the speaker should be sure they meet certain basic requirements. First, *be sure the visual aid meets a need.* In other words, if verbal means of developing ideas don't suffice, visual aids should supplement them. Second, *be sure the visual aid never becomes an end in itself.* It should support, not lead, the ideas. Third, *be sure to adapt the visual aid to the situation*—room size, audience size, time limits, time of day. Fourth, *be sure the visual aid has a professional appearance.* This doesn't mean that it must be commercially designed and prepared, but rather that it must be visually appealing and skillfully handled. Finally, if the visual aid meets the criteria of need, support, situation, and appearance, *be sure the visual aid is practical*—practical to develop, display, transport, and store.

As the speaker prepares and adapts the written technical report for an oral presentation, the five requirements for good visual aids may loom ominously ahead. The first two criteria of *need* and *support* may be more easily met than the others. Careful examination of the speaker's material can satisfy those two requirements. The third criterion, however, demands knowledge of the speaking *situation.* The speaker must ask such questions as

- How close is the nearest audience member?
- How far away is the farthest audience member?
- Can the visual aids be clearly seen?
- Can the colors be seen?
- Is the writing legible?

Other important questions include

- Are the visual aids simple and undetailed?
- Will the viewer have time to understand the content?
- Can the viewer focus quickly on the important elements?
- Will the information be effortlessly retained?

The fourth criterion, *appearance,* is closely allied with the analysis of the speaking situation and can make or break a presentation. Looks count in creating and affirming the credibility of a speaker's ideas. Common weaknesses in visual aids are improper lettering, myriad formulas, minute details, and excessive data. Visuals can achieve a professional appearance through carefully planned layout and vivid, clear lettering on posters, transparencies, or slides. (For the nonskilled letterer, dry-transfer or vinyl letters are impressive and quite easy to apply.)

Not only should professionalism apply to the visual quality of the aids but also to their handling. A skilled speaker knows how to use the aids to best advantage. For example, the speaker reveals the visual aid—poster, model, projection—at that moment in the speech where it will have the maximum impact and removes it from view when no longer needed; manipulates posters, charts, slides, and transparencies with ease; makes sure that the audience has a clear view of the visual aid; and knows the advantages and disadvantages of various visual aids and selects and uses them accordingly.

The fifth criterion, *practicality,* affects and is affected by the other four factors. The visual aids may be difficult, costly, and time-consuming to prepare; may necessitate cumbersome equipment, specialized facilities, and program assistants; and may present travel and storage problems for the speaker. When faced with these problems, a speaker must reexamine the use of particular visual aids.

Thus, the total effectiveness of whatever visual aid is selected to augment speech materials is dependent on whether the aid meets these five requirements.

Once the speaker has determined that visual aids should be and can be feasibly used, certain questions arise regarding the advantages and disadvantages of the many types of visual aids.

- What aid is most effective for my ideas and for this audience?
- What can I prepare easily and inexpensively?

TYPES OF AIDS

The task of answering the first question may be eased if the speaker has some basis for accepting or rejecting the major types of visual aids: chalkboard, posters and flip-charts, actual objects, models and mock-ups, slide projectors, overhead projectors, and handouts.

The chalkboard.   The chalkboard is probably the most often used type of visual aid. One is available in most conference rooms and therefore is convenient for spontaneous expression. However, the chalkboard may not be appropriate for data that are complex, data that ought to be saved, and extensive data the speaker must write while the audience waits.

Posters and flip-charts. Posters and flip-charts are frequently used by a speaker who wants freedom to refer to data without turning from the audience. These visual aids can be prepared before the presentation, can be prepared professionally, can be referred to several times during the speech, and, if needed, can be transported or stored. Disadvantages revolve around their limited effectiveness. Data on posters and charts should be clearly visible for at least 25 feet. When using prepared posters and charts, the speaker can't add data as easily as on chalkboards or transparencies, and these same posters and charts which offer limited space for data may also be too bulky to store and transport.

Actual objects. Actual objects may be considered for use by a speaker because they are obviously authentic and realistic; but, again, these objects may have limited effectiveness. They may be too large to be conveniently stored or transported, or they may be too small to be viewed by any but the closest audience members. A note of caution to the speaker planning to pass around objects among the audience—DON'T! Three audience members won't be listening at any moment: one will be passing the object, one receiving it, one waiting to receive it, and so on around the room.

Models and mock-ups of objects. The advantages and disadvantages of actual objects apply to the use of models and mock-ups. Although expensive or time-consuming to prepare, they are appropriate to focus attention on specific features of the actual object.

Slide projectors. Slide projectors offer advantages for displaying large, clear, photographic material with professional realism and comparatively low cost. The need for interesting layout, legible writing, and clarity are as important to slides as to other forms of visual aids. Slide projection equipment permits remote control by the speaker, as well as ease of storage and transportation. However, there are certain mechanical disadvantages in using slide projectors. Slides can easily "take over" a presentation and emphasize the visuals rather than the speaker. Another major problem is the need to dim room lights for viewing. In the subdued light, audience members may be unable to see the speaker and may thus lose interest. In addition, set-up and operation require skill, and a speaker must plan for such things as extra cords, outlets, screens, and light switches.

Overhead projectors. Overhead projectors provide much flexibility. There is no need to darken the room, and the speaker can face the audience. Although transparencies are simple and inexpensive to prepare, they allow for professional appearance. The speaker can add, remove, point out details, and may even create impressive, dramatic effects with overlays. Also, an air of spontaneity may result. Other than its cumbersome size for storage and transportation, one of the few disadvantages of the projector is that it may obstruct audience view if inappropriately placed. The projector should be angled so that it provides a clear view of the screen with minimal "keystone" effect.

Handouts.   Handouts, familiar visual aids, are frequently abused by their very familiarity. Yet they may be helpful for such items as budgets, financial reports, or proposed layouts and may be designed to be saved by the audience, consulted at a later date, or used for notes during the session. Professional quality should apply to these visuals as much as to any other type. Handouts are advantageous in providing a ready reference only if the listener is not distracted by any additional information on the handout and only if the speaker can control the audience by directing attention to specific items in it.

When using handouts, the speaker should pause until all are distributed in order to maintain control of audience attention. In addition, the speaker should *never* distribute the manuscript of a report before the presentation. Because the listeners' attention may be fragmented between manuscript and speaker, distribute it *after* the program.

Although other types of visual aids abound, the chalkboard, chart, actual object, mock-up, slide projector, overhead projector, and handout are the ones most frequently available to and used by a speaker. The advantages and disadvantages of these visual aids should be carefully analyzed and weighed by the speaker.

PREPARATION GUIDELINES

Once the most advantageous visual aids are selected, the speaker might consider these guidelines for using aids.

- Be sure the visual aid is visible from 25 feet.
- Make sure anything "written" is short and simple.
- Use large letters, solid lines from ⅛ up to ½ inch thick.
- Keep colors vivid and simple:
     Use black, red, deep blue, or green on white or pastel.
     Use white on black or dark green.
     Use no more than three or four colors.
- Use poster board at least 22 × 28 inches.
- Allow room for margins and ample spacing; don't crowd material.
- Eliminate unnecessary or distracting details.

- Keep the "horizon line" above or below the midpoint of the poster.
- Follow the rule of thirds: divide visual area into thirds both vertically and horizontally. Place your center of interest at one of the four places where the lines intersect.
- Use two or more aids to show separate parts of an idea.
- Practice in advance any drawing you plan to make.
- Plan ahead for an assistant.
- Know how much time is needed and know exactly when the visual aid will be used.
- Be sure all materials are ready and with you at the time of the presentation.
- Keep your eyes on the audience; don't block the audience's view of the visual aid.
- Don't reach across your body to point to items; stand to one side.
- Present one major idea at a time.
- Use a pointer carefully, not as a baton.
- Give the audience time to see the visual aid.
- Summarize after the visual aid is used.
- Cover or put away the visual aid before and after it is needed; plan ahead how this will be done.
- Don't make the visual aid the most important thing in the presentation.
- Don't rest posters on a chalkboard ledge; they tend to fall too easily. Use masking tape or clamps to secure them.
- Never apologize for the size of the visual aid or for its failure to work, or ask, "Can everyone see?" It's your responsibility to make sure your visual aid is in working order and is beneficial to the presentation.
- An old adage—*always* take along masking tape for any speech. It may help to secure visual aids, microphones, electrical cords, notes, etc. And if you don't need it for any of those things . . . it may help hold *you* together.

SUMMARY

The speaker who adapts a written report for oral presentation must consider using visual aids—visual aids planned and prepared to assure maximum listener response; visual aids analyzed and weighed for their advantages and disadvantages; visual aids prepared according to certain basic requirements; visual aids that enhance understanding, increase retention, and heighten the interest of the audience.

Appendix C

Ordering merchandise by mail can save you time and money and enable you to buy things unavailable elsewhere. But when you order merchandise by mail and it arrives months later—or not at all—what can you do? Despair not. You are protected. The Federal Trade Commission has ruled that you have certain rights.

The Right to Know When You Can Expect Shipment

Merchandise must be shipped exactly as stated in the ad or brochure (return mail, week, 10 days, other); within 30 days, if not specified.

The Right to Cancel Your Order

If the seller can't ship on time, you must be notified of the delay and given a free means of reply (postage-paid postal card, WATS phone number, other).

If the shipping delay is 30 days or less, you have the right to cancel the order and get your money back, the right to agree to the new shipping date, or the right not to answer. If you do not answer, the seller can assume you agree to the delay.

If the shipping delay is more than 30 days, you must give your express consent (preferably in writing) to the delay. Otherwise, the seller must return your money at the end of the first 30 days of delay.

The Right to a Refund If You Cancel

The seller must mail your refund to you within seven business days after you cancel your purchase. Where there is a credit sale, the seller has one billing cycle to "adjust" your account. (This rule does not apply to services such as mail-order photo finishing; magazine subscriptions and other serial deliveries except for the initial shipment; mail-order seeds and growing plants; Collect On Delivery orders; credit orders where the buyer's account is not charged prior to shipment of the merchandise; and sales under negative-option plans where you must notify the seller of your intent *not* to purchase.)

What to Do If You Have a Problem

If the mail-order seller does not comply with the rule as outlined, *write* the seller directly. If, within a reasonable amount of time, you don't get results, furnish the details in a letter accompanied by

- a copy of the advertisement
- a copy of your canceled check
- other pertinent information

Mail to

Director, Bureau of Consumer Protection (MO-P)
Federal Trade Commission
Washington, D.C. 20580

The commission does not intervene in private disputes between a buyer and a seller, but to properly enforce the rule, it keeps close track of companies that may be violating the rule. The commission will forward a copy of each consumer complaint to the U.S. Postal Inspection Service for action under its Consumer Protection Program.

Unordered Merchandise

If you receive merchandise in the mail that you did not order, federal law says you may consider it a gift and keep it without paying for it.

Only two kinds of merchandise can be sent legally through the mails to a person without his or her prior consent:

- free samples clearly and plainly marked as such
- merchandise mailed by a charitable organization asking for contributions

In all other instances, it is illegal to send you merchandise through the mails unless you have previously requested it.

You *do not* have to pay for *any unsolicited merchandise,* and it is illegal for the person or firm sending it to you to pressure you to return it or to send you a bill.

If you know of any violations of this law, or if you received unordered merchandise and are harassed with demands for payment, write to the Federal Trade Commission.

Postal Fraud and Misrepresentations

The U.S. Postal Service and the Federal Trade Commission both have jurisdiction over some areas of commerce by mail. The U.S. Postal Service is charged with protecting the public against fraud or misrepresentation by mail. Any information about these matters should be addressed to your Postmaster, your local Postal Inspector, or the Chief Postal Inspector.

DIRECT MAIL/MARKETING ASSOCIATION OPERATING GUIDELINES FOR ETHICAL BUSINESS PRACTICE[*]

1. Advertisers should make their offers clear and honest. They should not misrepresent a product, service or solicitation and should not use misleading, half-true or exaggerated statements. Advertisers should operate in accordance with the Fair Practice Code of the Council of Better Business Bureaus and be cognizant of and adhere to the Postal Laws and Regulations, and all other laws governing advertising and transaction of business by mail.
2. Advertisers should not make offers which purport to require a person to return a notice that he does not wish to receive further merchandise in order to avoid liability for the purchase price, unless all the conditions are first made clear in an initial offer that is accepted by the purchaser by means of a bonafide written order. Attention is suggested to more detailed specifications regarding negative option plans which have been formulated by the Federal Trade Commission.

*Courtesy, the Direct Mail/Marketing Association.

3. Mailings should not contain vulgar, immoral, profane or offensive matter nor should advertisers use the mails to promote the sale of pornographic material or other matter not acceptable for mailing on accepted moral grounds. Advertisers should not use the mails to promote the sale of products or services by means of lottery.

4. The terms and conditions of guarantee should be clearly and specifically set forth in immediate conjunction with the guarantee offer. Guarantees should be limited to the reasonable performance capabilities and qualities of the product or service advertised.

5. Advertisers should not make exaggerated price comparisons, claims on discounts or savings, nor employ fictitious prices.

6. A product or service which is offered without cost or obligation to the recipient may be unqualifiedly described as "free." "Free" may also be used conditionally where the offer requires the recipient to purchase some other product or service, provided all terms and conditions are accurately and conspicuously disclosed in immediate conjunction with the use of the term "free" and the product or service required to be purchased is not increased in price or decreased in quality or quantity.

7. Photographs and art work implying representation of a product or service offered should be faithful reproductions of the product or service. Photographs and art work implying situations under which a product or service would be advantageous to the purchaser should be in accord with written claims.

8. If laboratory test data are used in advertising, they should be competent as to source and methodology. Advertisers should not use excerpts of laboratory test material in support of claims which distort or fail to disclose the true test results.

9. Advertisers should not use unsupported or inaccurate testimonials; or testimonials originally given for products or services other than those offered by the advertiser; or testimonials making statements or conclusions the advertiser knows to be incorrect. If testimonials are used, they should contain no misstatement of facts or misleading implications and should reflect the current opinion of the author.

10. Advertisers who sell instruction, catalogs, mailing lists or merchandise-for-resale should not use misleading or deceptive statements with respect to the earning possibilities, lack of risk, or ease of operation.

11. Advertisers should not use promotional solicitations in the forms of bills or invoices (pro forma invoices) deceptively.

12. Advertisers should not mail unordered merchandise for which payment is demanded.

13. Advertisers should not use any list in violation of the lawful rights of the list owner, and should promptly bring to the attention of the lawful owner of any list any information they may have regarding any possible violation of the proprietary rights therein.

14. If products or services are offered on a satisfaction guaranteed or money back basis, refunds should be made promptly on request. In

an unqualified offer of refund or replacement, the customer's preference shall prevail.

15. Advertisers should be prepared to make prompt delivery of orders solicited in their copy. Unforeseen contingencies should be reported to the customer promptly when delivery is unavoidably delayed. A reply device should be included, enabling the customer, if he or she wishes, to cancel the order and obtain a refund of any purchase price already paid.

16. Advertisers should not use misleading or deceptive methods for collecting money owed by delinquent accounts.

17. Advertisers should distribute products only in a manner that will provide reasonable safeguards against possibilities of injury to children and/or adults.

18. All advertisers including those firms who use, create, produce or supply materials and/or lists for direct mail advertising should make conscientious efforts to remove names from their mailing lists when so requested either directly or in accordance with the DMAA Mail Preference Service.

MAILING LISTS

The moment you are born, you become a vital statistic. Your name is printed on a birth certificate, registered legally, placed in a newspaper notice. You become a matter of record—and an interested someone adds your name to some list.

Your parents may receive solicitations for insurance, for bronzing baby shoes, for preschool or day-care facilities. Both your name and your parents' names are worth money, possibly only a fraction of a cent, possibly more, depending on demographic variables.

And so it goes. As you mature, make purchases, join organizations, your name appears again and again, is added to new lists. Compiling and selling those lists is a multimillion-dollar business, a business vital to direct-mail sales.

Neil J. Katz, Director of Sales Service, Alvin B. Zeller, Inc., New York, mailing list compilers, explains:

When I tell someone I'm in the Mailing List business, the usual response is, "Are you responsible for filling my mail box with all that junk mail?" In all honesty, I have to admit that my business is responsible, in part, for what is called "junk mail"* by the general public. But if the recipient

---

*To remove your name from all mailing lists or to receive more mail on your favorite interests and hobbies, send instructions to Direct Mail/Marketing Association, 6 East 43rd Street, New York, New York 10017.

considers the mailing piece junk, then someone, somewhere, has used the wrong mailing list.

The Mailing List business is one area of advertising called Direct Mail/Marketing, Direct Mail Advertising, and Direct Response Advertising. Simply stated, Direct Marketing is the sale of a product or service directly to the consumer, usually through the mail, without an intermediary—such as a retail store. The producer reaches the consumer through the rental or purchase of a mailing list.

Proper selection of a list is not a haphazard operation. Most available lists—and there are thousands—are computerized, zip coded, and supplied on labels or magnetic tape. They can be chosen from broad categories with possible refinements based on

- geographic location
- sales volume
- executives by function
- Standard Industrial Classification (specific product, type of business or organization)
- parameters
- psychographics
- number of employees
- net worth rating
- institutions by type
- professionals by discipline or specialization
- families by income and children
- demographics

When you are certain which are your prime prospects, we supply exactly those names. When you are not certain, we are happy to offer advice. The object of acquiring a list is to match the offer with a list of those people most likely to react to the offer by buying, subscribing, responding in some way.

In general, there are two types of lists: *Business Lists* and *Consumer Lists.*

Business Lists are compiled from readily available sources such as telephone books, trade directories, and credit directories. They consist of *types* of businesses—florists, grocery stores, manufacturers, etc. Most lists are set up along the lines of the *Standard Industrial Classification* system, a system set up by the U. S. Government, wherein every type of business is assigned an identification number. This system is highly useful for the maintenance of a list on computer, since the operator has only to punch in a particular SIC number and a list of the selected businesses is produced.

Examples of use: A manufacturer has developed a new safety reflector for bicycles. We could easily address for him a list of bicycle dealers and, perhaps, a list of department stores addressed "Attn: Bicycle Department." A student graduating with a degree in television-radio wishes to send some résumés to TV and radio stations in a given geographical area. We can supply such a listing, including the name of the station general manager.

Consumer Lists are lists of individuals who subscribe to a particular publication or who have bought a particular product or service. These lists are usually maintained by the company owning the publication or selling the product. These companies are very selective as to whom the list is rented. Most of these list owners require that a sample mailing piece be submitted to determine if any competition exists between their product and that of the renter.

Examples of use: A new travel publication wishes to increase subscribership. Since they are in direct competition with other travel publications, they would not be able to obtain lists from competitive publications. Therefore, they would look for their potential subscribers among people who have bought luggage and other travel items, people who have charged airline tickets on their credit cards, people who have taken group tours, etc. A manufacturer has developed a new type of panty hose, plans to sell it by mail. We can supply several lists of subscribers to popular women's magazines to reach the target market.

Other facts: *Compilers* collect names and regularly "clean" the computer lists by deleting "Nixies" (undeliverable mail). Compilers deal directly with clients and brokers. Lists are rented for one-time use only, although multiusage or outright sale can be arranged.

Brokers, on the other hand, primarily manage consumer lists for the list owners. (If you compile your own list, you can rent or sell its use— become a broker.)

A client may consult with either a compiler, a broker, or both. Each controls different lists, exchanges, buys, and sells in order to service clients.

In addition, there are lettershops, either tied in with compilers or independently operated. Their job is to affix labels to envelopes, sort them according to zip codes, bag, and mail.

There is a complicated "mathematics of direct mail," depending on quantity, cost, printing, paper, postage of the mailing piece. For an *average* offer using 100,000 names, the rate of response is generally ½ to 1 percent. (Many different factors affect the rate—the mailing piece itself, design, size, timing, weather, etc.)

We urge clients to "look at the donut, not the hole."

So whether yours is a multimillion-dollar corporation with a broad sales program or a fresh new business just spreading its wings—whether you do large bulk mailings, dealer promotions by location, or want to saturate specific categories or areas, or seek pin-pointed sales leads only—the list is available, ready-made or custom-made, scientifically selected to give you an effective match: prime product to prime prospect.

Direct-mail/marketing lists are used for

- *one-shot mailings*—sending a single, persuasive letter to prime prospects for product (selling everything and anything, inexpensive or expensive, small or large, fragile or durable)
- *wear-out series*—sending out the same mailing piece again and again (new cover, new color, same *inexpensive* products such as gift items, holiday foods, books) until a predetermined percentage of prospects responds
- *campaign series*—sending a number of *preplanned* and *programmed* promotional letters and mailing pieces at regular intervals to create interest in final sales push for *one expensive product* (real estate, retirement development, office equipment)
- *continuous series*—sending own customers good-will or sales promotional mailings as variety of products are available (included with department store, credit card, utilities statements)

Whatever the product, whatever the type of mailing, the mailing lists should be restricted as far as possible to real prospects. And planning is essential. *What* you write is as important as *how* you write it. Before you write, then, think about your objective; think about your offer; think about your market. Do your research homework!

Appendix D

SELECTED LANDMARK LAWS FOR THE BUSINESS PROFESSIONAL*

Many federal laws directly or indirectly affect the forms of communication taught in the typical business communication course or used for the business of living, learning, and earning a living. This review introduces you to some of this significant legislation.

The Communications Act (1934), amended numerous times, slated for complete overhaul by Congress in the eighties, established the

- Federal Communications Commission, a centralized authority with the sole power to regulate interstate and foreign commerce in communication by wire and radio by American citizens, to make available, as far as possible, a rapid, efficient, nationwide and worldwide wire and radio communication service with adequate facilities at reasonable charges.
- Common carrier concept, whereby transmission capabilities are licensed to any citizen or group of citizens applying to and being approved by the FCC—provided a frequency is available for

*With the assistance of Don Leonard, College of Business Administration, Arizona State University; Harold W. Davey, Labor Arbitrator; Edmund G. Blinn, Department of Journalism and Mass Communication, Iowa State University; Donald S. Pady, Librarian, Iowa State University.

broadcast without interfering with others, applicant shows competency, adequacy of equipment, financial ability to make use of the assigned channel, and is primarily concerned with serving the public interest, convenience, and necessity.

(Dramatic changes in telecommunications—satellite, microwave, cable transmissions—since enactment of act opened up new channels for reception. Some channels are considered common carriers; others are not. Some channels are subject to federal antitrust laws; others are not. New channels opened doors for competition, new categories of entrepreneurial services. Each service is subject to possible court rulings and legislative regulation. Look for more medical, legal, educational uses, applications of data processing, electronic mail, teletext, two-way television for direct marketing-delivery such as QUBE system in Columbus, Ohio, electronic fund transfer, specialized mobile radio systems (SMRS), competing telephone systems. Consult a legal specialist for most recent rulings.)

The Social Security Act (1935), which has been amended 15 times, provides for

- social insurance programs for old age, survivors, disability, health insurance, and unemployment payments—the latter two also yield payments to the insured and their survivors
- public charity programs covering welfare services, institutional care, food, housing, and other forms of assistance

(Basic law recognizing responsibility of government for welfare and protection of individuals.)

National Labor Relations Act (Wagner Act, 1935), amended 1947, 1959, guarantees

- the right to form and join unions and bargain collectively through representatives of workers' own choosing
- the right to refrain from forming and joining unions

(Prohibits unfair employer/employee practices. Very complicated. Subject to many interpretations, rulings.)

Fair Labor Standards Act (1938), amended in 1974, is generally known as the Federal Wage and Hour Law. As amended, established

- minimum wage, overtime pay, equal pay, record keeping
- child labor standards for covered employment unless a specific exemption applies

(Job seekers should be aware of pay schedules.)

The Equal Pay Act (1963), amended in 1974, covers most private and public employees subject to the Fair Labor Standards Act (1938) and extends protection to executive, administrative, professional, and outside sales employees. Coverage includes most federal, state, and local government employees. The act prohibits discrimination on account of sex in the payment of wages. (An early and important antidiscrimination measure.)

Civil Rights Act (1964), Title VII, covers race, color, religion, sex, national origin. Companies may not hire, promote, or fire on the basis of any of the preceding distinctions. (Such prohibitions have made job seekers wary of including these details on their data/résumé sheets. However, *volunteering* this information is legal. Thus details may be included when an applicant believes they will be helpful.)

Executive Order 11246 (1965) provides equal opportunity in federal employment to all persons. Any organization or agency *holding a federal contract must maintain a continuing affirmative action program.* The order prohibits discrimination in employment based on race, color, religion, sex, or national origin. (As a result of this order, many organizations advertise widely, search actively for qualified job candidates.)

The Freedom of Information Act–FDIA (1966), amended 1974, 1976, was designed to speed and ease process of obtaining access to government records, procedures. (Popular with business people for information about IRS techniques, guidelines; information about enforcement strategies of federal agencies; information about competitors. Forty-eight states have enacted similar open-records legislation.)

Federal Wage Garnishment Law (1968)

- limits the amount of an employee's disposable earnings garnisheed in any one week
- protects the worker from discharge because of garnishment for any one indebtedness

(A safeguard for the over-extended, in-debt employee, offering protection from overzealous collection procedures.)

The Truth in Lending Act (1968)

- requires creditors to inform noncommercial customers in writing of the costs, terms, and conditions of a credit arrangement
- requires advertisements to specify any credit terms clearly and conspicuously

(Changed formats of direct-mail advertising and other business communications.)

Fair Credit Reporting Act (1970) covers credit bureaus, investigative reporting companies, detective and collection agencies, lenders' exchanges, and computerized information reporting companies. It

- requires these sources to adopt reasonable procedures with regard to confidentiality, accuracy, relevancy, and proper utilization of consumer credit, personnel, insurance, and other credit information
- requires credit refusers to tell applicant the *name and address* of the reporting agency if refusal is based on information from a third party transmitting *second-hand information* or a *subjective judgment* about the applicant's credit worthiness
- requires credit refuser to inform applicant of his or her 60-day right to learn the *nature* of information if the third party is a source reporting *first-hand, objective information* from only the company's experiences

(Helps applicant to correct inaccurate rating. Offers firm basis for complaint and adjustment.)

Title IX, Education Amendment Prohibition of Sex Discrimination (1972) prohibits sex discrimination in any educational program or activity receiving federal aid. (Increases participation and employment opportunities for females in subject and sport-related areas.)

The Privacy Act (1974)

- gives citizens access to information collected about them by the federal government
- enables citizens to learn how that information is used

(Information available in "due course" and for appropriate fee on application to government department. Significance: Believed to be forerunner to act broadly controlling the collection, storage, use, and dissemination of information by private industry.)

Family Educational Rights and Privacy Act (1974) gives parents and students 18 or older access to their files in public schools and colleges unless such students waive their rights. (Decreases credibility of references, inhibits statements. Files now designated "open" or "closed.")

Equal Credit Opportunity Act (1974). (Intent is to ban discrimination against any credit applicant on the basis of sex, age, or marital status.)

The Fair Credit Billing Act (1974)

- requires creditor to acknowledge written complaint about bill within 30 days, to investigate and resolve the problem within 90 days
- prohibits charging interest, closing the account, reporting the debtor to a credit-rating organization or pursuing regular collection procedures until 10 days after the creditor has answered the inquiry
- requires creditor to inform collection agencies of customer's opinion and inform customer of who received reports of delinquency
- penalizes creditor not following these rules by deducting first $50 of disputed amount and finance charges, even if the bill is correct

(Principle of good adjustment-letter writing—the quick response is now a federal dictate.)

Government in the Sunshine Act (1976) effective March 1977 (based on 1972 Federal Advisory Committee Act)

- promotes *open meetings* to increase public confidence in government, improve the quality of an agency's work, promote open discussion of issues, provide public access to government information, heighten public understanding of government decisions and the democratic process
- requires public bodies to give notice of meetings at least 24 hours in advance—time, place, and tentative agenda—by posting it on a bulletin board and notifying news media
- permits *closed doors* when such items as classified information, personnel matters, trade secrets, criminal accusations, and materials exempted by statute or private matters are discussed

(Called "formidable in spirit, but flimsy in fact," state and federal statutes differ. As of 1976, all states have some basic form of open-meetings law. All, however, have numerous loopholes, conflict with other laws, lack clear or specific language, have been the source of many legal disputes.)

U.S. Privacy Protection Study Commission Report (July 1977)

- contains numerous recommendations for legislation influencing the manner and content of communication in business

- covers consumer credit, banking, mailing lists, insurance, employment, medical care, investigative reporting
- urges businesses to adopt fair information practice codes voluntarily
- includes recommendation that employees be allowed to see, copy, correct own records in company files

(Some recommendations now state laws, may or may not become federal laws. Last item protects worker's privacy, endangers credibility of employment references.)

Fair Debt Collection Practices Act (1978) outlines what bill collectors (other than creditors or their lawyers) can and cannot do. Illegal abuses include

- threatening to tell debtor's employer or friends of delinquency
- contacting debtor's employer without specific permission
- calling before 8 A.M. or after 9 P.M. at home or at the office or making a rapid series of calls
- sending debtor letters that sound or look as though from a credit bureau, government agency; sending notices that look like court summonses
- using abusive language when speaking to debtor in person or over the phone
- trying to collect more than is due the creditor
- misrepresenting himself or herself to get entry to debtor's home to note or take something of value
- continuing to contact debtor—beyond one legal information call—after being informed *in writing* to stop

(Law may reduce telephone use, increase importance of written collection series.)

The New Copyright Law (effective January 1, 1978) is the first major revision of copyright legislation since 1909. It changed the term of copyright—previously two 28-year periods—to the life of the author plus 50 years. Protection exists from date of creation of work. Registration of works is a means to prevent loss of copyright protection and to enable one to sue for infringement. Permits "fair use" of a copyrighted work (for example, multiple copies for classroom use) if certain factors are considered, such as

- the purpose and character of the use, including whether of a commercial nature or for nonprofit educational purposes
- the nature of the copyrighted work
- the amount and substantiality of the portion used in relation to the copyrighted work as a whole

- the effect of the use upon potential market for or value of the copyrighted work

(*Single copies* permissible for use in teaching or scholarly research: chapter from book, article from newspaper or periodical, short essay, short poem, short story; graph, diagram, chart, cartoon, drawing or picture from periodical, newspaper, or book. *Multiple copies* for classroom use must meet tests for "brevity," "spontaneity," and "cumulative effect," subject to broad interpretation. Prohibitions seem more definite but equally difficult to enforce, especially with present sophisticated duplicating equipment.)

The New Bankruptcy Act (effective October 1, 1979) is the first major overhaul of bankruptcy law in 40 years. It attempts to establish a list of federal exemptions and give a bankrupt debtor a choice of federal or state exemptions.

State statutes vary widely. Generally, there is a homestead exemption, up to certain limits. In addition, the applicant may be allowed to keep a car, tools needed for work, and some personal property—up to a specified dollar limit. The law

- expands debtor's right to keep belongings away from creditors
- expands debtor's rights against harassment from creditors
- includes new reaffirmation (promises to pay debts erased by bankruptcy court) and lien-avoidance provisions more favorable to debtors
- liberalizes Chapter 13—Wage Earner Plan—making it easier for individual (or small business) to declare bankruptcy while reorganizing affairs and repaying all or part of debts

(Congress is considering amendments to the new code, for interpretations offer many escape hatches for debtors. Businesses are considering tighter lending policies designed to weed out doubtful customers, are requiring more collateral—larger down payments. Implications for collection series: earlier, faster requests for payment; shorter series; more emphasis on inquiries and appeals.)

Libel (Statutory and Common Law, as of 1981)*

Anyone who writes faces the possibility of a legal action alleging defamation. *Libel* is written defamation of character (defamation by radio or television is libel in most states, despite the spoken

*Interpreted by Edmund G. Blinn, Department of Journalism and Mass Communication, Iowa State University, Ames, Iowa.

nature of communication). *Slander* is spoken defamation. To *defame* someone is to expose him or her to the ridicule or contempt of other human beings. Damages awarded in a successful suit can be enormous, ranging up to millions of dollars. Even a successfully defended action, however, can be expensive in terms of legal fees and time.

For a *libel* to exist, three elements must be present:

- defamation
- publication
- identification

Publication legally exists when a third person sees or hears the material. A person may be *identified* by

- name
- physical description
- photograph
- drawing
- place of residence

Reference, for example, to an attorney practicing in West Swanzey, New Hampshire, will identify that person if only one lawyer is professionally active in that community. Generally, however, the published information must be false to be defamatory.

While libel should be a matter of concern for the writer, the legal defenses are effective. In almost all circumstances, if what has been written is *true* and presents information the public has a right to know, the writer can present an acceptable defense to the accusation. *Truth* is difficult to prove, particularly in a court of law; therefore most important is the defense that the material in question was presented in the public interest. But that defense will not succeed if the material was written with *actual malice.*

The legal definition of actual malice when the person written about is a public official or public figure (any person who is so well known as to be instantly recognizable or has participated actively in a public controversy) is: "Reckless disregard for truth or falsity." If the subject is a private person, the definition of malice varies with the jurisdiction—the state where the trial will take place. If, however, the writer writes with a "pure heart" (without intent to injure), that person will be immune from successful litigation in most circumstances.

In addition, writers enjoy a privilege to publish information obtained from government records (including statements made by public officials in the course of their official duties) without fear of a successful libel suit. Such publication, however, must be accurate to sustain the privilege. This defense, obviously, is of particular value to the mass media.

(Implications abound—caution is advised for writers of collection letters, recommendations, and all messages likely to be read by a third person or published. Morally, truth in writing is always important. Now the subject of one's writing is legally protected. Writers should keep informed of current legal rulings.)

Invasion of Privacy (Statutory and Common Law, as of 1981)[*]

The right to privacy has become a subject of vital concern to the writer in the past decade. Many aggrieved persons now sue for damages on the grounds of invasion of privacy rather than libel. Libel and invasion of privacy are *torts* (a tort is a civil injury) and frequently overlap. Some written or broadcast material may be both libelous and an invasion of privacy.

An examination of the cases alleging invasion of privacy reveals four distinct variations of the tort:

1. Appropriation of a person's name or likeness for commercial gain without consent
2. Placing a person in a false light in the public's perception
3. Publication of embarrassing private facts without warrant of the public interest
4. Physical intrusion on privacy

Generally, *appropriation* occurs in advertising; *false light* invasion is portraying someone as something he or she is not (falsely saying a person is a candidate for public office when that is not true, for example); *private life* invasion occurs when the material is based on gossip and not a desire to enlighten; *physical intrusion* is trespassing in person or through the use of electronic eavesdropping equipment (subterfuge, such as falsely identifying oneself as a law enforcement official in order to obtain information, is one example).

Truth may be a defense only in false light invasion. The most important defenses are consent (both written and implied) and newsworthiness. The courts have held that actions taking place in

*Professor Blinn's interpretation.

public are reportable in writing, broadcast, or photography, and that consent of the persons reported on is not necessary, except in the most extreme circumstances. (For example, a published photograph of a woman with her skirt over her head was ruled an invasion, although she was in a public place of entertainment when a jet of air revealed her undergarments.) Obviously, implied consent is difficult to prove legally, so it is wise to get written consent whenever possible, particularly when a photograph may be used for commercial purposes or when the writer will be unable to prove a public interest (as distinguished from curiosity) in the material.

As a matter of common law, the contents of a letter belong to the writer, not to the receiver. Clearly, this is an important fact as it concerns legal liability.

(Liability and invasion of privacy may also be claimed by a writer, should the receiver of a message publicize or publish the content without permission. Thus the writer has some safeguards. In addition, signing with the company's name above or below the writer's signature indicates that the writer is acting as an agent for the employers. Constant awareness of possible legal responsibilities will protect both receiver and writer.)

FURTHER READING

Christensen, Kathryn. "Taking Credit." *Wall Street Journal,* September 27, 1979.

"Fair Credit Billing: Principal Provisions." *Credit and Financial Management,* 78, March 1976, 24.

Gillmor, Donald M. and Jerome A. Barron. *Mass Communication Law,* 3rd ed. St. Paul, MN: West Publishing, 1979.

Hedge, Cynthia. "Pulling the Shades on Sunshine Legislation." *Matrix,* Summer 1979.

Hewitt, C. M. "Sociological Trends in the Law and Inflation." *American Business Law Journal,* 17, Spring 1979, 77–83.

Jackson, J. D. "Purchasing Law: How Uniform Is the Uniform Code?" *Purchasing,* 85, October 11, 1978, 83.

Jennings, Marianne. "Debt Collection and the Law." *Arizona Business,* 25, May 1978, 3–10.

Johnson, Donald F. *Copyright Handbook.* New York: R. R. Bowker, 1978.

Kovach, K. A. "Retrospective Look at the Privacy and Freedom of Information Acts." *Labor Law Journal,* 27, September 1976, 548–64.

Nelson, Harold L. and Dwight L. Teeter, Jr. *Law of Mass Communications,* 3rd ed. Mineola, NY: The Foundation Press, 1978.

Pember, Don R. *Mass Media Law.* Dubuque, IA: Wm. C. Brown, 1977.

Pertschuk, M. "Inflation Paradox: Business Regulation of Business." *Antitrust Law and Economic Review,* 10, 1978, 53–59.

Public Law 95–598, November 6, 1978. "An Act to establish a uniform law on the subject of bankruptcies." Washington, D.C.: Government Printing Office.

"Truth about Truth in Lending." *Credit and Financial Management,* 71, August 1969, 18–20.

Westermeier, J. T. Jr. and K. O. Polin. "Privacy Report to Alter Relation of Business to the Individual." *Data Management,* 15, September 1977, 30–33.

"What Does Fair Credit Reporting Mean to You?" *Credit and Financial Management,* 73, June 1971, 18–19.

"What Supervisors Should Know about Fair Employment Regulations." *Supervisory Management,* 16, May 1971, 29–32.

Handbook

Grammar, Punctuation, Mechanics, and Spelling

Grammar

In this section, the traditional definitions of the eight parts of speech are given; then the important grammatical terms are explained. The list of grammatical terms begins with the simplest terms and proceeds to the more complex.

PARTS OF SPEECH

Nouns

A **noun** is the name of a person, place, or thing. It answers the question *what?* or *who?*

> What is that? a *door*, a *book*, *liberty, Boston*
> Who is it? *John, Mother*, a *man*, a *Frenchman*

Substitute *what?* or *who?* for any word in a sentence. If the answer to the question is the word substituted, the word is a noun.

Varieties of nouns

1. A **common** noun names any one of a class of persons, places, or things.

   > boy   girl   desk   letter   car   street

2. A **proper** noun names one particular person, or one specified place, or one unique thing. The proper noun is always capitalized.

   > *Muhammad Ali*   *Robert Redford*   *John F. Kennedy*   *Saturday*   *July*
   > *America*   *Illinois*   *Hollywood*   *Main Street*   *English 101*   *Chevrolet*

3. A *collective* noun names a group of individuals who form a unit, or a group of objects that form a unit. The collective noun is singular in form; it may be either singular or plural in meaning, depending on how it is used in each particular instance.

> team   orchestra   jury   family
> A *number* of politicians *are* leaving the room.
> The *number* of complaints *has* increased.
> *Half* of the cake *was* eaten immediately.
> *Half* of the students *were* wrong.

4. A *concrete* noun names something that can be touched or seen or experienced by one of the other senses.

> table   sun   candy   smoke

5. An *abstract* noun names an idea or a quality that has no physical existence.

> beauty   hatred   patriotism   wisdom

Uses of nouns

1. Subject of a sentence

> The young *man* looked for a job.

2. Object of a verb

> The young man wrote his *résumé*.

3. Object of a preposition

> He gave his résumé to the *interviewer*.

4. Object of a verbal

> While the personnel director prepared to conduct the *interview*, the job candidate sat nervously in the outer office.

5. Predicate nominative

> It was a good *interview*.

6. Predicate object

> The interviewer called the job candidate the perfect *choice*.

7. Appositive

> The job candidate, a college *graduate* with prior sales experience, was obviously the better choice.

8. Nominative of address

> "*Phil*, you've got the job," the interviewer said.

Pronouns

A *pronoun* is a word that usually takes the place of a noun. Like the noun, it answers the question *what?* or *who?*

Varieties of pronouns

1. Personal

   I   you   he   we   they
   I wrote the letter.

2. Demonstrative

   this   that   these   those
   This is my letter.

3. Relative

   who   which   that   what
   I am the woman *who* wrote it.

4. Interrogative

   who   which   what
   Who wrote it?

5. Indefinite

   each   either   neither   one   none   few   some   several   many
   Each job applicant sent a cover letter and a résumé.

6. Reflexive

   myself   yourself   herself
   Many applicants saw *themselves* as the best candidates for the job.

Other characteristics of pronouns

Although its main function is to take the place of a noun, a pronoun may also substitute for another pronoun, a phrase, a clause, a sentence, a verbal, and other parts of speech. A pronoun agrees with its *antecedent* (page 513) in *gender* (page 514) and in *number* (page 514). For *person* in relation to pronouns, see page 516, and for *case,* page 515.

Verbs

A *verb* is a word that shows action, feeling, being, or state of being.

> I *ran;* I *jumped;* I *wrote.*
> I *loved;* I *hated;* I *hoped.*
> I *am;* I *seem;* I *become.*
> I *am* happy; I *have been* happy; I *have had* fun.

Varieties of verbs

1. A verb that needs an object to complete its meaning is called a **transitive** verb.

   > Please *lay* the application on the table.

2. A verb that makes a complete statement by itself and does not need an object to complete the meaning is called an **intransitive** verb.

   > I *sleep.*
   > I *lie* down.

Verbs that cause difficulty are *lie* and *lay, sit* and *set, rise* and *raise.*

Present Tense	Past Tense	Present Participle	Past Participle
TRANSITIVE			
lay (place)	laid	laying	(had) laid
set	set	setting	(had) set
raise	raised	raising	(had) raised
INTRANSITIVE			
lie (rest)	lay	lying	(had) lain
sit	sat	sitting	(had) sat
rise	rose	rising	(had) risen

Forms of verbs

1. A **regular** verb is a verb that forms its past tense and past participle by adding *d, ed,* or *t* to the infinitive.

bore	*bored*	*bored*
fear	*feared*	*feared*
deal	*dealt*	*dealt*

2. An ***irregular*** verb is a verb that forms its principal parts by changing the stem vowel or other parts of the infinitive.

> *come   came   come*
> *see   saw   seen*
> *write   wrote   written*

Voices of verbs

1. The ***active*** voice is the form of the verb that shows that the subject of the sentence performs the act.

> Jack *wrote* the letter.

2. The ***passive*** voice is the form of the verb that shows that the subject of the sentence is acted upon.

> The letter *was written* by Jack.

Tenses of verbs

Verbs have six tenses that are built on three principal parts: the present stem (infinitive), the past, and the past participle. (An ***auxiliary*** verb is a verb that helps form tenses of other verbs. Some of the common auxiliaries are *do, have, may, can, will.* [He *has* gone away.])

1. The ***present*** tense shows that an action is taking place now, or is generally true and customary.

> Barbara *looks* for a job today.
> It *is* hard to find a job these days.

2. The ***past*** tense shows that an action took place at a previous time.

> Michael *looked* for a job last year.
> It *was* easier to find a job then.

3. The ***future*** tense shows that an action will take place in time to come.

> Barbara's sister *will look* for a job next year.
> It *will be* just as hard to find a job then.

4. The ***present perfect*** tense shows that an action that began in the past is complete at present or extends to the present.

> David *has been looking* for an ideal job for years.
> He *has been* optimistic for years.

5. The ***past perfect*** tense shows that an action was completed by a definite time in the past.

> David *had been looking* for a job when he came across the ad in the classified section.
> He *had been* out of work up to that time.

Grammar

6. The *future perfect* tense shows that an action will be completed by a definite time in the future.

> David *will have looked* for the ideal job for a long time before he finds it.
> He *will have been* out of work for some time before then.

THE TENSES

IRREGULAR VERB

write, wrote, written

REGULAR VERB

decide, decide, decided

Built on the Infinitive

Present—I write

Future—I shall write

I decide

I shall decide

Built on the Past

(Note that the past tense form is **never** linked with an auxiliary verb.)

Past—I wrote

I decided

Built on the Past Participle

(Note that the past participle form is **always** linked with an auxiliary verb.)

Present Perfect—I have written

Past Perfect—I had written

Future Perfect—I shall have written

I have decided

I had decided

I shall have decided

Following are the principal parts of some familiar verbs.

Present Infinitive	Past Tense	Past Participle
REGULAR VERBS		
agree	agreed	agreed
apply	applied	applied
attack	attacked	attacked
deal	dealt	dealt
IRREGULAR VERBS		
arise	arose	arisen
awake	awoke, awaked	awoke, awaked
be	was	been

Grammar

Present Infinitive	Past Tense	Past Participle
bear	bore	borne
beat	beat	beat, beaten
become	became	become
begin	began	begun
behold	beheld	beheld
bend	bent	bent
bid (offer)	bid	bid
bid (command)	bade	bidden, bid
bind	bound	bound
bite	bit	bitten, bit
bleed	bled	bled
blow	blew	blown
break	broke	broken
bring	brought	brought
build	built	built
burst	burst	burst
buy	bought	bought
cast	cast	cast
catch	caught	caught
choose	chose	chosen
cling	clung	clung
come	came	come
cost	cost	cost
creep	crept	crept
cut	cut	cut
deal	dealt	dealt
dig	dug	dug
do	did	done
draw	drew	drawn
dream	dreamed, dreamt	dreamed, dreamt
drink	drank	drunk
drive	drove	driven
eat	ate	eaten
fall	fell	fallen
feed	fed	fed
feel	felt	felt
fell (cause to fall)	felled	felled
fight	fought	fought
find	found	found
flee	fled	fled
fling	flung	flung
fly	flew	flown

Present Infinitive	*Past Tense*	*Past Participle*
forbid	forbade, forbad	forbidden, forbid
forget	forgot	forgotten, forgot
forgive	forgave	forgiven
freeze	froze	frozen
get	got	got, gotten
give	gave	given
go	went	gone
grind	ground	ground
grow	grew	grown
hang (kill)	hanged	hanged
hang (suspend)	hung	hung
have	had	had
hide	hid	hidden, hid
hit	hit	hit
hold	held	held
hurt	hurt	hurt
keep	kept	kept
know	knew	known
lay	laid	laid
lead	led	led
leave	left	left
lend	lent	lent
let	let	let
lie (recline)	lay	lain
lie (deceive)	lied	lied
light	lighted, lit	lighted, lit
lose	lost	lost
make	made	made
meet	met	met
read	read	read
ride	rode	ridden
ring	rang	rung
rise	rose	risen
see	saw	seen
seek	sought	sought
sell	sold	sold
send	sent	sent
set	set	set
shake	shook	shaken
shine (give light)	shone	shone
shine (polish)	shined	shined

Present Infinitive	Past Tense	Past Participle
shoot	shot	shot
shrink	shrank, shrunk	shrunk
shut	shut	shut
sing	sang, sung	sung
sink	sank, sunk	sunk
sit	sat	sat
sleep	slept	slept
slide	slid	slid
sow	sowed	sown, sowed
speak	spoke	spoken
spend	spent	spent
spin	spun	spun
spread	spread	spread
spring	sprang, sprung	sprung
stand	stood	stood
steal	stole	stolen
stick	stuck	stuck
sting	stung	stung
stink	stank, stunk	stunk
strike	struck	struck
string	strung	strung
strive	strove	striven
swear	swore	sworn
sweep	swept	swept
swim	swam	swum
swing	swung	swung
take	took	taken
teach	taught	taught
tear	tore	torn
tell	told	told
think	thought	thought
throw	threw	thrown
understand	understood	understood
wake	waked, woke	waked
wear	wore	worn
weave	wove	woven
weep	wept	wept
win	won	won
wind	wound	wound
wring	wrung	wrung
write	wrote	written

Adjectives

An **adjective** is a word that modifies a noun or pronoun, usually by answering the question, *what kind?* or *how many?* or *which?* or *whose?*

> Résumés are often done in a *creative, contemporary* style. (What kind?)
> All résumés should provide the name of *each* company where the applicant worked. (How many?)
> *These* facts are important. (Which?)
> With *their* résumés, job seekers present *their* qualifications. (Whose?)

Notice that in these sentences, the words *all, these,* and *their* are adjectives. Only two adjectives require change of form to indicate number: *this, these; that, those.*

Adverbs

An **adverb** is a word that modifies a verb, an adjective, or another adverb, usually by answering the question, *when?* or *how?* or *where?* or *why?* or *to what degree?*

> Barbara used to send her résumés *everywhere*. (Where?)
> She *now* concentrates on places in which she is *really* interested. (When? To what degree?)
> She worked *efficiently, persistently,* and *relentlessly*. (How?)
> She was *not very* enthusiastic about some of the companies with which she interviewed. (To what degree?)
> She *therefore* tries to screen out the *less* desirable companies *before* she accepts interviews. (Why? To what degree? When?)

CAUTION

1. Adverbs and adjectives should be placed near the words or word groups that they modify.
2. Many adverbs are formed by adding *ly* to an adjective *(brave—bravely; beautiful—beautifully; quick—quickly)*. But many adverbs are not formed in this way *(well, now, right)*. And many adjectives end in *ly* (which in Anglo-Saxon meant "like" when affixed to a noun: *lovely, manly, fatherly, saintly, hourly, monthly).* When in doubt, consult the dictionary.
3. As a rule, *is, was, seems, becomes,* and the verbs pertaining to the five senses *(look, smell, feel, sound, taste)* are followed by an adjective.

> My résumé is *creative.*
> It seems *effective.*
> I feel *good* about getting the job.

Prepositions

A *preposition* is a word that shows the relationship between a noun (or noun equivalent) and another part of the sentence.

> Which *of* these résumés has the most information *about* job skills?
> Which *among* them has the least?

1. The noun or pronoun that follows the preposition is in the objective case.

> I brought my résumé into the *office.*
> Out of sixty *applicants,* only seven were granted interviews. Among *them* were the best educated.

2. The preposition usually comes before its object. But it may, and in idiomatic expressions it often does, follow its object. (In the following sentences, the prepositions are underlined once, their objects twice.)

> I'm not afraid of interviews.
> My boss has a lot on his mind.
> What are you talking about?
> Whom is it for?

CAUTION

The preposition is a tricky part of speech. Some words in English can be accompanied only by certain prepositions for correct usage. The most frequently used prepositions are *at, by, for, from, in, of, on, to,* and *with.*

Conjunctions

A *conjunction* is a word that joins two parts of a sentence.

1. A *coordinating conjunction* joins words, or word groups, that are of equal grammatical rank. The main coordinating conjunctions are *and, but, for, or,* and *nor.*

> I disagree with what you say, *but* I will defend your right to say it.

A *conjunctive adverb* is one of a small number of words in English that are primarily adverbs but are also often used as coordinating conjunctions, when the writer places them at the junction point between main clauses. (A *clause* is a group of words containing a subject and a predicate.) Some of the conjunctive adverbs are *accordingly, also, besides, consequently, furthermore, however, indeed, likewise, moreover, namely, nevertheless, still, then, therefore,* and *yet.*

> I am highly qualified; *consequently,* I have no problem finding a good job.

Expressions used between main clauses to form compound sentences are considered conjunctive adverbs: *that is, in fact, on the contrary, on the other hand, in the first place, to tell the truth,* and *for example.*

> There are many ways to write a refusal letter; *for example,* you might start with a buffer.

2. A ***subordinating conjunction*** is a word that connects a subordinate clause to the main clause. (A subordinate clause is simply another name for a dependent clause.) Some of the more common subordinating conjunctions are *after, although, as, as if, because, before, if, since, though, until, unless, when, where, while,* and *why.* The relative pronouns *(who, which, what, that)* may also be used as subordinating conjunctions.

> You probably won't find a good job *unless* you look for it.
>
> *Although* I was not as skilled as some of the other applicants, I was more motivated and more innovative.

CAUTION

1. You can distinguish a subordinating conjunction from a conjunctive adverb by remembering that the subordinating conjunction is **always** at the beginning of a subordinate clause; the conjunctive adverb, on the other hand, can be placed in various positions in the sentence **when it is being used as an ordinary adverb rather than as a conjunction.**

> She is a good letterwriter; *however,* she isn't as good as she thinks she is.
>
> She is a good letterwriter; she isn't as good as she thinks she is, *however.*
>
> *Because* she is a good letterwriter, she gets to write most of the company's business letters. (The word *because* cannot be shifted; it must be placed at the beginning of a subordinate clause.)

2. A comma is often used between main clauses that are joined by a coordinating conjunction. A comma separates a subordinate clause from the main clause in many cases. A semicolon is used before a conjunctive adverb when it joins two main clauses to form a compound sentence. A semicolon comes before an expression used as a conjunctive adverb, and the comma comes after it. But be sure that the conjunctive adverb is joining two main clauses. If it is used some other place in the sentence, set it off with commas, for it is not joining—it is interrupting.

Interjections

An ***interjection*** is an exclamation. It expresses emotion, greeting, or parting; it is independent of the rest of the sentence.

1. An interjection strongly expressed is usually followed by an exclamation mark.

> *Help! Help!*
>
> *Oh no, Mr. Bill! Not again!*

2. An interjection mildly expressed is usually followed by a comma or a period.

> *Hello*, Mary.
> *Ah*, there you are.
> *Oh*, I think I'll wait here.
> *Yes*, I do.

3. Some words that are usually used as other parts of speech may be used as interjections.

> *Well*, it took you a long time.
> *Why*, I did it as fast as I could.

   A part of speech, if it proves versatile, may become a member of several different groups. The word *round*, for example, can be five different parts of speech, depending on how it is used in a sentence.

> We're having a second *round* of interviews. (noun)
> This office is not *round*. (adjective)
> The string *round* the package tore loose. (preposition)
> *Round* up the applicants. (verb)
> They are walking *round* and *round*. (adverb)

It is not what a word *is* but what it *does* in a sentence that determines what part of speech that word is.

GRAMMATICAL TERMS

Subjects

The person, place, or thing about which something is said is called the **subject.**
1. A **simple subject** is the one word referring to the person, place, or thing.

> Many *employers* use executive search services.

2. A **complete subject** is the simple subject plus its modifiers.

> *Many employers* use executive search services.

3. A **compound subject** is more than one simple subject joined by *and.*

> *Executive search services and employment agencies* can be helpful to employers.

Predicates

That part of a sentence, including the verb, that tells what the subject is doing or being is called the **predicate.**

1. A *simple predicate* is the verb that indicates the subject's action or being.

> Letterwriting *is* an important activity in most companies.

2. A *complete predicate* is the verb plus its modifiers.

> Letterwriting *is an important activity in most companies.*

3. A *compound predicate* is more than one verb joined with *and*.

> Business people *write* letters and *read* reports.

Clauses

A *clause* is a group of words containing a subject and a predicate.

1. A *main clause* (also called an **independent** or **principal clause**) expresses a complete thought.

> A research <u>corporation</u> recently <u>made</u> a report.
>   **subject**   **predicate**
>
> <u>It</u> <u>forecast</u> a 50% increase in the number of employees at Company A.
> **S** **P**

Each sentence above is a main clause.

2. A *subordinate clause* (also called a *dependent clause*) is not complete within itself and cannot stand alone. It is used as a noun, adjective, or adverb, and it begins with one of the subordinating conjunctions listed on page 508.

> <u>Computers play an important role in the modern office</u>
> **main clause**
> <u>because they increase both speed and efficiency of operations.</u>
> **subordinate clause**

In the sentence above, both groups of words are clauses: each contains a subject and a predicate. The first group could stand alone as a simple sentence; the second—beginning with *because*—could not stand alone because it does not make a complete statement. Say it aloud and you'll hear the difference.

A subordinate clause can be used as an adverb.

> Computers are used *wherever they can save time and reduce human error.*

A subordinate clause can be used as an adjective.

> Offices *that use computers* are usually very efficient.

A subordinate clause can also be used as a noun.

> Another report revealed *that computers are being used more than ever before.*

CAUTION

You determine what the clause is being used for by asking one of the questions under "Parts of Speech." In the last three examples above, the subordinate clause answers *why? which?* and *what?*

Phrases

A *phrase* is a group of words used as a unit in a sentence. It does not have a subject and a predicate.

1. A *gerund phrase* is used as a noun (see Verbals).

> *Conducting interviews* is one way to screen job applicants.

2. An *infinitive phrase* is used as a noun, adjective, or adverb (see Verbals).

> *To know your audience* is most important in writing a sales letter. (noun)

3. A *participial phrase* is used as an adjective (see Verbals).

> *Having been trained,* the new employee is ready to begin work.

4. A *prepositional phrase* is used as an adjective or an adverb.

> I sent a letter to my *client.* (Where? adverb)
> The letter *in the blue envelope* is mine. (Which? adjective)

5. A *verb phrase* is used as a verb. It is part of the predicate.

> Interviews *were used* to screen the applicants.

Verbals

A *verbal* is a form of the verb that is used as a noun, an adjective, or an adverb. Since a verbal is not a verb, a sentence that has a verbal but no verb is not a complete sentence.

> *To write* a letter to your client
> *Going, going,* always *going,* but never *getting* there
> *Having written* two business letters

The three word groups above are all incomplete sentences because a verbal is not a substitute for a verb.

1. A *gerund* is a verbal ending in *ing* and used as a noun.

> *Working* is crucial.

2. A *participle* is a verbal used as an adjective. The present participle ends in *ing*; the past participle ends in *ed, d, t, en, n,* or makes an internal change.

> The *working* parts of a machine must be kept in good repair.

CAUTION

In the last two examples, both words (*working*) look alike. How the word is used in its own sentence determines what it is called.

3. An ***infinitive*** is a verbal, usually preceded by *to,* that may be used as a noun, adverb, or adjective.

> *To work* is crucial. (noun)
>
> He went *to work.* (adverb)
>
> I have employees *to work* the night shift. (adjective)

Substantives

A ***substantive*** is any word or group of words used as a noun. All such words or groups of words will answer *what?* or *who?*

> *Whosoever questions this* will find it true.

Appositives

An ***appositive*** is a word or word group that is placed after another word or word group and that has the same meaning as the original one. The test of an appositive is that one substantive can be substituted for the other without changing the meaning of the sentence.

> Mr. Jones, *my boss,* likes to write his own letters.

Sentences

A ***sentence*** is a group of words that express a complete statement.

1. A ***simple sentence*** has one main clause. It may have more than one subject or more than one predicate.

> I write letters.
> S   P
>
> I write letters and telephone clients.
> S   P   P
>
> My boss and I work together as a team.
>   S   S   P

2. A ***compound sentence*** has two or more main clauses.

> I write letters and my boss telephones clients.
> **main clause**   **main clause**

3. A *complex sentence* has one main clause and one or more subordinate clauses.

> It was Barbara who wrote the report.
> **main clause** **subordinate clause**

4. A *compound-complex sentence* has two or more main clauses and one or more subordinate clauses.

> Mr. Juarez interviewed the man who seemed so qualified for the job,
> **main clause** **subordinate clause**
> and the personnel assistant checked the references that the applicant had given
> **main clause** **subordinate**
> on his résumé.
> **clause**

Modifiers

A *modifier* is a word, phrase, or clause that describes, limits, or qualifies the meaning of another word or group of words. All adjectives and adverbs are modifiers.

1. *Restrictive* modifiers are necessary to the meaning of the sentence. They cannot be left out of the sentence.

> It was Mr. Juarez *who realized how well qualified the applicant really was.* (subordinate clause)
> Mr. Juarez asked for the *long* report, not the *short* one. (word)
> He grew tired *of reading the report after a few minutes.* (phrase)

Nonrestrictive modifiers add further information to the sentence, but may be left out. Such modifiers are set off by commas. The sentence can be clearly understood without the modifier.

> The interviewer was effective, *asking each man asking pertinent questions.* (verbal phrase)
> The applicant, *who thought Mr. Juarez a very good interviewer,* was generally impressed with the company. (subordinate clause)
> *Fortunately,* the applicant was offered the job. (word)

Antecedents

An *antecedent* is a word or word group to which a pronoun refers. There should never be any doubt as to which word is the antecedent of the pronoun. The reference should be clear and definite.

In the following examples, the reference is not clear, because the antecedent of each pronoun is not clearly identified.

> Mr. Juarez told the applicant that *his* statement had been incorrectly quoted.
> Mr. Juarez reviewed the applicant's test scores. *This* proved *his* superiority.
> The company announced that no persons were to be laid off without *their* consent.

The following example is correct.

> The applicant's text scores were reviewed. They proved his superiority. ("His" clearly refers back to "The applicant.")

Agreement

Every verb must agree with its subject in **number.** Every pronoun must agree with its antecedent in **number** and **gender.**

Definitions

Number is the indication of whether a noun, a pronoun, or a verb is one (singular) or more than one (plural).

Gender is the indication of whether a noun or pronoun is feminine, masculine, or neuter. The relative pronoun *who* usually refers to persons (either male or female), *which* to things, and *that* to either persons or things.

Rules for agreement

1. A singular pronoun is used in referring to such antecedents as *another, any, anybody, anything, each, each one, either, everybody, everyone, neither, nobody, none, no one, nothing, one, other, somebody, someone, something, man, woman,* or *person.*

   > *Someone* handed in *his* report three days early.

2. Two or more antecedents joined by *and* take a plural pronoun.

   > *Rena* and *her secretary* wrote *their* report.

3. Two or more singular antecedents joined by *or* or *nor* take a singular pronoun. If one of two antecedents joined by *or* is singular and one is plural, the pronoun usually agrees with the nearer.

   > Neither the *employees* nor *the company president* knows *his* exact salary.

4. Two or more subjects joined by *and* take a plural verb.

   > *Jon* and *Bill were* calling on their customers.

5. Indefinite pronouns *(each, either)* take singular verbs.

   > *Each was* sure he would bring in more sales.

6. Collective nouns *(team, orchestra)* usually take singular verbs (and are referred to by singular pronouns); but they take plural verbs when the individuals of the group are regarded separately.

   > The *committee issues* a monthly report.
   > The *team have* been unable to agree on a leader.

CAUTION

1. When the subject follows the verb, take special care to determine the subject and to make sure that the verb and subject agree.

> There were arguments after the last committee meeting.
>   **V**   **S**

2. The subject is not changed by the addition of such expressions as *together with, with, as well as, no less than, accompanied by,* or *including.*

> Bill, as well as the rest of the committee, was ready to adjourn by 6 P.M.
> **S**   **V**

3. A relative pronoun used as a subject is plural or singular, depending on its antecedent.

> Her message of appreciation, in the *memos and letters* that *were* distributed, was gratefully acknowledged by her employees. ("That" refers to "memos and letters" and has a plural verb "were." "Message of appreciation" is singular and uses the singular verb "was.")

4. A verb agrees with its subject, not necessarily with its predicate noun.

> Her chief *claim* to fame *was* her diplomacy and her knowledge of human nature.

5. A title of a book or a word used in a special sense takes a singular verb.

> *How to Communicate in Business was* written by Mabel Sanchez several years ago.

Predicate Nouns (Complements)

A substantive that completes the sense of the verb is called a **predicate noun,** or **complement.**

> Mrs. Juarez is a *member* of the board.

Case

Case indicates the relationship between a noun or pronoun and another element in the sentence. The three cases used in English are the **nominative** (for the subject), the **possessive** (to show ownership), and the **objective** (for the object). Nouns have a common form for the nominative case and the objective case, but all the personal pronouns except *you* and *it* have different forms for the nominative case and the objective case.

NOUN

	Nominative	*Possessive*	*Objective*
SINGULAR	boy	boy's	boy
PLURAL	boys	boys'	boys

PRONOUN

	Nominative	*Possessive*	*Objective*
SINGULAR			
First Person	I	my, mine	me
Second Person	you	your, yours	you
Third Person	he, she, it	his, her, hers, its	him, her, it
PLURAL			
First Person	we	our, ours	us
Second Person	you	your, yours	you
Third Person	they	their, theirs	them

RELATIVE PRONOUN

	Nominative	*Possessive*	*Objective*
SINGULAR AND PLURAL	who	whose	whom

Use the nominative case in the following situations:
1. When a noun or pronoun is the subject of a verb

> *Mrs. Lee* is a fine corporation president.
> *She* is a member of the board, and the other *members* appreciate her hard work.

2. After the conjunction *than* or the conjunction *as*

> Bill is better than *I* at letterwriting. One day as *he* entered the office, a client stopped him and complimented him on his fine letters.

3. As the predicate complement of a verb

> It was *he* who wrote that marvelous sales letter last month.

Use the possessive case in the following situations:
1. To show ownership

> *Bill's* sense of duty and *his* devotion to the *company's* tradition are well known.

2. Preceding the gerund (usually)

> *His* letterwriting skill has gained us many new clients.

CAUTION

1. Use an *of*-phrase instead of the possessive when writing of inanimate objects.

> The extent *of his achievement* is known by everyone in the company.

2. Do not use the apostrophe to form the possessive of personal pronouns (*his, hers, its*), which have already changed spelling to form the possessive case.

3. To form the possessive case of a noun, add either *'s* or an apostrophe (') to the noun. ***Never change the spelling of the noun itself to form the possessive***: only add to it the *'s* or the (').

   a. Nouns that do not end in *s* add *'s* to form the possessive.

   man—man's   men—men's   horse—horse's   bird—bird's   day—day's

   b. Plural nouns that end in *s* add only (') to form the possessive.

   horses—horses'   birds—birds'   day—days'   hens—hens'

   c. Singular nouns that end in *s* add either *'s* or ('), depending on pronunciation, to form the possessive.

   Phyllis—Phyllis's   lass—lass's   Moses—Moses'   bass—bass's

   d. Compound nouns form the possessive by adding (') only to the last noun.

   brother-in-law's interference   commander-in-chief's decision

   e. To show joint possession, add *'s* or (') only to the last noun.

   O'Connor and Goldberg's shoe store   Sauter-Finnegan's orchestra

Use the objective case in the following situations:

1. When the noun or pronoun is the object of a verb or preposition

   Most of *us* have written outstanding *reports* for the *committee*.
   We write *them* in different *formats*.

2. When the noun or pronoun is the subject, the object, or the objective complement of an infinitive

   To write *them* requires research.
   They wanted *him* to be head of the department.

The case of a relative pronoun is determined by how that pronoun is used in its own clause:

1. Use the nominative case when the relative pronoun is the subject of the clause.

   Members of the committee tell ***whoever*** will listen how many reports they
                                    S
   have issued so far.
   Mrs. Sanchez, ***who*** was vice-president last year, is president of the company this year.
                   S

2. Use the objective case when the relative pronoun is the object, subject, or objective complement of an infinitive.

   She is the kind of president ***whom*** employees respect.
                                  O

3. Use the objective case when the relative pronoun is the object of a verb or preposition.

   Mrs. Sanchez, ***whom*** Bill admired, was always courteous and respectful to her employees.
                   O

CAUTION

The case of a relative pronoun depends upon the part that pronoun plays *in its own clause*. If you have difficulty deciding whether *who* or *whom* should be used, substitute the third person personal pronoun (in the correct gender and number). Ignore the main clause; you are interested only in the subordinate clause in which the *who* or *whom* appears.

1. The rule holds even when the case in which the pronoun appears is the object of a preposition or a verb.

> The personnel director interviews **whoever** is qualified.
> The letter belongs to **whoever** writes it.

2. The rule holds, even when parenthetical expressions stand between the pronoun and its verb.

> It is Bill **who** some committee members think is our best letterwriter.
> Other committee members think that Barbara, **whom** I suppose you know, is the best.

Objects

An **object** is a substantive that receives the action of a transitive verb or follows a preposition.

1. A **direct object** is a substantive that receives the action of a transitive verb.

> Barbara writes creative *letters.*

2. An **indirect object** is a substantive for whom, or to whom, the verb performs its action. The indirect object comes before the direct object unless it is part of a prepositional phrase.

> She gave *Mrs. Juarez* a letter.
> She gave a letter to *Mrs. Juarez.*

3. The **object of a preposition** is any noun or its equivalent (substantive) used to complete the meaning of that preposition.

> When Bin Lim, our purchasing agent, got tired of *paying* top prices for stationery, he started to send out *requests* for *bids.*

Comparison of Adjectives and Adverbs

Adjectives and adverbs change form to indicate the degree of a particular quality that they possess. There are three degrees: **positive** (statement about one thing), **comparative** (statement about two things), and **superlative** (statement about three or more things).

> Barbara writes *long* reports.
> Bill writes *longer* reports.
> Bin Lim writes the *longest* reports of all.

Positive	Comparative	Superlative
good	better	best
high	higher	highest

Article

The definite article is *the.* The indefinite articles are *a* and *an. An* is usually used before nouns beginning with vowel-sounds (*a, e, i, o, u,* and *h* when it is not sounded—*honor*). *A* is usually used before words beginning with consonants. Articles are classified as adjectives.

1. **Omit** the article when writing of an indefinite quantity or quality.

> Creative letters are fun to receive.

2. **Use** the article when writing of definite people, places, or things.

> *The* letter I am writing may create new sales.

Inflection

Inflection is the change of form by which a word indicates its relationship to some other word or group of words.

1. **Declension** is the inflection of nouns and pronouns.

> *man   man's   man*—(nominative, possessive, objective)
>
> *I   my   me*—(nominative, possessive, objective)

2. **Conjugation** is the inflection of a verb to indicate *tense* (present, past, future, past perfect, present perfect, future perfect); *voice* (active or passive); *person* (first, second, third); *number* (singular or plural).

3. **Comparison** is the inflection of adverbs and adjectives.

> *fast   faster   fastest*—(positive, comparative, superlative)

Independent Element

An **independent element** is an expression that has no grammatical connection with the rest of the sentence. Such an expression must be separated from the rest of the sentence by a comma.

1. **Interjection**

> *Oh,* we're done at last!

2. **Direct address**

> I hope, *reader,* that you will like this.

3. *Parenthetical expression*

> The whole book, *we hope,* will help you.

4. *Absolute expression*

> *The exercises having been written,* the book is complete.

(An *absolute* consists of a noun plus an adjective—"exercises" is the noun and "having been written" is the adjective phrase.)

Mood

Mood is the distinction of form in a verb to indicate the manner in which an action or state is conceived. English has the indicative, subjunctive, and imperative moods.

1. The *indicative mood* states a fact or asks a question.

> The report is on the desk.
> Is the report on the desk?

2. The *imperative mood* gives a command or makes a request.

> Put the report on the desk.

3. The *subjunctive mood* expresses doubt, a condition contrary to fact, a wish, a regret, or a hope. The subjunctive is rapidly being replaced by the indicative.

> I did not think she *would put* the report on the desk.

Word Order

The natural word order in an English sentence is subject—verb—object. An inverted order puts the verb, or the object, before the subject.

> I wrote five letters today.
> S V   O
> Five letters wrote I today.
>   O   V S

Idiom

An *idiom* is a way of saying things that is peculiar to each language. The idiom may vary from the usual construction of that language, but it is perfectly acceptable. It is rarely possible to translate an idiom literally into another language.

> Mr. Lim *caught a cold.*
> He refused *to put up* with his doctor's restrictions.

Punctuation

PUNCTUATION AT THE END OF A SENTENCE (TERMINAL)

To indicate the end of a sentence, use one of these punctuation marks: the period, the question mark, or the exclamation mark.

By far the most frequently used mark is the period. It is put at the end of a declarative sentence. A declarative sentence is one making a statement. What a sentence declares may be foolish, dull, or fascinating, but that does not affect the punctuation. When a declarative sentence comes to an end, put a period after it, like this.

The question mark is used at the end of a sentence that asks a question. Did you know that? It is not used at the end of an indirect question.

The exclamation mark is not nearly as popular as it once was. It is used after an expression of strong feeling. Since modern society encourages people to restrain their emotions in public, they tend to understate things rather than shout them. Today, anyone who uses very many exclamations seems to be overexcited. Believe me!

Period (.)

Use a period in the following situations:

1. To indicate the end of a declarative sentence

> Political action committees are organizations formed to collect political contributions.

2. To show the omission of words in a quotation (These spaced dots are called ***ellipsis points.***)

> "Unions and trade associations have been able to form such committees since the 1940s. . . ."

521

(For other uses of the period and ellipses, see page 528.)

Question Mark (?)

Use a question mark in the following situations:

1. To indicate the end of an interrogatory sentence

    When were corporations allowed to form political action committees?

2. To indicate the end of an interrogatory quotation

    The writer asked, "Did the Federal Election Campaign Act of 1971 have any effect on political action committees?"

(For other uses of the question mark, see page 528.)

Exclamation Mark (!)

Use an exclamation mark after an exclamation.

    Yes!
    Hands off!

PUNCTUATION WITHIN A SENTENCE (INTERNAL)

Children can get along without any punctuation marks. When they are forced to use some, they usually find the terminal marks—period, question mark, exclamation mark—sufficient. Children tend to say things directly and briefly, in simple sentences that contain no series and no inverted order; hence their sentences need no internal punctuation.

Adults use a more complicated system of communication. Within a single sentence they may interrupt the flow of words more than once to express themselves accurately. On paper, these interruptions are shown by four major marks of internal (inside-a-sentence) punctuation: the comma, the semicolon, the colon, and the dash.

These marks serve different purposes. Each of them has a special job to do. Most people who use one punctuation mark where they ought to use another one are doing so simply because they don't know any better. It is very easy to know better. Follow these guidelines and watch your punctuation improve.

Comma (,)

Use a comma in the following situations:

1. To separate the units of a list or series. The comma before the last item of a series is optional.

The Federal Election Campaign Act of 1971, the amendment in 1974, and the amendment in 1975 helped corporations gain the right to form political action committees.

2. To set off nonrestrictive modifiers. A ***nonrestrictive modifier*** is one adding something *helpful* but not essential to the word or phrase it is describing. Usually, the meaning of the sentence would be clear even if the nonrestrictive modifer were omitted. To show that a modifier is nonrestrictive, put commas around it.

   A ***restrictive modifier,*** on the other hand, is one essential to a clear understanding of the sentence. For instance, in the sentence "I will vote against anyone who favors tyranny," the clause "who favors tyranny" is a restrictive modifier because without it the sentence is meaningless.

   a. To set off a nonrestrictive clause

      The law, *which says corporate funds can be used for the purpose of establishing political action committees,* is a combination of the earlier act and its amendments.

   b. To set off a nonrestrictive phrase

      Unlike corporate funding, the political fund is made up entirely of personal contributions.

   c. To set off a nonrestrictive appositive. An ***appositive*** is a modifier placed immediately after a word or expression. It means the same thing as that word or expression. When an appositive is nonrestrictive, it is set off by commas.

      PACs, *political action committees,* are funded by personal contributions because by law this is a right reserved exclusively for the individual, corporation, or union.

3. To set off parenthetical elements (interrupters)
   a. A word, phrase, or clause interrupting the flow of the sentence should be set off by commas.

      This right, *by law,* applies to the right to contribute to federal elections.

   b. Adverbs not joining clauses are usually set off by commas.

      There are, *however,* legal restrictions on PACs.

4. To separate independent clauses joined by *and, but, or, nor,* and *for*

      Corporate PACs may request contributions only from shareholders and members of management, and they may not make contributions of more than $5,000 to a candidate for each election.

5. To separate a direct quotation and the explanatory matter (unless stronger punctuation is needed)

      Lawyer Mark Tomes says, "You must understand that primary and general elections are considered separate elections."

6. To separate the components of a date

      An article about PACs appeared November 10, 1979, in a trade publication.

7. To separate the components of an address

      For further information, write the Federal Election Commission, Washington, D.C.

8. To set off nouns of address

> Employees, benefits provided by employers are many and varied.

9. To set off a subordinate clause preceding the main clause

> Although some benefits are required by law, employers may add numerous others.

10. To set off a long nonrestrictive phrase at the beginning of a sentence

> Over the last ten years, benefits offered by U.S. employers have risen twice as fast in value as salaries.

11. To prevent misreading

> To be sure, employers, in general, are more concerned about employees than ever before.

Semicolon (;)

Use the semicolon in the following situations:

1. To separate coordinate (equal) clauses *not* joined by a conjunction

> Benefits now average nearly 35 percent of payroll costs; it is estimated that by 1985 they will account for 50 percent.

2. To separate coordinate (equal) clauses joined by a conjunctive adverb

> Some employers totally absorb the costs of a life insurance plan; however, others pay for a basic policy and offer further coverage to the workers and dependents for an additional sum.

(Some of the more common conjunctive adverbs are *also, besides, consequently, furthermore, hence, however, likewise, moreover, nevertheless, so, still, then, therefore, thus*.)

3. To separate coordinate (equal) clauses joined by coordinating conjunctions, when those clauses contain internal punctuation

> Policies vary widely, with some employers covering the entire premium, while others offer voluntary plans; but one almost always saves by participating in a group plan.

4. To separate units, other than clauses, containing internal punctuation

> Such plans may include, among other things, medical and surgical insurance; dental maintenance; income disability and retirement plans; family and personal counseling.

Colon (:)

The colon does not serve the same purpose as the semicolon; the two marks are not interchangeable. The fact that they are similar in appearance is sometimes misleading.

Use the colon in the following situations:

1. To introduce a formal quotation

> Thomas E. Bolger expressed his views this way: "The telephone revolution began on March 10, 1876. . . ."

2. To introduce a formal enumeration

> Today, Total Communication Systems (TCSs) offer these qualities: reliability, flexibility, low cost, and security.

3. To separate two coordinate (equal) clauses *not* joined by a conjunction, when the second clause interprets, explains, or supplements the first

> The technology is already advanced for these systems: the economics are rapidly falling into place.

4. Following the salutation in a business letter or a formal speech

> Dear Mrs. Otis: Ladies and Gentlemen:

5. To separate the parts of numerical groups

> 10:14 A.M.   A 6:4 ratio

6. To introduce items in a list

> The usual documents required under an export letter of credit are the following: commercial invoice, consular invoice, bills of lading, and insurance policy.

Dash (—)

Use a dash in the following situations:

1. To show a sudden turn in the thought or construction of a sentence

> Innovations appear daily—you've already accepted some as normal, ordinary.

2. To set off interruptions in informal style

> Better planning, better decision making, better problem solving—in other words, better management—will yield increased productivity.

3. To indicate an unfinished statement

> And if we must adapt technology—

4. To indicate halting speech

> I walked up—all—the stairs. The elevators—weren't—working.

5. To give special emphasis

> No matter what you plan—remember, now—conditions change.

6. To bound a medially placed supplementary list containing commas

> We talk glibly about telephone communications—voice, data, video, facsimile—but how many of us understand how these work?

ADDITIONAL PUNCTUATION MARKS

In addition to the comma, semicolon, colon, and dash, other marks of punctuation help communicate our written meaning to our readers.

Apostrophe (')

Use the apostrophe in the following situations:

1. To form the possessive case of nouns and indefinite pronouns
   a. Add an *apostrophe* and *s* to a base word not ending in *s*.

   > Today's modern office community demands speed, versatility, and economy.

   b. Add just an *apostrophe* if the base word already ends in *s*.

   > The secretaries' salaries were increased by 7 percent.

   c. Add an *apostrophe only* or an *apostrophe* and *s* if the word is singular and ends with an *s*. (Choice depends on pronunciation.)

   > Tess's purse   Bess's car   Charles' book

2. To indicate the omission of letters in contractions

   > don't   won't   can't   it's
   > The company can't afford to offer raises to all of its employees.

3. To indicate the omission of figures

   > The Class of '81 has many important members.

4. To form the plural of figures, letters, and words referred to as words (optional)

   > Centralized typing pools and centralized data processing facilities, both fashions of the 1960's and early '70's, were driven by economic considerations alone. (1960s, '70s also acceptable)
   > He is too lazy to write out his *and*'s. (*and*s also acceptable)

Brackets ([   ])

Use brackets in the following situations:

1. To enclose an addition to, or comment on, the original text, when the addition is made by someone other than the author of the original material

> "The Industrial Revolution began in 1888 [sic]." (The *sic* indicates that the original author made the mistake in dates.)

2. To substitute for parentheses within parentheses (optional)

> There are various reasons for the change. (Economy, flexibility, speed [adaptability] are just a few.) All are important when considering a change in organization.

Parentheses (   )

Use parentheses in the following situations:

1. To enclose a statement not closely related to the thought of the sentence

> Electronic mail may or may not involve paper. (Mailgram and facsimile both use paper.)

2. To enclose asides, remarks made to the reader or audience

> Most electronic mail installations consist of a number of autonomous, self-contained networks that exist independently (yes, independently) of each other.

3. To enclose references, directions, and explanations

> Each electronic mail system (whether Telex/TWX, facsimile, or text-editing) has a specific purpose.

Punctuation with Parentheses

When the material within the parentheses forms a complete sentence, use a period before the second parenthesis.

> Communications on these systems are usually reserved for a limited number of high-priority documents. (The most common are urgent letters or messages.)

When the material within the parentheses does not form a complete sentence and requires punctuation after it, the punctuation should follow the second parenthesis.

> Manufacturers of analog and digital facsimile units include Graphic Sciences, Quip (a division of Exxon Enterprises), and Xerox.

Never use a comma before the first parenthesis unless the parentheses are used to mark divisions or enumerations run into the text.

> The office manager outlined her priorities: (1) re-organize the work flow, (2) hold weekly planning sessions, and (3) institute a new filing system.

Period (.)

In addition to its use at the end of a declarative sentence, the period is used for the following purposes.

1. To show certain abbreviations

    Business Communications Co., a Stamford, Conn., management research firm, says that text-editing machines are replacing typewriters.

2. To indicate fractions of dollars in sums of money

    The budget for office supplies was $9,466.71.

3. To show decimals

    This is only 1.04% of the total budget.

4. To indicate emphasis in advertising copy or selling letters (ellipsis points)

    Not $10.00 . . . not $5.00 . . . but only $1.00!

5. To indicate emphasis and replace the traditional salutation in a contemporary format business letter

    The Dairy Industry, Mr. Eves. . .

6. To show the omission of words from a quoted passage
    a. At the beginning of a sentence, or within it, use *three* spaced periods (ellipses).

    ". . . can likewise be enabled to talk to like machines or selected computers."

    b. At the end of a sentence, use *four* periods (ellipses), the first one serving as the terminal punctuation mark of that sentence.

    "Communicating text-editing equipment vendors include AM International and AM/Jacquard, Basic Four. . . ."

Question Mark (?)

In addition to its use at the end of an interrogatory sentence, the question mark is used to show that a statement may not be true.

    Most existing analog systems transmit an 8½-by-11-inch, 25-word (?) business letter in four to six minutes (?).

Quotation Marks (" ")

Quotation marks are used in the following situations:

1. To enclose direct quotations. To show that certain statements, word for word, were made by a particular person, quotation marks are placed around those statements. Some writers also

put quotation marks around thoughts. Others do not. Either method is acceptable as long as it is followed consistently.

> "By having in-house training, you will better understand our system," the marketing manager said.
> "By having in-house training," he said, "you will better understand our system."

2. To enclose quotations within quotations. Use *single* quotation marks around the material *quoted within* the quotation.

> "Excuse me," the secretary said, "but what did you mean by 'electronic mail'?"

3. To enclose slang and technical expressions

> The key word is "utilization."

4. To enclose titles of articles, chapters, short stories, and poems

> "Teaching Word Processor Operators Skills"
> "Stopping by Woods on a Snowy Evening" by Robert Frost

Punctuation Used with Quotations

Place a comma or period *before* the closing quotation marks.

> "By electronic mail, I mean," the manager said, "a form of rapid information transfer over telephone lines."

Place a question mark or an exclamation mark *before* the closing quotation mark when the mark is a part of the question or the exclamation. When the question mark or the exclamation mark belongs to the sentence containing the quotation, place the mark *after* the closing quotation mark.

> "Did I hear correctly," asked another employee, "that a business letter can be sent in less than 30 seconds?"
> Was the manager correct when he said, "Thirty seconds or less"?

Place a semicolon or colon *after* the closing quotation mark.

> The marketing manager replied, "Yes, I said 30 seconds or less"; then he went on to explain.

Quotation Marks in Relation to Paragraphs

Begin a new paragraph for each new speaker.

> "Are you interested in knowing more?" Jean asked.
> "Yes," Zora replied.
> "Sure?"
> "I'm sure."

Place the material accompanying the dialogue in the same paragraph as the dialogue.

"Will you come to the board meeting?" Mr. Hartner asked.
"Yes," Mrs. Gross replied. "I have a proposal to present."

Place quotation marks at the *beginning* of each paragraph but at the *end* of only the last paragraph when the speaker continues to speak through two or more consecutive paragraphs.

"Have you finished the letters?" Mrs. Smith asked.

"No, I haven't," replied the secretary.

"It's important that they go out today, you know. I gave you those letters yesterday and explained that they were needed today.

"Well, I suppose you've had too much to do with inadequate means of doing the work. When we install the new information processing machines, you'll have no need to apologize— or excuse for not completing the work."

Place quotation marks at the *beginning* of each paragraph, at the *end* of the last paragraph when you quote two or more consecutive paragraphs from someone else's writing.

"Down the road, widespread instant information exchange will become a reality when rooftop antennas link organizations together via satellite and optical fiber cables, supplementing or replacing current telephone lines.

"WP/AS managers, who assume responsibility for the various kinds of communicating equipment, will be in the avant garde to implement the decentralized and distributed communications systems of the future." (Willoughby Ann Walshe, "Electronic Mail Diversifies with Technological Innovations," *Word Processing World,* April 1979.)

Mechanics

Major marks of punctuation indicate the pauses within sentences and the termination of sentences. But there are many jobs these marks cannot perform. Several other devices will help you communicate effectively. (When in doubt, consult your dictionary.)

ABBREVIATIONS

Certain newspapers have adopted special abbreviations. Telex uses others. Advertisers shorten words. But it is still best to avoid abbreviations in formal writing. Use the following list sparingly. (Reminder: Titles are *usually* spelled out when only the surname—last—is used. Follow local traditions, preferences. Example—Rev. Nan Miller, Reverend Nan Miller, Reverend Miller. When responding, follow the other writer's signature and letterhead style.)

Common Business Abbreviations and Acronyms*

Usage is constantly changing. Periods come and go, so do capitals. Consult a recent dictionary for guidance.

A.A.A.	American Automobile Association, Amateur Athletic Association
AACSB	American Assembly of Collegiate Schools of Business
A.B.A.	American Bankers Association, American Bar Association

*Author's note: An *acronym* is a word formed from the initial letters of each of the successive parts or major parts of a compound term, for example, AWOL: *Absent Without Official Leave.*

abbr.	abbreviation
ABC	American Broadcasting Company
ABCA	American Business Communication Association
AC, a.c.	Area Code, alternating current
acct.	account
actg.	accounting
A.D.	*anno Domini* (in the year of our Lord)
ADP	Automatic Data Processing
ad val., a/v	*ad valorem* (in proportion to the value)
advt.	advertisement
AFL–CIO	American Federation of Labor and Congress of Industrial Organizations
AGC	automatic gain control
AGR	annual growth rate
agt.	agent
A.L.A.	American Library Association
ALC	automatic level control
AM	airmail, amplitude modulation (radio)
A.M.	*ante meridiem* (before noon)
A.M.A.	American Medical Association, American Management Association
AMS	Administrative Management Society
amt.	amount
anon.	anonymous
ans.	answer
AP	Associated Press
approx.	approximately
APS	Alphanumeric Photocomposer System
apt.	apartment
ASCII	American Standard Code for Information Interchange
ASK	American Simplified Keyboard
assn.	association

asst.	assistant
ATS	Administrative Terminal System
attn., atten., Att.	attention
atty.	attorney
ave.	avenue
AVT®	Audio Visual Tutorial (trademark of Media Systems Corporation)
AWOL	absent without official leave
bal.	balance
B.B.C.	British Broadcasting Corporation
bbl.	barrel
B.C.	before Christ
BCD	Binary-Coded Decimal representation
BE, b.e.	bill of exchange
BF	brought forward
BL, b.l.	bill of lading
bldg.	building
blvd.	boulevard
b.o.	buyer's option
bro., bros.	brother, brothers
BS	bill of sale
Btu	British thermal unit
bu.	bushel
bull.	bulletin
bx., bxs.	box, boxes
C, C., c	centigrade, Celsius, center, centimeter
CAP	Civil Air Patrol
cap.	capital, capitalize, capital letter
cat.	catalog
CBS	Columbia Broadcasting System
cc, c.c., cc.	carbon copy, cubic centimeter

CD	certificate of deposit
CDT	Central Daylight Time
CE	chemical engineer, civil engineer
cf.	*confer* (compare, see)
cfm	cubic feet per minute
chap., c.	chapter
c.i.f., C.I.F.	cost, insurance, and freight
cml.	commercial
co.	company
c/o	in care of
COBOL	*c*ommon *b*usiness *o*riented *l*anguage
c.o.d., COD	cash on delivery; collect on delivery
corp.	corporation
C.P.A., CPA	certified public accountant
CPM	critical path method
C.P.S., CPS	certified professional secretary
CPU	central processor unit
cr.	credit, creditor
CRT	cathode-ray tube
CST	Central Standard Time
CT/ST	Cassette Tape/Selectric Typewriter
cu.	cubic
cust.	customer
CUT	Coordinated Universal Time
c.w.o.	cash with order
cwt.	hundredweight
D.C., DC	District of Columbia
d.c.	direct current
dely.	delivery

DEO	department executive officer
dep.	deputy, depot
dept.	department
dft.	draft
dia., diam.	diameter
dis.	distant, distribute
disc.	discount
dist.	distance, district
div.	dividend, division
DL	Demand Loan
dld.	delivered
doz.	dozen, dozens
DP	data processing
Dr.	doctor
dr.	debit, debtor, dram
DSK	Dvorak Simplified Keyboard
DST	Daylight Saving Time
E.	East
ea.	each
ed., eds.	edition, editions
EDP	electronic data processing
EDT	Eastern Daylight Time
e.g.	*exempli gratia* (for example)
enc., encl.	enclosure, enclosed
Eng.	England, English
EOF	end of file
EOM	end of month
Esq.	Esquire (courtesy title used overseas and sometimes by lawyers—same meaning as Mr. but *follows* name; is used without a preceding title)

est.	estimated, estate, established
EST	Eastern Standard Time
et al.	*et alii* (and others)
etc.	*et cetera* (and so forth)
et seq.	*et sequentes* (and the following)
exc.	except, excellent
exch.	exchange
expy.	expressway
ext.	extension, extended
F.	Fahrenheit
FB	freight bill
fed.	federal, federation
ff.	folios, [following] and the following ones
FIFO	first in, first out (accounting)
fig.(s)	figure, figures
fl. oz.	fluid ounce
FM	frequency modulation (radio)
f.o.b., FOB	free on board
FORTRAN	*for*mula *trans*lation (programming language)
frt.	freight
frwy.	freeway
ft.	foot, feet
fwd.	forward
FX	foreign exchange
FYI	for your information
G., g.	gauge, gram(s)
gal.	gallon
GCT	Greenwich Civil Time
GMT	Greenwich Mean Time

GNP	Gross National Product
gov.	governor
govt.	government
gr.	grain, gross, gram, grade
gr. wt.	gross weight
GTC	good till canceled (market)
HF	high frequency
HMS	His or Her Majesty's Ship or Service
hon.	honorable
hp., HP	horsepower
hr.	hour
H.R.	House of Representatives (used with number for legislative bill)
hwy., hy, hy.	highway
I.B.A.	Investment Bankers Association
ibid.	*ibidem* (in the same place)
I.B.M.	International Business Machines
id.	*idem* (the same)
IDP	integrated data processing
i.e.	*id est* (that is)
IFB	invitation for bids
ill.	illustrated, illustration, illustrator
in.	inch
inc.	incorporated
incl.	including, inclusive
INS	International News Service, insurance
inst.	institution, institute (use if part of official name)
int.	interest, interior, international
I/O	input/output device
IOU	I owe you

IPN	information processing network
IPS	inches per second
IQ	intelligence quotient
ital.	italic, italicized
IWP	International Word Processing association
J.P.	justice of peace
Jr.	junior (follows name)
K.	Kelvin
kc.	kilocycle
kt.	karat, kiloton
kw.	kilowatt
kwhr., kwh	kilowatt-hour
l, l., ll.	liter, line, lines
lat.	latitude
lb., lbs.	pound, pounds
LC	letter of credit
LCL	less-than-carload lot
LIFO	last in, first out (accounting)
loc. cit.	*loco citato* (in the place cited)
long.	longitude
lph	lines per hour (typing)
L.S.	*locus sigilli* (place of seal)
LSI	large scale integration
ltd.	limited (use if part of official name)
M, m.	*mille* (thousand), meter, mile, million
MBS	Mutual Broadcasting System
MC	Master (Mistress) of Ceremonies, Member of Congress
MC/ST	Magnetic Card/Selectric Typewriter
mdse.	merchandise

MDT	Mountain Daylight Time
memo	memorandum
Messrs.	*Messieurs* (plural of *Mr.*, form of address sometimes used in international correspondence)
mfg.	manufacturing
mfr.	manufacture, manufacturer
mgr.	manager, monsignor
mi.	mile
MICR	magnetic ink character recognition
min.	minute
misc.	miscellaneous
mkt.	market
Mlle.	mademoiselle
Mme.	madame
mo.	month
mpg	miles per gallon
Mr.	mister (abbreviation of French *maister* [master])
Mrs.	Mistress
Ms.	Miss or Mrs.
MS., MSS.	manuscript, manuscripts
MSR	marketing service representative
MST	Mountain Standard Time
mt.	mountain
MTM	Methods Time Measurement
MT/SC	Magnetic Tape/Selectric Composer
MT/ST	Magnetic Tape/Selectric Typewriter
N	North
n/30	net in 30 days (invoice)
NAM	National Association of Manufacturers

Mechanics

nat., natl.	national
N.B.	*nota bene* (take notice)
NBC	National Broadcasting Company
n.d.	no date
N.E., NE	Northeast
NMA	National Micrographics Association
no., nos.	number, numbers
NS	New Style
nt. wt.	net weight
NW	Northwest
obs.	obsolete, observation
OCP	optical character printing
OCR	optical character recognition
op. cit.	*opere citato* (in the work cited)
orig.	origin, original, originally
OS	Old Style, out of stock
oz.	ounce
p., pp.	page, pages
PA	press agent, public address, per annum, power of attorney, purchasing agent
pat.	patent, patented
payt.	payment
PBX	private branch exchange (telephone)
pd.	paid
PDT	Pacific Daylight Time
PERT	program evaluation and review technique
pfd.	preferred
pk.	peck
pkg., pkgs.	package, packages

pkwy.	parkway
pl.	plate, plural
P.M.	*post meridiem* (after noon)
PO	post office, postal order, purchase order
PP, pp.	parcel post, postpaid, pages
ppd.	prepaid, postpaid
pr.	pair, pairs
prem.	premium
pres.	president
prof.	professor
pro tem	*pro tempore* (temporarily)
P.S.	postscript
PST	Pacific Standard Time
pt.	pint, part
PTA	Parent-Teacher Association
PWD	Public Works Department
q.	question, quire
Q.E.D.	*quod erat demonstrandum* (which was to be proved)
qr.	quarter, quire
qt.	quart, quantity
quot.	quotation
rd.	road
recd., rec'd.	received
ref.	referee, reference, referred
rep.	representative, republican, republic
retd.	retained, returned, retired
Rev.	Reverend
RFD	rural free delivery
RFQ	request for quotation

rm.	ream (paper), room
R.N.	registered nurse, Royal Navy
RPM	revolutions per minute
RR	railroad, rural route
R.S.V.P.	*réspondez s'il vous plaît* (reply, if you please)
rte.	route
rts.	rights (stock market)
S	South, Senate (used with number for legislative bill), series, saint
/S/	signed (before a copied signature)
SA	South America, South Africa, Salvation Army
SD	sight draft, special delivery
SD–BL	sight draft, bill of lading attached
SE	Southeast, service engineer
sec.	second, section
sec., secy.	secretary
Sen., sen.	Senator, Senate, senior
SNOBOL	*String Oriented Symbolic Language* (computer language)
SO	seller's option
soc.	society
sq. ft.	square foot
Sr.	Senior (use after name), Señor (Spanish *Mr.*)
Sra.	Señora (Spanish *Mrs.*)
SRO	standing room only
Srta.	Señorita (Spanish *Miss*)
SS	steamship, social security
st.	street
St.	saint
stk.	stock
Stk. Ex., St. Ex.	Stock Exchange

subj.	subject
supt.	superintendent
SW	Southwest
t., tps.	township, townships
TB	tuberculosis
t.b.	trial balance
temp.	temperature
tpke.	turnpike
treas.	treasurer, treasury
T/S	time sharing
TV	television
TWX	*tele*type*w*riter e*x*change (also called *telex*)
U.	university, upper, union, unit
u.c., uc.	uppercase
UFO	unidentified flying object
UL	Underwriters' Laboratory
UN	United Nations
univ.	university, universally
UP	United Press
UPS	United Parcel Service
U.S.	United States
U.S.A.	United States of America
U.S.M.	United States Mail
USO	United Service Organizations
v.	*vide* (see)
VHF	very high frequency
VIP	very important person (informal)
viz.	*videlicet* (namely)
vol., vols.	volume, volumes

Mechanics

VOR	voice operated relay
V.P.	vice president
vs.	*versus* (against)
VSC	variable speed control
vv.	vice versa, verses
W	West
WB	waybill
whf.	wharf
whsle	wholesale
w.i.	when issued
wk.	week
wkly.	weekly
WP	word processing
WPM	words per minute
wt.	weight
yd.	yard
yr.	year
ZIP	Zone Improvement Plan

Academic Degree Abbreviations

B.A. or A.B.	Bachelor of Arts
B.B.A.	Bachelor of Business Administration
B.C.	Bachelor of Chemistry; Classics; Commerce; Surgery; Civil Law; Canon Law; Commercial Law
B.C.E.	Bachelor of Civil Engineering; Christian Education; Chemical Engineering

B.E.	Bachelor of Education; Elocution; Engineering; English
B.LL, LL.B	Bachelor of Laws; Latin Letters
B.L.S.	Bachelor of Library Science
B.M.E.	Bachelor of Mechanical Engineering; Mining Engineering; Music Education; Music in Education
B.Mus.	Bachelor of Music
B.P.H.	Bachelor of Philosophy; Public Health
B.S.	Bachelor of Science; Surgery; Science in Pure Science
M.A. or A.M.	Master of Arts
M.B.A.	Master of Business Administration
M.C.E.	Master of Civil Engineering
Ed.M.	Master of Education
M.S.	Master of Science
D.A.	Doctor of Arts
D.B.A.	Doctor of Business Administration
D.C.L.	Doctor of Civil Law; Canon Law; Classical Literature; Commercial Law
D.D.	Doctor of Divinity; Divinity in Metaphysics
D.D.S.	Doctor of Dental Surgery; Dental Science
D.V.M.	Doctor of Veterinary Medicine
Ed.D.	Doctor of Education
Eng.D.	Doctor of Engineering
J.D.	Juris Doctor; Doctor of Laws
Litt. D.	Doctor of Letters; Literature; Humanities
LL.D.	Doctor of Law(s)
M.D.	Doctor of Medicine
Mus.D., Mus. Doc.	Doctor of Music
Ph.B.	Bachelor of Philosophy
Ph.D.	Doctor of Philosophy; Pharmacy

Military Abbreviations

Navy and Coast Guard Ranks

ADM	Admiral
CAPT	Captain
CDR	Commander
COMO	Commodore
ENS	Ensign
FADM	Fleet Admiral
LCDR	Lieutenant Commander
LT	Lieutenant
LTJG	Lieutenant (junior grade)
MIDN	Midshipman
RADM	Rear Admiral
VADM	Vice Admiral

Marine Corps Ranks (acceptable with Army and Air Force)

BGen	Brigadier General
Capt	Captain
Col	Colonel
Cpl	Corporal
1stLt	First Lieutenant
Gen	General
LCdr	Lieutenant Commander
LtCol	Lieutenant Colonel
LtGen	Lieutenant General
Maj	Major
MajGen	Major General
NCO	Noncommissioned Officer
Pvt	Private
2ndLt	Second Lieutenant
Sgt	Sergeant
SNCO	Staff Noncommissioned Officer

Selected Government Abbreviations

Departments, bureaus, agencies, and commissions change with needs and administrations. For an updated, complete list with addresses, consult your local post office or library. Another source of information is your congressional representative. Phone for quick and accurate information.

AA	Aging Administration
BIA	Bureau of Indian Affairs
BOR	Bureau of Outdoor Recreation
CAB	Civil Aeronautics Board
CAO	Consumer Affairs Office
CB	Census Bureau
CCC	Commodity Credit Corporation
CDC	Centers for Disease Control
CES	Cooperative Extension Service
CIA	Central Intelligence Agency
CSC	Civil Service Commission
DIBA	Domestic and International Business Administration
DOE	Department of Energy
ED	Education Department
EMS	Export Marketing Service
ERDA	Energy Research and Development Administration
ES	Employment Service
ETA	Employment and Training Administration
EWTB	East-West Trade Bureau
FCA	Farm Credit Administration
FCC	Federal Communications Commission
FDA	Food and Drug Administration
FDIC	Federal Deposit Insurance Corporation
FHA	Federal Housing Administration; Farmers Home Administration
FLRC	Federal Labor Relations Council
FNMA	Federal National Mortgage Association
FR, F.R.	Federal Reserve
FRB, F.R.B.	Federal Reserve Board; Federal Reserve Bank
FRO	Federal Register Office
FTC	Federal Trade Commission
FWS	Fish and Wildlife Service
HCFA	Health Care Financing Administration
HMOS	Health Maintenance Organization Service
ICA	International Communication Agency
ICC	Interstate Commerce Commission; Indian Claims Commission
INS	Immigration and Naturalization Service
IRS	Internal Revenue Service
ITC	International Trade Commission
NCAA	National Collegiate Athletic Association
NEH	National Endowment for the Humanities
NIE	National Institute of Education
NIH	National Institute of Health
NIMH	National Institute of Mental Health
NSF	National Science Foundation

Mechanics

OAVP	Older American Volunteer Program
OLMR	Office of Labor Management Relations
OMB	Office of Management and Budget
OMBE	Office of Minority Business Enterprise
OSHA	Occupational Safety and Health Administration
OST	Office of Science and Technology
OYD	Office of Youth Development
PC	Peace Corps
PHA	Public Housing Administration
PHS	Public Health Service
SBA	Small Business Administration
SEC	Securities and Exchange Commission
SSA	Social Security Administration
SSS	Selective Service System
TVA	Tennessee Valley Authority
USA	United States Army
USAF	United States Air Force
USCG	United States Coast Guard
USCS	United States Customs Service
USES	United States Employment Service
USMC	United States Marine Corps
USN	United States Navy
USNR	United States Naval Reserve
USPS	United States Postal Service
VA	Veterans Administration
WAC	Women's Army Corps
YCC	Youth Conservation Corps

State, District, Territory Abbreviations

On envelopes, spell out the complete name or use the two-letter abbreviation—all capital letters, no period—always followed by the zip code. You'll help the Optical Character Reader (OCR) used in many United States Post Offices to speed mail sorting. And your mail will arrive more quickly.

Alabama	AL	Montana	MT
Alaska	AK	Nebraska	NE
Arizona	AZ	Nevada	NV
Arkansas	AR	New Hampshire	NH
California	CA	New Jersey	NJ
Canal Zone	CZ	New Mexico	NM
Colorado	CO	New York	NY

Connecticut	CT	North Carolina	NC
Delaware	DE	North Dakota	ND
District of Columbia	DC	Ohio	OH
Florida	FL	Oklahoma	OK
Georgia	GA	Oregon	OR
Guam	GU	Pennsylvania	PA
Hawaii	HI	Puerto Rico	PR
Idaho	ID	Rhode Island	RI
Illinois	IL	South Carolina	SC
Indiana	IN	South Dakota	SD
Iowa	IA	Tennessee	TN
Kansas	KS	Texas	TX
Kentucky	KY	Utah	UT
Louisiana	LA	Vermont	VT
Maine	ME	Virginia	VA
Maryland	MD	Virgin Islands	VI
Massachusetts	MA	Washington	WA
Michigan	MI	West Virginia	WV
Minnesota	MN	Wisconsin	WI
Mississippi	MS	Wyoming	WY
Missouri	MO		

Canadian Abbreviations, Foreign Abbreviations

Avoid foreign abbreviations except for U.S.S.R., U.A.R., B.C.C. (Union of Soviet Socialist Republics, Union of Arab Republics, British Crown Colonies). Use either the standard abbreviation, two-letter abbreviation, or full name for all Canadian mail.

Alberta	Alta.	AB
British Columbia	B.C.	BC
Labrador	Lab.	LB
Manitoba	Man.	MB
New Brunswick	N.B.	NB
Newfoundland	Nfld.	NF
Northwest Territories	N.W.T.	NT
Nova Scotia	N.S.	NS
Ontario	Ont.	ON
Prince Edward Island	P.E.I.	PE
Quebec	P.Q.	PQ
Saskatchewan	Sask.	SK
Yukon Territory	Y.T.	YT

Mechanics

AMPERSAND (&)

The *ampersand* is a symbol for the word *and*. It should not be used in formal writing. However, use the ampersand and any other abbreviations if they appear in a company's official title.

> Standard & Poor's Corp.   Coopers & Lybrand

ASTERISK (*)

The *asterisk* is used to show that a word or expression is being used in some special way, explained elsewhere in the text, usually at the bottom of the page.

> Communication* is a necessity in the business world.

> _____

> *Total communication includes all electronic, mechanical, and personal modes of interchange.

CAPITALS

Capitalize the first word of every sentence. Capitalize all proper nouns and adjectives derived from proper nouns. In addition, use capitalization as an attention or emphasis device. General rules are listed below; however, usage changes with time, purpose, and individual company style.

Academic Degrees

Capitalize the abbreviation but not the name of the degree when combined with the word *degree*.

> B.A.   a bachelor of arts degree
> M.B.A.   a master of business administration

Academic Fields

Capitalize each word in the name of a *specific* course but not the general field of study.

> Accounting II   cost accounting
> English 302   business communication

Advertising Material and Trademarks

Capitalize emphasized words, registered trademarks—accepted by general use.

> Coca-Cola   The Pause That Refreshes
> Seven-Up   The Uncola Cola

Astronomical Bodies

Capitalize the names of astronomical bodies, except the words *earth, moon, sun, star.* When these are used with the names of other astronomical bodies, all are capitalized.

> Venus   Mercury   Milky Way   Big Dipper
> Have you seen the pictures taken of the Moon, Jupiter, and Earth?

Books, Booklets, Magazines, Newspapers, Theses

Capitalize the first word in the title, the last word, and all other words except those prepositions, conjunctions, and articles shorter than four letters. (Titles may be typed in all capital letters or in caps and lowercase, then underlined.)

> STYLE MANUAL FOR WRITTEN COMMUNICATION *A Guide to Communication*

A period is not needed at the end of the title. Use other punctuation—question mark or exclamatory mark—if needed.

Business Products

Capitalize the name of the *specific* product. Follow the form used by the manufacturer.

> Randustrial products   Kodak Film   System 84 information processor   Xerox paper
> pageAmerica   Quadex200 systems   R.I.S. reinking fabric ribbon   Kleenex tissues

Do not capitalize the class of products.

> text-editing or computer terminal systems   typewriter ribbons   pagers

Compound Words

Capitalize the individual parts of a compound word in a title or heading. In text copy, capitalize only the proper noun or proper adjective.

> East-West Center   Sixty-Second Gourmet   Type-Rite

but

> The IBM mag-card units use a code operating at very high speed.
> Moncton, New Brunswick, is in the French-speaking section of Canada.

The Deity (Religious Terms)

Capitalize words referring to the deity, holy books, holy days, and creeds.

> God   Allah   Koran   Psalms   Easter   Ramadan   Buddha   Apostle's Creed

Do not capitalize adjectives derived from the Bible or the word *bible* when used figuratively.

> apocryphal   biblical   scriptural
> This guide is my bible.

Directions

Capitalize *north, south, east,* and *west* when these words are used to name parts of a country, *not a direction.* Capitalize the compass points when used with other proper names.

> They selected the East for their new firm.
> Move the machine to the east side of the plant.
> They live at 711 South First Street.
> South Pacific   Southeast Asia   North America   West Coast

Formal Writing

Capitalize the first word of any statement following the words RESOLVED or WHEREAS.

> RESOLVED, That the American Business Communication Association. . . .
> WHEREAS, The Japanese members have contributed so actively. . . .

Geographic Terms

Capitalize proper names of geographic locations, places.
Caution: (1) The common noun following two or more such terms is usually not capitalized. Follow specific organization style preference. (2) Do not capitalize a common adjective before the proper name. (3) Capitalize geographic nicknames in common use. (4) Do not capitalize words derived from the names of places when the words have a specialized meaning.

> the Great Lakes   the Cascade Mountains   New York   Pacific Ocean
> the Atlantic and Pacific oceans
> the state of Iowa   the countries of Southeast Asia
> the Twin Cities   the Hawkeye State   the Big Apple   Cyclone Country
> china   french leave   japanned metal   brussel sprouts   india ink

Government Terms

Usually capitalize *constitution, federal, government, national,* and other such terms when they refer to specific organizations, institutions, or are used as shortened forms of full names. Always capitalize all governmental and political bodies and all branches of the military.

Federal Reserve Bank   State Department   House of Representatives
Democratic Party   Republican Party   Federal Constitution   Sixth Fleet
Marine Corps   Government of the United States   Congress

but

government spending *or* Government spending
congressional immunity *or* Congressional immunity

Many publications omit capitals when terms are used as adjectives or when referring to specific governmental bodies.

Historical Periods, Holidays

Capitalize all such proper names.

World War II   Labor Day   Reformation   Thanksgiving
Golden Age   Yom Kippur

Institutions

Capitalize the names of churches, schools, libraries, government agencies, and other public institutions.

The Boston First Unitarian Church   a local Unitarian church
Asbury Junior High *but* the junior high school I attended
the Seattle City Library *but* the city library in Seattle
The University of Texas   Iowa State University (capitalize and include *The* if it is part of the formal name)
Los Angeles Department of Health *but* a public health agency

Letters

When writing or typing letters in traditional form, capitalize as follows:

Inside address: Capitalize name, title(s); street and state; company name, company department.
Attention line: Capitalize the first word and all the principal words.
Salutation: Capitalize the first word and all nouns.
Subject line: Capitalize the first word and all the principal words.
Complimentary close: Capitalize only the first word.

Prof. Hazel Lipa
Department of English
Iowa State University
Ames, Iowa 50011

Attention: Director of Personnel   Attention: Sales Manager
Dear Ms. Jones: Dear Friend: To: Department Heads
Subject: Mid-Term Grades   Subject: Absenteeism
Cordially yours,   Yours truly,   Sincerely yours,

For special effect or emphasis, use capital letters, underline words, center on page.

ATTENTION—ALL PERSONNEL   SUBJECT: Ad Hoc Committee Structure

Names

Capitalize the first letter of each name and the nickname of a person.

Thomas (Tex) Carter   Catherine (Cindy) Olson   Cooky Cohan
Andrea Wise   Pinky Anderson   Fran Weeks   James T. Jones

Nouns with Numbers or Letters

Usually capitalize nouns followed by numbers or letters unless the noun refers to minor items such as page, paragraph, line, sentence, or verse. Abbreviate the word *number* and use *No.* or *Nos.* if preceding the numeral.

Purchase Order No. 1066   Chapter X   Section V   Unit 3
page 3, line 5   paragraph 2   Lesson 6   Section B   verse 9

Outlines

Capitalize the first word of each section of an outline. Individual style determines subsequent capitalization.

V. Grammar, Punctuation, Usage
  A. Spelling
    1. General rules
  a. Doubling final consonants
    (1) Double . . .
      (a) Before . . .

Plays

Choose one of three methods: (1) type the title in all caps; (2) underline the title, capitalizing principal words; or (3) enclose the title in quotation marks after capitalizing the principal words.

CAT ON A HOT TIN ROOF   *Cat on a Hot Tin Roof*   "Cat on a Hot Tin Roof"

Poetry

Capitalize the first word of each line of poetry unless the author uses lowercase letters.

He was found by the Bureau of Statistics to be
One against whom there was no official complaint. . . .—W. H. Auden

by the rules of the game something has gone.
Not people die but worlds die in them. . . .—Yevgeny Yevtushenko

Prefixes

Use a lowercase letter when a prefix is added to a capitalized word.

non-English   un-American   trans-Pacific   pre-Colombian

Races, Nationalities, Languages, Religions

Capitalize the proper nouns and adjectives derived from names of races, nationalities, languages, and religions.

Chinese   Caucasian   Latin   Spanish   Methodist   Hebrew   Catholic

Relatives

Capitalize the words naming family members when followed by the person's name.

Call Uncle Arno quickly.
My mother is ninety-five years old.
I told Mother to phone before eight o'clock. (optional)

Statement Following a Colon

1. Always capitalize a quotation following a colon.

Take, for example, her realistic stand on skateboard accidents: "The problem is behavioral."

2. Capitalize or lowercase an expression following a colon if it is a complete sentence. Do not capitalize an expression that is *not* a complete sentence.

> She explained her concern: flimsy locks.
> She explained her concern: The locks on the doors were flimsy.
> She explained her concern: the locks on the doors were flimsy.

3. Capitalize or lowercase a list of items following a colon if the list is tabulated. Do not capitalize the list if it follows the colon.

> The Olympic Committee announced the following competitions:
> Figure skating
> Speed skating
> Cross-country skiing
> Slalom
>
> The Olympic Committee announced the following competitions: figure skating, speed skating, cross-country skiing, slalom.

Time Periods

Capitalize the names of the days of the week, months of the year, holidays, specially designated days and periods. Do not capitalize the seasons of the year unless personified.

> Monday　January　Labor Day　Easter　Clean-Up Week　Year of the Child
> The rain in spring brings early summer flowers.
> All too soon Winter enters, with gray hair, sore limbs, sagging skin. . . .

Titles

Capitalize professional, business, civic, military, religious, and family titles *preceding* personal names. Preferred but optional—do not capitalize such titles *following* names unless they are part of an inside address of a letter, on the envelope, or the title of a high government official.

> John D. Petty, D.V.M. *or* Dr. John D. Petty　General Robert E. Lee
> Alfred Knopf, Publisher　Editor Maxwell Perkins *or* Maxwell Perkins, Editor
> Mayor Lee Fellinger　Jerry Brotman, Personnel Director　Rabbi Jane Byman
> John Culver, the senator　The Honorable John Culver　President Robert S. Parks
> Robert S. Parks, our president　The Reverend Al Beng
> The President of the United States is hoping to be reelected. (optional)

Check your dictionary for forms of address, salutations.

CARET (⌃)

A *caret* shows where a letter, word, or phrase has been omitted.

> most important
> Information is the⌃raw material of thought and creativity.

HYPHEN (-)

Check your dictionary for accurate use of the hyphen with specific words. Hyphen use changes as the language changes.

Word Division

1. Words should be divided only between syllables.

   > ex-po-sure   im-pu-ni-ty   sim-u-la-tion   wom-an-hood

2. Repeated consonants are usually split.

   > par-al-lel   nec-es-sary   mis-sion   rec-om-mend   re-fer-ring

   But if the root or base word is destroyed by dividing the double letters, divide *after* the double letters.

   > bill-ing   kill-ing   sell-out

3. Words ending in *cial, tial, cion, sion, tion, sive, tive,* and other suffixes, usually keep the syllable intact.

   > bene-fi-cial   im-par-tial   trans-mis-sion   sat-u-ra-tion

4. One-syllable words cannot be divided.

   > naught   asked   night   bring

5. Abbreviations, figures, and words containing apostrophes cannot be divided.

   > U.S.A. $10,000   mustn't   you'll

6. Hyphenated words should be divided only at the hyphen.

   > self-evident   self-employed   self-addressed

7. Compound words written *without a hyphen* should be divided between the elements of the compound.

   > business-men   letter-head   foot-ball   room-mate   more-over

8. Do not divide a word beginning with a one-letter or two-letter syllable after that syllable.

>   before, *not* be-fore   abort, *not* a-bort   polar, *not* po-lar

9. Avoid dividing the last words of more than two consecutive lines. Avoid dividing the last word of a paragraph or the last word on a page. Carry over at least three letters to the next line or do not divide a word. It's best to avoid word division. Use a short line rather than divide a word.

10. In text, if it is necessary to divide parts of a date, proper name, or address—*although these do not require hyphens*—divide them at a logical point for ease of reading.

>   January 28,/ 1985   (between the day and the year)
>   Miss Mary/Jones   (between the first and last name)
>   John/Murray, J.D.   (between the first and last name, not the degree)
>   San Diego,/California   (between the city and the state)

Hyphenated Words

The use of the hyphen is rapidly changing. Use hyphens primarily to avoid ambiguity—to make sure your reader understands exactly what you mean. Some words may appear as one word, as two, or connected by hyphens. Check the dictionary for recent form. Use common sense as the final criterion. (*Note:* Current practice is to eliminate hyphens.)

Prefixes

Hyphenate words with prefixes as follows:
1. Proper nouns or adjectives derived from proper nouns

>   pro-American   anti-American   un-American   pre-Columbian   semi-Gothic

2. Many words beginning with *self, ex, vice*

>   self-esteem   ex-president   vice-chancellor

3. Ambiguous words—likely to be misunderstood

>   re-form (form again)   re-cite (cite again)   re-ally (join with again)

Suffixes

Hyphenate words with suffixes as follows:
1. Ambiguous words—words likely to be misunderstood

>   crack-up (noun)   bull's-eye (noun)   common-law (adjective)

2. Root words—when suffix begins with a consonant and root word ends with same double consonant

> shell-less   hull-less   bell-like

Compounds

Hyphenate compound words as follows:
1. Nouns

> court-martial   right-of-way   go-between   charge-a-plate   one-arm bandit

2. Adjectives

> open-end (mutual fund)   well-known (person)   low-pressure (system)

3. Words with prepositions

> follow-up letter   out-of-date   brother-in-law

Form the plural of some compounds by adding *s* to the most important word.

> follow-up letters   rights-of-way   brothers-in-law

4. Possessives. Some compounds formed with a possessive noun are hyphenated.

> bird's-brain   calf's-eyes   crow's-feet

Double compounds

Hyphenate compounds modifying the same noun. The first hyphen is followed by a space, used to carry the modifier over to the noun *(suspending hyphen).*

> long- and short-term investments   state- and federal-tax-exempt bonds

Improvised words

Such words are always hyphenated to form adjectives and verbs; sometimes hyphenated to form nouns.

> L-shaped   T-shirt   mail-o-gram   blue-gray   double-space

Dual titles

Hyphenate as follows:

> secretary-treasurer   accountant-secretary   executive director-publisher

Mechanics

Numbers

As words

Hyphenate compound numbers from twenty-one through ninety-nine. (But use figures if the number requires more than four words.)

> sixty-five   ninety-eight hundred   seven hundred ninety-nine   450,032

With compound adjectives

Hyphenate numerals used before words to form compound adjectives.

> 45-minute trial   ten-year-old boy   90-story skyscraper   ten 18-cent stamps

If a number immediately follows another, the smaller number is usually spelled out. For other number rules, see page 000.

As fractions

Hyphenate a fraction used as an adjective.

> a three-fourths majority   one-half year's salary   half-time help

But *do not* hyphenate fractions used as nouns.

> three fourths of the voters   one half of the holdings

Double compounds

Hyphenate compounds modifying the same noun. The first hyphen is followed by a space, used to carry the modifier over to the noun *(suspending hyphen)*.

> a two- or three-page memo   ten- and twenty-pound notes

ITALICS *(Italics)* or <u>UNDERLINE</u>

To indicate italic typeface, underline. Use a solid line, including the space between words, in titles. Otherwise, underline each word.

For Titles

Italicize (underline) titles of publications—books, magazines, musical works, plays, theses—and movies, radio and television programs, names of ships, and art work. These may also be typed in *all* capital letters. If underlined (italicized), articles, conjunctions, and short prepositions are not capitalized unless used as the first word of the title.

Asian Laughter　　*Mash*　　*Omni*　　<u>Ninth Symphony</u>　　*Business Week*　　<u>Mona Lisa</u>

For Foreign Words or Phrases

tour de force　　*sine qua non*　　*illegitimi non carborundum*

For Emphasis

You are *not* my boss.　　*Use a solid line.*　　*Read the fine print.*

NUMBERS

The "appropriate" way to use numbers when writing has been standardized by custom. Most widely accepted are the rules established by the Associated Press and the United Press for use by journalists.

Follow general conventions but rely on your own judgment to help your reader. Business messages use figures more often than words.

As Words

1. Number ten and under—except when used with a number above ten

    . . . seven or eight good stocks　　. . . ten times value

2. Number beginning a sentence—rephrase sentence if number is large, awkward to express in words

    Sixty-eight investors. . .　　Shares traded totaled 1,450,789. . .

3. Round or indefinite numbers

    $25 billion　　about a thousand bushels

4. Fractions standing alone

    The widow's share equaled one third of the estate. (noun)
    The broker recommended investing a one-third share of the profits. (adj.)

5. Approximate age

    The company is ninety-six years old.

But

    The company is 96 years, 3 months, 10 days old. (optional commas)

6. Periods of time—unless such figures are financial terms
   a. Formal datelines—on invitations, legal documents

> January twenty-eight, nineteen hundred and ninety
> Twenty-eighth of January
> January twenty-eighth, 1990

   b. Exact time; with o'clock

> The market opens at five minutes to eight.
> The market opens at eight o'clock.
> The brokers arrive at seven-thirty.

   With P.M. or A.M. use figures.

7. Days of the month, preceding the month

> sixth of May   tenth of October

8. Decades and centuries (use words or figures, lowercase or capitalizes)

> the twentieth century   20th century   in the Sixties   in the 60's (60s)

9. Political divisions and sessions of Congress (optional)

> Forty-first Congress   41st Congress   Twenty-first District   21st District

10. Addresses
    a. Street names from one to ten

> 6132 North First Street   3221-F Tenth Boulevard

    b. House and building numbers (optional)

> One Fifth Avenue   1 Fifth Avenue   Thirty Dupont Circle   30 Dupont Circle

11. Legal use
    a. Sums of money—words *and* figures

> the sum of seventeen hundred (1700) dollars
> the sum of seventeen hundred dollars ($1700)

    b. Dates—write in full or use ordinal ending *st, d, th*

> WITNESSETH this first day of January, 1990
> WITNESSETH this 1st day of January, nineteen hundred and ninety

As Figures

Figures are used preferably in tabular and statistical matter, records, election returns, times, speeds, latitude and longitude, temperatures, highways, distances, dimensions, heights, ages, ratios, proportions, military units, political divisions, orchestra instruments, court districts or divisions, handicaps, betting odds, and dates.

1. Numbers over ten

>   105 dealers   15 years   58 separate polls

2. Numbers in series—even if one or more is under ten

>   3 MT/ST, 5MT/SC, and 15 manually operated machines

3. Two numbers together—spell out shorter number

>   105 twenty-four-hour convenience shops   seven 18-cent stamps

4. Directions—use figures for all

>   Drive 5 miles east, 15 miles west.
>   Type the manuscript with 1½-inch margins, 60 characters to a line.

5. Exact age

>   She is 18 years, 3 months, 6 days old. (commas optional)

6. Distance—round off numbers unless exact figures are essential

>   72 meters   11 miles   105 yards

7. Numbers with nouns—use figures following *chapter, volume, page, floor, apartment, room, line, verse, exhibit, figure, appendix*—whenever figures are the names of something.

>   Chapter 6 (VI), page 85   Figure 4A   Apartment 701   Room 11   U.S. 66
>   page 72   sentence 7   6th Fleet   1st Army   5th U.S. Circuit Court

8. Addresses
   a. Street names, street numbers 11 or above

>   3221-F 17th Street   621 East 49 Place (ordinal *st, d, th* optional)

   b. House and building numbers

>   111 Lynn   7810 East Monterosa   1019 North Woodbine   One 71 Street

   c. Zip codes

>   Scottsdale, AZ 85251   Topeka, KS 66611   Washington, D.C. 20013

9. Dates
   a. Civilian—in letterhead, heading, text

>   January 28, 1990   . . . bills dated July 1 are now overdue.

   b. Military form

>   1 January 1990   1 JAN 1990

   c. Short form—in interoffice mail, reports, billings

>   1/1/1990   1-1-1990   1-1/31-90

10. Exact time; with A.M., a.m., P.M., p.m. (be consistent)

>   6:08   7P.M.   7 p.m.   8a.m.   8 A.M. (space or omit space after number)

11. Military time—identifies hours from 1 through 24, beginning with midnight

1:00 A.M.	0100	1:15 A.M.	0115
Noon	1200	12:45 P.M.	1245
6:00 P.M.	1800	6:15 P.M.	1815
Midnight	2400	11:30 P.M.	2330

12. Fractions and decimals
   a. Series

   Your retirement contributions may be divided between CRET and TIAD in 1/2, 1/3, or 2/3 proportions. (Be consistent—not ½, 1/3, 2/3. . . .)

   b. Mixed numbers—use figures for both whole numbers and fractions

   2½   102¼

13. Money, interest, percent
   a. Sums of money—use the dollar sign for $1 or over; omit the decimal point and ciphers for even sums; spell out the word *cents* for less than $1.

   $65 $8.91 $10,000   90 cents   9 cents

   b. Interest periods—use figures without commas if including year, month, day (optional)

   This statement includes your interest for 1 year 8 months and 2 days.

   c. Percentages

   Worldwide footage drilled in 1982 is projected to rise about 10%.
   discounts of 25, 35, or 50%   25%, 35%, and 50% discounts
   a 12% T-bill   42 percent discount   42 percent of the market

14. Numbers with symbols—omit space—use for statistical matter, technical papers, tabulations, invoices, serials

   #99 $5.00   100%   75¢   11*   +11.1%   72°   18″   6′5″

15. Tables and data reports
   a. Sums of money—determine style and be consistent in tabulations, memos, forms, reports

   70¢ $.70 $0.70

KEY PATTERNS IN THE ECONOMY
Non-Standard & Rich's Projections

	Est. 1979	Est. 1980	Est. 1979	Est. 1980
	—(Billions)—		—% Change—	
Gross National Product	$2,363	$2,548	+11.1%	+7.4%
Inflation Rate for Year	8%	8.8%	. . .	. . .

b. Terms—use appropriate symbols in context

the S&P 500 Index, at 7.4 times estimated 1979 earnings . . .
net 50, 2% ten days or n/30, 2/10

c. Stock quotations, items, serials, policy numbers—use *No.* in text; use symbol (#) before a figure in tabulations and short forms

OTC 3½–4¼   (96, NYSE)   yield 13.165 or 13.165%   earn 15% or 15 percent
Policy No. 889976   Lot #25 (memo form)   Lot No. 25 will be auctioned
Serial No. KH113345   SS No. 338-00-000

d. Measures, dimensions, temperature readings

72 degrees or 72° CO_2 10 gallons   10 pounds or 10 lbs.   6 bushels

16. Plural forms—add *'s* or *s*

7's or 7s   40's or 40s

17. Group numbers
a. Telephone numbers—use parentheses around area code

(515) 294-0037   1-(800)555-1212

b. Serial numbers, policy numbers, year, page, and room numbers—no punctuation

Form No. 66879   Policy No. 895543   1990   page 1780   Room 1124

c. Four or more figures—separate with commas

524,641 Independents   population of 4,657,992 $775,989,231.71
1,800 F-16 fighter aircraft

18. Outlining, references—use arabic and roman numerals or a decimal system (see Chapter 13)

SLASH OR DIAGONAL (/)

The slash is a time-saver for the typist and reader.
a. With abbreviations, symbols, and business terms

P/E   C/c   2/10, n/30 $1.55M $4.75, 2/$9, 3/$12

b. To indicate uncertainty

The money will be used to buy stocks/bonds. (Either one or both)

c. To type fractions not on the typewriter keyboard
(Space between whole numbers and fractions. Be consistent.)

9 3/4, 6 7/8, 8 1/2, 7 1/4, 11 1/16 (not 9 3/4, 6 7/8, 8½, 7¼, 11 1/16)

Mechanics

Spelling

You may find some consolation in this remark by a leading scholar: "Its system of spelling is one of the blackest marks against the English language." Until some form of official standardization takes place, misspellings will continue to appear.

The rules given here can help you learn to spell correctly. Repeated use of the words appearing in the two lists at the end of this section will familiarize you with the words most frequently misspelled.

USE THE DICTIONARY

Because there are so many exceptions to the rules, because so many English words are not spelled as they are pronounced, and (to complicate the problem further) because so many words are pronounced differently in different sections of the United States and Canada, the dictionary remains the most useful teacher of spelling.

When you look up the spelling of a word, take time to read the additional information. The preferred spelling is given first. Use it unless you have a good reason for choosing a variant spelling. The dictionary also tells you how the word is divided into syllables and whether it is ordinarily capitalized or hyphenated. Having learned the exact meaning or the variety of meanings the word has, you are more likely to remember that word and add it to your vocabulary.

PROOFREAD

Proofread your paper, underlining lightly the words you are not sure of. Then look up those words in the dictionary. If you find that the usual way of proofreading does not help you catch misspelled words, you might try reading your paper backward. Or you might use any one of the many suggestions on page 97.

GENERAL RULES

A *prefix* is a syllable that can be placed before a word or before the *root* (base) of a word to make a new word.

> *dis*appoint   *im*possible   *un*likely

A *suffix* is a syllable that can be placed after a word or after a root to make a new word.

> suppos*ition*   bring*ing*   fam*ous*

Doubling Final Consonants

1. Double the final consonant before a suffix beginning with a vowel in words of one syllable ending in a single consonant preceded by a single vowel.

> bat + er = batter   plan + ed = planned   stop + ing = stopping
> big + est = biggest   man + ish = mannish   rob + ery = robbery

2. Double the final consonant only if the accent is on the last syllable in words of more than one syllable.

> confer + ed = conferred   occur + ence = occurrence
> begin + ing = beginning   control + able = controllable

but

> develop + ed = developed   benefit + ing = benefiting

Final Silent *e*

1. Drop the *e* before a suffix beginning with a vowel in words that end in a final silent *e*.

> hope + ed = hoped   shine + ing = shining   create + or = creator
> sense + ible = sensible   grieve + ous = grievous   value + able = valuable
> persevere + ance = perseverance

Exceptions: *e* kept in *dyeing* and *singeing* (to distinguish from *dying* and *singing*); in *noticeable* and *courageous* (to keep *s* and *j* sounds).

2. Keep the final *e* before a suffix beginning with a consonant.

> hope + ful = hopeful   shape + less = shapeless   sure + ly = surely
> achieve + ment = achievement   nine + ty = ninety

Exceptions: *ninth, truly, duly, argument, wholly.*

Words Ending in *y*

1. Change the *y* to *i* before a suffix beginning with a consonant in words ending in *y* preceded by a consonant.

       hungry + ly = hungrily   greedy + ness = greediness   plenty + ful = plentiful
       merry + ment = merriment   penny + less = penniless   beauty + fy = beautify

2. Make the same change before the suffixes *-ed, -er, -es,* and *-est.*

       occupy + ed = occupied   busy + er = busier   satisfy + es = satisfies
       shiny + est = shiniest

3. Keep the *y* before the suffix *-ing.*

       hurry + ing = hurrying   study + ing = studying   bury + ing = burying

Adding Prefixes

The prefixes *dis-, mis-,* and *un-* end with a single consonant. When they are attached to a base word beginning with the same letter, there will be two *s*'s or two *n*'s. Otherwise, there will be only one.

       mis + spell = misspell   dis + agree = disagree
       un + natural = unnatural   un + usual = unusual
       un + necessary = unnecessary   un + conscious = unconscious
       dis + satisfied = dissatisfied   mis + take = mistake

Adding Suffixes

1. Do not drop a letter from the base word when the suffix *-ness* or *-ly* is added.

       stern + ness = sternness   mean + ness = meanness   plain + ness = plainness
       real + ly = really   final + ly = finally   general + ly = generally

2. But if the base word ends in *y* preceded by a consonant, change the *y* to *i.*

       happy + ness = happiness   weary + ly = wearily

Words Containing *ei* and *ie*

1. Use *ie* when the sound is long *e* (as in *see*).

       believe   relieve   grief   thief   niece   field   priest   chief

    Exceptions: *either, neither, leisure, seize, weird.*

Spelling

2. Use *ei* after *c* or when the sound is not long *e*.

> receive   deceive   sleigh   neighbor   height   weight   heir   skein

Exceptions: *friend, mischief, handkerchief, sieve, view, fiery, financier, species, leisure.*

I before *e*
Except after *c*
Or if sounded like *a*
As in *neighbor* or *weigh*

RULES FOR FORMING THE PLURALS OF NOUNS

The rules below cover the usual ways of forming the plurals of most nouns. To form the plurals of "irregular" nouns, look in your dictionary. Numerous rules and exceptions make it difficult to generalize.

1. Add *s* to the singular to form the plural of most English nouns.

> dog—dogs   table—tables   house—houses

2. Add *s* to form the plural of nouns ending in *y preceded by a vowel.*

> money—moneys   boy—boys   donkey—donkeys

3. Change the *y* to *i* and add *es* to form the plural of nouns ending in a *y preceded by a consonant.*

> company—companies   monopoly—monopolies   fly—flies   baby—babies

4. Add *es* to form the plural of nouns ending in *s, x, ch,* or *sh,* for the plural results in an extra syllable.

> mass—masses   box—boxes   bunch—bunches   bush—bushes

5. Add *s* to the most important word of the compound in order to form the plural of compound nouns written with hyphens.

> officer-in-charge—officers-in-charge   brother-in-law—brothers-in-law
> goodbye—good-byes

6. Change a vowel inside the word to form the plural of certain frequently used nouns.

> foot—feet   goose—geese   louse—lice   man—men   mouse—mice
> tooth—teeth   woman—women

7. Use either the original plural form or the anglicized plural form of certain foreign nouns.

> stadium—stadia or stadiums   curriculum—curriculums or curricula

8. Use only the original plural form of certain foreign nouns.

> datum—data   basis—bases

HOMONYMS AND NEAR HOMONYMS

(Words similar in sound but different in meaning)

accept, except
adapt, adopt
advice, advise
affect, effect
aisle, isle
all, awl
all ready, already
all together, altogether
allowed, aloud
allusion, illusion
altar, alter
angel, angle
arc, ark
ascent, assent
ate, eight
aunt, ant
bale, bail
bare, bear
base, bass
be, bee
beech, beach
beet, beat
bell, belle
berth, birth
bier, beer
blew, blue
born, borne
break, brake
breath, breathe
buy, by
cannon, canon
canvas, canvass
capital, capitol
ceiling, sealing
cell, sell
cellar, seller
censor, censure
cent, sent, scent
cereal, serial
cite, site, sight

clause, claws
clothes, cloths
coarse, course
complement, compliment
corps, corpse
costume, custom
council, consul, counsel
credible, creditable
creek, creak
currant, current
dear, deer
decent, descent, dissent
desert, dessert
device, devise
dew, due
die, dye
dining, dinning
dual, duel
earn, urn
faint, feint
fair, fare
feat, feet
fir, fur
flea, flee
flew, flue
for, fore, four
formally, formerly
foul, fowl
fourth, forth
freeze, frieze
gait, gate
gamble, gambol
great, grate
grown, groan
hail, hale
hall, haul
hare, hair
hear, here
heal, heel
heard, herd

heart, hart
heir, air
hew, hue
holy, wholly
hose, hoes
hour, our
idol, idle
in, inn
ingenious, ingenuous
instance, instants
irrelevant, irreverent
its, it's
kernel, colonel
knead, need
knew, new
knot, not
know, no
later, latter, ladder
lead, led
lesson, lessen
lie, lye
load, lode
loan, lone
loath, loathe
lose, loose
made, maid
male, mail
mane, main
manner, manor
mantle, mantel
meat, meet
medal, meddle, metal
might, mite
minor, miner
moan, mown
moral, morale
morn, mourn
night, knight
pail, pale
pain, pane

passed, past
patience, patients
peace, piece
peal, peel
pear, pair, pare
personal, personnel
plane, plain
pour, pore
pray, prey
precede, proceed
presence, presents
principal, principle
profit, prophet
quiet, quite
rain, rein, reign
raise, raze
read, red
read, reed
respectively, respectfully
right, write, rite
ring, wring
road, rode, rowed

role, roll
sail, sale
scene, seen
sea, see
seam, seem
serf, surf
sew, so, sow
shone, shown
slight, sleight
soar, sore
soul, sole
staid, stayed
stair, stare
stake, steak
stationary, stationery
statue, statute
straight, strait
suit, suite, sweet
tale, tail
than, then
there, their, they're
threw, through

throne, thrown
tied, tide
to, too, two
toe, tow
vale, veil
vary, very
vein, vane, vain
vice, vise
wade, weighed
waist, waste
wait, weight
wander, wonder
ware, wear
wave, waive
way, weigh
weather, whether
week, weak
won, one
wood, would
your, you're

Index